SEARCHING FOR CERTAINTY

Also by John L. Casti

SEARCHING FOR CERTAINTY

What Scientists Can Know

About the Future

John L. Casti

WILLIAM MORROW AND COMPANY, INC.

New York

Library of Congress Cataloging-in-Publication Data

Casti, John L.
    Searching for certainty : what scientists can know about the future / John L. Casti.
        p.   cm.
    Includes index.
    ISBN 0-688-08980-1
    1. Science—Methodology.   2. Science—Forecasting.   3. Science—Social aspects—Forecasting.   4. Forecasting.   I. Title.
    Q175.C434   1991
    501'.12—dc20   90-43889
                                                                              CIP

Printed in the United States of America

First Edition

1 2 3 4 5 6 7 8 9 10

BOOK DESIGN BY PAUL CHEVANNES

To the memory of my mother, who taught me that knowledge is always preferable to faith—but that there are many kinds of knowledge

PREFACE

Long, windy prefaces are boring. So let me tell you in one short paragraph what this book is about:

> In some areas of nature and life, such as celestial mechanics and short-term weather forecasting, science has good methods for predicting what will happen next and why. Yet in other areas, like the stock market, we are basically powerless either to predict or to explain any interesting aspect of the system's behavior. Why should this be the case?

So there it is. This is a book about the degree to which the science of today is in a position to predict and/or explain everyday events occurring in the worlds of natural and human affairs.

To explore this prediction/explanation duality, I've chosen to employ the case study method, focusing on five topical areas of general concern scattered along a spectrum ranging from the natural sciences to the life sciences to the social sciences and beyond. Specifically, these areas are:

- *Weather and climate:* Can we predict/explain changes in weather and climate?
- *Developmental biology:* Can we predict/explain the development of the physical form of living things?
- *Stock markets:* Can we predict/explain the behavior of stock market prices?
- *Warfare:* Can we predict/explain the outbreak of war?
- *Mathematics:* Can we predict/explain the true relations among numbers?

In addition to the chapters addressing these problems of nature and life, I have included an introductory chapter providing essential background information about how the everyday terms *prediction* and *explanation* are interpreted and used in the world of science. Taken together, this spread of topical areas gives a fair snapshot of the status of modern science as a tool for telling it not only like it is, and why, but also like it will be.

To add a small game-playing component to the book, as well as to assess the relative capabilities of science to scale these twin peaks of prediction and explanation, I have assigned "term grades" for the five topical areas. These grades reflect my rather personal view of how science stands today in its capacity to predict and explain phenomena of daily concern to virtually everyone. The grading system I've employed is the conventional A, B, C, D, and F system of American educational institutions. For readers unfamiliar with this scheme, A is the highest grade, F the lowest. I have also exercised the option of attaching a + or a − to any letter grade as a means of adding a bit more resolution to the scale. As my students would no doubt confirm, I'm pretty subjective in assigning these grades. So it wouldn't surprise me a bit if, after seeing the evidence, the reader arrived at a quite different valuation as to the ability of modern science to predict and/or explain any particular kind of phenomenon. Frankly, I hope so, since there's nothing I'd like better than to have even the feeblest of excuses for engaging in that much-too-common modern academic sport popularly known as grade inflation.

In this same spirit, reader reaction to my earlier trade science book, *Paradigms Lost,* provided me with a wealth of new ideas and perspectives that have, I hope, been put to some use in this volume. So again I encourage interested readers to agree or disagree with my prejudices expressed here by dropping a note to me with their views.

The appropriate mailing address is c/o Institute for Econometrics, OR, and System Theory, Technical University of Vienna, Argentinier-strasse 8, A-1040, Vienna, Austria.

Since I promised a short preface, let me rein in my congenital and professorial impulses toward pontification, equivocation, elaboration, obfuscation, extemporization, and, in general, everything except illumination and elucidation of the material composing the book. Besides, it's far better to see the arguments for yourself just by floating along these mainstreams and backwaters of nature and everyday life, watching scientists on the shore in their noble, and even sometimes successful, attempts to hunt down and capture that ever elusive wild beast called everyday reality. Enjoy the cruise.

J.L.C.
Vienna, 1990

ACKNOWLEDGMENTS

As occupations go, the writing of books must surely rank as one of the most solitary. But appearances can be deceiving and vices do sometimes turn into virtues. And there's no better illustration of these old adages than to start counting the number of friends, relatives, professional associates, and loved ones who put their collective shoulder to the wheel in the thankless task of providing encouragement and support at every stage of the book-writing process. Without their good spirits and wise counsel, it's hard to imagine how any book would ever be completed. Happily, this book is definitely no exception. So it's indeed both a pleasure and a privilege to applaud the generosity of these noble spirits in print.

First of all, let me acknowledge with thanks conversations with and helpful suggestions from my Viennese "brain trust": Manfred Deistler, Gustav Feichtinger, Eckehart Köhler, Paul Makin, Werner Schimanovich, and Michael Zillner. Without their collective and constructive in-

II

put, this would have been a quite different book—and not for the better.

For undertaking the not entirely trivial task of trying to make sure that I didn't slip up by including more than my allotted share of technical howlers, I am greatly indebted to several maestros of the more arcane scientific arts, who did their best to ensure that I stayed on the straight and narrow, technically speaking at least. In alphabetical order, let me cite Jesse Ausubel, William Brock, Gregory Chaitin, Brian Goodwin, Ray Pierrehumbert, and Karl Sigmund in this connection. As is the custom, and certainly in this case the fact, whatever factual errors and misinterpretations remain are sadly, but most assuredly, my own.

As in my earlier books, my hat is off to Eddy Löser for librarianship above and beyond the call of both duty and friendship.

For copyediting par excellence, Bruce Giffords is in a class by himself. His sharp eye and deft touch have saved me from the kinds of embarrassments that authors have nightmares over.

My literary agent, John Ware, as is his wont, has been a pillar of enthusiasm and encouragement—in addition to a source of honest, well-meant, and valued constructive criticism. No author could ask or hope for more.

For her by-now-customary editorial wizardry, honors, *summa cum laude,* are in order for Maria Guarnaschelli. Without having had the dubious benefit of seeing the draft version of these chapters, readers will never know how lucky both they and I are to have had the manuscript cleaned and pressed by the "Guarnaschelli wash and wringer." But I know. And if the text is not yet grammatically, structurally, and conceptually squeaky clean, it can be attributed only to my own indelible brand of stubbornness.

Combining the functions of both editor and technical adviser, my longtime friend, boss, and tireless correspondent Hugh Miser has served as a tower of intellectual and moral strength from the project's very inception. Not only did he read and comment constructively on every single line of every single page of the book, but he was also generous enough to supply me with a steady stream of anecdotes, queries, references, and other bits of scientific arcana garnered from his many years of service to academia, government, and intellectual life in general.

Finally (why do families always come last?), my wife, Vivien. If there's anything I'm certain about, now that I've written this book on certainty, it's that absolutely the last thing in the world she wants to see is her name enshrined in print. But I'm just perverse enough to insist on dragging her out onstage anyway. Technical advice, editorial help, and moral support are one thing; no-strings-attached loyalty and tender, loving care are quite another. There just aren't many Vivien B. Castis in this world.

CONTENTS

CHAPTER ONE: **Correlations, Causes, and Chance**
Prediction and Explanation in Science and in Life

CHAPTER TWO: **Whither the Weather?**
Can We Predict/Explain Changes in Weather and Climate?

CHAPTER THREE: **Shaping Up**
Can We Predict/Explain the Physical Form of Living Things?

CHAPTER FOUR: **Meanwhile, Over at the Casino**
Can We Predict/Explain the Behavior of Stock Market Prices?

CHAPTER FIVE: **A Nice Little War**
Can We Predict/Explain the Outbreak of War?

CHAPTER SIX: **Proof or Consequences**
Can We Predict/Explain the True Statements of Arithmetic?

SUMMARY: **The Letters of the Laws**
What Can We Know for Sure?

CHAPTER ONE

CORRELATIONS, CAUSES, AND CHANCE

Prediction and Explanation in Science and in Life

Who controls the past controls the future. Who controls the present controls the past.

—GEORGE ORWELL

Only by taking an infinitesimally small unit for observation (the differential of history, that is, the individual tendencies of men) and attaining to the art of integrating them (that is, finding the sum of these infinitesimals) can we hope to arrive at the laws of history.

—LEO TOLSTOY

"Please would you tell me," said Alice, a little timidly, "why your cat grins like that?" "It's a Cheshire Cat," said the Duchess, "and that's why."

—LEWIS CARROLL

THE LAWS OF THE GAME

Reno, Nevada, advertises itself as "The Biggest Little City in the World" and, unlike Las Vegas, its brasher, glitzier big sister to the south, Reno still retains some of the frontier charm of its rough-and-ready silver- and gold-mining past. While both Reno and Las Vegas are pretty strange places as cities go, what with their freewheeling ways, round-the-clock gambling, slot machines in every drugstore and rest room, and general ambience of easy money, one thing they are definitely not noted for is encouraging the spirit of rational inquiry and scientific experimentation. The last thing the casino bosses want is for their patrons actually to *think* about what they're doing. Yet in March 1961 Reno served as the venue for a scientific experiment that was not only to change forever the face of the gambling industry, but also to initiate the now widespread use of the computer as a tool for doing experimental mathematics. To find a down-to-earth, practical example of scientific prediction and explanation in action, we can hardly do better than return for a moment to that fateful day in 1961 when the academics rode into Reno to shoot it out with the casinos.

At the annual meeting of the American Mathematical Society in Washington, D.C., in January 1961, a young mathematics instructor from MIT, Edward O. Thorp, presented a short paper with the provocative title "Fortune's Formula: The Game of Blackjack." The essence of Thorp's revolutionary idea was to note that the card game of blackjack (or twenty-one) as played in casinos around the world has an abstract structure totally unlike most of the other popular casino games, such as craps, roulette, or keno. In these other games there is no memory from round to round, so that each play of the game is independent of every other. Thus, for example, when you see the dice total seven on a given roll, the likelihood that seven will appear on the next roll remains exactly the same as it was before—one chance in six. But in twenty-one things are different. If on the current round of play you observe a lot of face cards and tens (collectively and colloquially termed tens) on the table, then for the next round the likelihood of these ten-counting cards' turning up is reduced, since the deck from which the next hand will be dealt is now depleted in tens. Hence, unlike the other house offerings, twenty-one is a game in which the sequence of plays is what probability theorists call a set of *dependent trials*.

By conducting extensive computer simulations of the play of many millions of hands of twenty-one, Thorp discovered that as the composition of the deck shifts downward from being "ten-rich" to "ten-poor," so do the player's chances of getting a winning hand. The simulations showed that the greater the fraction of tens remaining in the deck, the greater is the player's advantage; conversely, the more low-counting cards in the deck, the larger the advantage to the house. Since the player can choose how much to bet on each hand, the essence of Thorp's strategy is clear: Keep a running count of the proportion of high to low cards in the deck, and make big bets when the odds swing in your favor and low bets when they move in the direction of the house. Along with this strategy for bet sizing, Thorp also developed a playing strategy, based upon the same high/low ratio, which specified the best action for the player to take at any stage of play. Armed with this information, Thorp was ready for a showdown with the house.

Following presentation of his paper at the AMS meeting, Thorp was besieged by phone calls, telegrams, and letters offering to stake him to an on-site test of his radical, but still theoretical, ideas in Nevada. Since Thorp has given a very complete and entertaining account of his thoughts and experiences in his best-selling book *Beat the Dealer*, it's sufficient to report here only a few highlights, as well as the immensely pleasurable fact that the test was completely satisfactory in every way (except to the casino owners).

During the course of his experimental tests in the "laboratories" of Reno and Las Vegas, Thorp was able not only to empirically validate the results of his computer simulations, but also to discover that it takes a lot more than just mathematics to emerge unscathed from the felt-top jungles of casinoland. Hypersensitive to even the hint of a threat to their bloated coffers, the casino owners are eternally on the lookout for players like Thorp who stand out from the crowd, either by the size of their bets or, what's infinitely worse, by the size of their winnings. In his book Thorp details several episodes in which the success of his twenty-one strategy attracted unwelcome attention from the pit bosses, heat that ranged from plying him with lots of free booze and ladies of the evening to cheating dealers and finally to outright banishment from the twenty-one tables. In fact, so successful was Thorp's brand of applied probability theory and statistics that for a while the gambling industry threatened to abolish entirely the game of twenty-one.

As usual with such overreactions, cooler heads eventually prevailed, especially since twenty-one was by far the most profitable game for the casinos prior to Thorp's bursting of their bubble. What ultimately emerged was the plain fact that making money, even with a surefire winning method, is still lots of hard work, since effective employment of Thorp's ideas and techniques requires far more time and effort than most people are willing or able to invest. But just to be on the safe side, the casino owners, always ready to protect their investment in absolutely any way they can, modified the rules of the game in order to make it more difficult for the "card counters" to walk off with the store. These changes involved imposing restrictions on bet doubling, taking insurance when the dealer shows an ace, bonus payments awarded for special types of hands, and other playing options tending to favor the player. And so things stand to this day in casinos around the world—making money at twenty-one is still possible, but the rate of return for even the best players is probably less than what they could earn employing the same talents as tax examiners, bookies, or bank tellers. For us, what's interesting about Thorp's pathbreaking accomplishment is not so much the psychic gratification we get from seeing the greedy casino owners knocked flat on their fat derrieres, but the real-life illustration of scientific explanation and prediction in action.

From a scientific perspective, we can express Thorp's investigation of twenty-one in more formal terms in the following way. Over many decades of empirical observation, people had noted that there appeared to be winning ways for your twenty-one plays. And, in fact, casino folklore is filled with stories of legendary players like Sonny, Greasy John, and "the little dark-haired guy from California" who regularly cleaned the casinos' clocks at the blackjack tables. Thorp's first task was to explain how this could have occurred. Solving the explanation part was easy, as outlined above. Twenty-one is a game with *dependent* trials; as a result, the odds continually shift back and forth between the house and the player. Thus, scientifically speaking, the explanation lies in the laws of probability governing dependent trials. But what about prediction? After all, who cares about knowing *why* we can beat the game of twenty-one? Tell us *how*.

It's evident that just by keeping track of the ratio of high to low cards remaining in the deck, Thorp couldn't predict *exactly* what the next hand dealt would be. However, what his card-counting strategy can do is predict with some accuracy the statistical distribution of future hands. In other words, the Thorp high/low count can predict that some types of hands are more likely to appear than others, thus enabling the players to weight their bets accordingly. How did Thorp make these statistical predictions? Basically, he arrived at them by using a computer to discover the "laws" of twenty-one. That is, by playing tens of millions of hands under the prevailing rules, Thorp discovered what the odds are for any given state of play. With these "laws of the game" in hand, he was able to forecast not only when the deck would favor the player, but also what the most advantageous playing strategy would be in each situation. Note carefully, though, that at no point could Thorp say with assurance that such-and-such a hand would definitely appear next. Thus, the laws he discovered are what we call probabilistic, or *stochastic,* admitting only probabilistic kinds of predictions. Keeping this colorful example in mind, let's now look at more general issues surrounding randomness, uncertainty, prediction, and explanation.

Making sense of the things we see and predicting the future course of events have always played an essential role in the formation of each individual's world view. We see evidence of this need to know and understand the future in everything from the popularity of newspaper astrology columns and daily weather reports to the eager anticipation of government trade figures and the outcome of superpower summit meetings. In every case, what's really involved is the human need to try to make the patterns of what we see or expect to see somehow fit into the overall framework of what we know, or at least *think* we know. In short, we want to use either our personal knowledge or someone else's to push back the shadow of ignorance. To get a better grasp of what's involved in lifting this veil of uncertainty, let's take a moment to look at what it might mean to say we have *certain* knowledge of any kind.

In 1761 in a letter to a German princess, the Swiss mathematician Leonhard Euler identified three types or senses of certainty. As we pursue our goal of looking at the degree to which science can help to narrow the boundaries of uncertainty, Euler's taxonomy of what it means to be certain can be helpful in focusing our thoughts. Euler distinguished among:

• *Perceptual certainty:* This is the type of certainty that comes from saying, "I saw it with my own eyes." Thus, certain knowledge of the perceptual type is exemplified by personal attendance at, say, a literary reading or a rock concert.

• *Demonstrative certainty:* When you use the tools of deductive logic to prove the Pythagorean Theorem's claim about the relation among the lengths of the sides of a right triangle, you are gaining certain knowledge by virtue of demonstration. Thus demonstrative certainty, according to Euler, is what would be exemplified by our saying, "It's a logical certainty."

• *Moral certainty:* Suppose I tell my students that Euler was a famous Swiss mathematician. Normally, students are gullible enough to believe me when I make statements of this kind, and so they leave the classroom with a third type of certain knowledge— the kind based upon what they've been told by others. This sort of knowledge is what Euler called morally certain.

In the search for what science can say for sure about either the past or the future, our concerns in this book will be mainly with logical certainty, i.e., the sort that comes from discovering the laws governing the behavior of natural and human phenomena. This is not to say that the other categories of certainty are less important, but only that they are, for the most part, outside the bounds of scientific inquiry.

Roughly speaking, we can identify two main sources of the uncertainty we want to banish from our daily lives: randomness and imprecision. The latter term refers to the kind of uncertainty that arises from an imprecision or vagueness in language. This type of uncertainty shows up in simple statements like "Ty Cobb was a *great* hitter," or "Richard M. Nixon was a *lousy* president." Here I have italicized the imprecise words that serve as the source of the uncertainty. How great a hitter was Cobb? And just how lousy a president was Nixon? Linguistic imprecision lies at the heart of the uncertainty expressed by these queries.

While I suspect that a lot more uncertainty than most of us realize comes about from imprecision of this type, our main interest in this book lies more with the uncertainty resulting from randomness than that arising from imprecision. Again, this is not because randomness is any more important than imprecision, but only because it is a type of uncertainty generator whose symptoms are more readily treated using the tools and tricks of the scientific medicine man. So onward to randomness.

What does it really mean when we say that some sequence of events is "random"? Common sense would probably say that a set of events is random if it is, in some sense, unpredictable—i.e., the events follow no readily apparent pattern. Intuitively speaking, this description of randomness seems to be the one that jibes best with our everyday use of the term *at random*. But if there's one thing that science, and especially mathematics, teaches us it's not to trust everyday, garden-variety common sense and intuition. And so it is with randomness, too, as the following simple geometrical problem illustrates.

Take a circle and draw an equilateral triangle inside it, as in the figure below. Now let's draw a straight line (a chord) from the apex of the triangle to a "randomly chosen" point on the circle, and ask: "What is the likelihood that the length of the line is longer than a side of the triangle?"

The geometry of the situation makes it clear that the chord will be shorter than a leg of the triangle if the randomly chosen end point lies on either the arc *AB* or the arc *AC*. Since these two arcs together form two thirds of the circle's circumference, we conclude that the desired likelihood is $\frac{2}{3}$. Thus, by this argument, a chord chosen "at random" has probability $\frac{2}{3}$ of being shorter than a leg of the triangle. All neat, tidy, simple—and maybe wrong!

Unfortunately, there is another solution that's equally neat, simple, and tidy. First pick a point *C* within the circle and draw the line (radius) from the center *O* through the point *C*. Next, through the midpoint of the line *OC* draw the line perpendicular to the original line. This new line will be a chord that intersects the boundary of the circle in two points. The situation is shown in the following diagram:

Elementary geometry shows that for the chord with midpoint *C* to be shorter than a leg of the triangle, the point *C* must lie in the shaded region between the two circles, whose area is three-fourths the area of the bigger circle. Thus, if we select our chord by "randomly" choosing its midpoint *C*, then we're led to conclude that the desired probability is $\frac{3}{4}$.

Which of these different answers is "correct"? Mathematically, they both are. The difference is attributable only to the ways in which we interpret the phrase *at random* in the construction of the chord. In the first case, we interpreted it to mean that with one end point of the chord fixed, we choose the other end point with equal likelihood from among the points on the circumference of the circle. In the second case, our assumption was that the midpoint of the chord is chosen with equal likelihood from the points in the interior of the circle.

The moral of this simple example is not a mathematical one; mathematically, there is no problem at all. The point is to emphasize the fact that the words *at random* do not have an absolute, totally objective meaning. Since the subjective interpretation we attach to randomness infects even such a simple situation as this, it should come as no surprise that when we encounter far more subtle and complex situations in natural and human affairs, what we mean when we say "at random" can dramatically influence the validity of our claims about being able to explain and/or predict the course of events. Now let's temporarily leave this theme and shift our attention to some of the intellectual constructs that science has at its disposal for the banishment of ignorance and uncertainty.

As it's usually taught, the process of science consists of the following stages:

As indicated by the double arrow, this process, or method, involves a continual interplay back and forth between experimentation and theory construction. Since the philosophy-of-science bookshelves sag under the weight of scholarly treatises expounding on the pieces of this diagram, let's just touch lightly on one or two aspects of each component that are of particular importance for our later needs.

Observations: The observing of events or "happenings" in the external world is where most explanatory schemes, scientific or otherwise, are anchored. Such observations may take the form of sensory impressions like the sight of a bolt of lightning, the smell of freshly baked bread, or the smooth feel of satin. On the other hand, the observations of the external world may be more indirect, such as reading the pointer position on a voltmeter or noting the ticking of a Geiger counter. Usually, we're not interested in one-time-only isolated events, but in sequences of observations. This is especially true when it comes to matters of prediction, where our concern is with attempting to divine how a sequence of observations of some phenomenon will carry on into the future. But whether the observations are multiple or not, they constitute what we call the facts. And it's the facts that the process of science is geared up to explain.

Empirical laws: After observing several occurrences of particular types of events, an irresistible next step is to try to organize the observations into some meaningful pattern. This is the essence of what we mean by an empirical law: a relation characterizing compactly the observed facts. So, for example, after taking many observations of sunspot activity over the course of time, we might notice a rhythmic cycle that peaks about every eleven years. This pattern of highs and lows of sunspot activity constitutes an empirical relation linking the amount of activity with the time of observation. Another example closer to home arises when we observe fluctuations of the U.S. dollar exchange rate on the international currency markets in response to the U.S. Federal Reserve's setting of the discount rate. We note that whenever the Fed raises the discount rate, the dollar tends to rise in value against most foreign currencies. The amount of the rise varies according to many factors, but the overall relation between the rise or fall of the discount rate and the value of the dollar constitutes an empirical law. In fact, what distinguishes the winners from the losers in the currency-trading game is the degree to which a trader can ferret out a good approximation to the exact nature of this law.

Laws of nature: An empirical law has a kind of contingent aspect to it; new observations can rather easily persuade us to modify the law. On the other hand, a law of nature has the air of something cast in concrete—permanent, fixed, immutable. At what stage does an empirical law become a law of nature? The ontological status of such laws is very unclear. They seem to be more than just a constant conjunction of observations (like an empirical relation), since they support events that could have occurred but didn't. On the other hand, they are far from being inevitable logical truths. Exactly where the dividing line is placed varies from situation to situation, and we will find ourselves criss-crossing this fuzzy boundary many times as we move from topic to topic throughout the book. So for now it's best just to leave the point hanging, my hope being that its resolution will emerge in an evolutionary fashion during the course of the next few hundred pages.

Theories: A law explains a set of observations; a theory explains a set of laws. The quintessential illustration of this jump in level is the way in which Newton's theory of mechanics explained Kepler's laws of planetary motion. Basically, a law applies to observed phenomena in one domain (e.g., planetary bodies and their movements), while a theory is intended to unify phenomena in many domains. Thus, Newton's theory of mechanics explained not only Kepler's laws, but also Galileo's findings about the motion of balls rolling down an inclined plane, as well as the pattern of oceanic tides. Unlike laws, theories often postulate unobservable objects as part of their explanatory mechanism. So, for instance, Freud's theory of mind relies upon the unobservable ego, superego, and id, and in modern physics we have theories of elementary particles that postulate various types of quarks, all of which have yet to be observed.

Prediction and explanation are the twin pillars upon which the goals of the scientific enterprise rest. The whole point of science, along with religion, mysticism, and all of science's other competitors in the reality-generation game, is to make sense somehow of the worldly events we observe in the course of everyday life. Thus, the point of the practice of science as science is to offer *convincing* explanations for these events, as well as to back up those explanations with accurate, reliable predictions about what will be seen next. But what do we mean by a "scientific" prediction and/or explanation? In what way does it differ from predictions and explanations generated by employing the tools and techniques of other predictive and explanatory schemes, e.g., those associated with the practice of astrology or procedures involved with the *I Ching*?

While the long answer to this query will unfold over the remainder of the book, the short answer is rather easy to give here. Scientific explanation and prediction is explanation and prediction *by rule,* or, as it's sometimes put, *by law.* To take a simple example, the observed fact that copper is a good conductor of electricity, while silicon is not, is explained by invoking the rule that chemical elements or compounds having a lot of easily detached electrons in their outer shell can use those electrons to conduct heat and electricity. On the other hand, the rule states that those elements like silicon that do not have an abundance of such "free" electrons are not good conductors. The situation is similar with regard to prediction. For instance, we can accurately predict that there will be a full moon on October 30, 1993 by appealing to the rules of celestial mechanics, essentially Newton's equations of gravitation and motion. And, in fact, when a rule like Newton's proves useful enough over a long enough period of time, it's often enshrined in the lexicon of science by being upgraded to a "law," viz., Newton's *laws* of motion.

At this juncture a neutral skeptic might well object, saying that other prediction and explanation schemes are also based on rules. For example, many brands of mysticism involve following the procedures of various sorts of meditation exercises, exercises that their adherents claim will result in a kind of self-realization and enlightenment. It is then sometimes asserted that this enlightenment, in turn, will enable one to at least explain, if not predict, the vagaries of everyday life. And just about everyone is familiar with Sunday-supplement seers, stock market gurus, and other types of visionaries who predict coming events on the basis of crystal-ball gazings, tarot card readings, the interpretation of celestial configurations, the outcome of the Super Bowl, divine inspiration, and/or other procedures that might charitably be thought of as based on the following of a set of rules. So in what way *exactly* do these rule-following schemes part company from what is customarily considered to be a "scientific" procedure?

Basically, there are two properties tending to distinguish scientific rule-based schemes for prediction and explanation from their many competitors. The first is that scientific schemes are *explicit,* i.e., the rules and the way they are to be applied are spelled out with sufficient clarity and in enough detail that they can be used by anyone. In short, it doesn't require any special insight or inspiration to make use of scientific laws or rules. Of course, it may take years of training and a laboratory full of equipment to actually follow the rules. But what it doesn't take is any sort of private interpretation of what the rules mean or how they are to be followed. Loosely speaking, such a set of rules can be encoded in a computer program, and the prediction and/or explanation encapsulated in the rules can be obtained by running this program on a suitable computer.

The second distinguishing characteristic of scientific rules is that they are *public.* Unlike many religions and other belief systems, science has no private truths. The laws and theories of science are publicly available to all interested parties. And, in fact, it's a necessary part of the scientific enterprise that the rules underlying any scientific claim for prediction or explanation be made freely available so that anyone who wishes may test the claim using the same set of rules. This is the essential content of the testability of claims, one of the fundamental tenets underpinning the ideology of science.

While there is a certain degree of explicitness and public availability of the rules underlying many nonscientific belief systems, it's in science that these features are most clearly seen. And it is these key features of science-based procedures for explaining and predicting that the reader should keep uppermost in mind as we proceed through the remainder of this book.

Now let's get back to our main goal. What do all these musings

about observations, laws, and theories have to do with scientific prediction and explanation? In what way do we employ scientific theories
to explain and make projections of the events of daily life? Since
pictures always speak louder than words, the connections are displayed
in Figure 1.1.

In the figure, note the manner in which the operations of logical
inference, experiment, induction, and deduction interact. Induction,
the process of arguing from specific instances to general conclusions,
is employed on the experimental side of science to generate laws
(empirical and of nature) from observations. The complementary operation of deduction, the drawing of specific conclusions from general
instances, is then used to generate predictions and explanations from
scientific theories. The dotted leg of the triangle with two arrowheads
represents the fact that we also speak in everyday language when we
make predictions based on observations. However, we still often use
the methods of science to test those predictions experimentally.

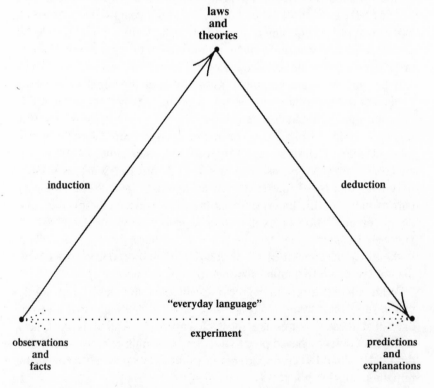

Figure 1.1. *The process of science*

Before leaving this figure, it's worth noting that the usual path around the triangle starts at the top with a theory. We use the objects and logical structure of that theory to make predictions, which are then tested in the lab. So, contrary to popular belief, the starting point of science is not generally observation at all, but theory. Since in this book we will dwell at great length upon these matters, further elaborations are not called for at the moment. So let's shift our immediate attention to the main vehicle by which science actually produces its explanations and predictions—a model.

In broad terms, a *scientific model* is an abstraction of some slice of reality that the model claims to represent. Just as a model of an F-16 fighter aircraft omits many of the features of the real plane and retains only those aspects that the modeler intends to portray (mainly the external shape, colors, and principal components), scientific models also omit many aspects of the real world and retain only those features that relate directly to the model's purposes.

A good illustration of this abstracting process is provided by the well-known billiard ball model of an ideal gas contained in an enclosed cylinder. In this setup, the molecules of the gas are thought of as hard little spheres moving along their appointed Newtonian rounds inside the cylinder. Just like the balls on a billiard table, the molecules collide from time to time, changing their paths in accordance with the usual rules governing inelastic collisions. It turns out that by thinking in terms of this model, one can readily envision and understand many important properties of the gas, such as its temperature and pressure. However, it's clear that a number of real-world features of the molecules have been abstracted away in the model. For instance, real molecules are not geometric points, nor do they collide in the inelastic manner of billiard balls (neither do real billiard balls themselves, for that matter). Nevertheless, the model is useful for the purposes to which it is applied.

Helpful as the above types of mental and physical models are, most of theoretical science relies upon another kind of model involving its own peculiar sorts of abstractions—a *mathematical model*. The basic idea underlying the modeling relation between the real world and the universe of mathematical objects is displayed in Figure 1.2.

The central idea of a mathematical model is somehow to mirror the observable quantities of the real world in the abstract structures making up the world of mathematics. This idea is illustrated in Figure 1.2 by the "encoding" arrow, which establishes a dictionary we can use to

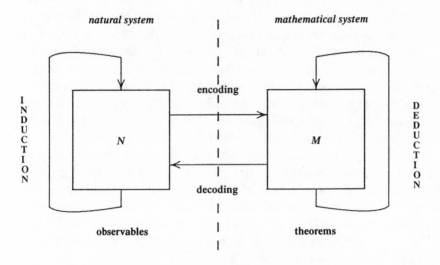

Figure 1.2. *The modeling relation*

translate the real-world observables into mathematical objects. Once this match-up is in place, the rules of deductive inference can be used to generate new relations (theorems in *M*) linking the mathematical objects. These valid mathematical assertions (the theorems) can then be "decoded" into statements (predictions) about the natural system *N* that's *modeled* by the mathematical system *M*.

It's of more than passing interest to inquire as to why we should bother going through all this translation back and forth between the down-to-earth, practical world of reality and the abstract, hard-to-get-your-hands-on world of mathematics. If we want to know about the doings of nature and the animals, why can't we just stay within the realm of real life and real people and leave the mathematicians to worry about their abstractions? This question is especially pertinent in the light of recent research indicating that not only all humans, but probably also all birds and mammals share the same fundamental cognitive machinery and use the same processes to conceptualize the world. Yet there's not a bit of evidence to suggest that birds, whales, and elephants use mathematics. So why do humans?

The only really convincing answer we can give to this commonsense query is that the world of mathematics is the only one in which there is a systematic, reliable procedure for generating new truths from old—the rules of logical inference. These rules include things like the familiar syllogisms of elementary logic: "All fish can swim. A trout is a fish. Therefore, trout can swim." The conclusion of this deductive argument is arrived at by means of one of Aristotle's rules of logical inference; namely, the rule "If A is true, and B is an instance of A, then B is also true." Since accurate predictions in the natural world are the counterparts of logical truths in the world of mathematics, until we can come up with direct, systematic, testable, and reliable procedures for creating good predictions straight from physical observables, we're stuck with the indirect route of prediction generation via the detour of mathematical abstraction. Incidentally, this argument shows rather clearly that what laymen often call the "useless abstractions" of the mathematician are very far from being useless; in fact, they're critical for the success of the kinds of predictive schemes that these very same laymen hunger for. As the famed mathematician David Hilbert once remarked, "There's nothing more useful than a good [mathematical] theory."

Now armed with these basics about how science is supposed to operate and the methods and techniques scientists employ, let's crank up our conceptual microscope for a somewhat more in-depth look at the book's two primary foci—explanation and prediction, scientific style.

THE WHY OF THINGS

On November 29, 1978, an earthquake measuring a whopping 7.8 on the Richter scale rocked the Pacific coastal state of Oaxaca in Mexico. While this quake was an unmitigated disaster for the people of the region, it served as a major milestone in the centuries-long struggle by seismologists to understand the nature of earthquakes and to predict accurately the time and place of these geophysical rumblings. To understand why, let's quickly review the prevailing scientific reasons for how earthquakes come about.

According to the theory of plate tectonics, the world's land masses can all be thought of as gigantic slabs floating about on top of a denser, semimolten material in the earth's mantle. As these slabs move about, they collide with one another in various ways. Head-on collisions form some of the world's great mountain ranges, like the Himalayas, for instance. Oblique collisions give rise to more ominous effects—they generate earthquake zones. Generally in these oblique encounters, the slabs collide and stick together. As time goes by, this bond is put under increasing stress as the two slabs try to move apart in different directions. Eventually the bond fractures under the tension, resulting in a rapid, jerky type of separation of the two slabs—an earthquake. This picture indicates rather clearly why the magnitude of the resulting earthquake is directly dependent upon the strength of the bond between the slabs and the slabs' relative speed and direction of separation.

A fairly recent discovery in the earthquake-modeling business is that in the region where the two slabs are joined, even small stress-relieving tremors may cease shortly before a major quake. This quiescent period, termed the *alpha phase,* may persist for a number of years. Then a *beta phase* ensues in which a number of small shocks occur over a period of a few days to a few months, culminating in a major quake. In 1977 a group headed by Gary Latham at the University of Texas Geophysical Laboratory programmed a computer to look through the world's seismological data, searching for likely-looking seismic "gaps" of this sort as indicators of major earthquakes in the making. The computer discovered one such alpha-phase gap for a region about 200 miles long on the coast of the Mexican state of Oaxaca.

The Texas group published its findings along with a very precise prediction of where it expected the quake's epicenter to occur: between 16 and 17 degrees north latitude and between 96 and 97 degrees west longitude, an area on the coast smack-dab in the middle of the Oaxaca location. The seismologists further predicted that the magnitude of the quake would register between 7.25 and 7.75 on the Richter scale—a major jolt. The only thing they didn't predict was the exact timing of the event, although they did note that the quiescent phase had already existed "substantially longer" than similar time periods in the past that had preceded large quakes.

At this stage politics began to intrude its ugly head into the affairs of science. The Mexican press got wind of the earthquake prediction and splashed it across the front pages of newspapers in the capital, Mexico City. The result was panic in Oaxaca, as a number of residents sold their homes at bargain-basement prices and fled the area. Many local politicians denounced the prediction as irresponsible, a sentiment reflected in the words of experimental seismologist Karen McNally when she remarked that "predicting an earthquake in somebody else's country . . . is something you do with great trepidation." Ironically,

McNally herself was to play a central role in carving out the scientific triumphs later salvaged from the rubble of Oaxaca.

Operating on the basis that there's no such thing as too much data when it comes to testing models of earthquake prediction, McNally and her co-workers set up a number of monitoring stations in the suspect region, including one right on top of the spot where the Texas group claimed the quake would be centered. Its instruments in place by early November 1978, the McNally group started seeing increased seismic activity around November 15. The activity then decreased until November 28, when there was another round of shocks. The next day there was a major quake located exactly in the center of the area where McNally's group had placed its array of monitoring stations—the strongest possible vindication of the concepts and methods employed by Latham and the Texas group.

While this story only scratches the surface of the human, political, and scientific drama associated with the 1978 Oaxaca quake, it serves admirably as a case study of how the scientific world understands the terms *explanation* and *prediction*. In brief, the theory of plate tectonics was used to *explain* how the earthquake would occur and where it would strike, while a different theory involving the alpha and beta phases of activity was employed to *predict* the timing of the quake. Since both the explanation and the prediction were based on scientific theories and their concomitant laws, a natural starting place for considering scientific explanation, in general, is with an investigation of the lawful relations between events and the theories used to explain such lawful relations.

In everyday conversation we think of an explanation of some event as the answer to a question that begins with *why*. Why is my wife yelling at me for not taking out the garbage? Because the remnants of last night's trout amandine are smelling up the kitchen. Or, why haven't I heard from my broker recently? Because my portfolio has declined 10 percent over the past week on the strength of his hot tips. Simple cause and effect. The search for explanation in science also often involves looking for causal relations of a similar type.

Perhaps the first such causal scheme was that advocated by Aristotle in his *Physics*, where he identified four collectively exhaustive and mutually exclusive causal categories: material, efficient, formal, and final causation. Each of these categories provided the answer to a "why" question, and together they were supposed to give a complete explanation for why things are as we observe them. To use one of Aristotle's own favorite examples, we might ask, ''Why is my house the way it is?'' The Aristotelian answers are that the house is as it is because of the materials from which it is constructed (material cause), because of the labor that the workmen put into building it (efficient cause), because of the architectural plans describing the structure of the house (formal cause), and because of my desire to have a comfortable shelter from the elements (final cause). In this setup we see the essence of the commonsense view of explanation: causal connection.

As noted in the previous section, the key concept in science is that of a law, and all scientific explanations in one way or another invoke scientific laws to legitimize their assertions. But not all laws are causal, and it has been forcefully argued that our preoccupation with causal laws is deeply tied up with the subconscious tendency of humans to re-create the universe in our own image. Thus, since *we* feel psychologically comfortable with cause-and-effect relationships, we try to impose that pattern on nature as well. We'll come back to this point in a moment. For now let's take a short detour into the labyrinthine world of causality to look at a couple of the more notable landmarks.

What is it that typifies causality? Given two events *A* and *B*, how can we say that one of them acts as the ''cause'' of the other? Again speaking in everyday terms, we would probably say that *A* causes *B* if the occurrence of *A* at one moment necessarily brings about the occurrence of *B* at a later time. Note here how the idea of law has been brought in to link the two events: *A* today *requires B* tomorrow. Employing the terminology of logic, we would express this lawful relationship by saying that *A implies B,* showing that causality in the physical world is intimately tied up with the idea of deduction in the austere world of logical abstraction.

It's of considerable interest and importance to compare the idea of causality with that of *correlation.* Suppose we have two events *A* and *B* such that whenever *A* takes place, *B* is always observed to follow. To take a familiar example, in one study it was noted that there is a high positive correlation between the number of storks seen nesting in English villages and the number of children born in these same villages. Such a correlation is rather similar to what we earlier termed an empirical law or relationship. But in today's high-tech world, it's difficult to see any more of a causal connection between storks and infant births than between black cats and bad luck. There's just no causal relationship at all. What's lacking here is a theory that summarizes a number of interacting laws, all of which taken together would provide a logical chain leading from the appearance of storks in the villages to the appearance of babies. The interested reader may want to consult the "To Dig Deeper" section for this chapter, where an illustration of what *might* constitute one such chain is given.

The foregoing distinctions between causation, correlation, and explanation can be considerably sharpened by introducing the idea of *determination*. Roughly speaking, in science this term refers to a constant and unique connection among things or events. To illustrate, suppose we note a high positive correlation between the advertising outlays and the net profits of a business. Suppose further that we see an empirical relationship between the advertising expenditures and profits, showing that the ratio of advertising expenses A to profits P is a constant quantity k—i.e., we observe the fixed ratio $A/P = k$ at all times. What this means is that we have a "law" saying that profits are a fixed fraction $1/k$ of the advertising expenditures. Or, more formally, $A = kP$. This is a determinate relationship between advertising and profits. But on the basis of the information at hand, we can't really say whether the advertising outlay causes profits or high profits stimulate more advertising. So the relationship is not causal. Suppose we had not noticed the constant of proportionality k between A and P, but instead observed only the high positive correlation between profits and advertising expenditures. In that case we would still have a determinate relationship, but it wouldn't be an explanation; the explanation resides in the law $A = kP$.

Before leaving this point, I should mention that the notion of determinacy has nothing to do with randomness. The advertising example involves a *deterministic* relationship, the law $A = kP$. But even the tossing of a coin is a determinate process, since the outcome is not lawless but rather obeys a different kind of law—a statistical one. Thus one event can determine another without causing it. Causal determination is only a special type of determination. So again we see that from a scientific standpoint the nub of the matter is whether or not the explanation we offer is based upon a lawful relationship. But there are many kinds of laws, not all of them causal. So let's explore this point in just a bit more detail.

The philosopher of science Mario Bunge has provided a convenient categorization of the many types of explanations possible for observed events, distinguishing between those explanations that *may* be causal and those that aren't. As a summary of the idea of explanation as science understands that term, it's useful to reflect on Bunge's list.

I. TYPES OF CAUSAL EXPLANATIONS

A. Inclusion in a sequence

Example: Today is Tuesday because yesterday was Monday.
General Rule: B is true because it was preceded by A, and whenever A occurs it is known or assumed to be followed by B.

B. Tracing origins and evolution

Example: Tina lost her baby teeth because all children lose their baby teeth at her age.
General Rule: A is a necessary stage in a developmental or evolutionary pathway.

C. Connection with other facts

Example: Iron rusts when it's brought into contact with moisture and air.
General Rule: A follows from other facts of a different order.

D. Analysis

Example: Compressing a gas in an enclosed cylinder raises its temperature because the gas molecules have more collisions with the walls of the cylinder.
General Rule: A is the aggregate or composition of simpler facts that are known or assumed to be true.

II. TYPES OF NONCAUSAL EXPLANATIONS

E. Membership in a class

Example: Rover doesn't talk because he's a dog and dogs don't talk.
General Rule: All members of class X possess property P. The object x is in X. Therefore x has property P.

F. Description

Example: The refrigerator motor functions the way it does because of the laws of thermodynamics.

General Rule: A takes place because of phenomenological laws having no causal component.

G. Static structures

Example: The reason this stone pillar is placed here is because of the role it plays in the overall structural integrity of the building.

General Rule: The entities composing a structure hold a certain place in the structure, which accounts for the peculiarities and functions of the overall structure.

H. Reference to a lower level

Example: The thought of a nice, cool beer is explained by neurophysiological processes in my brain.

General Rule: A is the outcome of a set of qualitatively different events belonging to a lower level of organization.

I. Reference to a higher level

Example: The behavior of a molecule of water in a container full of water is explained by the state of all the water, e.g., whether it's liquid or ice.

General Rule: A is explained by showing the place of the given object in the whole, and then showing the influence of the whole on the part.

J. Statistics

Example: The pressure-volume relationship of an ideal gas is explained by means of the billiard ball model of gas, together with statistical hypotheses and rules about the individual interactions.

General Rule: The object to be explained is a member of a population whose behavior can be accounted for only by statistical aggregates.

K. Teleology

Example: Wars are consciously planned by politicians and bankers in order to prevent economic crises or to placate social unrest.

General Rule: The object's behavior is explained by invoking goals or purposes for the object.

L. Dialectics

Example: The composition of the atomic nucleus is the result of the conflict between two opposing tendencies: the equalization trend arising from the conversion of neutrons to protons, and the reduction of the proton number owing to electrical repulsion.

General Rule: A is explained as being the result of the inward and outward conflicts that keep certain processes going, or that bring about the emergence of entities having new qualities.

There may be many readers, myself included, who would take exception to one or more of Bunge's classifications into causal and noncausal categories. Nevertheless, the overall trend is evident: Causal explanation will be found only within the laws of science and nature, not outside them. In short, scientific explanation is explanation by law, not by causes. As we examine the many natural and human activities dealt with in later chapters, the reader should keep this point uppermost in mind. Now let's shift attention to our other primary focus—prediction.

POLISHING THE CRYSTAL BALL

Marcus Tullius, better known as Cicero, as well as being a statesman and poet, was reputed to be ancient Rome's greatest orator. He claimed that two things underlay the Roman government: ritual and divination. And in his work *De Divinatione,* Cicero presents an extended discussion of the pluses and minuses of divination, eventually rendering the verdict that the liabilities far outweigh the assets. Having himself served for a time on the Roman Board of Augurs, presumably Cicero knew whereof he spoke! In light of the feverish and increasingly profitable activities of the Beltway Bandits, the deep-thoughts-for-hire industry ringing Washington, D.C., it seems safe to say that after two millennia we haven't moved much further along the road to enlightenment than the Romans. We still want to know the future and are willing to shower riches and glory upon those who present even the most superficial appearance of being able to foretell it.

While our interest here is in scientifically based prediction methods, history is full of all sorts of wild schemes aimed at revealing the future. For instance, there is the method of gelomancy, in which predictions are obtained by translating hysterical laughter into tangible terms— undoubtedly a useful procedure to employ at academic and political conventions. Or there's the daffy method of daphnomancy, in which questions of great import are answered in varying degrees of yes or no by throwing laurel leaves onto a fire. The louder the leaves crackle, the better the omen; the deeper the silence, the worse the prospects.

Of course, some prediction "methods" are not really methods at all, but only statements of the beliefs of so-called experts in the area the prediction addresses. These are the kinds of predictions about the future made by seers, mediums, and mystics that often appear at year's end in Sunday supplement articles. A particular favorite of mine along these lines came from Henry Freedman, an expert on long-range prospects for the graphics arts and communications industry. In a prediction made specially for *The Book of Predictions,* Mr. Freedman claimed that by the year 2000, "Authors will have complete control over the publication process, from editing and printing to distribution of the finished work, thus ending the relationship between author and publisher." To live to see that glorious day is almost motivation enough to turn me into a teetotaling, fried-egg-avoiding jogger with an addiction to granola. Almost. But interesting and entertaining as these divination methods are, I don't think even their proponents would be prepared to argue that they are in any way scientific. So let's look at what it would take to say we had a scientific method of forecasting the future.

In his immensely entertaining science-fiction novel *The Stochastic Man,* Robert Silverberg tells the tale of a certain Lew Nichols, a man who makes his living practicing "stochastic prediction," the art of plotting extrapolations from all possibilities to arrive at the most likely course of events. This technique makes Nichols an almost infallible short-range prophet, who uses his skills to help push forward the cause of a colleague in a presidential campaign. Later Nichols meets a sultry, mysterious Indian beauty, who shows him that genuine second sight can be developed with comparative ease. Then one day in March of '99, the sullen and eccentric millionaire Martin Carval appears on the scene with the chilling pronouncement that "Your computer models allow you to guess the future. Now I will show you how to *control* it." Could such a scene really take place? Is it even possible, in principle, for someone like Nichols to have a computer scheme that would be capable of predicting the future with complete accuracy?

To show the impossibility of a perfect prediction scheme, let's suppose you have the most powerful computer imaginable, a machine that's capable of computing anything that can be computed—and within a reasonable timespan to boot. For all practical purposes, any systematic scientific method for making predictions is tantamount to carrying out some sort of computation (the justification for this claim will occupy much of our attention in the final chapter of this book). Let's attach a light to this mega-monster computer, and wire it up so that the light turns off when the computer prints the statement YES, and stays on if the computer serves up a NO. Initially, the light is turned on. Now let's ask the machine to tell us if the light will be on at some definite time in the future, say a hundred years from now.

Clearly, there's no way the machine can give the correct answer. If it says YES, the light turns off; but if the machine says NO, then the light stays on. Either way, the machine makes the wrong prediction about what will be the case in the future. Of course, the knowledgeable reader will recognize this situation as just another illustration of the standard self-reference type of paradox so cherished by logicians. Nevertheless, it shows in particularly simple terms the impossibility of ever attaining a state of perfect foreknowledge of everything. However, the example doesn't rule out the possibility of predicting some types of events with complete certainty. So let's take a moment to classify the kinds of forecasts of the future that may be possible.

In contrast to the prediction schemes discussed earlier, scientific predictions, just like scientific explanations, are based in law. Speaking more formally, a scientific prediction involves deducing a relationship between as yet unknown or unexperienced facts using general laws and pieces of specific information. Note the way in which prediction is superficially the same as explanation—i.e., both are consequences of the use of deduction to obtain new facts from laws and individual bits of information. So, logically speaking, both prediction and explanation are deductive processes. But epistemologically the two are quite separate, as prediction has a type of uncertainty all its own. In addition to the uncertainty of incompleteness found in explanation, prediction also has the kind of uncertainty involving the unforeseen emergence of novelty. Now let's have that promised look at the types of predictions that may arise. Just like with categories of explanations considered in the last section, this classification of types of predictions is also due to Mario Bunge.

III. TYPES OF PREDICTIONS

A. Taxonomic rules

Example: All mammals are warm-blooded.
General Rule: Every *a* is *A*.

B. Structure laws

Example: The existence of some light isotopes of certain chemical elements can be predicted on the basis of the assumed structure of their nuclei.
General Rule: Assumptions about the structure allow us to formulate predictive rules.

C. Phenomenological laws

Example: By knowing the refractive index of a transparent body, and by measuring the angle of incidence of a light ray entering the body, we can use Snell's Law to predict the angle of refraction.
General Rule: Appeal to a static law of nature.

D. Time patterns

Example: The full moon will occur on May 16, 1992.
General Rule: Appeal to a dynamical law of nature.

E. Statistical ensemble

Example: Mendelian genetics predicts the overall statistical distribution of genetic traits in a population, but cannot predict with certainty the appearance of a given hereditary trait in a certain offspring at a certain time.
General Rule: Use of statistical laws of nature to predict aggregate quantities among a population of objects or events.

In passing, it's of some importance to note that a prediction need not necessarily involve a statement about the future from facts in the present. For example, in the structure law example above, the inference is from the known to the unknown. Similarly, the invocation of Snell's Law to predict the angle of refraction of a light ray doesn't involve any essential temporal component. But, for the most part, the kinds of predictions that we'll concern ourselves with in later chapters will fall into the categories D and E, in which timing is indeed of the essence.

With these ideas of prediction in mind, we may wonder where causality fits in. If prediction is just deduction in disguise, at least logically speaking, and if causality is the real-world counterpart of logical deduction, then it seems sensible to suppose that there should be a deep connection between the two. But, in fact, this is not the case. It is just not true that prediction depends in any way on causality. To think that it does is to confuse a trait of the natural world (causation) with a criterion (predictability) for the empirical test of scientific assumptions that need not involve the notion of causality at all. If we insist on the equation prediction = causality, then we are also forced to accept the consequence that scientific law = causal law, which we know is not the case. In fact, even a causal law doesn't ensure that predictions made using it will have any greater level of accuracy than those arising out of noncausal laws. For example, Newton's laws of motion are causal but lead to great errors in the prediction of planetary orbits if the initial planetary positions are not known very accurately. In summary, there is no necessary relation between prediction and causality, any more than there is between causality and explanation. The preceding line of thought naturally leads to the question of how much trust we can place in even scientific predictions.

In a 1946 paper in the *Journal of Philosophy,* Nelson Goodman put forth what has come to be termed the Grue-Bleen Paradox as a vehicle to sharpen our thinking on the question: How do we justify our inductive inferences? In other words, if I see the Sun come up in the east every day for forty-five years, how do I justify the prediction that it will rise again in the east tomorrow? Since this kind of assertion certainly constitutes a scientific prediction as we have been using that term here, based as it is on the laws of celestial mechanics, Goodman's thoughts on the matter of the validity of the entire prediction process are of considerable interest for us.

Imagine a situation in which I want to buy an emerald ring as a present for a certain lady of my acquaintance. So I head for Guttmann's jewelry shop down at the end of my street to look over his offerings. Like almost every other Viennese shopkeeper, Guttmann keeps the lights in his shop down at a level so low that only a mole could actually see the merchandise. So before handing over my square of plastic to finalize the purchase of the ring, I ask Guttmann if I can take it outdoors to examine the stone's true color. As well as being a mole, every Viennese is also a philosopher, so as we're walking to the door Guttmann casually mentions that the color of the stone is "grue." This strange pronouncement stops me dead in my tracks, and I ask him just what kind of "color" he has in mind. Guttmann says that *grue* is a common term in the world of gemologists: A stone is grue if, when it's observed before January 1, 2000, it's green, and after that time it's blue. Similarly, he says, a stone that's blue before the turn of the century and green afterward is called *bleen* by the cognoscenti. Not wanting to get into a detailed discussion with Guttmann—especially about matters linguistic or philosophical—I shrug my shoulders, hand back the ring, and tell him I'll sleep not only on the idea of grue and bleen, but also on whether or not I really want to buy the ring. Of course I studiously avoid Guttmann thereafter, but his claim about these odd colors for describing what to my eye looked to be a perfectly normal green emerald continues to haunt me as I ponder the nature of inductive reasoning and prediction. Here's why.

Let's consider a green emerald that I buy today from Guttmann's archrival, Schlecter. The fact that this emerald is green certainly adds confirmatory evidence to my belief that all emeralds are green. However, it also adds support to Guttmann's claim that "all emeralds are grue." And since all emeralds observed up to now have been green, and all such emeralds have been observed before the year 2000, I sadly conclude that both the "green" and "grue" hypotheses are equally strongly confirmed by the emerald I bought from Schlecter. A similar argument would hold if I had bought a blue sapphire today, in which case the twin hypotheses "blue" and "bleen" would have been equally strengthened.

Now what can we expect on the stroke of midnight, December 31, 1999? Will my emerald be green or grue? The commonsense answer is that it will be green rather than the weird color grue. But why should this be the case? All the evidence at hand supports either prediction equally well, yet we intuitively feel that "green" is the only way to bet. The question Goodman asks is simply why we instinctively feel that the color green is more "projectible" into the future than the color grue. Goodman himself feels that the resolution of the paradox hinges on the fact that certain predicates like *blue* and *green* are more firmly entrenched than others. That is, they are more acceptable than others because of what the philosopher David Hume called "custom and habit." Basically, blue and green are preferable to bleen and grue because the observational procedures for them are always simpler— e.g., they don't involve any timed switches. For our concerns, the main point of the paradox is just to single out the fact that the validity of predictions may involve a lot more subjectivity than many scientists would care to admit—even when the predictions arise from so-called scientific laws. In short, a hypothesis or theory is not necessarily made more certain when its predictions are confirmed.

Despite the fact that we've been speaking rather negatively here about the inherent logical limitations of prediction, let's not be too gloomy. As we'll see later, there are many situations in life in which very accurate, reliable predictions can be offered about phenomena of great interest and importance. But what the above remarks do show is that it's very rare to find a situation in which we can speak with complete certainty about anything. Thus, our predictions are almost always enshrouded within a murky haze of uncertainty or imprecision, forcing us to speak like a TV weatherman and talk about the outcome being *A* with a 10 percent chance, *B* with 50 percent, and *C* with 35 percent probability, keeping the final 5 percent in reserve for novelty. But if we're going to speak in probabilistic terms, we need to be conversant with at least the rudiments of elementary probability theory and statistics. So let's devote a few pages to an introduction/review of the standard way science has chosen to formalize our intuitive ideas about the uncertain.

THE GOOD, THE BAD, AND THE PROBABLE

Some years ago in New York, I had a barber named Benny who regularly distracted me with his version of the age-old game "divide and conquer," in which he would classify people into mutually ex-clusive groups. As a sample play of this game, I recall Benny's re-marking one steamy summer afternoon, "You know, Doc, there are two kinds of people in this world: Italians, and those who wish they were Italian," a dichotomy no doubt attributable to Benny's Sicilian background. As my own family hails from this same part of the world,

Benny's expression of ethnic pride and prejudice fell upon rather sympathetic ears, which was probably why he brought the matter up in the first place. However, despite my weaknesses for spaghetti, gondolas, and exotic sports cars, I tend to divide the world along quite different lines.

As an inveterate letter writer, I find nothing more difficult to understand or more annoying than someone who dawdles over correspondence. So my own pet global dichotomy involves classifying the world into those who answer correspondence promptly and those who don't. In fact, at one point I became so irritated by the reluctance of certain parties to respond to my entreaties that I started keeping a record of incoming correspondence just to see how tardy, inattentive, and generally disorganized some of these "correspondents" really were, when measured against the general run of mankind. While I never thought this information would be useful for much of anything other than as confirmation of my deeply held beliefs about such laggards, it turns out that we can make good use of this database of delinquents as a way of introducing a short review of one or two of the basic ideas of elementary statistics and probability needed for our subsequent development.

Table 1.1 displays a record of the number of items of personal correspondence I received over a recent one-year period. This record includes letters, cards, faxes, telexes, and telegrams, but omits things like magazines, journals, promo brochures, books, and other nonpersonal correspondence (especially bills). There are a total of 292 items registered in the table, with an obvious clustering around the Christmas-card period in December and January, and a counterbalancing thinning-out in the summer months when academics tend to do their annual disappearing act.

Jan.	Feb.	Mar.	Apr.	May	June	July	Aug.	Sept.	Oct.	Nov.	Dec.
31	24	28	19	23	20	18	12	21	29	25	42

Table 1.1. Monthly count of incoming postal items

The most important single statistic that can be gleaned from this record is the *average*, or *mean*, number of items received each month. This critical quantity is obtained simply by taking the total number of items received and dividing by the number of observations in the record. Since there are a total of 292 items recorded in 12 monthly data points, the average, usually denoted in statistics by $\bar{x}$, is just the quantity

$$\bar{x} = \text{expected number of postal items per month} = \frac{292}{12} = 24\frac{1}{3}$$

In the absence of additional information, the average is the best estimate I can make of how many cards and letters will be coming in during the course of a given month. But, as can be seen, only in the months of February, May, and November are receipts anywhere near the average. So it's of at least as much interest to know how my mail fluctuates around the average as it is to know the average itself. For this we need to compute another quantity, the *variance*.

The way to calculate the variance is to add up how far each monthly level is from the mean, and then take the average of these differences. This gives a measure of how far the individual monthly observations are from the mean. But since each monthly level can be either larger or smaller than the mean, the difference between the individual levels and the average can be either positive or negative. Therefore, to avoid having negative and positive differences cancel each other out, thus giving a misleading estimate of the real deviations from the mean, we make all the differences positive in order to reflect all departures from the average. The most mathematically convenient way to accomplish this is simply to square each difference. Thus, the variance is computed by adding up the quantities (level of mail in month i − average level)^2, and then dividing by the total number of months. Thus, for our numerical example above, we would have

$$\text{variance} = \frac{[(31 - 24\frac{1}{3})^2 + (24 - 24\frac{1}{3})^2 + (28 - 24\frac{1}{3})^2 + \ldots + (42 - 24\frac{1}{3})^2]}{12} = 53.722$$

Of course, this number is the average of the *squares* of the deviation of the monthly postal receipts from the mean. To get a more realistic estimate of the average deviation itself, we simply take the square root of the variance. This quantity, termed the *standard deviation*, is usually written as s in the world of statistics. For the above data, we find that $s = \sqrt{\text{variance}} = \sqrt{53.722} = 7.329$. Thus, there is a fairly substantial average deviation of more than 7 items from the expected level of $24\frac{1}{3}$ items per month.

We can use the correspondence database in a different way to illustrate another key statistical concept, the idea of *correlation*. From Table 1.1, we see that the number of postal items I received each month ranged from 12 to 42 during the course of the year. Suppose I also kept track of the number of incoming phone calls during this same period. If I had actually done this and plotted the number of calls against the postal items using crosses as labels, I might have seen a graph like that shown in Figure 1.3. The figure also displays what statisticians call the *regression line,* which is simply the best straight-line fit to the data.

The data in Figure 1.3 rather strongly suggest that as the postal input increases, the number of incoming phone calls declines. This

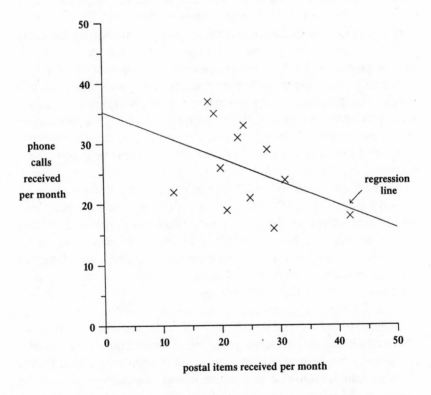

Figure 1.3. *Postal items received versus phone calls*

rather evident inverse relationship is made explicit by the negative slope of the regression line (its actual value is around -0.39). For any set of data points relating two quantities, it turns out that a positive slope of the regression line indicates that as one quantity increases, so does the other (positive correlation); a negative slope like that seen here means that as one variable increases, the other decreases (negative correlation).

Before leaving the world of statistics, a couple of amplifying remarks about correlation are in order. The most important point to clarify is the relationship between strong correlation (positive or negative) and causality. That relationship is simple to describe: no relation at all! In general, strong correlation implies nothing about causal connections between the variables that are correlated. Confusion on this point has probably been responsible for more misuses and abuses of statistics than any other single misperception, as will be especially vividly illustrated in Chapter Four when we come to consider stock market prediction and explanation schemes. For now, let's just note that in the example treated here it seems plausible to assume that there might be some causal explanation for the fact that as my phone calls go up, the postman's life gets easier, since at least some of those phone messages presumably substitute for a written communication. But this is injecting additional information into the situation that's not inherently part of the given data itself. So on the basis of the correlation alone, we are *never* justified in imputing a causal relationship between two quantities—even if they have perfect positive or negative correlation.

What about zero correlation? Does this imply that the quantities involved are entirely unrelated? The answer depends on what you mean by the term *unrelated*. As used in probability and statistics, *unrelated* usually means that the quantities are *statistically independent*—i.e., knowledge of one gives no information whatsoever about what the other is doing. In this sense, which we'll make more precise in a moment, zero correlation does *not* imply independence.

With the foregoing limitations of correlation in hand, we see that knowledge of the correlation doesn't really help much in furthering our understanding of the relationship between observed quantities. So let's move away from the world of raw data and simple statistical tricks, stepping into the universe of possible events to examine a few of the concepts and methods that probability theorists have developed for characterizing the likelihood of things.

*   *   *

Virtually all of my correspondents fall into one of three groups: academics, publishers, and relatives/friends. Of course, these categories are not mutually exclusive. So let's suppose I dig into my files and label each item with as many of the symbols A, P, and F as are appropriate for the item at hand. For instance, if I have a postcard from my colleague and friend Karl telling me how warm the sun is this winter in Luxor, then this item would get two symbols—an A since Karl is an academic colleague and an F since he's also a friend. On the other hand, a letter from my sister would be labeled solely with an F. For the sake of discussion, let's imagine I actually carried out this onerous chore, coming up with the following distribution:

Category	Number of Items	Fraction of Total
A	175	0.60
P	73	0.25
F	146	0.50

Table 1.2. Different categories of postal items

Now let's play the all too common "Looking For the Letter" game. LFL involves a furious rummaging through the files in a generally fruitless search for some long-forgotten or never-before-seen item of correspondence. The figures in the last column of Table 1.2 show the likelihood that any single draw from my filing cabinet will turn up an item carrying one or more of the labels A, P, and F. Now how did I arrive at these likelihoods?

The process is elementary, my dear reader: I took the total number of items of each type as shown in the second column of the table, and divided that quantity by 292, the total number of items in my correspondence file. In everyday terms, these likelihoods are what we would call the "probability" of my fishing out a correspondence item carrying the labels A, P, and/or F. What justifies the validity of this approach to setting probabilities is the assumption that a random dip into the files is equally likely to turn up any one of the 292 items in the drawer. This idea forms the basis of what probability theorists call the *relative frequency* approach to likelihood estimation. Let's see how it looks in more formal clothes.

Assume we have a set $\mathcal{U}$ consisting of all the possible events that can occur in a given situation. Suppose that A is some event in $\mathcal{U}$. Under these circumstances, the relative frequency approach tells us that the probability of A, denoted by $P(A)$, is given by the following rule:

$$P(A) = \frac{\text{the number of ways that the event } A \text{ can occur}}{\text{the total number of ways that all events in } \mathcal{U} \text{ can occur}}$$

In other words, $P(A)$ is just the "size" or "frequency" of the event A relative to the size of the entire set of possible events $\mathcal{U}$.

To connect this notion with a familiar example, think about the game of five-card draw poker. Suppose that the event A we want to know about is the appearance of a royal flush on the deal (what poker addict wouldn't be interested in *this* event?). Thus, $A = \{a \text{ royal flush on the deal}\}$. The universe $\mathcal{U}$ of all possible events is simply the number of possible five-card hands we could receive on the deal. From a normal fifty-two-card deck, this number is just the number of ways we can draw five cards from a deck of fifty-two. Elementary combinatorial theory gives this number as 2,598,960. Since there are only four different ways we can get a royal flush, the desired probability is

$$P(\text{royal flush}) = \frac{4}{2,598,960} = 0.0000015 \approx \text{a bit better than 1 in 1 million}$$

Maybe this is where the expression *one in a million* came from!

It's fairly evident, I think, that when it comes to predicting a future happening on the basis of past and current events, it's crucial to know whether what's predicted *depends* in any meaningful way on the events used to make the prediction. If the two are genuinely independent, then the prediction scheme is vacuous (at least from a scientific standpoint); no information about one event can be obtained from knowledge of the other. But what does it mean for two events to be independent?

Suppose we are concerned with the events A and B. Our question is whether they are statistically independent—i.e., does the probability of the occurrence or nonoccurrence of one have any bearing on the probability of the occurrence of the other? Note carefully that this is *not* the same thing as logical independence, which was discussed earlier. The essential difference is that logical independence deals with specific, single events *A* and *B*; statistical independence deals with the probability distributions for events that *might* or *might not* occur in a universe $\mathcal{U}$ of possible events. Probability theory *defines* the events *A* and *B* to be statistically independent if we have the relation

$$P(A \text{ and } B \text{ both occurring}) = P(A \text{ occurring}) \times P(B \text{ occurring})$$

In words, *A* and *B* are independent if the likelihood of their joint occurrence equals the product of the likelihoods of their occurring separately. Now why should this be a good definition of independence? In what way does this formula jibe with our everyday intuition about two events being independent? Basically, the answer comes down to an analysis of the conditional probability of the event *A*, *given that the event B has already occurred.* If the events *A* and *B* are statistically independent, then common sense and intuition say that the occurrence or nonoccurrence of *B* should have no influence at all on this conditional probability. In short, the probability of *A* given *B* should be exactly the same as the probability of *A* alone. Tracing through the mathematical implications of this requirement leads to the expression above.

This is about as good a place as any to end our far too abbreviated refresher course on the elements of probability and statistics. These ideas about how to get a grasp on uncertainty are crucial for understanding many of the approaches to explanation and prediction of real-world phenomena of the sort we'll be looking at throughout the remainder of the book. However, without further strengthening, they don't do much to help us deal with the process of change, i.e., dynamics. Since change is the very essence of most people's ideas of prediction, it behooves us to take a few pages to consider the way science talks about time-varying phenomena. Thus we devote the next section to an overview of what we mean when we speak of a dynamical system.

THE TRACKS OF TIME

In the introduction to his book *Théorie analytique des probabilités,* the eighteenth-century French mathematician Pierre Simon de Laplace made the following oft-quoted statement:

> Given for one instant an intelligence which could comprehend all the forces by which nature is animated and the respective positions of the

beings which compose it . . . nothing would be uncertain, and the future
as the past would be present to its eyes.

This Laplacian vision of the universe stands as the high-water mark of
the mechanistic Newtonian world view, claiming that events of the
future and past would be an open book for one who could know the
forces that act upon the "particles of life," together with the positions
and velocities of those particles at some given instant of time. What
possible scientific justification could Laplace have had for making this
outrageously extravagant claim? By what mechanism could he have
hoped, even in principle, to predict the future with certainty on the
basis of knowledge of the present? Laplace's answer to these questions
involves what we call today a *dynamical system*.

As I write these words, there's a pesky fly buzzing about in my
office creating quite a disturbance as it moves about on its path of
intricate, seemingly aimless dives, loops, and rolls. Just now the fly
has landed on my desk and is wandering around on the surface, presumably in accordance with a plan allowing it to fulfill its destiny as a
fly. But what if this fly has no overall plan of any kind? Or, more
precisely, that the plan wired into its brain says only: "Wherever you
are, read the signal from that location on the desktop (a "flyomone,"
perhaps) and move to wherever the signal tells you to go." To carry
this fantasy one step further, imagine that every single point on my
desktop carries such a message, stating unambiguously in "fly language" what location on the desk the fly should move to from that
point. Under such circumstances, the fly's path might look something
like that shown in Figure 1.4.

Within the confines of the above fantasy, the fly's movements
about the top of my desk capture exactly the key elements of a dynamical system: (1) a region or space (technically a *manifold*) M on
which the motion takes place (the desktop), and (2) an unambiguous
rule specifying where to go to next from wherever you currently find
yourself. Mathematicians call such a rule a *vector field*. In more general situations, the "points" of the manifold M may not be real spatial points like those forming the two-dimensional surface of my
desktop, but only the "points" of some higher-dimensional abstract
space. A good example is the four-dimensional spacetime of relativity theory, in which the "points" are a combination of the three
spatial dimensions and time. But in all cases, the points of M are
termed the possible *states* of the system, leading to the often-

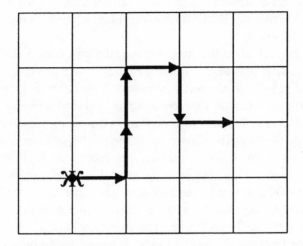

Figure 1.4. *A fly's path along the desktop*

encountered terminology *state space* for *M*. With these ideas in mind, we see that

dynamical system = manifold of states + vector field

Generally, we think of the fly's motion on a tabletop as being continuous, implying that the grid spacing in Figure 1.4 shrinks to an infinitesimal, essentially to zero. In that case, the fly's path becomes a continuous curve along the surface of the desk, and it's natural to think of this path as unfolding in continuous time. We term such a dynamical process a *continuous-time system*. On the other hand, if instead of a fly on my desk there had been a grasshopper, then the movement from point to point would have been in jumps made at discrete moments. In this case, it's more natural to think of the points on the path as changing at discrete instants, leading to what we call a *discrete-time system*.

In either continuous or discrete time, the fly-on-the-desktop example illustrates perfectly how Laplace could assert his idea of predictability. All we need to know is the fly's original position on the desk, along with the vector field telling it where to move from any point. Thereafter we can predict exactly where the fly will be at any time in the future by just repeatedly applying the rule of motion specified by the vector field. But note carefully for future reference that the success of this predictive scheme is totally dependent on knowledge of the rule, or "law," of motion. Without knowing this law, there's no prediction, scientifically speaking.

As it turns out, all of the laws of classical physics, such as Newton's laws of motion, Maxwell's equations for electromagnetism, and even Einstein's equations of special relativity, can be used in this same fashion to trace out the time behavior of physical processes. These dynamical laws of motion are described in formal mathematical terms by what are technically known as differential equations, which are easily obtained by simple mathematical operations from the corresponding vector fields. For both theoretical and practical reasons, it turns out that the most important thing we can know about the behavior of a dynamical system is where its trajectory ends up in the long term. Let's return to the fly on the desktop and see why.

Suppose I eventually get tired of waiting for the fly on my desk to buzz off, and so decide to put down a few pieces of flypaper at strategically chosen locations. As the fly wanders about on my desk, I hope it will soon encounter one of these traps, which in effect carry the message: "Stop right here!" In dynamical systems jargon, a point where the vector field broadcasts such a message is called a *fixed point*. Obviously, once the fly gets stuck at such a point, its tour of my desk comes to a bad end and its motion and later its life terminate. But there's another possibility for the fly's long-run behavior.

A fly like the one pestering me now might get lucky and avoid the flypaper, in which case the rules of the vector field could eventually force the fly onto a sequence of points that repeat themselves over and over indefinitely. Now the fly's ultimate behavior is just to "go around in circles," forever visiting and revisiting the same sequence of points. In this case, the fly has been attracted to what is technically termed a *limit cycle*. These two types of long-run behavior, a fixed point and a limit cycle, are shown in Figure 1.5.

In the classical theory of dynamical systems, fixed points and limit cycles are the *only* types of long-run behavior. All the recent excitement about chaos, fractals, and the like has come about from the discovery of a third type. We'll come to that in a moment. First let's tie down some of the ideas about classical systems by looking at an important example.

Vito Volterra was an outstanding Italian mathematician of the first part of this century, whose work strongly influenced the development

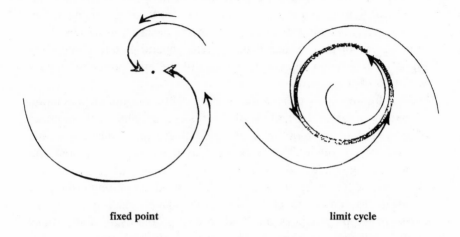

fixed point   limit cycle

Figure 1.5. *Types of long-term behavior for a classical dynamical system*

of modern calculus. Like a lot of other mathematicians, Volterra held rather definite political views, and was finally forced to leave both his position at the University of Rome and Italy itself in 1931 when he refused to take an oath of loyalty to Mussolini's Fascist regime. Just as with his political ideas, Volterra was also ahead of his time when it came to putting mathematics back into contact with reality, devoting most of his research after World War I to investigations in mathematical biology. But unlike most blackboard speculators, Volterra was not afraid to get his hands dirty, and often engaged in field expeditions of various sorts to gather data for his studies in what we would now term *mathematical ecology*.

In one of his experimental forays in the early 1920s, Volterra gathered a considerable volume of data on two fish species found in the Adriatic Sea. These two species displayed what we today call a *predator-prey* relation to each other—one species was regularly served up as the preferred blue-plate special for the other. The empirical part of Volterra's study involved keeping track of the population levels of these two types of fish over a substantial period of time. The theoretical side of the investigation focused on the distillation of this mass of observations into a pair of rather simple differential equations expressing the fluctuation of the two populations over the course of time. The particular form of the equations (i.e., the vector field) is not especially important for us at the moment. But what is of great interest is the geometrical description of how Volterra's predator-prey system behaves. The general picture is shown in Figure 1.6, where x represents the size of the prey population and y is the number of predators.

This figure shows clearly that starting from any initial population levels, the long-term behavior of the system is cyclical, the number of prey and number of predators each fluctuating inversely to the fortunes of the other. This is because as the prey are captured and eaten, the resources available to the predators are reduced and they, too, begin to die off. But with fewer predators around, the prey can start to reproduce at higher levels again, leading to an increase in the prey population. And so emerge the cyclic fluctuations in the predator and prey populations. The figure also shows that the larger the initial populations, the larger the subsequent fluctuations. But in all cases, Volterra's simplified model leads to behavior

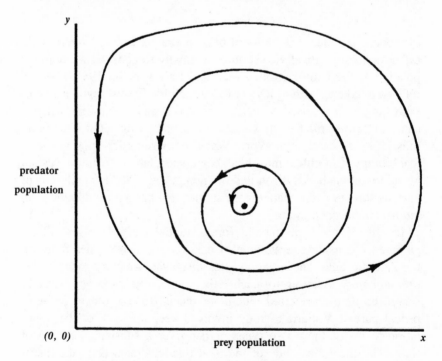

Figure 1.6. *Predator-prey dynamics*

that is cyclic regardless of the starting levels of the predator and the prey.

Some straightforward embellishments upon Volterra's assumptions about predation rates, birth rates, natural attrition, and the like bring his model more into line with physical reality, leading to a modified vector field describing the predator-prey fluctuations. A picture of the dynamics of this new system is shown in Figure 1.7. In this case, we see that regardless of the initial predator and prey populations, the system eventually settles down to a single cyclic behavior. In other words, all trajectories are attracted to this single orbit, which is an example of a *limit cycle*. Thus, in contrast to the case of Figure 1.6, in which each initial population level gives rise to its own characteristic cyclic orbit, here we have only a single cyclical fluctuation of

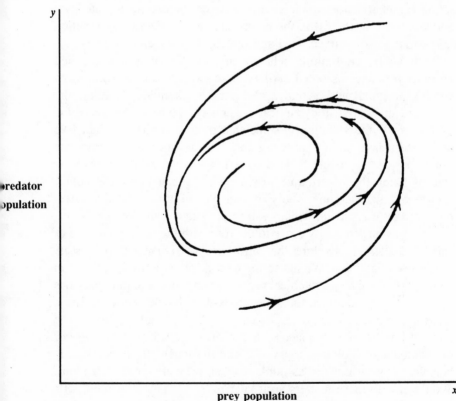

Figure 1.7. *A predator-prey limit cycle*

predators and prey to which all starting populations are eventually attracted.

Finally, let's consider a limiting case in which either the predators or the prey die off (a case in which either $y = 0$ or $x = 0$). Suppose the prey die out, perhaps due to a not so unlikely chemical poisoning of their habitat. Then the predators would eventually die out, too, since they would be deprived of their source of food. Under these circumstances, as time goes on both populations die off—i.e., the limiting populations are $x = y = 0$—a single point in the two-dimensional space of possible fish populations. This is an example of the kind of fixed point, or *equilibrium point,* introduced earlier. If the predators had died out instead of the prey, there would be a population explosion of prey since no predators would be around to eat them. In the oversimplified world of Volterra, such a situation would also eventually lead to an equilibrium point at $x = \infty, y = 0$. But since nature abhors infinities, other factors would always intervene before this infinite level could ever be reached. But the point remains that the prey population would rise to some fixed level and remain there indefinitely.

Technically, the limiting behavior of a dynamical system is called an *attractor,* and, as noted earlier, these two types of attractors, an equilibrium point and a limit cycle (periodic motion), constitute the two ways that classical dynamical systems can come to the end of the line. In fact, the situation is somewhat more complicated than I've described it here, as it's quite possible for the trajectories from some initial population levels to lead to a limit cycle, while from other starting points the system trajectory moves to a fixed point. Moreover, it turns out that there is actually another type of attractor that a trajectory can get trapped in. This possibility, usually called a *strange attractor,* has only recently come to the fore with the widespread use of supercomputers to explore the intricacies of dynamical processes. These investigations have led to the current obsession with *chaos,* in which virtually every dynamical process from physics to philology has been feverishly examined for signs of possibly chaotic behavior. These ideas are of crucial importance to us as well, especially as they forge a direct link between Laplace's idea of the complete predictability of the behavior of a dynamical system and the inherently unpredictable behavior of what most of us think of when we call a process random. We'll come to these matters a bit later in the chapter. For now, let's explore how we can use the language of dynamical systems to talk mathematically about "catastrophes."

THE MATHEMATICS OF THE UNEXPECTED

In the early seventeenth century, Isaac Newton showed that the path of a planet moving under the influence of the Sun's gravity would trace out an ellipse, and that the period of this motion would depend only on the planet's average distance from the Sun. In mathematical jargon, Newton showed that this "two-body problem" was integrable. In plain English, this means that we can find a set of mathematical equations (Newton's laws of motion) from which we can derive a complete system of relations (Kepler's laws) enabling us to predict any future positions and velocities of the two bodies with arbitrary precision for all time—at least in principle.

But the solar system is not composed of just two bodies. So while it's a good approximation to think that each planet moves around the Sun in an elliptical orbit, the planets also influence each other's motion, causing their individual orbits to depart from perfect ellipses. For example, the Earth's orbit is not fixed in space but gradually rotates, or precesses, at a rate of 1.7 degrees per century due to perturbations by other planets, mainly Jupiter. There are no simple, explicit mathematical relations describing this motion that would allow us to predict with complete accuracy where the planets will be in the future. This fact gives rise to the so-called Three-Body Problem, in which we ask whether these small perturbations in the planetary orbits will eventually cause one of the planets to "fly off" into outer space or have a catastrophic collision with another celestial body. In short, "Is the current configuration of the solar system stable?" It was this very question, incidentally, that led to Laplace's famous remark about predictability via dynamical systems, quoted at the beginning of the preceding section.

In everyday terms, if we call an ecosystem or a bridge or a person stable, it means that that object remains more or less unchanged in the face of various disturbances acting upon it. Thus, I would certainly regard my wife as having a very stable personality, since she's able to remain unflustered in the face of the very great pressures exerted upon her in having to deal with me on a day-to-day basis. On the other hand, I might be tempted to describe one of my past editors as a rather unstable personality type, in light of her manic-depressive fits over what I could see as only the most innocuous of suggestions from me about the processing of my sterling prose. In short, the essence of instability resides in the idea that small changes can lead to disproportionately large effects. And so it is in mathematics, too.

There are two fundamentally different ways we can perturb a dynamical system: change the starting point or change the vector field. With the first type of change, the stability question can be stated as

The Classical Lyapunov Stability Problem

If the initial point on the state manifold is perturbed to a nearby point, do the two trajectories emanating from these points remain "close" for all time? In particular, do the trajectories end up in the same attractor?

A change of the vector field itself can arise in several ways. Probably the most common is when the vector field depends upon some physical parameter in the system, human or natural interventions acting to modify that parameter. For example, in Volterra's predator-prey system, specification of the appropriate vector field requires inclusion of terms representing the birth rates of both the predator and the prey. If we specify different birth rates, the corresponding vector fields give different rules for how the population trajectory should move in the two-dimensional "predator-prey space." This change from one vector field to another by variation of parameters may do wild things to the kinds of trajectories that the corresponding dynamical processes will follow. This illustrative example leads to the general

Structural Stability Problem

Given two "nearby" vector fields, do trajectories starting from the same initial point, but following the different vector fields, end up in the same, or at least "nearby," attractors?

The importance of these two stability problems for questions of explanation and prediction is clear, especially in the case of prediction. If the attractor of the mathematical model (dynamical system) constituting the explanation of the system is unstable in the Lyapunov sense, then we can have little faith in the long-term predictions arising from such a model, since imprecise knowledge of the initial point is one of the principal crosses that scientists always have to bear. On the other hand, if the model is stable relative to perturbations away from the starting point, then small disturbances tend to wash out as time goes by, and all trajectories ultimately come back to the same attractor. In this case, we might be willing to bet at least a salary check or two on the predictions of future events arising from the model.

Similar remarks apply to the structural stability/instability problem, but now with the inevitable inaccuracies in the model arising from a disturbance to, or, equivalently, an imprecise knowledge of, the vector field rather than from a perturbation away from the starting point. Since this kind of instability plays the central role in *catastrophe theory,* one of the most heralded (and controversial) mathematical developments of recent years, it's worth taking a few pages to acquaint ourselves with these "catastrophic ideas," showing us how mathematics can be used to expect the unexpected.

About a half-hour train ride southeast from the center of Paris lies the small village of Bures-sur-Yvette. Like most bedroom communities it's rather nondescript, the principal local diversions being watching the commuter trains go by, a trip to the local shopping center, and a *steak frites* at the Café des Sports. But for mathematicians and physicists there is one thing that sets this community apart from its carbon-copy cousins along the RER "B" train line from Paris, drawing them from around the world like flies to honey. This is the presence of the Institut des Hautes Études Scientifiques (IHES), the French equivalent of the famed Institute for Advanced Study in Princeton, New Jersey. Many visitors to the IHES, myself included, have noted that the institute's lovely location in what was formerly a private estate, its secluded and heavily wooded grounds, as well as its rarefied intellectual climate far from the hustle and bustle of Parisian life, make for an environment that conjures up images of the retreat for scholars described in Hermann Hesse's classic novel *The Glass Bead Game.*

Unlike its bigger role model in Princeton, the IHES has no social scientists or humanists; it devotes all of its intellectual energy and financial resources to the austere rigors of pure mathematics and theoretical physics. And what resources they are. The small permanent staff of the IHES numbers more Fields Medal winners (the mathematical equivalent of the Nobel Prize) than any other institution in the world. So, a priori, this is not a place from which you would expect major bombshells to burst forth into the world of developmental biology, linguistics, and philosophy. But then, mathematician and philosopher René Thom, the IHES's most publicly visible (and outspoken) scholar, is not exactly your plain-vanilla, garden-variety genius either.

In the November 30, 1973 issue of *The Times Higher Education Supplement,* Professor Clive Kilmister of the University of London wrote in a review of a recently published French book:

It is impossible to give a brief description of the impact of this book. In one sense the only book with which it can be compared is Newton's *Principia*. Both lay out a new conceptual framework for the understanding of nature, and equally both go on to unbounded speculation.

And thus did Thom's pioneering book *Stabilité structurelle et morphogènése* burst into the scientific public's consciousness. When the English translation appeared in 1975, similar glowing statements appeared, not only in all the science journals but also in general circulation publications like *Newsweek* and *The New York Times*. And as one has come to expect whenever a laborer in the vineyards of mathematics receives even a small measure of public acclaim, the naysayers of the mathematical community came crawling out from under their rocks. In this instance the charge was led by Hector Sussman of Rutgers University, who "selflessly" traveled the world for the better part of two years claiming not that Thom's mathematics was no good, but that the way his ideas were being employed by some of his more enthusiastic acolytes would give mathematics a black eye in the world at large. These outbursts were enough to make one wonder if the mathematics of Archimedes, Gauss, and Newton rested on such shaky grounds that the whole edifice would come tumbling down over the excess enthusiasm displayed by a few theoreticians trying to reestablish a measure of contact between the worlds of pure mathematics and reality. So what were these ideas that Thom put forth and that created such a tempest in the mathematical teapot?

Basically, what Thom presented was an outline for a mathematical theory of discontinuous phenomena. The mathematics of Newton deals with *continuous* processes like the motion of the Earth around the Sun and the trajectory of a pendulum bob as it swings back and forth in a grandfather clock. In such situations, the position of the Earth or the bob changes only a small amount over a small interval of time—i.e., the system's change of state is a continuous function of time. On the other hand, many of the most interesting and important phenomena in life are discontinuous—an earthquake, the breaking of a wave, the collapse of a speculative market. While Thom's book carried the imposing and academically impenetrable title *Structural Stability and Morphogenesis,* what captured the imagination of the general public was his topic's popular name: catastrophe theory. Apparently, in French the word *catastrophe* is not quite as catastrophic as its English counterpart. But the graphic image conjured up by the term *catastrophe,* coupled with the public's hunger for any kind of magic that will help avoid or precipitate one, ensured a microscopic examination of Thom's theory under the harsh glare of both the scientific and media spotlights. While the mathematical details are much too onerous to enter into here, the basic ideas are easy to describe geometrically.

Earlier we spoke about fixed points, one of the main types of attractors of a dynamical system. The kinds of "catastrophes" (discontinuities) that catastrophe theory addresses are simply the sudden transitions that a system can make when it moves from one stable fixed point to another. To see how this can happen, think of a man jumping from a window on the upper floor of a house on fire. The exact distance away from the house where he lands is determined by Newton's laws of motion, which contain variables (technically termed *parameters*) specifying the two main factors determining the point of impact—the force of gravity and the air resistance. Therefore, the exact location where the man lands is a function of these two quantities (and also, of course, a function of the initial velocity with which he jumps).

Now let's engage in a little science fiction by supposing that the air resistance is held constant, but that we have the ability to vary the gravitational force. As we twist the "gravity knob" and increase the gravitational attraction, air resistance becomes increasingly less important and the man's final distance away from the house changes. Similarly, if we "turn down the gravity," air resistance becomes more important, again leading to some kind of change in the man's final point of impact. Usually, a small change in the gravitational force generates only a small change in the place where the man ends up— i.e., the final position is a continuous function of the gravitational force. However, as the gravity knob moves across the critical level of zero gravity, the final impact location undergoes a discontinuous change, since at that value the man no longer reaches the ground at all but just floats outside the window in an unstable equilibrium. And if we foolishly continue to turn down the gravity, antigravity sets in and the man sails off into outer space. The general idea is shown schematically in Figure 1.8, where the "catastrophic" jump (no pun intended) is represented by the separation between the two point-of-impact curves as the gravity knob passes through zero. This kind of small change in a parameter (or parameters) leading to a large "jump" in the final position of the system is what Thom called a catastrophe.

The vector field defining the rule of motion of a dynamical system almost always contains parameters like the gravitational force and air resistance in our man-in-the-burning-house example. These parame-

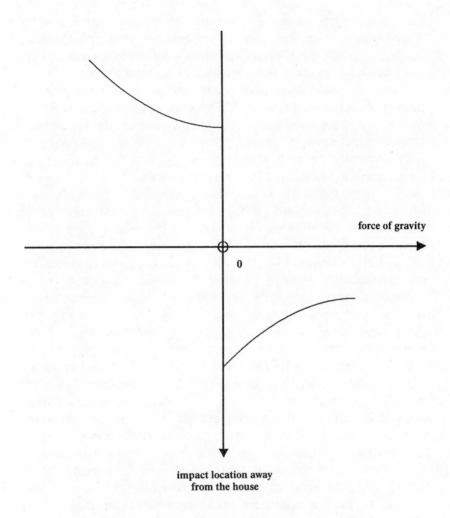

Figure 1.8. *Impact location versus gravitational force*

ters specify the exact physical situation, and often correspond to aspects of the problem that can be modified or controlled by the investigator. For example, things like the reaction rate of a chemical process, the stiffness constant of a spring, and the length of the arm of a pendulum enter as parameters in the dynamical equations characterizing the behavior of these objects. In a given equation, for each value of the parameters the system usually has a different stable equilibrium position to which it moves, an equilibrium corresponding to a fixed point of the dynamical system. Consequently, there is a whole surface of points, each of which is an equilibrium (stable or unstable) for the dynamical process under consideration—one equilibrium point or more for each set of values of the parameters.

Figure 1.9 shows such an equilibrium surface for the case of a system in which we consider the equilibrium position of one variable x as we vary independently two parameters a and b. Here the convoluted surface in the upper part of the figure is the sheet of equilibrium values that x can assume, while the plane lying below it represents the two-dimensional space of the system's parameters a and b. The upper and lower sheets of the equilibrium surface correspond to stable equilibria, while the shaded middle sheet represents the unstable equilibria. The figure shows how, as the parameters a and b are varied, the equilibrium state of the system can "jump" discontinuously from the upper sheet to the lower sheet, and conversely, depending upon exactly how the two parameters are changed. This discontinuous jump as a

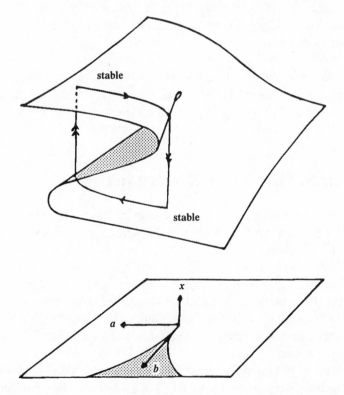

Figure 1.9. *The cusp geometry for a system with two parameters*

result of the parameters crossing the boundaries of the lower shaded region are examples of catastrophes in Thom's sense.

Thom's theory allows us to assert that if the number of independent parameters is small (less than six), then there are only a small number of mathematically distinct types of equilibrium surfaces that can occur in a structurally stable manner, i.e., in a way that the geometric character of the equilibrium surface cannot be destroyed by a small change in the vector field defining the dynamical system. Hence, the geometry in Figure 1.9 is essentially the only picture that can turn up for the equilibrium surface of a dynamical system with two parameters and one observed output. For technical reasons, this surface is called the *cusp* manifold.

I should note, however, that the mathematical theory is at present on a sound footing only for those dynamical systems whose long-run behavior consists solely of fixed points. For systems having limit cycles and strange attractors, a complete mathematical characterization of the geometry of their attractor region remains but a dream.

Since Thom originally developed these ''catastrophic ideas'' in an attempt to account for the emergence of physical forms, especially those arising in living organisms, we'll have plenty of opportunity to see catastrophe theory in action when we come to consideration of these matters in Chapter Three. So let's leave the world of catastrophes for now and pass on to the even wilder and more untamed corner of the mathematical jungle where chaos reigns supreme.

A STRANGENESS IN THE ATTRACTION

The greatest unsolved problem of classical physics is to give a mathematical explanation for the onset of turbulence in fluid flow. Anyone who's ever watched the lazy flow of a meandering stream quickening to become a rushing torrent of white water, as in the Colorado River as it flows through the Grand Canyon, will recognize the essence of the problem. How can we mathematically characterize that transition from the simple-to-understand, parallel streamlines of smooth water flow to the complicated, seemingly random whorls and eddies of fully developed turbulence?

Around 1970 David Ruelle, a Belgian physicist working down the corridor from René Thom at the IHES, was investigating a mathematical model of the onset of turbulence with a visiting Dutch colleague,

Floris Takens from the University of Groningen. At the time of their work, conventional wisdom regarding the onset of turbulence had it that turbulence came about as the breakdown of smooth flow (a fixed point) into an ever-increasing succession of higher and higher order superimposed periodic orbits as the *Reynolds number,* a parameter relating the flow velocity and the viscosity of the fluid, increased. Thus, in this classical Landau-Hopf scenario, named after the Russian physicist Lev Landau and the German mathematician Eberhard Hopf who originally proposed it, the streamlines of the flow begin by being smooth and parallel in what's termed *laminar flow.* As the Reynolds number increases, there is a critical value at which the parallel flowlines give way to small whorls, the physical counterparts of limit cycles. Increasing the Reynolds number further leads to another critical value at which these whorls develop whorls of their own, generating an even more complicated type of flow pattern. And so the process continues at higher values of the Reynolds number, ultimately leading to fully developed turbulent flow. Ruelle and Takens disputed this picture, creating an alternate mathematical model in support of their objections and reservations.

The crux of the difficulty with the Landau-Hopf picture is that it is mathematically unlikely that the process of whorls piled upon whorls can be continued indefinitely to form turbulent flow in the manner the scenario requires. In their alternate model, Ruelle and Takens accept the first Landau-Hopf transition from a fixed point (laminar flow) to a limit cycle (whorls) as the Reynolds number passes its first critical level. But at the next critical value, the Ruelle-Takens scenario has the limit cycle give way to what's called *quasiperiodic motion,* a sort of combination of two interacting limit cycles. But that's the end of the standard attractors. At the next critical value of the Reynolds number, the Ruelle-Takens model has the system entering a type of attractor totally unknown to classical physics—and mathematics. Proving the point that a graphic terminology is just as good a vehicle for directing attention to one's work in science as it is in the rest of life, Ruelle and Takens christened this kind of long-term behavior associated with the onset of turbulence a *strange attractor.* And it is exactly this unexpected, new kind of dynamical behavior that has given birth to the flourishing "chaos" industry. To see the intimate connection between strange attractors and prediction, let's leave the complicated physical setting of fluid flow, and consider instead just about the simplest kind of dynamical process imaginable: multiplication by a single number.

* * *

Suppose we have a dynamical system involving a point moving on a state manifold M, consisting of a circle of circumference 1. Thus, we can describe where the point is at any moment by a number between 0 and 1. Suppose that the vector field determining how the point moves on the circle is given by the rule: "If you're at the point x, go to the point $10x$." With this rule, the circle is stretched to ten times its length, and wrapped ten times around itself. For future reference, I'll call this example the *Circle-10 system*. Let's now try to follow the path of a given point as this rule is applied over and over again, i.e., iterated.

First of all, we divide the circumference of the circle into ten sectors, labeled 0, 1, . . . , 9. In terms of numbers between 0 and 1, sector 0 corresponds to all numbers between 0 and 0.099999 . . . , while sector 1 runs from 0.1 to 0.19999 . . . , and so on to sector 9, which runs from 0.9 to 0.9999. . . . Let's suppose our starting point is 0.379762341. This is a number living in sector 3, nearly 80 percent of the way to sector 4.

When we apply the rule of the vector field to the starting number and wrap the circle ten times around itself, the circle's length expands by a factor of ten. Thus, the starting point moves to 3.79762341. But note that one time around the circle just gets you back to where you began, and so do two tours, and so do three. So, the result of applying the vector field is just the same as coming to the point 0.79762341. This is a point in sector 7. Therefore, on the first iteration the starting point moves from sector 3 to sector 7. As we continue to iterate the vector field in this manner, we generate the following results:

Time	Number		Point on Circle	Sector
0	0.379762341			3
1	3.79762341	→	0.79762341	7
2	7.9762341	→	0.9762341	9
3	9.762341	→	0.762341	7
4	7.62341	→	0.62341	6
5	6.2341	→	0.2341	2
6	2.341	→	0.341	3
7	3.41	→	0.41	4
8	4.1	→	0.1	1
9	1	→	0	0

This table shows that the action of the Circle-10 rule is the ultimate in simplicity: At each stage, just multiply by 10 and delete the digit to the left of the decimal point. Examining the sequence of sectors that the system visits, we find our starting point's itinerary is sectors 3, 7, 9, 7, 6, 2, 3, 4, 1, 0, 0, . . . If these numbers look familiar, they ought to: They're just the decimal digits of the starting point! And this is no accident, either. For *any* starting point, the itinerary of sectors visited will match exactly the decimal digits of the starting point, for the simple reason that the rule "Multiply by 10 and chop off the first digit" corresponds to nothing more than shifting the decimal point one position to the right. It's hard to imagine a more straightforward, easy-to-calculate, deterministic dynamical system than this one.

But simple to describe and calculate doesn't necessarily mean simple in behavior, and the Circle-10 system captures almost all of the interesting behavioral features of the kind of strange attractors that concerned Ruelle and Takens, and that eventually led to the theory of chaotic processes. Let's look at these features in more detail.

• *Divergence:* Just for fun, consider Champernowne's number,

$$C = 12345678910111213141516 . . .$$

which is obtained by writing down the positive integers in order. Now suppose the decimal digits of the starting point of our Circle-10 system agree with Champernowne's number in the first 100 million places, but thereafter continue with . . . 33333 . . . forever. Call this new number c. Thus the itinerary of the system starting from C agrees with that starting from c for the first 100 million steps. But then the itinerary from c stays put in sector 3 forever, while that from C goes its merry way, whatever that might be, but which certainly is not a total absorption by sector 3.

This example shows that two starting points C and c, closer together than we could ever hope to measure, end up following completely independent paths. More formally, we say that the itineraries *diverge,* and that systems having this kind of divergent behavior are displaying *sensitivity to initial conditions.*

• *Randomness:* Imagine we wander over to the local casino and watch a few rounds of play at the roulette wheel. Further, suppose we record the numbers as they come up, which might yield the intuitively random sequence 5, 23, 12, 30, 2, 18, 4, 17, 31, 24, 1, 00, 11, 32, 25, 17, 27, and 33. Just as we formed Champernowne's number by writing down the integers in order, we can form a random number by writing down this sequence in the same way, obtaining 5231230218417312410011322517273. There is a point x on the circle whose decimal expansion mimics this sequence, namely, the point in sector 5 given by $x = 0.52312302184173 \ldots$ So if we iterate the dynamical system, using this value x as the starting point, we generate the sequence from the roulette wheel. But by most everyday tests this is a random sequence; yet we have succeeded in generating it from what to all appearances is a totally deterministic dynamical system. What this experiment shows is that a deterministic mapping, applied to the point x, can generate a sequence that's every bit as random as the spin of a roulette wheel.

As we'll spell out in some detail in Chapter Six, almost *every* number has a decimal expansion that's random. Therefore, our purely *deterministic* dynamical system behaves in a random manner, and not just for a few special starting points, but for almost every starting point.

• *Instability of itineraries:* If almost all itineraries are random, it's of considerable interest to ask which ones are not. That is, which starting points are periodic, leading to itineraries that repeat themselves over and over again? Clearly, the answer is those points whose decimal expansion is either finite, like our test sequence, or repeats (technically speaking, they're actually the same thing). And it is a well-known mathematical fact that a number will have such a repeating expansion if and only if it is rational, i.e., if it is a number like $\frac{1}{2}$, $\frac{7}{16}$, or $\frac{207}{399}$, each of which is the ratio of two whole numbers.

In the interval between 0 and 1 there are an infinite number of rational numbers, as well as a much larger infinity of irrational numbers like $\sqrt{3}$, π, and Champernowne's number. It can be shown that between any two irrational numbers there is a rational one, although they do not alternate (almost all the numbers are irrational). Thus, the starting points leading to periodic itineraries are totally mixed up with those *aperiodic points* that do not lead to such cyclic itineraries. This fact also shows that the periodic points are unstable, since if we perturb them just a little bit to a nearby irrational, they cease to be periodic. As it turns out, it's the case that *all* possible motions are unstable. That is, regardless of whether you start at a periodic or an aperiodic point, the itinerary is unstable (technically, in the sense of Lyapunov, as discussed earlier).

The set of itineraries followed by the starting points on our Circle-10 system is an example of what Ruelle and Takens called a strange attractor. Such an attractor is characterized by the properties just discussed: instability of all motions, deterministic randomness, and sensitivity to initial conditions. Furthermore, it turns out that most dynamical systems have a strange attractor for some region of the parameter values describing the system. In the more general setting of a continuous-time dynamical system, a typical strange attractor looks geometrically something like the object shown in Figure 1.10.

Asked to describe this figure, the closest we can come is to say it looks a lot like a bowlful of spaghetti. Each strand, or orbit, is as close as we like to the others, yet separate from them. This picture makes it clear that as the dynamics unfold on such an attractor region, even a small nudge of the system can push the current point from one strand to another from which the system will take off on a totally different course. This kind of pathological sensitivity to perturbations is one of the fingerprints by which chaotic dynamics are often discovered. Sensitivity of this sort already shows up in the Circle-10 system above, where a mistake in, say, the thirtieth digit of the initial point (one part in a million trillion trillion) will cause the system trajectory to be in the "wrong" sector after only thirty steps. Thus, unless the starting point is known *very* accurately, we can't even predict what sector of the circle the system will be in after just thirty steps. But in most real problems we're lucky if we can measure things to an accuracy of even

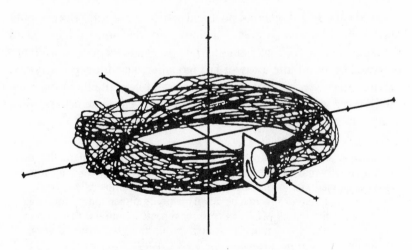

Figure 1.10. *A strange attractor*

one part in ten, let alone a million trillion trillion. Thus, the Circle-10 example shows us just how bad things can get, even in simple systems, if we want to use such a mathematical model to make long-range forecasts. Since we'll see plenty of real-life examples of strange attractors and deterministic randomness as we proceed, let's finish our introduction to such behavior by considering just what it is *exactly* about the dynamics of the Circle-10 system that gives rise to the pathological sensitivity in its behavior.

Basically, the sensitivity in the Circle-10 system stems from a combination of two competing factors in the system dynamics: stretching and folding. The transformation $x \rightarrow 10x$ stretches distances locally near the point x by a factor of 10. Thus, nearby points are moved far apart. But the circle is a bounded region, so we can't stretch it everywhere. Thus, to fit it all in after distances have been expanded by 10, the circle's circumference has to be folded around itself many times. This means that some points that previously were far apart move closer together. So the stretching moves nearby points apart, while the folding moves distant points closer together. The stretching shows how points that start off nearby can lose sight of each other as the stretching continues, eventually failing to "keep in touch." Of course, the folding means that some points move closer together again. But it's impossible to know beforehand which points these will be. This is as good a definition as any I know of for what constitutes the essence of "chaos."

In 1941 the late Argentine poet and writer Jorge Luis Borges published "The Library of Babel," a short story that some critics regard as his greatest work. This haunting tale gives an account of a library composed of an infinite array of hexagonally shaped levels, or floors, containing every book that has or ever could be written. In one passage, Borges writes that the discovery of the twenty-five orthographic symbols in which the books are written

> made it possible, three hundred years ago, to formulate a general theory of the Library and solve satisfactorily the problem which no conjecture had deciphered: the formless and chaotic nature of almost all the books. One which my father saw in a hexagon on circuit fifteen ninety-four was made up of the letters MCV, perversely repeated from the first line to the last. Another (very much consulted in this area) is a mere labyrinth of letters, but the next-to-last page says *Oh time thy pyramids*. This much is already known: for every sensible line of straightforward state-

ment, there are leagues of senseless cacophonies, verbal jumbles and incoherences.

This passage is a precursor to the kind of problem that the discovery of chaotic dynamical processes poses for prediction schemes in science.

Chaotic dynamical systems are, in effect, mathematical models that "read" the initial conditions or starting points. We saw an illustration of this in the behavior of the Circle-10 system, and it can be shown that this phenomenon is completely general. Thus, such systems are like the librarians in Borges's library, who read every word and character of every book in their care. On the other hand, regular or nonchaotic systems are like browsers in the library, who read only the title and just thumb through the text. The sensitivity of chaotic systems to the starting point corresponds to choosing different books in the library telling different tales.

Another aspect of the inherent unpredictability of chaotic processes is that their time evolution is what is sometimes termed *computationally irreducible*. In other words, there is no faster way of finding out what such a process is going to do than just to turn it on and watch it unfold. In short, the system itself is its own fastest computer. If we place this idea within the context of Borges's library, we can see that for most books in the Library of Babel the only way you can find out whodunit is to read the entire book through to the end. Unfortunately, most books in the library are nonsensical gibberish; however, somewhere in the library is a book containing the entire history of the universe—past, present, and future. The problem is that consulting the card catalog in the Library of Babel to find this "universal history" is no less taxing than the gargantuan task of reading through every book!

So from the standpoint of prediction, if we claim that a given dynamical system governs the biological population, stock market index, or wind flow pattern under consideration, and that mathematical model displays chaotic behavior, then we're in deep trouble when it comes to making predictions on the basis of this model. In fact, it may be impossible, at least in practice if not in principle, to predict the future behavior of such processes. You might object that, although this kind of chaotic behavior is displayed by the *mathematical* system, perhaps real-life processes don't work that way at all. Comforting as such an argument might be, it just doesn't seem to hold up under detailed scrutiny. Numerous experiments with chemical reactions, electrical oscillators, insect populations, and other real systems have shown exactly the kind of aperiodicities, sensitivity to initial conditions, and deterministic randomness characteristic of chaotic behavior. Thus, when it comes to assessing the predictability of any real-world process, we have to keep the possibility of chaos continually in mind.

Explanation is an easier case, as the existence of chaotic dynamics poses no theoretical barrier to the development of good models. In fact, just such models as these are now being put forward as some scientists' best guesses at the laws that govern processes as physically dissimilar as the human heartbeat and stock market price fluctuations (well, maybe they're not so unrelated, after all!). It may well be the case that after the smoke and fire clear away, science will render the verdict that certain phenomena, like long-range weather patterns, that have resisted prediction for ages really are governed by chaotic laws of motion. This conclusion, suitably buttressed by convincing theoretical and empirical evidence, would certainly merit high marks for explanation. But the scientific laws of explanation would then be basically useless for any sort of prediction.

Now let's get up from the philosopher's armchair and see what all these ideas we've been talking about have to do with real life. On this world tour, our first port of call will be that perennial conversation filler of taxi drivers, waitresses, postmen, and cocktail-party bores the world over—the weather.

CHAPTER TWO

WHITHER THE WEATHER?

Can We Predict/Explain Changes in Weather and Climate?

Some [people] are weatherwise, some are otherwise.
—BENJAMIN FRANKLIN

Red sky at night, sailor's delight.
Red sky in the morning, sailor take warning.
—OLD WEATHER PROVERB

Climate models are dirty crystal balls.
—STEPHEN H. SCHNEIDER

A TOWER, A BOY, AND A GIRL

Not far from the Acropolis in Athens stands a white Pentelic marble tower 46 feet high. Were it not located so close to the unapproachable beauty and majesty of the Parthenon, this tower would doubtless be regarded as one of the world's most striking examples of ancient Grecian architecture. Instead it's generally given a couple of sentences in the guidebooks and a two-minute "quick look" on the itinerary of Greek tour guides. But for those who are weatherwise, a visit to the Horologion of Andronicus (or, as it's more commonly called, the Tower of the Winds) is like kissing the Blarney Stone for an Irishman or worshiping at the Black Stone of the Ka'bah for a Moslem. Why? Simply because it was at the Tower of the Winds that its architect, Andronicus of Cyrrhus, began the first systematic approach to weather forecasting, leading to the modern sciences of meteorology and climatology.

The Tower of the Winds, much of which is still standing today, was octagonal in shape, each of its sides being carved with the figure of one

77

of the eight principal winds. In addition, the sides of the tower were individually inscribed with lines that were visible from a great distance, and that could be used as sundials. It's strong testimony to Andronicus's architectural and scientific genius that these clocks showed the time with an error of only about three minutes. And for evenings or those periods when there was no sunlight, the tower once contained a water clock. Finally, the tower was capped with the world's first weathervane, a bronze statue of Triton, the mythological demigod of the sea. In fact, the custom of placing weathervanes on steeples arose from this very model at the Tower of the Winds. Using these devices in his tower, Andronicus was able to link time and wind direction, arriving at predictions about the weather for the sailors of the day, who apparently congregated at the tower as a kind of waterfront hangout. But as in all matters pertaining to observational science in ancient times, to uncover the reasons why Andronicus thought that the weather and the winds had something to do with each other, we must go back a couple of thousand years and look at the writings of Aristotle.

In the fourth century B.C. Aristotle wrote the *Meteorologica,* the first "scientific" treatise on weather. This book, from which the modern term *meteorology* is taken (from the Greek word *meteoron* meaning "something that falls from the sky"), dealt with a variety of astronomical, geological, and oceanographic topics. Although Aristotle thought of meteorology as a science, we would be hard put today to regard his view of how weather changes as being in any way scientific.

To illustrate this point, Theophrastus, Aristotle's student and successor, wrote: "We must now show that each wind is accompanied by forces and other conditions in due and fixed relation to itself; and that such conditions in fact differentiate the winds from one another." Of course, we can discern some germ of truth, however slight, in this sort of statement. For instance, it is true that some of the great persistent seasonal wind patterns like the trade winds or the Asian monsoons are governed by a small number of basic physical processes. But to suppose, as Aristotle did, that each of the "eight winds" is governed by its own distinct cause (i.e., law) would strike a modern scientist as tantamount to a complete disavowal of the idea of the universality of physical law. Thus, while Aristotle and Andronicus clearly perceived some kind of relation between the winds and the weather, it's evident that whatever that relation was, it was not what we think of nowadays when we look for a lawful explanation and/or prediction of atmospheric phenomena. So let's move the clock forward a couple of thousand years and consider a prototypical example of what we *do* mean by climatic prediction and explanation—scientific style.

On February 8, 1983, a massive duststorm blanketed much of Melbourne, Australia, turning midday skies as dark as midnight and smothering the city in half a million tons of topsoil. Eight days later the outskirts of Melbourne were struck by a raging firestorm, driving kangaroos to invade farms and forcing farmers to use guns to relieve the suffering of their burned sheep. At the same time, on the other side of the world there was massive flooding in Ecuador and on the gulf coast of the United States, as well as devastating cyclones in Tahiti. For the story of the scientific how and why of these dramatic meteorological happenings, the appropriate place to start is in British colonial India at the turn of the century.

Gilbert Walker was a Cambridge University mathematician who was appointed to the position of Director General of Observatories in India in 1904. Arriving at his post just a few years after the catastrophic failure of the monsoon and the ensuing famine of 1899–1900, Walker focused his efforts on the problem of predicting the monsoons. He correctly saw these hurricanes as a global rather than regional phenomenon, and set out to relate yearly variability to global climatic fluctuations. While ultimately failing in his efforts to develop an effective predictive scheme for the monsoons, Walker did succeed in uncovering three large-scale oscillations in climate, the most important of which is now termed the Southern Oscillation. In Walker's own words, "When pressure is high in the Pacific Ocean it tends to be low in the Indian Ocean from Africa to Australia; these conditions are associated with low temperatures in both these areas and rainfall varies in the opposite directions."

For several decades the Southern Oscillation was ignored or just dismissed as a meteorological curiosity, primarily because Walker offered only statistical correlations as evidence with no accompanying theoretical mechanism to explain the data. All that changed in 1958 with the International Geophysical Year. During the IGY, extensive measurements were made of the Earth and the atmosphere. Some of this data was analyzed by meteorologist Jacob Bjerknes, who made a connection between Walker's Southern Oscillation and the well-known El Niño conditions in the eastern Pacific. To see what this connection is, let me summarize the El Niño, or, as it's sometimes termed, the El Niño–Southern Oscillation (ENSO) phenomenon.

Normally in the Pacific, trade winds from the southeast drive ocean currents westward, forcing surface waters away from the South American shore. This relatively warm surface water is then replaced by colder water from below, bringing massive amounts of plankton and other nutrients from the lower levels. This upwelling of nutrient-rich colder water generates the rich fish population off the coast of Peru. Generally around December this cycle is interrupted when the trade winds slacken, thus blocking the upwelling of the cooler water. The water temperature then rises by as much as 7 degrees. (Note: Throughout this chapter, all temperatures will be expressed in degrees Celsius.) This warm water then leads to massive amounts of rainfall. Generally these conditions pass after a few weeks. But every now and then they persist, giving rise to the infamous El Niño condition (so termed from the Spanish nickname for the Christ Child, *el niño* or "small boy," since the condition is usually encountered around Christmas). The overall situation in both normal and ENSO times is shown in Figure 2.1.

What Jacob Bjerknes discovered is that the Southern Oscillation and El Niño are mutually reinforcing phenomena: El Niños occur when the regions of high pressure in the east and low pressure in the west both weaken, and the trade winds slacken. While these empirical facts are of great interest, from a scientific standpoint they are only the starting point for an explanation of the occurrence of these two oscillations. Why do these pressure zones weaken? And why do they usually change back after a few weeks? Only in the last few years have climatologists put forward convincing answers to these questions.

Based on Bjerknes's observations, Stephen Zebiak and Mark Cane at the Lamont-Doherty Geological Observatory of Columbia University developed a computer model demonstrating that the underlying reason for the El Niño phenomenon involves a change in the warm-water volume in the Pacific. In broad outline, their argument goes as follows: Just before El Niño, the volume of surface water across the Pacific at the equator is greater than usual because the thermocline (the barrier between the warm and cold layers) fluctuates due to natural oceanic cycles and is, on the average, deeper prior to El Niños. So near South America, cool surface temperatures and brisk trade winds prevail. But, on the whole, the equatorial Pacific holds more heat. Therefore, some part of the atmosphere eventually warms up, thereby altering the air pressure pattern. This then disrupts the trade winds, and

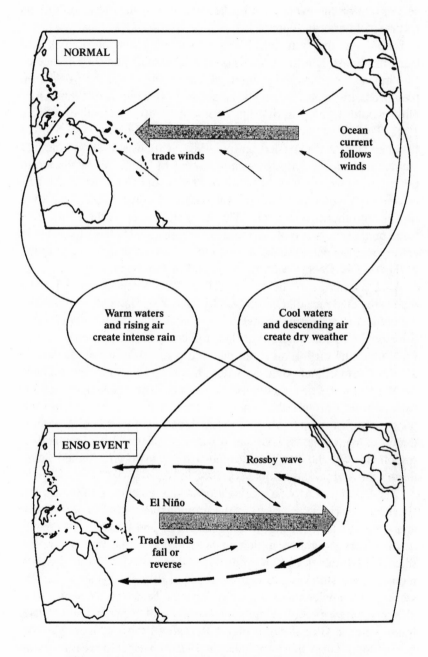

Figure 2.1. *The El Niño–Southern Oscillation phenomenon*

sets in motion the events that lead to El Niño. When these conditions reverse, El Niño disappears.

Employing this principle of thermocline movement, Zebiak and Cane used past data to forecast correctly the onset and the absence of El Niños as much as two years in advance. And to put the frosting on their predictive cake, they made an actual forecast in early 1986: An El Niño would develop during the middle of 1986 and decline in early 1987. Their prediction came true with the appearance of an El Niño in October 1986 that persisted on into 1987. This was the first time that anyone had successfully forecast a coming El Niño. Let me hasten to point out, however, that the work of Zebiak and Cane, while the first to actually predict an El Niño, was based upon results obtained by a number of other investigators. The story leading up to the Zebiak and Cane prediction is one of the more absorbing case studies of science in action over the past decade, a brief chronology of which can be found in the To Dig Deeper section at the end of this book.

As a postscript to the successful El Niño forecast, there is now increasing evidence that not only is El Niño a regular and not a random phenomenon, appearing periodically as part of an internal oscillation in the global climate system, but that it alternates with an opposite twin La Niña (''the girl''), an abnormally cold stretch of equatorial water. Thus, current climatological wisdom has it that El Niño and La Niña are the two poles of a continuous back-and-forth action, in which the surface waters around the equator in the eastern Pacific go from one temperature extreme to another every three to six years. And, in fact, there are many who believe that it was the effect of La Niña that was responsible for the terrible drought in the midwestern United States during the spring and summer of 1988.

The El Niño–La Niña explanation and prediction by Zebiak and Cane are clearly a far cry from the gropings and guesses of Aristotle and Andronicus about the ways of the winds and weather. Of course, in the intervening two millennia both experimental and theoretical science have developed enormously. Galileo's invention of the thermometer, his student Torricelli's invention of the barometer, and the work of the nineteenth-century physicists on heat and mechanics have all contributed greatly to our understanding of weather and climate. Moreover, the Global Atmospheric Research Program, a decade-long international effort that concluded in 1979, provided a wealth of empirical data upon which many of today's theoretical studies are anchored. And this is not to mention the two most important factors in the understanding and prediction of the weather, the digital computer and the weather satellite. But we're getting ahead of our story. So to get a better handle on just exactly what Zebiak and Cane had at their disposal to explain and predict atmospheric phenomena that the ancient Greeks didn't, let's start with an examination of how weather patterns actually form.

THE WEATHER MACHINE

As American presidents go, the sixth, John Quincy Adams, was most assuredly a man of mediocre tone, his sole mark of distinction being that he was the only President who was also a published poet. By his own statement, he was "a man of reserved, cold and forbidding manner," a rather generous self-evaluation if one trusts the judgment of W. H. Lyttelton, who described Adams as having "a vinegar aspect, cotton in his leathern ears and hatred in his heart." All in all, not one of America's finest.

During the course of his single term of office, Adams demonstrated his lack of charm and vision by his shameful treatment of James Espy, the first man to recognize the role of warm air in the creation of thunderstorms. Such storms begin with thermals, which are rising currents of warm air coming from heated land. These masses of hot air lose temperature as they rise, eventually cooling to the dew point. Clouds then form, ultimately having their moisture wrung out as a thunderstorm. Espy wanted to use his ideas of storm generation and form a national weather service. Making use of influential congressmen, Espy finally managed to arrange a meeting with Adams to present his plan. The result? In his diary Adams wrote:

> Mr. Espy, the storm breeder. . . The man is methodically monomaniac and the dimensions of his organ of self esteem have been swollen to the size of a goiter by a report of a committee of the National Institute of France, endorsing all of his crackbrained discoveries in meteorology.

In short, Adams thought Espy was a crank! But it was Espy's vision, not Adams's vitriol, that finally carried the day and was ultimately realized as today's National Weather Service. And the underlying principles that the Weather Service employs in its forecasts are fundamentally the same as those espoused by Espy. To see why, let's take a longer look at the process of weather generation.

The key to understanding the weather lies in one simple principle: Nature abhors a nonuniform distribution of energy. This basic idea lies at the core of every aspect of what we see as changes in the weather. All of the familiar aspects of weather and climate like wind speed, temperature, and rainfall are corollaries of this foundational principle. In short, the world's weather can be thought of as the output of a machine that moves energy from one place to another in an ongoing effort to achieve a homogeneous distribution of energy throughout the atmosphere. But, you might inquire, why doesn't the energy distribution equilibrate after a transient period, stopping the weather machine dead in its tracks? In other words, why is the Earth always in a state of energy disequilibrium?

There are three principal reasons for the ever-present energy imbalance on Earth and throughout the atmosphere: clouds, mountains, and the surface albedo. Clouds clearly interfere with the transmission of the solar radiation in areas that they cover. Mountains act to diffuse and diffract energy in various ways, while the surface albedo, a measure of the fraction of incident solar radiation that is reflected back into the atmosphere, influences how much energy is absorbed at a given location on the Earth's surface. Thus regions covered by highly reflective materials like water or ice have much higher albedos than areas like cities or agricultural land. As a result, in regions of high surface albedo there is not as much thermal energy absorbed as in lower-albedo areas; hence, an imbalance in energy distribution develops. But it's not only clouds, mountains, and the surface albedo that generate the energy imbalance.

The various energy sources (mainly the Sun's radiation) and the Earth's orbital and planetary motion are themselves in a continual state of change. Thus, the energy balancing act is continuously being disturbed at the source level as well. The end result of nature's juggling of all these factors is what we see as the daily and seasonal changes in weather. Keeping the "Energy-Balance Principle" in mind, let's now examine the five main subsystems of the weather system in a bit more detail.

• *Atmosphere:* For weather formation, the most important layers of the atmosphere are the two closest to the Earth: the troposphere and the stratosphere. The schematic diagram in Figure 2.2 shows these layers. The troposphere contains most of the water vapor and atmospheric pollution, and is where most clouds form and precipitation occurs. The stratosphere, on the other hand, consists of a comparatively low-density, dry air mass, and is where jet aircraft fly to avoid the weather and to save fuel.

• *Bodies of water:* For weather formation, by far the most important such bodies are the world's oceans, which act not only as massive storehouses of thermal energy, but also as vehicles to transport this energy from one location to another. But rivers and lakes, especially large ones like the Great Lakes or Lake Baikal, also play important roles in forming local weather.

• *Ice:* The great polar ice sheets are crucial to the formation of the world's weather, as are slabs of floating ice in the seas. Other types

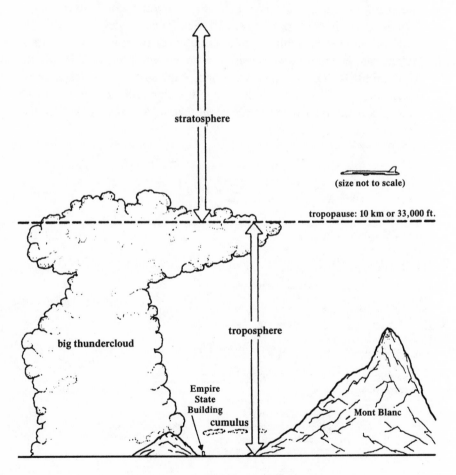

Figure 2.2. *The troposphere and the stratosphere*

of ice sheets, such as mountain glaciers and surface snow cover, also contribute to the weather by their reflection of incident solar radiation.

• *Land masses:* The world's land masses, including mountains, soil, and rocks, enter into the weather-formation process by their topography as well as by their ability to absorb heat.

• *Mankind, plants, and animals:* Living organisms affect the weather by their transforming of the world's land masses, as well as by the gases and particles they discharge into the atmosphere.

So how do all these subsystems interact to produce tomorrow's weather? Figure 2.3 displays the various interactions between these pieces of the overall mosaic we call the *climate system.*

Everything starts with the solar radiation striking the Earth's atmosphere and penetrating to the surface. As shown in Figure 2.4, the tilt of the Earth's axis causes each portion of the surface to receive sometimes more and sometimes less of this solar radiation as the Earth moves around the Sun (the reader will recognize this fact as the cause

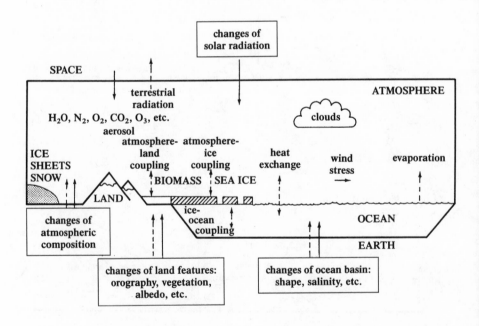

Figure 2.3. *Components of the world's weather system*

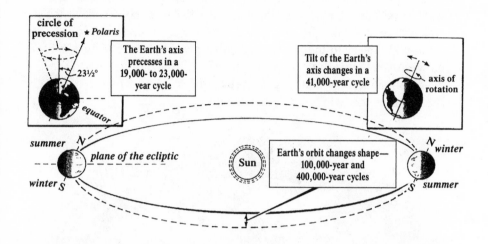

Figure 2.4. *The tilt of the Earth's axis and the incident solar radiation*

of the change of seasons). But at all times, the further the region is from the equator, the less solar radiation it receives. The result is an excess of heat at the equator and a deficit at the poles. Figure 2.4 also shows the long-term wobbles and other periodic fluctuations in the Earth's orbit that are collectively termed the *Milankovitch cycle*. We'll speak more about their influence on climate in a later section.

In accord with the Energy-Balance Principle, heat is transferred from the equator to the poles by the process of thermal convection. This process is called *Hadley circulation*, and terminates at about 30 degrees north and south of the equator on account of the Earth's rotation. Poleward of this, heat transport is carried out by turbulent, large-scale horizontal eddies, which "boil off" heat from the warm equator to the cold poles. These eddies are the mobile low-pressure regions we know as storms.

The foregoing picture suggests that air would rise at the equator and drift toward the poles, where it would be cooled and then drift back to the equatorial zone. Such a wind pattern would create steady northerly winds in the Northern Hemisphere, while southerly winds would prevail in the Southern Hemisphere. But there are no such wind patterns. Why not? Basically, because the Earth is not a stationary ball, but rotates on its axis. This rotation induces what's called a *Coriolis force*, which, together with frictional effects, the distribution of land and water, and the influence of mountains, results in a movement of the atmosphere that, on the average, is from west to east outside the equatorial zones. In the tropics and subtropics where the trade winds blow, movement is in the opposite direction, from east to west. Thus, over a broad band of latitudes, the prevailing winds blow west to east. A picture of this wind system is shown in Figure 2.5.

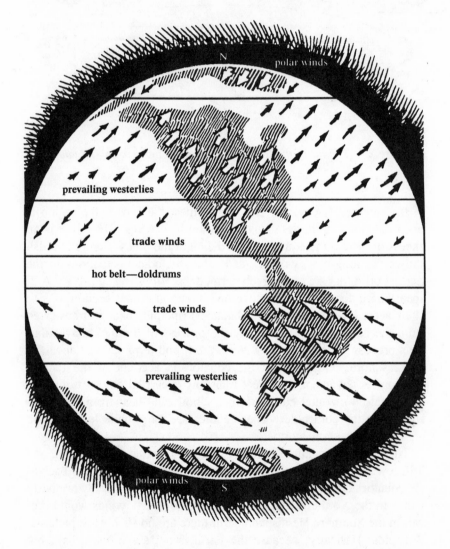

Figure 2.5. *The Earth's wind system*

The general atmospheric circulation described above, along with the oceans, is the main mechanism for redistributing excess heat from the tropics to the poles. But there are auxiliary mechanisms that also contribute to this process. The most important is the evaporation-condensation cycle of water. In this cycle, thermal radiation from the Earth forces moisture from the land and oceans to enter the atmosphere as water vapor, where it can then be carried by the winds to the polar regions. During the course of this transport, the water vapor forms clouds leading to various types of precipitation like rainfall, snow, and more violent storms such as tornadoes and hurricanes. With this weather blueprint at hand, let's see how meteorologists and climatologists try to formalize the whole system into a model of the general circulation of the atmosphere.

We have already discussed the Earth's weather system as a kind of machine into which we put energy and different types of information and out of which emerge quantities like temperature, pressure, and humidity at each point of the atmosphere. Consequently, to formalize this machine metaphor for the weather, there are three main components that must be addressed: (1) the *inputs,* consisting of the incoming solar radiation, the current atmospheric state, the physical properties of the Earth like its rotation rate and land topography, and the various surface albedos, (2) the *mathematical relations* (equations) expressing how the inputs are transformed into new quantities by the laws of mechanics, thermodynamics, hydrodynamics, and chemistry, and (3) the *outputs,* which are the variables that we want to forecast, such as the wind velocities, temperature, barometric pressure, and humidity. Let's talk about each of these items in more detail.

• *Inputs:* The inputs to the weather model consist of several quite different sorts of things. First, there are the energy inputs, involving the incoming solar radiation and its diurnal and seasonal variations. In some types of models, other energy inputs from terrestrial sources like volcanoes might also be included. But the energy inputs are usually just taken to be the energy received from the Sun. The second kind of input is what mathematicians call a *parameter.* This is a quantity that specifies the experimental situation itself. In the context of the weather there are many parameters that must be fixed in order for the model to be determined. Such parameters include the various albedos in the region the model covers, the topography and geography of the land, as well as the surface temperatures of the oceans. Finally, there are the initial conditions. Part of the input to the weather machine is a statement of the values of all atmospheric quantities at "time zero" of the weather simulation represented by the model.

• *Equations:* Several of the most revered laws of physics and chemistry are involved in the dynamical transformation of the inputs during the course of weather formation. Conservation laws for energy, mass, water substance, and heat appear, as does the equation for the state of an ideal gas. Furthermore, we have the dynamical equations arising from Newton's Second Law, which, for fluid flow, go under the name of the Navier-Stokes equations. Each of these mathematical relations acts in its own characteristic way to move energy from one point of the atmosphere to another or to transform substances from one physical state into another. The values of the various physical quantities that ultimately generate "the weather" arise from the collective effect of all these competing transformations.

• *Outputs:* The point of the model is to produce values of variables like temperature and pressure that can finally be translated into an everyday statement such as "The chance of rain tomorrow is 10 percent." The quantities needed to formulate such a statement are the output of the model. As already noted, they consist of variables like wind speeds, temperature, specific humidity, barometric pressure, and the like.

Once the inputs have been prescribed and the atmospheric variables have been encoded into mathematical symbols and linked according to the rules specified by the system's equations, the weather machine is turned on and the desired outputs come pouring (no pun intended) out the other end. The entire situation is schematically depicted in Figure 2.6.

The process of predicting the weather using a mathematical model is identical in spirit, if not exact form, to the determination of the fly's path along my desktop in the example considered in the last chapter. In practice, however, it is considerably more complicated. In the language of a general dynamical system, the mathematical relations for the weather system define the system's vector field. The manifold of states is composed of a complicated subset of a multidimensional space, specified by the various constraints imposed by the numerous

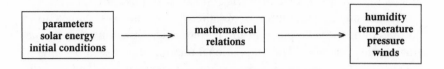

Figure 2.6. *The weather machine*

conservation laws that keep the mathematical model in contact with physical reality. Since we'll have occasion to speak in somewhat more detailed terms about the entire process in the next section, let's leave the modeling problem now and turn to our two main concerns: prediction and explanation.

It's impossible to discuss meaningfully the questions of prediction and explanation of weather and climate without first considering the matter of time scale. Even the most casual observer will be sensitive to the fact that predicting the weather tomorrow is an inherently different task from trying to guess what effect our profligate use of fossil fuels today will have on the climate in the year 2084. Thus, when someone speaks of prediction, our first response should be to say, "Over what time frame?" This is the question that separates weather forecasting and meteorology from climate prediction and climatology. And it is this temporal distinction that determines our criteria for success, both in matters of prediction and in those of explanation.

While the difference for researchers has narrowed considerably in the past few years, the distinction between *weather* and *climate* remains basically as it's always been: One represents the weather today, while the other is the daily weather averaged over some appropriate period of time. What is an "appropriate" period for defining *climate* varies from situation to situation, but is generally taken to be anywhere from a few months to a few thousand years. More explicitly, we have:

weather = the state of the atmosphere at a given place and time

climate = the average weather in a region over a long period of time

When it comes to weather prediction, the obvious criterion is to ask for tomorrow's weather page today. Let's admit at the outset that no weather model even comes close to offering this degree of precision. We'll see why in the next section. For now, let it suffice to say that there are severe, probably even insurmountable, theoretical and experimental obstacles to reaching this level of predictive bliss.

On the side of explaining the weather, the whole issue comes down to the confidence we place in the mathematical relations that go into our weather machine. The foundational relations like Newton's laws of mechanics, the conservation principles, the ideal gas law, and so forth, are well-tested, generally accepted laws of nature in the sense that we used that term in the opening chapter. However, in weather modeling we combine these basic laws into new, higher-level mathematical relations. This process introduces two new questions calling for a resolution before we can assess the model's explanatory power. The first involves the degree to which the new relations match physical reality. In other words, do our new *mathematical* quantities reflect the behavior of the *physical* quantities they purport to represent? The second basic question is whether the model is complete. Do our mathematical relations encompass all the interactions relevant for the purposes of the model? The degree to which we can give affirmative answers to these two queries is a measure of how well our models actually explain the weather.

When it comes to the question of prediction and explanation of climate, the basic theme song is the same, only the tempo changes. Good climatic prediction would mean being able to predict accurately the average levels of things like rainfall and temperature over a fairly extensive geographic region such as a large country. Thus, climatic prediction involves long-term trends, and completely ignores short-term fluctuations or seasonal variations. An example of the kind of prediction that a good climate model might provide would be an accurate statement of the average temperature in the United States in the year 2030, resulting from a doubling of the amount of carbon dioxide discharged into the atmosphere today.

As for climate models and explanation, at first glance we might think that since climate is just weather averaged over a long period of time, explanation of climate is the same as explaining the weather. While possibly true, at least in principle, this argument is analogous to trying to explain the behavior of biological organisms by studying the motion of their constituent atoms as they go about their business in accordance with the laws of chemistry and physics. It doesn't work for the simple reason that when we pass to a new level of organization of matter, new principles and phenomena emerge. And it is these emergent properties that constitute the distinguishing features of the system of interest. When we move from weather to climate, factors that were irrelevant in weather take on leading roles. For example, the Milankovitch cycle shown earlier in Figure 2.4, involving variations of the Earth's rotational motion and solar orbit, is generally conceded to be the trigger that sets off periodic ice ages. The large time scale involved in this cycle makes it completely irrelevant to forecasting the daily weather. Yet when it comes to climatic models, ice ages are of great interest. So we need to include the Milankovitch cycle in any kind of explanation of really long-term climatic change. In the opposite direction, daily temperature fluctuations have little meaning when averaged over a period of many years. So today's temperature in Tallahassee is a quantity that plays no role in explaining climatic change in Florida over the coming fifty years.

With these introductory notions of weather, climate, prediction, and explanation under our belts, let's now move on to a more detailed consideration of each of them, starting with the problem of greatest everyday concern: rain or shine tomorrow.

A TEMPEST IN A TRANSISTOR

The time-honored, socially acceptable way for conscientious objectors to discharge their duty to God and country during a war is to serve in the medical corps. During World War I, both the philosophy and the practice of science benefited from this tradition as one of the pivotal works of modern meteorological thought was written by a man serving as an ambulance driver. This work, by the British mathematician and physicist Lewis F. Richardson, represented the first genuinely scientific program for predicting the weather numerically. Given the seminal nature of Richardson's work, not to mention the less than optimal circumstances of its development, it's definitely worth our while to spend a bit more time looking into it.

Richardson was a Quaker who studied physics at Cambridge under J. J. Thomson, discoverer of the electron. In 1913 while working at the Eskdalemuir Observatory on the problem of weather forecasting, Richardson was already encountering difficulties in trying to find explicit solutions to the governing differential equations. Feeling himself at an impasse, he started experimenting with various types of difference schemes in order to approximate the solutions of the equations numerically. Following the outbreak of the First World War, Richardson joined the Friends Ambulance Unit and continued his work while attached to a motor ambulance convoy in France. During the period 1916–1918 he completed the draft manuscript of his pioneering book *Weather Prediction by Numerical Processes,* which was published in 1922. As an odd aside, during the Battle of Champagne in April 1917, the working copy of his manuscript was sent to the rear for safekeeping. In the confusion following the end of the war, the manuscript was mislaid, only to be found later under a pile of coal in Belgium and returned to England.

What Richardson did in his book was to attempt to work out a six-hour forecast for May 20, 1910. To this end, he imposed the checkerboard grid shown in Figure 2.7 (where each cell is about 200 kilometers on a side) over England and part of Europe. He then stacked four vertical layers on top of the grid, and assigned three variables to each cell: temperature, water vapor, and wind velocity. Using mathematical relations for the conservation of mass, momentum, water vapor, and energy, Richardson proceeded to calculate (by hand!) how the values of these variables would change over the course of time. The results? Disastrous! The computation produced very rapid changes in air pressure that were up to one hundred times too large, resulting in super-hurricane-like winds more like those seen in Martian duststorms than anything ever observed on Earth. So, despite the fact that the great novelty and imagination of Richardson's book got him elected to a fellowship in the Royal Society, it's really the account of a grand failure. This is a verdict Richardson himself accepted, as indicated by his statement in the preface to the book: "Perhaps some day in the dim future it will be possible to advance the computations faster than the weather advances and at a cost less than the saving to mankind due to the information gained. But this is a dream."

As it turned out, the flaws in Richardson's work were only technical and technological, not conceptual. The outlandish predictions he came up with for the weather of May 20, 1910, were due primarily to three factors: (1) the coarseness of his checkerboard grid, a constraint imposed by the fact that the number of computations increases geometrically as the grid size is reduced, (2) the rather inaccurate and spotty observational data available for the initial values of the variables on the preceding day, May 19, 1910, and (3) a mathematical condition relating the spatial grid size to the size of the time step that can be taken

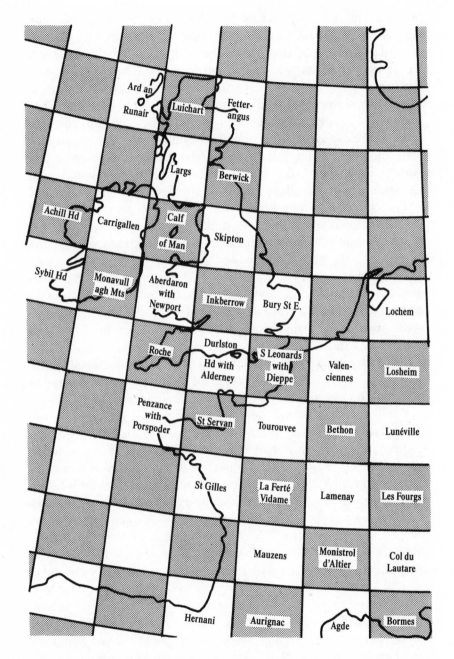

Figure 2.7. *Richardson's weather-forecasting grid and notation*

before the numerical calculation becomes what's termed *computationally unstable*. This last condition, known now as the Courant-Friedrichs-Lewy condition, was discovered only in 1928, more than ten years after Richardson carried out his work. The condition states that the time step in the model must be shorter than the time it takes for a sound wave impulse to move from one grid point to another. Thus, if the time increments are too long or, equivalently, the grid points are spaced too close together, the numerical solution will become unstable and "blow up." And, as fate would have it, Richardson chose temporal and spatial grid sizes that grossly violated this condition, leading to the physically unrealistic levels of air pressure in his predictions.

Following the Second World War, John von Neumann became interested in the possibilities of the digital computer. An important part of his sales pitch to the governmental funding agencies was to stress the need for such computing power to manage the national economy and to predict the weather. This last area was of great interest to the military, and resulted in Navy and Air Force funding for much of the cost of the Institute for Advanced Study Meteorology Project. As noted above, two of the main reasons why Richardson's work failed were because the Courant condition had not yet been discovered and because high-speed computers did not then exist. But von Neumann knew about both of them and wanted to use the weather-forecasting problem as a way to show the benefits that computers could bring to society.

While von Neumann was the spiritual leader and overseer of the IAS numerical weather work, the intellectual leader of the project was Jule Charney, later a professor of meteorology at MIT. In the spring of 1950, Charney, Ragnar Fjörtoft, and von Neumann published the first paper from the IAS project. It consisted of an analysis of the weather-forecasting equations, as well as a summary of a series of twenty-four-hour forecasts made for four days in early 1949. These computations showed that numerically calculated predictions of the atmosphere's large-scale motions were comparable to what an experienced meteorologist could forecast based on subjective experience. By the end of June 1953, the IAS project was able to make a twenty-four-hour forecast in about six minutes of computing time. Richardson's "dim future" had finally arrived—after less than thirty years! Now having paid our respects to the pioneering efforts of Richardson and von Neumann, let's look at how things stand today in the world of numerical weather prediction.

*   *   *

In a 1904 paper titled "Weather Forecasting as a Problem in Mechanics and Physics," Norwegian meteorologist Vilhelm Bjerknes set the modern tone for the study of the weather. In this first complete formulation of the weather-forecasting problem, Bjerknes anticipated the dual experimental/theoretical components that underlie all numerical weather-forecasting models: (1) knowledge of the initial state of the atmosphere at every point in a spatial grid, and (2) use of the mathematical relations governing the atmospheric dynamics to see how the state at each grid point develops from the states at other points.

As we saw in the work of Richardson, the first step in building a numerical weather-forecasting model is to discretize the spatial region of interest by superimposing a cellular grid upon it. Figure 2.8 displays the nature of such a grid, along with some of the variables whose values we would like to know in each cell of the grid at each moment

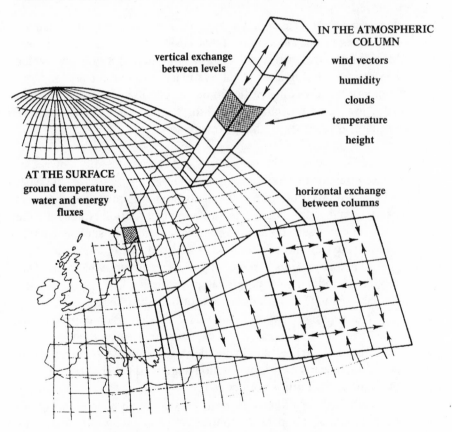

Figure 2.8. *A numerical weather-forecasting grid*

of time. The basic idea is then to take the first step of the Bjerknes program and specify the values of each of these variables in each cell at some initial instant. Of course, this can be done only by getting actual observations of the weather via satellites, airplane pilots' reports, weather ships, and all the other devices of the world weather-reporting network. With this information at hand, we move to Bjerknes's second step and use the mathematical relations to tell us how these initial values change during the course of time. This computational step involves solving the differential equations of the atmosphere, yielding solutions which, as Richardson discovered, cannot be expressed in closed form. Thus, we discretize them using a variety of mathematical schemes, and then solve the resulting approximate system numerically. What separates a good prediction from a bad one is the skill with which these two steps—observation and computation—are carried out.

For weather forecasting, the type of model employed is usually termed a *general circulation model* (GCM). This is a model that uses a three-dimensional grid like that shown in Figure 2.8, together with a quite detailed set of mathematical relations. We have considered these relations in broad outline earlier in our discussion of the weather machine. Now let's dig into them a little deeper. In a GCM we have mathematical relations of the following sort:

• *The Navier-Stokes equations for horizontal air movement:* These equations describe the movement of air masses in the east-west and north-south directions. This motion is related to the force exerted on the air by the Earth's rotation (the Coriolis force), by the horizontal pressure gradients, by dissipative forces such as friction and turbulence, and by the sources and sinks of momentum.

• *The Navier-Stokes equation for vertical air movement:* This motion is influenced by vertical pressure gradients, gravity, the Earth's rotation, and frictional and turbulence effects.

• *The continuity equation for mass:* This equation expresses the conservation of mass, relating changes in vertical motion to the divergence of the horizontal wind field. Integrating ("solving") this equation gives the vertical motion and predicts the atmospheric pressure at the Earth's surface.

• *The thermodynamic equation:* This equation relates changes in the potential air temperature to the heat supplied by radiation, condensation, and other heat sources.

• *The continuity equation for water:* This is a conservation relation for the total water content in all its phases. The equation relates changes in humidity of the air to sources and sinks of moisture.

For those masochistically oriented readers of a slightly technical leaning, the mathematical transliteration of these relationships can be found in the To Dig Deeper section for this chapter at the end of the book.

So much for equations. But as we know from our weather machine discussion, GCMs also include parameters. Here are the main ones:

• *Geophysical:* These are parameters involving the size, rotation, geography, and topography of the Earth.
• *Radiative:* Such parameters refer to the incoming solar radiation and its daily and seasonal variations.
• *Reflectivity:* This category includes those quantities having to do with the radiative heat conductive properties of the land surface according to the nature of the soil, vegetation, and snow or ice cover.
• *Oceans:* These are the parameters representing the surface temperatures of the various oceans.

Finally, we come to the punch line: the variables that the GCM actually forecasts. These are usually some combination of

• *Winds:* the east-west, north-south, and vertical components of the wind velocities;
• *Temperature:* the surface temperature as well as the potential atmospheric temperature;
• *Pressure:* the changes in height of the lines of constant pressure (*isobars*) in the atmosphere, along with the surface pressure;
• *Water vapor:* the specific humidity and the precipitation.

As a specific example of such a GCM, let's consider the British Meteorological Office model, which is divided into fifteen atmospheric layers starting at the surface of the Earth and rising to a height of twenty-five kilometers (80,000 feet). In this model, each level (layer) is divided into a network of points about 150 kilometers apart, giving a total of around 350,000 grid points. Each of these points is assigned values of temperature, pressure, wind, and humidity every twelve hours from observations taken over the entire globe. The equations expressing the change in these quantities are updated numerically, using a computer time step corresponding to fifteen minutes of real time. These forecasts are made for up to six days into the future. To get some idea of the computing resources required, a one-day forecast involves 100 billion computations and four and a half minutes on a Cyber 205 semi-supercomputer. Just for the sake of scale, one billion is the number of ping-pong balls it takes to circle the Earth at the equator. So what does the British Meteorological Office get for its computing pound sterling? How well do these forecasts match the reality of the weather in a place like Britain, where everybody talks about the weather but nobody brags about it?

When it comes to assessing weather models, there are two basic approaches: the objective and the practical. The first involves making statistical comparisons between the model outputs and the actual weather. The practical criterion, on the other hand, is more subjective. It rests on the pragmatic consideration of how useful the model outputs are to those actually charged with making forecasts. In other words, to what degree do weathermen at the National Weather Service rely upon the model outputs in formulating their verbal forecasts? Let's consider the case from the objective standpoint first.

In Figure 2.9 we see the correlation coefficient between the predicted and observed values of the changes in height of the 1,000 millibar (mb) level for forecasts made by the British Meteorological Office (BMO) during the period 1968–1984. The 1,000 mb surface is the height at which the atmospheric pressure is 1 bar (about 14.5 pounds per square inch, slightly less than the pressure at sea level). Since a positive correlation of 1.0 would represent perfect agreement between prediction and measurement, this diagram shows the substantial improvement in the BMO's modeling efforts during this sixteen-year period. Note, incidentally, the very major strides forward after introduction of the more detailed models in 1972 and 1982.

Another standard statistical criterion for assessing predictions is the so-called *root-mean-square* (RMS) criterion. This measure is a very close relative of the ordinary standard deviation of a data set considered in Chapter One, involving the formation of the average of the squares of the differences between the model predictions and the observations and then taking the square root of this average. By this RMS criterion, in 1974 the error of the three-day forecast was only 20 percent less than the *persistence error,* which is the error made by predicting that the weather tomorrow will be the same as it is today. In other words, the *persistence forecast* is the no-skill (or, more euphe-

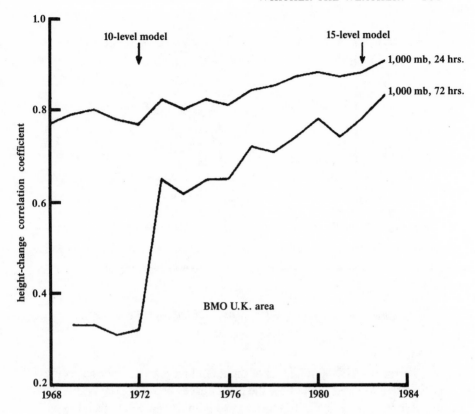

Figure 2.9. *Correlation coefficient for predicted and observed 1-bar levels*

mistically, the zero-change) prediction, and is often used as a benchmark against which to measure the performance of "skillful"
prediction methods. Thus, in 1974 the models were not really doing
very well, being able to reduce the persistence error by only a meager
20 percent. But by 1984 the corresponding figure was 52 percent, and
the degradation to the 20-percent level did not take place until day 6 of
the forecast. This points to an improvement in predictive skill of three
days over the ten-year period.

Using the RMS error, we can recast the results of Figure 2.9 by
slicing the same cake in another direction, looking at the way errors
build up as the length of the forecast increases. Figure 2.10 shows the
results of a 1980 study using the model of the European Centre for
Medium-Range Weather Forecasting (ECMWF), a multinational
agency headquartered in the United Kingdom. The figure shows the

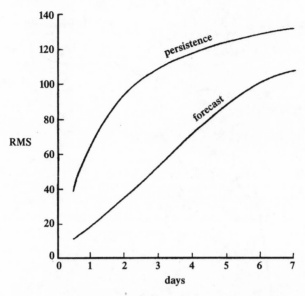

Figure 2.10. *The 500 mb forecasts from the ECMWF in 1980*

RMS error for the 500 mb level of the model forecast as opposed to the persistence forecast. Note how the error curves begin to converge after about forecast day 5. We'll return to this point in more detail a bit later.

Moving to another hemisphere and another continent, in Figure 2.11 we see a similar result for 48-hour rainfall forecasts in Australia for 1970–1986. Here the scale of evaluation is something called the normalized S1 Score. The normalized value is the departure of the forecast from the persistence forecast, large negative values representing large improvements over a persistence forecast.

As a final example of the accuracy of GCMs, Figure 2.12 shows the sea-level pressure predictions versus observations at different latitudes obtained by a number of mostly climate-forecasting models over the decade 1974–1984. This figure has several instructive aspects, the two most significant being that the farther one gets from the equator, the worse the predictions become, and the more recent the model, the better the prediction in general. Now let's turn to the more subjective matter of how useful the predictions of such models are in formulating the forecasts we see in the newspaper each day.

Experience has shown that weather forecasts are no longer useful if their RMS error exceeds 75 percent of the persistence error. Using this

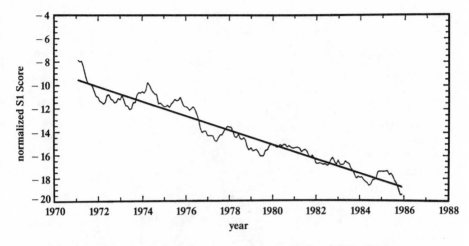

Figure 2.11. *Rainfall forecasts in Australia, 1970–1986*

criterion, the average useful predictive range of forecasts in 1984 was 5.3 days for extratropical regions in the Northern Hemisphere and 5 days in the Southern. On balance, the best models appear to provide good, i.e., useful, forecasts for 4 to 5 days in the mid-latitude regions.

Looking at things from the standpoint of the user, the European Centre for Medium-Range Weather Forecasting assessed the utility of its model outputs to forecasters for the period March 3, 1980, to March 9, 1981. During this one-year period, the ECMWF looked at fifty-two cases that were rated by the forecasters as to whether the model output provided (A) good guidance, (B) no major error, or (C) misleading input to the worded forecasts. The summary of this subjective assessment of the ECMWF model output is displayed in Table 2.1.

The message of this table comes through loud and clear: Very few errors of significance to a medium-range forecast occur by day 3, but at least half of the predictions become misleading beyond day 5. It's worth noting that when this assessment was carried out by the fifteen member states of the ECMWF, all the verdicts were in rough agreement as to how long the model predictions were useful.

Taken together, these pieces of evidence point to the conclusion that current weather prediction models give useful information in the extratropical regions for a period of four to five days. Of course, in some regions this period can be considerably extended. For example, who

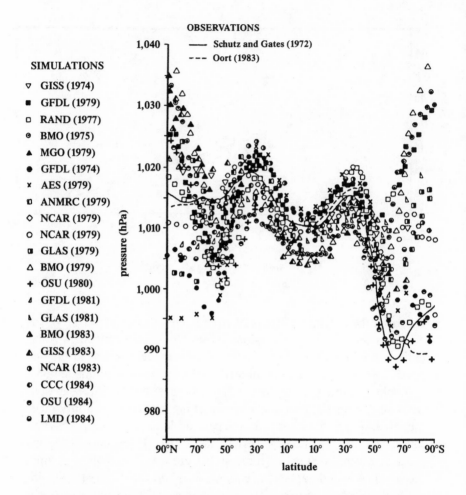

Figure 2.12. *Sea-level pressure predictions of several models, 1974–1984*

among us wouldn't like to have his or her salary depend upon success in forecasting the weather in the Sahara (hot, hot, and more hot) or in Antarctica (cold, cold, and more cold)? But for the parts of the world where most of us live, work, and play, about the best that the computer models can offer by way of useful short-term forecasting is a few days. And even then the spatial range is limited to grids on the order of 100 kilometers ($\approx$ 62 miles) on a side. Thus, pinpointing *exactly* where a particular low-pressure zone will center or where a cloud bank will

	Day						
	1	2	3	4	5	6	7
N. Atlantic/Europe (surface)							
A	50	44	21	10	2	2	1
B	2	8	25	21	71	7	7
C	0	0	6	21	33	43	44
(500 mb)							
A	52	48	30	13	2	2	1
B	0	4	19	25	25	15	8
C	0	0	3	14	25	35	43
U.K. area (surface)							
A	49	37	30	17	9	5	2
B	3	15	16	19	19	18	14
C	0	0	6	16	24	29	36
(500 mb)							
A	51	47	37	21	16	10	4
B	1	5	12	19	19	17	11
C	0	0	3	12	17	25	37

Table 2.1. Subjective assessment of the ECMWF model

form is still part of Richardson's "dim future." But when can we expect to reach this future? Are there properties of the weather system that impose inherent limitations on our ability to provide good forecasts over a period of weeks, or even months? Or is extending the range of useful forecasts just a matter of more powerful computers and more accurate measurements of the atmospheric state? Before closing the book on matters of weather forecasting and moving on to climatic prediction, let's take a few pages to discuss these crucial questions.

There are many types of filters in life, like those for coffee, tea, motor oil, and air, each performing exactly the same function: to allow some material quantity to pass through a membrane while preventing the transmission of other substances with which the desired material is mixed. Engineers and applied mathematicians also have their own kinds of filters, except that the quantities these filters pass are not matter but information. In the engineering business, for example, filters are used to extract the message contained in a signal corrupted by noise. With the development of computers, transistorized electrical circuitry, space travel, and all the other wonders of postwar technology centering on the processing of information, the mathematical study of filtering of signals of all types became a discipline in its own right in the mid-1950s. And it was some of the early fruits of this work that led by a somewhat circuitous route to what has eventually developed into the modern mathematical theory of chaos.

In 1949 the famed MIT mathematician Norbert Wiener published a book in which he set out a new mathematical approach for filtering noisy signals of all types—audio, visual, electronic, chemical, economic, and biological. Now a filter can be thought of as a kind of "black box": We feed the time series constituting the noise-corrupted signal into one end and the filtered estimate of the message emerges from the other. A *linear filter* is a box in which the estimate of the message is formed by summing the individual elements of the input signal as they arrive. Thus, each component of the signal is given a weight in accordance with the dictates of the filter. Wiener showed how to calculate the weight appropriate for each term, based upon assumptions about the statistical properties of the noise corrupting the transmitted message. In short, a linear filter forms its estimate of the true message by taking a special weighted average of the noisy observations, where the noisier components are given less weight than the "cleaner" ones. As a result of Wiener's work, by the mid-1950s the idea that linear filtering methods would perform as well as any other procedure was circulating in certain quarters.

Of course, Wiener was far too savvy about the many assumptions that went into his result ever to claim that linear filtering was the best that could be done. And, in fact, he devoted considerable energy to the study of various types of nonlinear filtering schemes for extracting the message from signals whose noise processes were not compatible with the assumptions of a linear filter. But practitioners are well known for ignoring such delicacies of the mathematician's art as assumptions. And one applied area in which Wiener's work was greeted with great enthusiasm was statistical weather forecasting, where the weather is predicted by using empirically established formulas. As a result of various types of misinterpretations of Wiener's work, claims were circulating in the statistical weather-forecasting community that linear filters would work as well as any nonlinear filter for squeezing good weather predictions out of noisy, incomplete observations. However, not everyone was convinced of the validity of this claim.

Edward Lorenz, then a young theoretical meteorologist at MIT, found the idea of the universal superiority of linear filtering schemes implausible, and set out to create a system of nonlinear equations whose solution could be used as the "observations," or inputs, for a linear filter. Lorenz's idea was that if the output from the filter didn't match the actual behavior of the known nonlinear system, then there must be a better nonlinear filter for extracting the message from the signal. Lorenz eventually concocted a nonlinear model involving thirteen variables that revealed the limitations of linear filtering. The famed *Lorenz equations* of modern chaos theory can be obtained from this original model by imposing a number of simplifications. Since the historical events shed considerable light on the prospects for long-term numerical weather prediction, let's take a moment to examine them in more detail.

During the course of analyzing his system, Lorenz used a computer that every minute or so would print out a set of thirteen numbers representing the weather system's "state"—one day's worth of weather prediction. At one point Lorenz was interested in looking at a particular situation over a longer period of time, and didn't want to have to go back to time zero and start the process from scratch. So instead he started at a time T much greater than zero, entering the state at time T that had been computed on a previous run. But while his computer carried out computations to an internal accuracy of six figures, to save typing time Lorenz inserted the initial values at time T only to three-digit precision.

To his great surprise, when Lorenz examined the computer's output from the run he had started at time T, it differed greatly from the original run that had been started at time zero, once both processes had run beyond time T. The situation Lorenz found himself facing is shown schematically in Figure 2.13. At first Lorenz suspected computer trouble, but later he discovered that the problem was the high sensitivity of his equations to the initial data. As it turned out, Lorenz's weather-forecasting equations were unstable in exactly the same way that the Circle-10 system studied in the opening chapter displays unstable behavior with respect to its initial conditions. In particular, a modern analysis of these same equations strongly suggests the presence of deterministic randomness, i.e., inherently unpredictable, chaotic behavior.

Lorenz's pioneering studies led the way to a host of additional work, all pointing to one conclusion: The equations of the atmosphere are unstable in the sense that they have strange attractors. So there is no

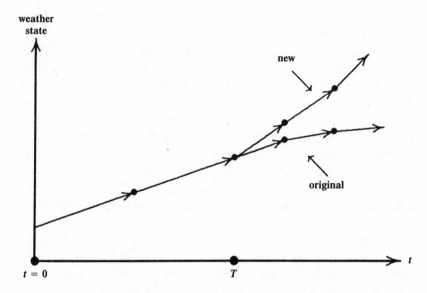

Figure 2.13. *Lorenz's experiment*

hope for really long-term prediction. From a mathematical point of view, this is a fatal blow. But what about the real atmosphere? After all, mathematical models are not the same thing as the physical world they claim to represent. So maybe the real atmosphere is not irregular, even if we can never hope to predict its behavior with our numerical models. What this boils down to saying is that, while the mathematical models of the weather have strange attractors, maybe the real atmosphere has a long-run behavior that is not chaotic.

Extensive investigations of this proposition show that there is little doubt but that the real atmosphere is indeed a chaotic system, too. If all known or suspected periodic oscillations are subtracted from the observations, too much variability still remains. For example, there is no evidence to show that migratory storms pass a given location at regularly spaced times. In fact, with periodic behavior there would be no weather-forecasting problem at all, and no new weather extremes either. For instance, a heat wave in which a new temperature record was set would correspond in system-theoretic terms to encountering a rarely visited part of the weather system's attractor. In a world in which the weather was truly periodic, new records could never be set, but only tied.

However, let's not be too pessimistic. From *some* initial weather states it is possible to predict the weather with considerable accuracy. Figure 2.14 shows the evolution in weather-state space of two ensembles of weather forecasts over a certain period. For the first cluster of initial conditions in (*a*), the forecasts diverge only a little, suggesting good predictability. On the other hand, in (*b*) the paths from different initial states diverge considerably, indicating that the atmosphere is in a chaotic state over the period of the forecasts. So in this case we can't make any meaningful prediction.

As an illustration of the kind of empirically based work that supports the claims for chaotic behavior in the weather system, there is a study by A. Tsonis and J. Elsner, in which they examined ten-second averages of vertical wind velocity 10 meters above the ground over an eleven-hour period on September 26, 1986, in Boulder, Colorado. Thus Tsonis and Elsner ended up with a database consisting of 3,960 observations. Using some of the statistical and dynamical systems tricks of the chaologists, they discovered that the wind velocity subsystem appears to have a strange attractor. As additional evidence of this sort mounts, the case for periodicity in the weather looks increasingly weak. This fact, in turn, tells us that there are inherent limitations on the length of time for which we can expect to be able to make useful forecasts. Let's talk for a moment about what those limits might be.

The diagram in Figure 2.15 shows the average RMS error for forecasts of the height of the 500 mb level made by the British Meteorological Office in 1984. These forecasts were made to predict the weather ten days ahead in the Northern Hemisphere (outside the trop-

(a) *(b)*

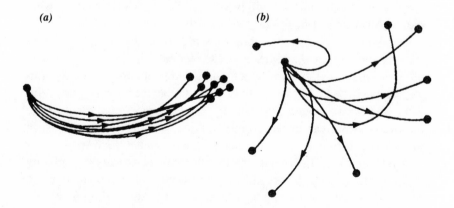

Figure 2.14. *Weather trajectories from different initial states*

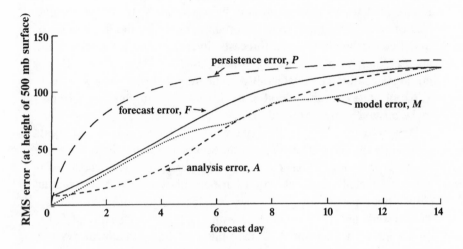

Figure 2.15. *Contributions to forecast errors*

ical regions). The figure shows the contributions to the total forecast error made by the error in the analysis of the initial data, and the error due to approximations made in the model itself, i.e., errors due to the incompleteness of the set of mathematical equations. The error in the zero-skill persistence forecast is also shown. We see that the forecast error reached 75 percent of the persistence error in forecast day 6, and was up to the 90 percent level by day 9. Thus, although the actual errors do not grow much after day 9, the differential advantage of using the model over just guessing is by then basically nil.

Detailed studies of the possibilities of reducing the two types of errors indicate that with realistic levels of development in computing power, observational accuracy, and general knowledge of atmospheric dynamics, we can hope to do no more than about double the length of the useful forecasts. So we come to the perhaps sad conclusion that the ultimate limit of what we can expect from numerical weather forecasting is, in general, good forecasts for a period of approximately two weeks.

If the outer limit of what the meteorological community can offer by way of outguessing the weather is two weeks, how can we hope to speak of climatic studies that purport to tell us what the effects our excesses of today will have on the climate fifty years from now? At first glance, it seems paradoxical to suggest that we can say anything of interest about the climate years, or even decades, from now if we cannot even say whether or not it will be raining in England next month. For the resolution of this dilemma, let's start by reexamining the differences between weather and climate in more detail.

THE COLD AND THE DARK, THE WARM AND THE WET

Selby Maxwell was an astronomer who for a time in the 1920s served as the science editor of the *Chicago Tribune*. Following the signing of the Treaty of Versailles ending World War I, the paper's editors realized that crop conditions in Europe would be a crucial factor in the new peace. As a result, Maxwell was assigned the task of plotting potential famine spots in Europe for a war atlas that the *Tribune* was planning to publish. This assignment introduced Maxwell to the influence of climatic conditions on human affairs, ultimately leading him to the development of a weather-energy cycle that he claimed governs all weather—past, present, and future.

According to Maxwell's theory, the weather cycle is based upon the interrelationships in the movements of the Sun, Earth, and Moon, although the lion's share of the interaction takes place between the Earth and the Moon. He claimed to have determined the correct time lags that cause the turbulent upper air masses to act in a predetermined manner. The underlying idea is that air masses on the Earth are subject to the same kinds of tidal forces as the oceans, and that they run in the same kinds of cyclic patterns. Maxwell's assertion was that all weather cycles of the same length complete a cycle and start over again at the same time, and that all such cycles are related in one way or another to his basic energy cycle. The formula he used for weather prediction involved plotting the movement of the jet stream, a narrow band of swiftly moving air in the high altitudes of the Northern Hemisphere, as a function of the motion and declination of the Moon. By Maxwell's reasoning, the storm activity is always at the center of the jet stream. This center drops lower during the warmer seasons, and shifts back up during the winter months because of the tilt of the Earth's axis. Thus his weather cycles come about from the tides of the jet stream. Using these "weather tides," Maxwell claimed to be able to predict storms not only days but months or even years in advance.

At about the same time that Maxwell was developing his ideas about cyclical weather patterns, Raymond Wheeler, a psychologist at the University of Kansas, was exploring the effects of climatic change on human behavior. In an attack on the behavioristic psychology theories in vogue at the time, Wheeler claimed that human behavior was not built up piece by piece from elementary primitives, but was an integrated pattern of responses to the individual's environment. This view forced Wheeler to consider that fluctuations in the environment might play a determining role in the way that people behave, a notion that caused him to look at the role of climatic variation in human affairs. To his great surprise, Wheeler discovered strong correlations between weather cycles of the Maxwell type and historical factors such as types of governments, wars, cultural styles, and human achievements. More specifically, he discovered a one hundred-year cycle, divided into four almost equal parts, indicating that mankind has behaved differently during periods of warm-wet, warm-dry, cold-wet, and cold-dry weather.

Illustrating Wheeler's theory, Figure 2.16 shows the Drought Clock correlating weather with the major wars of history. In the figure, C stands for cold periods. As the Clock shows, most international wars are waged during warm periods, while civil wars take place during cold-dry times. The Clock also shows that a major cold drought and a period of anarchy occur about every 510 years. Perhaps ominously, the Drought Clock also indicates that we are now entering a major cold-dry era—a time of great civil unrest, lower agricultural productivity, and social revolution. If newspaper headlines over the past few years are any indicator, Wheeler's theory certainly can't be dismissed out of hand.

The detailed empirical studies of Maxwell and Wheeler give us a hint as to how we might resolve the paradox between the strong reasons meteorology gives us for believing the weather system to be aperiodic, and the claims of many climatologists that there is a cyclic pattern to the weather. The difference lies in the fact that the two systems are qualitatively *similar* but far from quantitatively *identical*. In the context of weather versus climate, the difference shows up in the time scales of the processes of interest, together with the variables we employ to measure the system. Weather prediction is concerned with phenomena taking place over a period of hours in regions whose spatial scale is measured in kilometers. Climatic variability, on the other hand, involves processes whose duration is measured in years or centuries over regions the size of large countries. And while both mete-

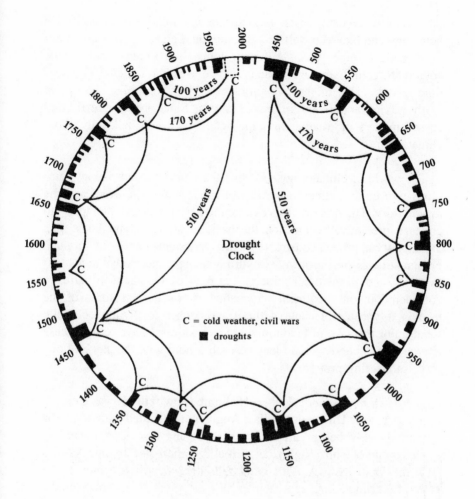

Figure 2.16. *The Drought Clock*

orologists and climatologists are concerned with variables like
temperature and precipitation, the weather forecaster wants to know
about the *exact* values of these quantities in a particular location; the
climatologist is concerned about the *average* values, spaning large
segments of both space and time.

So when we say that the weather system is aperiodic, we are referring to the interests of the meteorologists and their concern with precise
levels of weather variables, not to the average values, which are of

interest to the climatologists. With this view in mind, we can easily see how someone like Maxwell or Wheeler could claim a cyclical pattern of climatic change, while a meteorologist like Lorenz could argue equally forcefully for aperiodicity in the weather system. The spatiotemporal scales of the two problems are so dissimilar that we're really talking about two different systems. Since we've already discussed matters of weather in some detail, let's now talk only about climate.

The world of climatology, just like the world of meteorology, employs two quite distinct categories of models: the *empirical* and the *explanatory*. The first involves examining past trends and attempting to create a predictive scheme on the basis of statistical methods. The explanatory approach constructs predictive models based not so much on statistics as on the laws of hydrodynamics, thermodynamics, astronomy, and all the other principles of physics and chemistry already considered in our treatment of weather. Let's discuss some of the leading advocates of each of these approaches to divining climatic trends. For the sake of taxonomy and exposition, I have termed these approaches "schools," and labeled each school with the name of one of its pioneering proponents.

• *The Lamb school:* Hubert H. Lamb, now retired, was a climatologist at the University of East Anglia in the United Kingdom. His work is now being carried on there by his associates under the leadership of Tom Wigley, as well as by others like Jerome Namias in the United States. This work falls directly in the center of the empirical modeling approach to climatic prediction. Much of the efforts of the Lambians is devoted to quantifying historical sources like ships' logs and accounts of climatic patterns recorded by ancient court scribes. Given the fondness of the modern climatologist for high-tech solutions, Lamb's work, like Maxwell's and Wheeler's, appears to have been overshadowed in recent years by the computer-modeling wing of the climatological community. However, the historical record and its analysis are still proving to be very useful to the other schools as background data.

• *The Smagorinsky school:* Joseph Smagorinsky cut his meteorological teeth on the von Neumann–led IAS Weather Project. Later he headed a major numerical weather-forecasting research center in Princeton. The approach of this school is basically to adapt the

weather-forecasting GCMs for use in climatology. Thus, the Smagorinskians are, in effect, meteorologists in disguise, using the same
types of philosophy and models, as well as the same computers,
only looking into doings climatological rather than meteorological.
At present, I think it's fair to say that this is the dominant school of
activity in the climatology game.

• *The Budyko school:* Mikhail Budyko heads the Global Meteorological Institute in Leningrad, and was one of the first scientists to
warn about the greenhouse effect more than twenty years ago. He
has championed the somewhat idiosyncratic view that all atmospheric motions are dependent on the thermodynamic effect of a
heterogeneous distribution of energy on the Earth's surface. Thus,
this school of climatology focuses on developing energy-balance
models, drawing upon observational data derived from descriptive
climatology of the Lamb type. Since these models employ much
simpler parametrization schemes than the GCMs, they can be applied to longer time-scale changes. It's of interest to note that many
of the ideas of the Budyko school have now been incorporated by
the Smagorinskians, so it may no longer be appropriate to draw a
clear-cut distinction between the two.

With these categories in mind, let's now turn to one of the favorite
testing grounds of climatological ideas and models: ice ages.

The giant sequoias of northern California are among the oldest
known living things, some of them having survived for more than three
thousand years. From the patterns of the rings left behind as these
majestic trees shed their bark, skilled dendrochronologists can read the
long-term record of the annual amount of solar energy that has struck
the Earth. It was from readings like these that Raymond Wheeler
developed his theory of human events and their correlation with climatic cycles. More recently, climatologists have found evidence to
indicate that about every two hundred years the Earth experiences a
"little ice age" due to peaks in solar activity. As solar activity again
rose to a peak at the end of 1989, it's of more than passing interest to
ask if climatological analyses can tell us if we will return to the cold
conditions of the early nineteenth century. Or will things really freeze
over in a great ice age of the sort that ten thousand years ago buried
what is now New York City under hundreds of meters of ice? And how
soon can we expect either of these two senarios to unfold?

One of the first to warn of the possibility of a new ice age was Reid Bryson of the University of Wisconsin, who argued that the Northern Hemisphere is returning to normal weather after having experienced a fifty-year period of abnormally mild conditions. He based his arguments on the same kinds of statistical information used by the Lamb school, indicators like tree rings and pollen counts. Further evidence of the same sort is provided by Cesare Emiliani of the University of Miami. He notes that over the past 7 million years the global mean temperature has been as high as it is in this century only 5 percent of the time. These are hard facts. Let's take a moment to see the different ways these facts can be interpreted as being precursors of long-term climatic change.

Basically, there are four possible scenarios for an ice age, depending upon the severity of the freeze (little or great) and its speed (slow or fast).

• *A little/great ice age:* Most climatologists, starting with Bryson, believe that the evidence points to the kind of climate that prevailed from the seventeenth century to about 1850. During that time northern Europe lived in the twilight of permanent winter, with cool, dry summers and poor harvests and cold, snowy, bitter winters. Some of the consequences of such a picture would be wetter weather in the winter-wheat sections of the high plains in the United States, but with yields remaining more or less unaffected. In other parts of the world, the little-ice-age scenario would result in major droughts in India and China every four years or so, as well as loss of half the food production capacity in Canada. A great ice age, on the other hand, would see Chicago under a sheet of ice miles thick, while most of Canada, southern Alaska, and the northern United States would be covered by a single sheet of ice the size of Antarctica. Such a world would mostly consist of dry equatorial zones, occasionally experiencing short bursts of very heavy rainfall.

• *Fast/slow freeze:* The prevailing notion is that an ice age would occur slowly beginning with the formation of ice packs from snowfall. The basic mechanism in this scenario is a positive-feedback effect in which increased snow cover would raise the surface albedo, thereby reflecting more incident solar radiation back into the atmosphere. This, in turn, would further reduce temperatures, contributing to even greater snowfall. An alternate view holds that the freeze would occur because of the migration of Arctic snowpacks southward. But either mechanism would take thousands of years. There are fast-freeze theorists, however, who say that an ice age could be brought on by a "snowblitz"—massive snowfalls that never melt. A process like this might bring on an ice age in only seven to ten years.

So there we have it. All possible ways to go into the deep freeze, with even the most benevolent of the scenarios holding out the prospects of an apocalyptic future for most of the world. Cold-Earth climatologists may disagree on exactly how far and how fast we'll fall into the freezer, but the one thing upon which they all concur is that fall we will—gradually or with alacrity. But why should we have these ice ages at all? Predicting them is one thing; explaining the reasons for their occurrence is quite another. What do the climatologists have to say about the actual mechanism(s) underlying the development (and disappearance) of an ice age?

In an earlier section, we briefly mentioned the Milankovitch cycle. This consists of slow, regular oscillations in the shape of the Earth's orbit around the Sun, and in the parameters of the Earth's rotational motion (see Figure 2.4, page 87). While for many purposes it's useful to pretend that the Earth is a perfect sphere, spins like a Harlem Globetrotter's basketball, and moves around the Sun in a perfectly elliptical orbit, this mathematically convenient picture is only a gross approximation to the true state of affairs. The Earth is not a sphere, but shaped more like a fat pear. And the orbital motion is not a perfect ellipse, but an irregular kind of curve with no mathematical name. Moreover, it's a curve that changes its shape over the course of thousands of years, sometimes bringing the Earth closer to the Sun, sometimes taking us farther away. Finally, the Earth's axis of spin does not always point in the same direction, but wobbles. This wobbling (more precisely, *precession*) of the axis also affects the amount of solar radiation reaching the Earth's surface.

As a result of pioneering work in 1976 by Jim Hays, John Imbrie, and Nick Shackleton on the changing pattern of ice cover revealed by radioactive isotopes in core sediments, the consensus of the climatological community today is that the periodic occurrence of an ice age is due primarily to the Milankovitch cycle, together with a little help from the periodic fluctuations in solar output (the sunspot cycle). Thus we can regard the Milankovitch cycle as the primary pacemaker of the ice ages. But there is one puzzling aspect of this theory that is still not entirely settled. The Milankovitch cycle is a gradual, smooth change in the astronomical parameters of the Earth's motion. Yet when ice ages end, the climatic record shows relatively rapid shifts in the weather from periods of warm to cold and back to warm again. Question: How could the gradual, essentially linear, astronomical forcing of the Milankovitch cycle result in such a nonlinear, back-and-forth type of response in the climatic system?

Over the past few years, work led by John Imbrie of Brown University has suggested that the astronomical cycles exert their strong influence on the climate through an intermediary—the carbon-dioxide-based greenhouse effect. The basic conclusion of this work is that carbon dioxide amplifies the changes that the Milankovitch process is trying to produce: the more carbon dioxide, the greater the global temperature. But how does carbon dioxide in the *atmosphere* mediate the effect of ice on the *surface*?

Recently, Jonathan Overpeck and his co-workers have used a GCM to study this question, coming to the conclusion that changes in the melting history of the Laurentide Ice Sheet (a massive sheet covering much of high-latitude North America) offer an explanation for the observed nonlinear response of the climate system. The main mechanism they propose involves a major diversion of the Laurentide meltwater into the Mississippi and St. Lawrence rivers, causing the North Atlantic sea-surface temperature initially to decrease, then to warm again. Tests of this theory with a GCM support the dominant role of these sea-surface temperature fluctuations in generating the high-latitude temperature changes needed to end the ice age.

Our discussion of the prediction and explanation of ice ages has included the possibility of our being put out into the cold at nature's whim over a time frame measured in tens, if not hundreds or thousands, of years. But there is another possible scenario—one whose timing can be measured in days. Furthermore, this is a path that banishes nature to the sidelines, leaving the playing field and the decisions entirely to us humans. This road to the cold and dark is the cul-de-sac of a global nuclear war. Since the climatic effects of such an exchange of nuclear weapons has been a front-page news item in recent years, an examination of the question from the perspectives of this chapter would not be amiss.

*   *   *

Ambio is a highly respected environmental journal published by the Royal Swedish Academy of Sciences. Around 1980, the editors asked Dutch scientist Paul Crutzen and his American colleague John Birks to prepare a paper addressing the atmospheric effects of nuclear war. As atmospheric chemists, Crutzen and Birks originally intended to look only at increased amounts of ultraviolet radiation reaching the Earth's surface as the result of a nuclear war. But by one of those strokes of serendipity that often unaccountably occur in the history of a major scientific breakthrough, they inexplicably decided to consider the smoke from fires as well. Preliminary calculations convinced Crutzen and Birks that there could be enough smoke in a major nuclear exchange to blot out the Sun from half the Earth for weeks on end. Publication of their paper in the November 1982 issue of *Ambio* stimulated work by many other scientists on the relationship between fire and smoke from nuclear blasts and the darkening of the Sun, leading to a major study and meeting in late 1983 that sparked off scientific and public concern over the problem of "nuclear winter."

Subsequent studies indicate that the principal environmental consequences of nuclear war are likely to be: (1) obscuring smoke in the troposphere, (2) obscuring dust in the stratosphere, (3) fallout of radioactive debris, and (4) partial destruction of the ozone layer. This list, incidentally, shows why no such climatic effects were observed during the period of atmospheric testing of nuclear weapons prior to the 1963 Limited Test Ban Treaty. The reason is quite simple: The tests were all conducted over desert scrubland, coral atolls, tundra, and wasteland. Thus they set no fires; hence, there was no smoke.

The basic nuclear winter scenario involves the following sequence of steps:

nuclear blasts → fires → smoke → reduced sunlight → darkness and cold

Let's look at the pieces of this gloomy picture in somewhat more detail.

A. The nuclear explosions send dust, radioactivity, and various gases into the atmosphere. The dust expelled from the surface is enough to build a dam across the English channel 500 yards high and 30 yards thick.

B. The explosions ignite fires, burning cities, forests, fuel, and grasslands in the warring countries.

C. The fires send up plumes of smoke and gases high into the troposphere. Within a couple of weeks, some of the dust, radioactivity,
   and smoke is carried around the world by the winds.
D. At the same time, clouds of smoke spread around the Earth in the
   mid-latitude zones from Texas to Norway. The dust eventually
   settles to the ground in a period of weeks or months.
E. Beneath the clouds of smoke and dust, daylight is reduced to
   darkness for days and to twilight for weeks.
F. Temperatures drop on the land under the clouds of smoke and
   dust. If the nuclear exchange takes place in the spring or summer,
   this drop in temperature is comparable to the difference between
   winter and summer ("nuclear winter"). Average temperatures
   probably do not return to normal for more than a year, and the
   climate is disturbed for a much longer period.
G. When the dust and smoke clear, the Earth's surface is exposed to
   additional damaging ultraviolet radiation resulting from partial destruction of the ozone layer.

These are the main steps on the road to nuclear winter. Can we really
expect such dramatic temperature reductions for such an extended
period? Or are these just worst-case scare stories manufactured to
direct media attention to a hitherto unappreciated facet of the horror of
nuclear war?

Following publication of the Crutzen-Birks study, Carl Sagan and
two of his former students, James B. Pollack and O. Brian Toon from
NASA's Ames Research Center, together with Richard Turco and
Thomas Ackerman, undertook an extensive set of calculations to check
the back-of-the-envelope estimates in the *Ambio* paper. The Sagan
group had already been sensitized to the possibilities of major climatic
disruptions due to dust in the atmosphere by their work on the
Mariner 9 probe to Mars in 1971. It seemed that when the probe
arrived, a massive Martian duststorm was under way. While waiting
for the storm to abate, Sagan noticed that the instruments on the probe
recorded atmospheric temperatures considerably higher, as well as
surface temperatures much lower, than normal. Later, Sagan's group
began to apply some of the same techniques used to analyze the Martian duststorm data to similar phenomena generated by volcanic erup-
tions on Earth. So when the Crutzen-Birks report came out, the NASA
team was well positioned to do a detailed computational investigation
of the situation.

Using its model, the Sagan group produced a paper that has become famous in nuclear winter circles—and not just for its science. This paper, known under the label "TTAPS" from the last names of its five authors, was published in the prestigious American journal *Science* just before Christmas 1983. To maximize the public exposure of the paper's conclusions, Carl Sagan arranged a prepublication press conference on Halloween to announce the paper's frightening conclusions. As a bit of unsubstantiated scientific gossip, in certain corners of the climatological community it was rumored that Sagan chose this especially dramatic moment to call public attention to the nuclear winter scenario in an effort to garner support for a Nobel Peace Prize nomination. Well, why not? After all, the subsequent East-West dialogue on scientific and political issues surrounding the nuclear winter scenario spawned by the paper's conclusions certainly merits some kind of prize. But I should add that if any such accolades are forthcoming, let's hope the prize committees remember to recognize the paper's senior author, Richard Turco, too, since he was the man primarily responsible for carrying out most of the actual computational work supporting the paper's conclusions.

The TTAPS group concluded that a major nuclear exchange in the Northern Hemisphere would result in a short-term temperature change of almost 40 degrees and a total recovery time of nearly one year. By way of comparison, even a 1-degree long-term drop in temperature would eliminate all wheat growing in Canada, and a 10-degree drop is typical for an ice age. But the TTAPS model was not beyond reproach: It was one-dimensional in its assumption that particles of dust and smoke could move vertically but not spread in latitude and longitude. This kind of assumption implies that the atmosphere is passive—i.e., it just sits there and radiates energy up and down.

In the years since the pioneering TTAPS study, a number of investigators have substantially extended the scope of the modeling of nuclear blast effects using three-dimensional GCMs. One of the leaders in this effort has been Stephen H. Schneider of the National Center for Atmospheric Research (NCAR) in Boulder, Colorado. In a 1988 summary of the state of nuclear winter modeling, Schneider and his coworkers concluded that the climatic effects are likely to be much less severe than reported in the TTAPS paper. I hasten to emphasize that this does *not* imply that there is no problem. Far from it, in fact. However, the projected summertime temperature drops of 5 to 15 degrees would be more like the difference between summer and fall than that between summer and winter. This conclusion has led Schneider to relabel the overall situation "nuclear autumn." His general conclusion is that "it is unlikely that climatic effects of nuclear war alone will be more devastating to the combatant nations than the direct effects of the use of many thousands of nuclear weapons." But the report cautions that the entire assessment hinges upon human behavioral assumptions of what constitutes a plausible scenario for nuclear attacks. It's also worth mentioning here that the nuclear winter scenario doesn't have to involve a two-sided war; a preemptive aggressor would produce the same atmospheric and biological backlash upon itself as it would receive from an attack by another country.

Both the ice age projections and the nuclear autumn scenario involve drastic global coolings. Interestingly, however, the most topical climatological issue before the house at the moment involves just the opposite effect: a worldwide warming due to increased atmospheric carbon dioxide (CO_2) and the so-called *greenhouse effect*. If the "hot-Earth" climatologists are correct, our long-term future is not to shiver in a deep freeze at all, but rather to sweat things out in a global steam bath. In order to assess the merits of these climatological arguments, let's first take a look at the basic greenhouse mechanism.

The Bible says that the meek shall inherit the Earth, while many entomologists are putting their money on the insects. Hot-Earth partisans, however, would probably advise that your betting dollar will yield a higher return by placing it on the radishes! Reason? As has been well chronicled in virtually every magazine, newspaper, and TV science show over the past five years or more, industrial activity has been pumping more and more CO_2 into the atmosphere as each year goes by. And this excess CO_2 will benefit some plants like the radishes by its fertilizing effect. On the downside, this same excess CO_2 is also draping a blanket over the Earth, preventing solar radiation reflected at the surface from escaping out through the atmosphere. This is the famous greenhouse effect, familiar to all gardeners. It is schematically shown in Figure 2.17. In rough outline, the mechanism follows these steps:

1. Increased temperature causes more evaporation from the oceans.
2. Water vapor in the air adds to the greenhouse effect, possibly also changing the cloud cover.
3. Less snow and ice cover in a warmer world implies that more

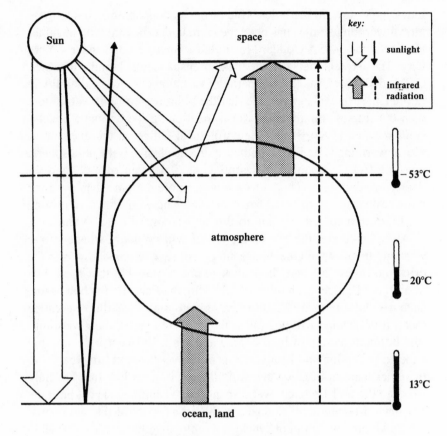

Figure 2.17. *The greenhouse effect*

incoming solar radiation is absorbed at the Earth's surface, thereby perpetuating the cycle.

The questions for climatologists are, as always, how much warming can we expect, how fast will it take place, and what are the likely consequences?

Since greenhouse warming became a front-page issue, virtually every climatological research center in the world has taken a stab at predicting the effects of, say, doubling the amount of CO_2 discharged into the atmosphere. The dominant, although far from uniform, view appears to be that the global mean temperature will rise about 3 degrees over the next fifty years. This increase will be smaller in the tropics and much larger toward the poles. One of the leading contributors to these global warming studies has been the team under the direction of James Hansen at the NASA Goddard Institute for Space Studies in New York City. These researchers dispute the consensus view, claiming that their GCM model suggests less temperature variation but more variability in rainfall. But they also conclude that the polar regions will warm more than the tropics. Finally, it's worth mentioning the dramatic conclusions reached at the British Meteorological Office on the question of global warming. The BMO predicts a drastic change if the atmospheric level of CO_2 is doubled: a warming of 5 degrees overall, and 12 degrees at the poles. This outcome is far more extreme than even the most pessimistic of the Goddard scenarios, and would involve turning the Earth into something akin to the hellish conditions on Venus.

At this juncture, the perceptive reader will no doubt wonder if the warming trend of the greenhouse effect will save us somehow from the drift into a new ice age. Is it even remotely possible that these two trends could cancel each other out, leaving the Earth in much the same state we find it in today? Sad to say, climatologists see almost no hope that a little ice age will neutralize the projected greenhouse warming. The difficulty is one of both degree and kind. By most accounts, the expected warming will be about 3 degrees over the next fifty years. On the other hand, a little ice age would result in a cooling trend of only between 0.5 and 1 degree over a span of two centuries. Thus, both the amounts of temperature change and the time frames of the two opposing trends are too far out of synchrony for them to have any appreciable chance of canceling each other out. On balance, if the climatologists are correct, our likely future is in the sauna and not in the freezer.

Ice ages, CO_2 warming, nuclear autumn or winter: all major climatic disturbances, but over radically different time scales running from thousands of years to a matter of days, and over the entire globe. What about an intermediate kind of climatic prediction, one made for a local region over a period of time measured in just a few years? What can we expect from GCM simulations carried out to obtain far more modest (and probably more useful), albeit less attention-getting, sorts of climatic forecasts?

As an illustration of just such a study, Figure 2.18 displays the projected and observed record of rainfall and temperature from two GCMs over a five-year period in the Amazonian regions. The models were those of the Canadian Climate Centre (CCC) and the Goddard Institute for Space Studies (GISS). The regions covered by the models

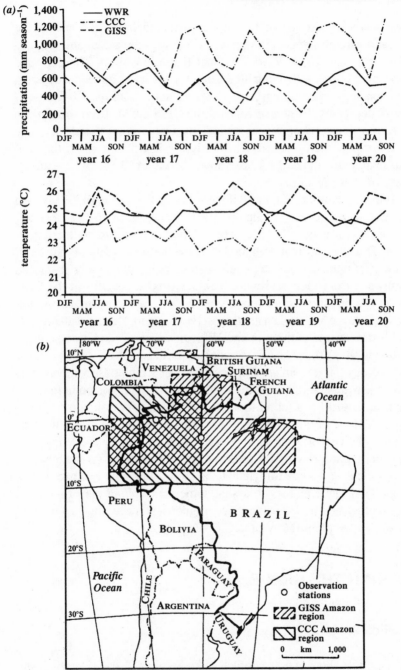

Figure 2.18. *Different GCM predictions in the Amazonian regions*

are shown in part (b) of the figure, while their projections for the climatic variables appear in part (a), along with the actual observations taken from data in the World Weather Record (WWR). The CCC and GISS predictions were computed using GCMs with somewhat different grid spacings, nine 5-degree-by-5-degree squares in the CCC model, four 8-degree-by-10-degree cells for the GISS GCM. Both simulations were run over a twenty-year period, by which point the steady-state behavior had been reached. Thus only the last five years of the simulated climatic trajectories are shown in Figure 2.18. What can we make of these results?

The seasonality of the rainfall record is stronger in both GCMs than in the observed record. While the WWR observations do show a strong seasonality, it is out of phase between the northern and southern Amazon. Thus the fact that both models show the seasonality of the southern region indicates that the mathematical rain belts may be displaced northward from their real-world counterparts, especially in the CCC model. Although these factors do not necessarily prove much, particularly since the WWR data are themselves far from "clean," the results do illustrate some of the principal difficulties involved in assessing climatic GCMs. To quote Ann Henderson-Sellers, a lively player in the climatology game, "In specific locations for which observational data can be ascertained, slight shifts in the model circulation combine with the coarse [grid] resolution to make validation very difficult."

As the tone of this somewhat inconclusive comment seems to characterize the current state of much of long-term climate modeling, this seems an appropriate place to bring our deliberations on matters meteorological and climatological to a close. Let's now move into a judgmental mode and try to assign some measures of performance to the weathermen and the climatic prognosticators as they attempt to predict and explain the weather.

MAKING THE GRADE

Prediction

By now, just about every schoolchild knows that Charles Darwin spent the years 1831–1836 sailing the Pacific aboard the British ship HMS *Beagle,* where he gathered the data upon which he based his theory of natural selection. What is not so well known is the fate of the *Beagle*'s captain, Robert Fitzroy. Upon the ship's triumphant return to England, Fitzroy was appointed governor of New Zealand, where his support of the native Maori population generated such outrage among the British settlers that he was recalled to London. In good Peter Principle fashion, Fitzroy was then rewarded with a promotion to admiral. And in 1859 the British Admiralty gave him the job of developing a weather-warning service for the British Navy.

By 1861 Fitzroy was so confident of his forecasting skills that he began sending his predictions to the newspapers. The forecasts created considerable controversy, the Royal Society claiming that Fitzroy was making predictions without enough scientific data to support his conclusions. And this was not the only scientific controversy that engaged Fitzroy's attention.

Being a deeply religious man, Fitzroy wrote many criticisms and preached many sermons warning Darwin against his pernicious, anti-Christian ways. Unfortunately, the good admiral's talents as a ship's captain far outweighed his abilities as a polemicist, and Darwin's supporters crushed the arguments with such finality that Fitzroy ended up slitting his throat with a razor in 1865. Such was the fate of one of the world's first weather forecasters. But despite the fact that many of us have occasionally felt the desire to apply Fitzroy's razor to our own local TV weatherman, the facts support the claim that weather forecasting, scientific style, has progressed enormously since Fitzroy's day.

When it comes to weather forecasting, the most common reason for predictions to diverge is differences in the analyses of the raw data that goes into making up the initial conditions. These errors in the initial conditions, coupled with the intrinsic sensitivity to initial conditions of the dynamical equations, are the primary obstacles to the creation of good forecasts over virtually arbitrary periods of time. Studies have been carried out to test long-range predictability using the so-called *perfect-model assumption,* in which the mathematical model of the atmospheric dynamics is taken to be an exact representation of the actual physical process itself. These studies show that errors reach their asymptotic, or saturation, level after a period of 14 to 20 days. Thus the limit of deterministic predictability is generally taken to be about two weeks. Another way to describe this situation is to say that the error growth rate during the early stages has a doubling time of around two days.

The pioneering work by Lorenz has shown why this kind of intrinsic limit seems to exist for the numerical weather models and not for the prediction of phenomena like the tides. The weather system is governed by dynamics that have a strange attractor, and every such attractor is filled with unstable orbits of every possible period, as well as an uncountable number of aperiodic trajectories. Thus, the long-run dynamical behavior of such a system can be thought of as being tantamount to a random walk through this uncountably large forest of unstable paths. So, as we saw in the opening chapter, unless the modeling, the analyses of initial conditions, and the computations are all carried out with infinite precision, errors unavoidably creep in that eventually bury the useful information in the prediction. For weather-forecasting models, this "eventually" appears to be a time horizon of about two weeks. Thus, in assessing the current state of the numerical weather forecaster's art and awarding a grade, we should measure our judgment against this theoretical barrier.

Forecasting climate patterns is a different kettle of fish entirely. In fact, the difference between climate forecasting and weather forecasting is just about as great as the difference between looking at rocks from the perspective of elementary particle physics and from the vantage point of geology—especially when the time horizon of the prediction is very large. For instance, when we start talking about climatic predictions over a period of many years, crucial roles are played by things like sea-ice variations, surface glacier effects, and temperature in the deep ocean layers, not to mention the astronomical factors associated with the Milankovitch cycle. None of these factors has much bearing on daily weather forecasting. Thus, despite the fact that many climatic forecasts are carried out using the same types of GCMs employed by the weather people, the criterion for assessing predictability is radically different. So we must respect these differences in coming to our term grade for the climatologists.

In rather marked contrast to the weather forecasters, the climatological community has much less confidence about the ability of its models to tell us what we'd really like to know. For instance, at a recent meeting in New York held to assess the likely effects in the United States of CO_2 warming of the atmosphere, three major models were presented. Two of them showed an increase in summer rainfall in the southeastern part of the country, while the third showed a decrease. But when the region of interest shifted to the Great Plains, a different pair of the models predicted a drop in rainfall, while the third projected an increase. As James Hansen of Goddard remarked about the regional effects of global warming caused by a buildup of greenhouse gases in the atmosphere, "[They] cannot be predicted with any confidence." Dissident climatologist S. B. Idso put the matter more forcefully when he stated in 1984 that "there is no a priori reason to believe that the computer models of the atmosphere currently employed to investigate the effects of increasing atmospheric CO_2 are reasonable representations of reality."

Further testimony to the uncertainty surrounding climate models came in a debate held at MIT in early June 1990 between Stephen Schneider and Richard Lindzen. While Schneider supported the view that current climate models can reasonably predict a mean rise in global temperature of at least 2 degrees over the next century, Lindzen argued that these models are, in fact, weak, and that the picture presented by Schneider and others is "misleading." Lindzen based his arguments on the fact that climatological models are "inconsistent with observations of landbased global average temperatures," contain documented errors, and have done a poor job of predicting climatic change in the tropics. Moreover, Lindzen noted that the models do not adequately account for the role of feedback from the oceans. In his rebuttal, Schneider acknowledged that the issues raised by Linden are legitimate, but still stated that it is "unlikely that the models are off by more than a factor of three."

On the positive side, climatologists of the Lambian stripe have found numerous long-term patterns in the climatic record that cannot be easily dismissed. Maxwell and Wheeler's weather cycles are good examples of this kind of repetitive picture, standing as strong testimony to some sort of regularity and exploitable structure in the world's climate. Moreover, even the GCMs do a fair job on climatological questions as long as their time horizons are limited to a few years or less, and not measured in decades or centuries. We saw some evidence of this in the nuclear winter simulations, as well as in the work done on the Amazonian basin. These cases show that while climatic prediction may not be at the level of precision or development as that of weather forecasting, it's still far from worthless.

So predicting weather and predicting climate are two very different problems. Thus, in putting the foregoing evidence together and coming up with a grade, it's necessary to consider the predictability of each separately. Upon weighing the merits of each case in the light of the evidence at hand, we come to the following report card on the two problems:

Term Grade—Prediction (Weather): B⁺
Term Grade—Prediction (Climate): C

Explanation

Scientific explanation is explanation by law. Therefore, the grade we assign for weather and climatic explanation is directly proportional to the degree to which we can feel confident that we know the laws governing these atmospheric processes.

For the dynamics of the weather, at least since the time of Vilhelm Bjerknes early in this century, we have had a reasonably good grasp of the various laws and equations of physics, chemistry, and the geosciences that regulate the basic atmospheric processes. This fact has been made ever more clear by the subsequent success of Richardson and the von Neumann group in writing down and numerically solving these equations, as well as by the work of Lorenz and his followers in showing the inherent limitations of these models. But the real proof is in the pudding, as they say, and the pudding in this case is the fact that very few people in the weather-forecasting business worry much about the underlying laws when it comes to planning future research. Rather, their concern lies overwhelmingly in improving the observational equipment and the worldwide reporting network. This is not to say that the models are perfect. But it is to say that the refinements that appear to be needed in the models are just that—refinements and polishing of the apple to a little brighter shine. No one seems to believe that there are any major missing pieces in the equations (read: laws) still requiring attention.

On the climatic side of the house, the picture is, as usual, not quite so rosy. Many of the major factors in long-term climatological change are reasonably well understood, such as the Milankovitch cycle, sunspots, the Southern Oscillation, and the like. Yet there are numerous "missing links" that climatologists claim must be put in place before we can really say we understand and can explain why processes unfold as they do. For example, there is evidence that, for predictions longer than two years, it's necessary to take into account broad-scale volcanic activity. Yet no one really knows how this factor should be incorporated into the numerical models. Another crucial factor in long-term climatic change is the ocean temperature at various depths, along with the sea-ice interface. While there is some hazy understanding of the relation of these matters to things like ice ages, what's currently known is very far from being what scientists would term a law. So with all these ifs, ands, buts, and disclaimers, I don't think anyone could seriously argue that we can explain the climate with anywhere near the degree of fidelity with which we can explain the weather. All this having been said, our final assessment of scientific explanation of the atmosphere comes down to:

Term Grade—Explanation (Weather): A⁻
Term Grade—Explanation (Climate): C⁺

Atmospheric phenomena are an area in which the processes involved are governed mostly by the laws of physics, chemistry, and astronomy. While we may not know every detail of those laws, we have some confidence that they do indeed exist and, moreover, that steadfast perseverance will reveal their nature to us. Our next case study of prediction and explanation also involves an area in which the processes are governed at one level by these very same laws of physics and chemistry. But the essence of the phenomena of interest lies at another level entirely, a level at which new laws enter that are not reducible to those of the physical sciences. What's involved here is the kind of level jump separating the physical from the life sciences. It forms the basis for our next story of prediction/explanation—the emergence of the physical form of living organisms.

CHAPTER THREE

SHAPING UP

Can We Predict/Explain the Physical Form of Living Things?

The history of man for the nine months preceding his birth would probably be far more interesting, and contain events of far greater moment, than all the three-score and ten years that follow it.

—SAMUEL TAYLOR COLERIDGE

It is not birth, marriage, or death, but gastrulation, which is truly the most important time in your life.

—LEWIS WOLPERT

Theoretical biology should be done in Mathematical Departments. . . . We have to let biologists busy themselves with their very concrete—but almost meaningless—experiments; in developmental biology, how could they hope to solve a problem they cannot even formulate?

—RENÉ THOM

FROM BLOBS TO BABIES

On its cash register receipts, Foyles in London advertises itself as "The World's Greatest Bookshop." Perhaps. But one thing is certain: Foyles undoubtedly ranks among the world's most *disorganized* bookshops, a fact due in no small measure to the quaint, but completely incomprehensible, practice employed by many British booksellers of shelving their titles by publisher rather than by subject, author, or any other rational, coherent, useful scheme. A few weeks ago I dropped into Foyles in search of some volume of ancient and forgotten scientific lore. As I was rummaging through what I thought were the science stacks, my eye was struck by a garishly covered, lavishly illustrated book that turned out to be a history of the great science fiction and horror films of the 1950s. Since I had nothing but time to kill anyway, having exhausted my patience in futilely trying to locate the right section of the store in which to look for the item I really wanted, I picked up this book in the hope that a short trip down memory lane might ease my irritation a bit. Opening the book at random, I began my tour through monsterland with an account of the 1958 classic *The Blob,* a sci-fi epic that, if for no other reason, is worth a footnote in cinema history books as marking the screen debut of the late Steve McQueen. The story involves a slimy monster from outer space that almost engulfs a small middle-America town before McQueen discovers its Achilles' heel—the cold of a deep freezer. Recollection of this story set my thoughts off onto further contemplation of this gelatinous nightmare, including its weird, otherworldly way of carrying out the universal biological imperative to survive.

Just like all earthly organisms, The Blob started its life as—a blob. However, unlike terrestrial plants and animals, as it digested the good citizens of McQueen's town, The Blob only grew into a bigger blob and never developed arms, legs, teeth, hair, eyes, or any of the other organs characterizing life forms on Earth. And The Blob also never assumed a shape other than its original, slightly flattened spherical form, again unlike all earthly organisms larger than a bacterium. Since no one in the film could dispute The Blob's survival skills (at least in a warm environment), the obvious question is: Why don't all organisms just stay blobs? Or, putting it another way, we could ask: How and why do organisms here on Earth develop their characteristic physical forms from their beginning as microscopic blobs of protoplasm hardly larger than the period on the question mark at the end of this sentence? In biological terms, the how and why of physical form is called *development,* and it constitutes the true terra incognita of the biologist's world. Let's have a quick look at the general features of the problem.

A good starting point is the development cycle of a typical terrestrial organism, the frog, which is shown in Figure 3.1. (For the most part in this chapter, we'll focus on the developmental aspects of the higher animals. The situation for plants and more primitive organisms is similar, but with a few technical differences that need not concern us here.) Starting at ten o'clock, the development cycle consists of the four stages:

fertilization → **cleavage** → **gastrulation** → **organogenesis**

along with the optional postnatal stage of **metamorphosis,** which occurs in some species like frogs. Since it's during these stages that the physical shape of the organism is fixed, and the stages themselves are universal for all known living things, understanding the problem of

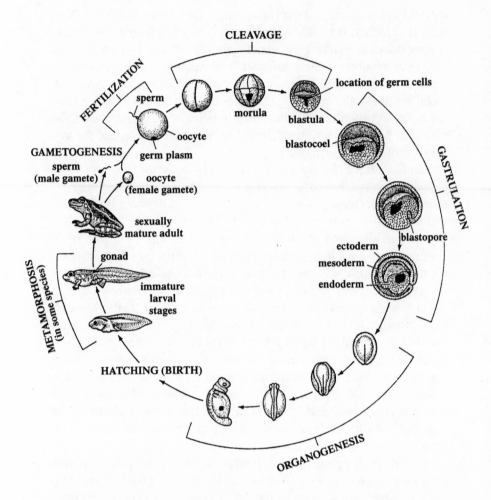

Figure 3.1. *The development cycle of a frog*

development is really tantamount to understanding what's going on at each stage of this cycle. So let's take a moment to discuss the steps in a bit more detail.

- *Fertilization:* During this stage the male sperm and female egg (technically, an *oocyte*) come together to produce a fertilized egg, the *zygote*.
- *Cleavage:* In this part of the cycle, the fertilized egg divides

rapidly several times, forming a ball of cells termed the *morula,* i.e., a blob. In the final stages of cleavage, the morula develops into a hollow sphere, the *blastula* (a bigger blob).

• *Gastrulation:* After the rate of cell division slows down, the cells undergo dramatic movements and change their positions. This cellular rearrangement involves the blastula's "caving in" on itself and forming a kind of deeply dented ball, something rather similar to one of those beanbag chairs that were in vogue in certain circles in the 1960s. This process gives rise to three cellular regions, or *germ layers:* the *ectoderm, endoderm,* and *mesoderm.* The ectoderm produces the cells that later form the outer skin layer and the nervous system, while the endodermal cells eventually become the lining of the digestive tube and its associated organs like the liver and pancreas. The mesoderm ultimately develops into the other inner organs, such as the heart and kidneys, as well as into the blood cells and the connective tissues like muscles, bones, and tendons.

• *Organogenesis:* Once the germ layers are established, the cells interact and rearrange themselves into the various bodily organs. As many organs involve cells from more than one germ layer, some cells may have to undergo long migrations during this period to reach their final positions. From the diagram, we also see that a portion of the fertilized egg serves to produce the *germ cells* (not to be confused with the earlier germ layers), which are set aside for reproductive purposes. All the other cells of the body are called *somatic cells.*

From this picture, we see that the cells are undergoing two quite separate and distinct kinds of activities during the process of development: (1) an *internal* change in which the original "uncommitted," general-purpose cell becomes a brain cell, a heart cell, or some other kind of specialized cell in a process called *differentiation,* and (2) an *external* process in which the cell migrates to a new spatial location and, in general, interacts with other cells to form a local part of the organism's overall spacetime pattern in the process termed *morphogenesis.* Putting all these considerations together, we can state

The Fundamental Problem of Development

During every stage of development, how does the developing organism maintain the correct spatial and temporal arrangement of cells for the species to which it belongs?

Since our primary concern here is how and why organisms take on their characteristic forms, we could rephrase the fundamental problem in morphogenetic terms as: "How does the organism come to assume the shape that it does?" Let's listen to what some of the deep thinkers of the past have had to say about the matter.

One of the miscellaneous bits of wisdom I managed to retain from my university studies is the remark made by one of my professors to the effect that he didn't think anyone should be allowed to practice under the title *philosopher* unless that person had demonstrated expertise in some specialized area as a basis for his or her philosophical stance. Today, twenty years and what seems like twenty thousand books of philosophy later, this admonition sounds even better to me than it did when I was a student. Unlike the current crop of philosophical philosophers, almost all of the great philosophers of the past—Plato, Aristotle, Aquinas, Descartes, Leibnitz—conformed to the stricture of being experts in something besides philosophizing. And most of them held some rather definite, and often contradictory, views on the matter of biological form. Let me briefly outline the position of three of the most prominent, as their conflicting ideas constitute the basis for the principal competing schools of thought today on the problem of development. The main positions are expressed in Table 3.1.

Philosopher	View on Biological Form
Plato	A reflection of eternal forms; transcendent mathematical laws
Aristotle	A property of nature, not transcendent; arises from nonmaterial principles inherent in the organism itself
Descartes	Organisms are machines; form is determined from a "blueprint"

Table 3.1. Philosophical views on biological form

Aristotle's field of expertise was biology, while that of Plato and Descartes was mathematics. And when it comes to a philosophy of form, Aristotle's vision is probably most consistent with what many laymen today think of when they consider the general workings of life. Namely, that there is something going on in living entities that is fundamentally inexplicable by the laws of chemistry and physics. On the other hand, Plato, the geometer and champion of idealized, archetypal forms, saw each group of animals and plants as representative of an archetype, the individual species within the group being variations on the archetypal theme. Finally, Descartes, who in today's world would be termed an applied mathematician, argued that life is just a particular manifestation of material reality, hence governed by nothing more or less than natural physico-chemical principles. With the views of these philosophers in hand, let's allow the biologists to take the floor and tell us what they think about the emergence of form.

When we examine the form of an adult organism of any kind, one of the first questions that comes to mind is whether the future adult form is present in the fertilized egg in *actual* or *codified* form. During the seventeenth century, many biologists took the position that an entire adult organism was already present in miniature in the egg. Thus, the final adult structure and shape was "preformed" in the egg, leading to the label *preformationism* for this theory of development. In this picture, the problem of development becomes simply a problem of growth, as the final adult form just "grows up" from the miniature, preformed version in the egg.

From the modern vantage point, the difficulties with the outrageously simplistic notion of preformationism as a theory of development are many, both logical and biological. In the first category, we have the problem of infinite regress. Preformationism, if true, would imply that the miniature adult form contains an even smaller adult form which itself contains a still smaller version, *ad infinitum*. From the biological side, preformationism fails to account for even the most rudimentary, pre-Mendelian facts known about heredity, such as the fact that the offspring of one black and one white parent generally turn out to have an intermediate skin color. For a long list of reasons like these, biologists abandoned preformationism in the latter part of the eighteenth century.

Around 1767 Kaspar Wolff, a German embryologist working in St. Petersburg, Russia, proposed the idea that biological form is an *epigenetic* phenomenon, in which the fertilized egg contains a set of instructions from which the adult form is built. Thus, epigenesis means that *all* of the adult organism is present in codified, rather than actual, form in *all* fertilized eggs in *all* species. Basically, every theory of epigenesis argues that there are two types of codified instructions: (1) a *genetic set* encoded into the cellular DNA and from which the entire adult organism is generated, and (2) a *cytoplasmic set* that takes the form of informational molecules floating about in the cellular cytoplasm (the part outside the nucleus), and that acts to switch certain genes on or off during the course of development. The difficulty with Wolff's theory is that it says nothing about *how* the set of instructions in the fertilized egg becomes translated into the final adult form.

The arguments in developmental biology today all center on the manner in which epigenesis actually occurs. There are three more or less distinct schools of thought on the matter, operating under the rubrics *vitalism, organicism,* and *mechanism,* in rough correspondence to the three philosophical positions noted earlier. Let's briefly sketch the arguments of each of these competing views of epigenesis.

Vitalism

Figure 3.1 showed the separation of the developed organism into two distinct kinds of cells—the germ cells (germ plasm) and the somatic cells (somatoplasm). This distinction between cell types dates back to work in the 1880s by the German biologist August Weismann, who proposed the idea that somehow the germ plasm is the active agent that shapes or molds the somatoplasm. Weismann suggested that organisms can pass along their germ cells only to offspring, and that there is no transfer of information from the soma cells to the germ cells. This idea probably arose from Weismann's work with insects, where the germ plasm tends to be segregated from the somatoplasm more sharply than it is in higher animals. Moreover, he argued that no modification of the germ plasm could take place as a result of what happens to the body— i.e., organisms could not inherit acquired characteristics. Weismann's basic scheme is depicted schematically in Figure 3.2.

Using his scheme, Weismann asserted that whatever it is that determines each component of the adult body, that determinant is distributed to various parts of the embryo during development. Thus, the developing embryo could be thought of as a kind of mosaic, containing parts that develop in an independent, yet harmonious, fashion to generate the final adult form.

Not long after Weismann advanced his theory, another German

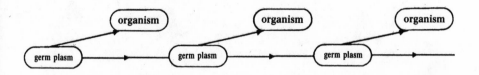

Figure 3.2. *Weismann's theory of cell types*

embryologist, Hans Driesch, performed a set of experiments on sea urchin embryos, showing that Weismann's ideas of mosaic development couldn't possibly be the whole story. In these experiments, Driesch bisected the embryos at the gastrula stage. Assuming Weismann's theory was correct, Driesch expected some kind of partial sea urchin–like monster to develop, since each part of the bisected gastrula would have only half the determinants of the full adult. To his surprise, Driesch found that each half was still capable of producing smaller, but perfectly formed, adults. A diagram of this experiment is given in Figure 3.3. In addition, Driesch also discovered that when he fused two embryos artificially, what emerged was not a double sea urchin, but a normal single one.

This ability of embryos to adjust to damage is called *regulation,* and is a process very closely related to *regeneration.* Both processes form an impassable barrier to the ideas of mosaic development as postulated by Weismann. As a result of his work on regulation, Driesch eventually came to the view that the inherent organizing principles in plants and animals are "vital factors," or *entelechies,* inexplicable by the natural forces of physics and chemistry. In short, the organism has some sort of overall plan for its growth, a plan that resides outside the matter from which it's constructed. For want of a better term, we can think of this plan as a "life force," which vitalists regarded as being beyond the bounds of physical science. Driesch was so distraught by the inability of the physics of his day to give a coherent explanation of development that he gave up biology and ended his career as a professor of—philosophy!

So we see that the vitalist school of biological development regards the organism at all levels of complexity as being imbued with a life force transcending its material composition. This plan can be thought

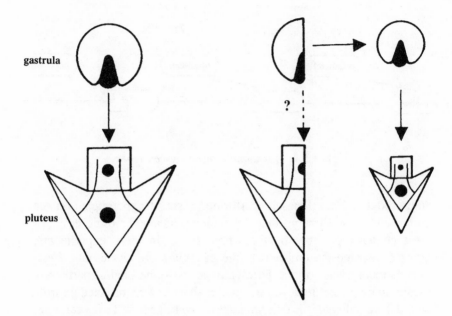

Figure 3.3. *Driesch's experiment on sea urchin embryos*

of metaphorically as a kind of internal psyche of the organism, or as a "will" to accomplish its goals despite obstacles put in its path. Moreover, this inner desire or will (entelechy) need not be seen as a physical force, yet it is immanent in nature and inherent in the organism itself. So in this manner does the vitalist school revive the Aristotelian notion that the sources of material form reside in nature, but are not necessarily part of the material composition of the organism.

Organicism

During the first half of the nineteenth century, the comparative study of form revealed deep similarities between body plans and other structural features of large groups of organisms. The so-called *rational morphologists* of this period developed the concept of the typical form or archetype of each group of animals and plants, regarding the individual species as being just variants of the basic pattern. In this manner, such rational morphologists as Richard Owen and Geoffroy Saint-Hilaire applied Plato's original notion of idealized, transcendental forms to problems of biological development. (Owen, by the way, was also the man responsible for coining the term *dinosaur,* literally meaning "terrible lizard.") The basic tenet of the rational morphologists was that Plato's eternal laws of form and organization are reflected in the biological realm. So, for instance, they argued that the five-fingered forelimb of a vertebrate might be transformed into a whale's flipper, a bat's wing, or a human hand. Nevertheless, each of these appendages is a reflection of an archetypal form—the five-fingered forelimb.

Darwinians rejected the whole notion of laws of form and transcendent archetypes. Rather, they tried to account for the archetypal forms by purely historical means, using the argument of descent from common ancestors. This kind of historical explanation departs radically from the concepts of the transformation and unfolding of an idealized form held by the rational morphologists. And with the ascendancy of Darwinian thinking, the ideas of the rational morphologists were relegated to the backwaters of the biological world until rather recently. But with the work of Paul Weiss, C. H. Waddington, and others on morphogenetic fields in the first half of this century, as well as the current ideas of Brian Goodwin, René Thom, and their co-workers on a structuralist approach to biology, an *organicist* school of thought has begun to rise up out of the ashes of rational morphology. This new school is characterized by thinking of organisms as wholes, and replacing Driesch's nonphysical entelechies with physically based morphogenetic fields to account for the observed wholeness.

Mechanism

The Darwinian emphasis on heredity—coupled with the discovery by James Watson and Francis Crick in 1953 that the material basis for heredity is the genetic pattern residing in the cellular DNA (the *genome*)—has served to catapult Descartes's view of the body as a machine into the spotlight as the dominant paradigm today for biological development. Since the characteristics of a cell depend on its proteins, and it is known how the proteins are specified by the DNA, the central problem of morphogenesis for mechanists is to specify the control of protein synthesis. As Robert Sinnsheimer of the University of California at Santa Barbara remarked recently, "The human genome is the complete set of instructions for making a human being."

In mechanistic terms, the only way the development of form can be understood is through the action of physico-chemical influences, or *morphogens,* on the cell. A number of schemes have been proposed to explain what these influences are, including chemical gradients, electrical gradients, and mechanical contact between cells. One popular view that we'll consider in great detail later is that whatever these morphogens might be, they serve to provide *positional information* in the developing tissue. The cells then interpret this information in accordance with their genetic programs in order to switch on the production of the right proteins at the right time in the right place. So the mechanistic assumption is that everything about form can be explained in terms of known physical processes and interactions.

Some of the difficulties in the mechanistic argument derive from the fact that both the DNA and the proteins of rather different species may be very similar. For instance, humans and chimpanzees have DNA strands that are more than 99 percent identical. By way of contrast, closely related species of mice have *larger* differences in their DNA than do humans and chimps. Thus, a mechanist has a hard time explaining why we're not much more like chimpanzees than we are if DNA content by itself is the sole consideration. Other difficulties come from the fact that, even within the same organism, different patterns of development take place while the DNA remains the same, since each and every cell (except the sex cells) contains exactly the same complete set of genetic instructions. So, for example, the human arm and leg both contain exactly the same DNA. Consequently, the very great differences between an arm and a leg must be attributable to factors other than the genes, factors that act differently in the development of the two appendages. Thus, to understand development, it's necessary to know more than just molecular composition; some sort of overall organizing principle is also required.

This completes our cursory review of the current contenders in the developmental biology game. Table 3.2 summarizes the positions of the competing schools of thought.

Before moving on to a more in-depth account of the strengths and weaknesses of each of these lines of argument, let's note that we can superimpose either a top-down or a bottom-up approach to morphogenesis on the arguments given by each school. This observation comes from the fact that every living organism is simultaneously the end point of two very different developmental histories: (1) an *ontogenetic* his-

School	Thesis
Vitalism	biology greater than physics; entelechies outside natural law
Organicism	biology greater than physics; organizing principles within natural law, but unknown
Mechanism	biology < physics

Table 3.2. Comparison of competing schools of developmental biology

tory arising from what we will be calling here the developmental pathway of the organism, and (2) a *phylogenetic* history coming about from the organism's belonging to a particular species that has experienced a characteristic evolutionary path of development.

For example, a typical vertebrate like a frog goes through the ontogenetic sequence shown in Figure 3.1 (page 134). But the *species* "frog" is the result of evolutionary alterations in previously existing species, beginning over 4 billion years ago with the first living cell. The sequence of evolutionary changes by natural selection leading from the primordial cell to the modern frog is the frog's phylogenetic sequence. An organism's ontogenetic history, or *ontogeny*, is confined to the organism itself; its *phylogeny* is a consequence of the organism's belonging to a species, and is a property of the species, not of the individual organism. It's natural to wonder whether there is some connection between these two radically different kinds of developmental histories. The nineteenth-century German biologist Ernst Haeckel coined the famous phrase "ontogeny recapitulates phylogeny" to express the claim that the two sequences were, in fact, isomorphic, i.e., abstractly equivalent. Nowadays no one really believes "Haeckel's Law," at least not in the strong form in which Haeckel originally stated it. But I digress. For the purposes of our discussion, the main point is that the two developmental paths present us with alternate vantage points from which to examine the question of how the adult organism comes to assume its final physical form.

The bottom-up view of morphogenesis involves taking the ontogenetic stance. From this perspective, we regard the organism's form as arising in some fashion from a set of rules that are applied to the fertilized egg, causing it to develop eventually into the adult form. Whether these rules are the known laws of physics and chemistry, or the as yet unknown laws governing various types of morphogenetic fields, or even principles underlying entelechies, the rules work from the fertilized egg at the bottom upward to the adult form at the top.

Turning the telescope around and focusing on the phylogenetic path, we take a top-down, evolutionary view of morphogenesis. Here we regard the organism's form as being the result of a long chain of evolutionary adaptations. This is basically a Darwinian point of view, in which the ancestral protoplasmic blob is shaped by environmental forces and the dictates of survival into the physical forms we see around us today.

We'll have plenty of opportunities as we go along to examine the interplay between the competing schools and the different ways of looking at the emergence of biological form. For now, and as a prelude to our investigation of the organism as a machine, let me devote a few pages to a slightly more detailed account of how the living cell actually functions.

THE GENOCENTRIC VIEW OF THE WORLD

The unraveling of the double helix structure of cellular DNA by James Watson and Francis Crick in 1953 undoubtedly represents one of this century's most publicly visible scientific triumphs, its place in the spotlight secured by Watson's colorful and controversial account of the process in his best-selling memoir *The Double Helix*. Much less publicly celebrated, but perhaps of even more lasting scientific value, was the discovery of exactly how the instructions for protein synthesis are coded into the twin strands of the DNA molecule. That story also unfolded at Cambridge University, just a few years after the momentous work of Watson and Crick.

In 1956 Sydney Brenner, a young biologist from South Africa, took a position with the Medical Research Council Laboratory in Cambridge where, as luck would have it, he shared an office with Francis Crick for the next twenty years. As Brenner tells the story, there was one inviolable rule in their office: "You could say anything that came into your head." Brenner goes on to note some of the consequences of this rule, remarking that "at one stage or another we [he and Crick] have convinced each other of theories which have never seen the light of day. . . . I mean completely crazy things.'' But one of the not so crazy things that Crick and Brenner talked about in the late 1950s was how to go from the nucleic acid language of DNA to the amino acid language of the proteins, the building blocks from which all living objects are formed.

The Watson-Crick theory saw the cellular DNA as a sort of long, flexible ladder whose top and bottom ends are given half-twists in opposite directions. At each end of every rung on this ladder is attached one of four *nucleotide bases:* adenine, thymine, guanine, and cytosine, written A, T, G, and C for short. Watson and Crick discovered that these bases always occur in the pairings A ↔ T and G ↔ C on the two ends of each rung. It was this pairing, incidentally, that suggested the way in which DNA could act to store the cellular hereditary information and pass it along during the process of replication. Since there are only 4 nucleotide bases but 20 types of amino acids from which the proteins of life are formed, Brenner and Crick immediately saw that if the rungs on the DNA ladder were to serve as an encoding for the amino acids forming the proteins of life, then the code would need to involve at least 3 bases per amino acid, since 2 bases per acid could account for at most $4 \times 4 = 16$ of the necessary 20 types of amino acids. In short, they thought it would be a triplet code. The physicist George Gamow, working independently, suggested such a scheme involving an overlapping triplet code in which the amino acids would plug directly into "holes" in the DNA. Most everyone thought this procedure would never work, but the problem was to suggest something to put in its place. One day while wrestling with the matter over a few beers at the famed Eagle Pub in Cambridge, Brenner and Crick hit upon the correct solution: a nonoverlapping triplet code. But this was not the end of the gene translation problem, only the beginning.

It's now known that the information coded into the cellular DNA is first transcribed onto a strand of RNA, which is a molecule very similar to DNA. This "working copy" of the genetic information in the DNA is then decoded by special-purpose cellular enzymes called ribosomes, resulting in the formation of the proteins from which all living organisms on Earth are formed.

Following these spectacular molecular-biological successes, Francis Crick spread the frosting on the cake when he put forward what has come to be termed the Central Dogma of Molecular Biology. In short form, the Central Dogma states that information in the cell flows along the one-way path: DNA → RNA → protein. By making the substitutions DNA/RNA → germ plasm, protein → soma, and comparing with Figure 3.2, we see that Crick's Central Dogma is essentially just the translation of Weismann's germ plasm/soma scheme into molecular biological terms. An even cruder way of stating the Central Dogma is just to say that the *genotype* determines the *phenotype*. The cellular DNA constitutes the organism's genotype, while the final physical form, behavior patterns, and functional activities constitute what is known as the phenotype. The hope (and sometimes claim) of the molecular biologist is that a deep enough understanding of the ways in which proteins interact to form a living organism will be sufficient to show us *exactly* how the phenotype emerges from the information encoded into the genes.

But if you put the hundred thousand or so different types of proteins composing a tiger into a bag of water and shake it up, the resulting mixture is still very far from having a tiger in your tank. We need to know how some of those proteins are organized into living cells, and how others cause those cells to arrange themselves into the four-footed, orange-and-black-striped vertebrate we call a Bengal tiger. From a bottom-up cellular perspective, the problem of development involves explaining just how the proteins can act to cause the cells to carry out three rather different types of activities: growth, movement, and differentiation.

A fascinating experiment serving as a major milestone on the way toward understanding development, mechanistic style, was carried out in 1984 by Brenner's group at Cambridge. They succeeded in mapping the entire developmental history of each of the 959 cells composing the tiny nematode worm *C. elegans*. But this work is only a beginning, and Brenner states that to understand how the information coded in the genes relates to the means by which cells assemble themselves into an organism may require an appreciation of what he calls "the grammar of it all."

According to the mechanist's view of development, encoded in the DNA there is a "genetic program" that serves to tell the cellular protein-manufacturing machinery what proteins to manufacture, when to manufacture them, and in what quantities they should be produced in order to generate the final adult organism. The basic mechanism by which this might be carried out was discovered by François Jacob and Jacques Monod in their *repressor-derepressor* theory of genetic action. Fundamentally, this theory says that some of the genes do not code for proteins used in formation of the organism's structural form or internal organs, but rather code for proteins that act to regulate the activity of other proteins. Thus, by the Jacob-Monod theory, these *regulator* genes can serve as spatiotemporal "switches," ensuring that the cells' chemical outputs are properly coordinated so as to produce whatever organism is coded for in the DNA. But we're already starting to veer dangerously close to some of the gory details of the mechanist school's claims. So without further ado, let's give the floor over to its spokesmen for an account of just how and why they think "it's all in the genes."

THE GENE MACHINE

In September 1987 the Los Alamos National Laboratory was host to the First International Workshop on Artificial Life, a gathering of computer scientists, theoretical biologists, system scientists, and others interested in exploring the possibility of creating life not *in vitro,* but *in silico.* One of the more entertaining papers given at the workshop was by the well-known Oxford University zoologist Richard Dawkins, who gave the audience a short tour of what he calls Biomorph Land, a mythical territory so named in honor of the vaguely lifelike creatures called biomorphs appearing in the surrealistic paintings of the anthropologist Desmond Morris. Let's take a quick tour through Biomorph Land ourselves as a painless way of making contact with the essential ingredients of the mechanistic view of biological development.

The elementary objects of Biomorph Land are simple treelike figures that we can represent on a piece of paper by a sequence of short lines. A typical object in this universe is shown in Figure 3.4, which consists of a "seed biomorph" at the top, followed by a sequence of more elaborate relatives. The seed biomorph was generated by having the computer start by drawing a single vertical line. Next the line branches in two, and then each of the branches splits into two sub-branches. Continuing with this same splitting-and-growing process, we obtain the more elaborate biomorphs shown in the rest of the figure, which can be thought of as the "children" of the "parent" seed.

As a model of development, this splitting-and-growing operation corresponds to the process of cell division and growth. So where do the genes come in? How can we introduce the idea of genetic influence on

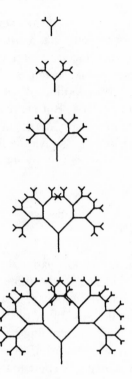

Figure 3.4. *A typical biomorph seed and its progeny*

form into the model of biomorph development? Dawkins's answer is to introduce into the program nine elements—or "genes"—that influence things like the angle of branching, the length of a branch, the number of subbranches, and so on. For genetic variability, each gene is assumed to come in both a "plus" and a "minus" form. An idea of how this works can be seen in Figure 3.5, which shows a central tree (biomorph) in the middle surrounded by eight variants. All biomorphs in the figure are the same as the central one, except that one gene has been changed, i.e., "mutated." For example, the biomorph labeled Gene 1⁻ shows the effect on the central tree if Gene 1 mutates to its minus form.

Each of the gene actions has its own characteristic "formula" in Dawkins's program, but the formulas themselves are, as Dawkins points out, meaningless. Just as in real life, where genes mean something only when they are translated into proteins and growing rules for developing embryos, in Biomorph Land, too, the genes are meaningful

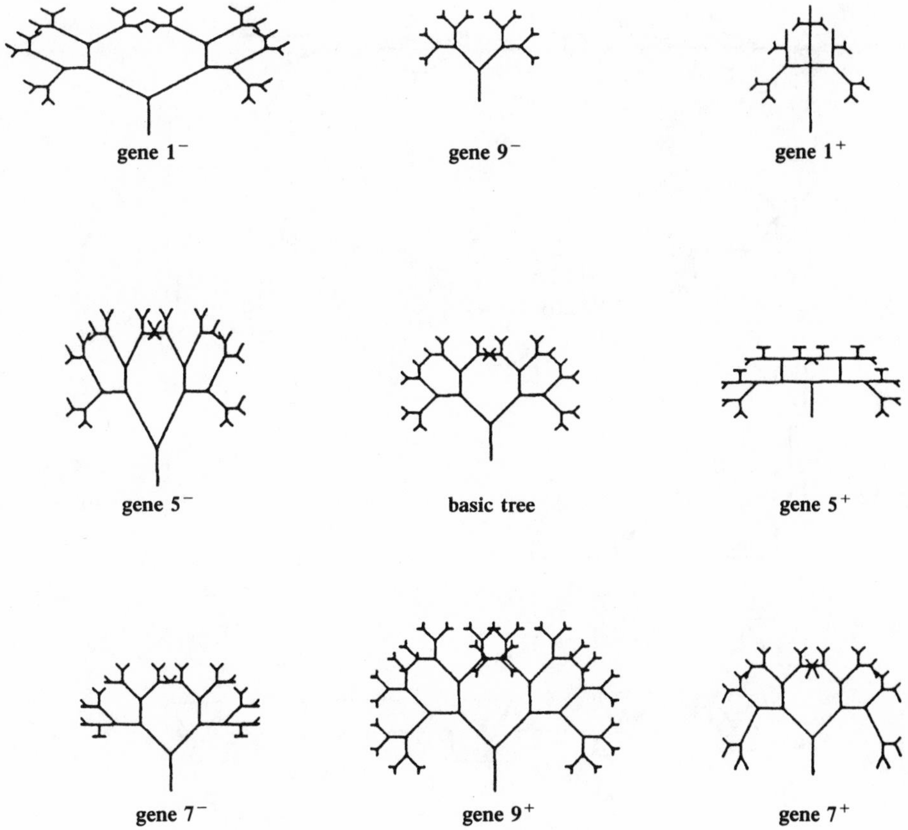

Figure 3.5. *The effect of genes in Biomorph Land*

only when they are translated into rules for creating a branching tree pattern.

With these rules for genetic action in hand, Dawkins starts with a parental biomorph and "grows" a litter of children, each differing from the parent by a mutation in one gene. At this stage, evolution steps in to play a hand by selecting just one of the offspring to go on to the next generation. In practice, Dawkins himself plays the role of the "natural selector." Figure 3.6 shows twenty-nine generations of such a biomorph history, starting from the dot (blob) in the upper left-hand corner. The figure also shows a few of the evolutionary dead ends that Dawkins rejected during the process of selecting those forms that would survive to reproduce for the next generation. Figure 3.7

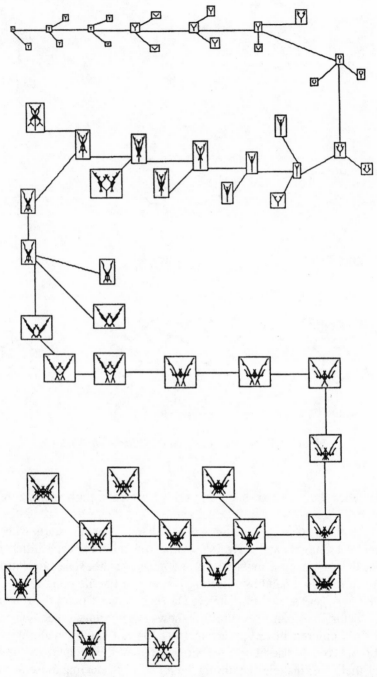

Figure 3.6. *A biomorph developmental pathway*

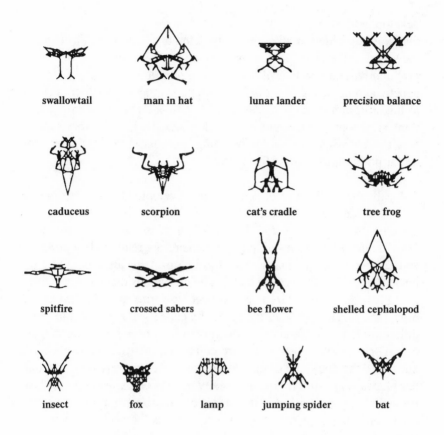

Figure 3.7. *Some residents of Biomorph Land*

displays some of the other inhabitants of Biomorph Land arising out of the combination of random genetic mutations and Dawkins's "natural selection."

While Dawkins developed his biomorph model to illustrate the basic aspects of the Darwinian theory of evolution—random mutations and the principle of natural selection—his setup can serve equally well to illustrate the mechanistic view of development by making two simple changes: (1) assume that the gene action is chosen in a deterministic fashion according to the dictates of a "genetic program" rather than being chosen at random, and (2) let there be only a single offspring at each step, thereby eliminating the need for any kind of selection (actually, we'll see later that some versions of the mechanist program for development also incorporate natural selection, so even this change may not be needed in all cases.) Thus, the essence of the mechanistic view is that the process of development is completely governed by a program written into the cellular DNA, a program that is expressed via genetic action during the course of protein synthesis. We'll come back to this program metaphor later, but for now let's see how mechanists think such a program might tell developing cells in the embryo where they are and what they should be doing. In other words, let's get back to the problem of pattern formation.

By the mechanist's creed, embryonic development results from spatially and temporally ordered "readouts" of genetic information into proteins. As we have seen, this idea is a consequence of two facts: (1) virtually all activities of living organisms are regulated by proteins, and (2) the amino acid sequences forming proteins are ordered by the nucleotide base sequences in DNA. The problem is that we don't know how proteins are organized so that specific forms arise in developing organisms at a level higher than that of a cell. Even knowing how cells differentiate into different types is not enough to explain morphogenesis. For example, your biceps are composed of striated muscle cells, but so are the markedly different muscles stretching across your shoulder blades. What the mechanists really need is an explanation for how these different sorts of spatial patterns could arise from initially rather homogeneous sheets of cellular tissue. This is the problem of pattern formation.

Mechanists have suggested two fundamentally different ways in which spatial patterns could arise. The first involves the cell's having access to "historical" information. For example, the cell could somehow register each time it divides, and keep a record of the number and orientation of the divisions it has undergone. A second approach is to assume that in some fashion the cells "know" where they are situated within a developing organism and behave accordingly. It's very difficult to see how historical information alone could account for observed phenomena like the regulation of sea urchin eggs or the regeneration of an amputated limb, both processes seeming to require that the cells redirect their programs to take account of the disturbances to their developmental pathways. Thus, for the most part, mechanistic embryologists have concentrated their efforts on providing an answer to how the cells might obtain positional information.

The idea of positional information was originally suggested by

Driesch in the early part of this century, while its modern formulation dates to the work of Lewis Wolpert in the late 1960s. The basic assumption is that a developing organism is divided into regions, and that within each region a coordinate system is established somehow, much like the letter-number combination schemes often used on city maps to pin down the locations of individual streets. The coordinate system enables every cell to determine its location within the region by reference to the coordinate grid. Knowing its position, the cell can then decide what it should be doing, i.e., what kind of proteins it should produce and when. Clearly, the plausibility of the whole idea rests upon providing a scheme for how this coordinate grid might be set up.

The most thoroughly studied mechanism by which a grid system could be established is for the positional information to be given by chemical gradients. Concentrations of various chemicals would then control the subsequent biochemical reactions within individual cells. Wolpert introduced the famous French Flag Problem to illustrate the basic idea. Figure 3.8 displays the essential aspects of this setup. In

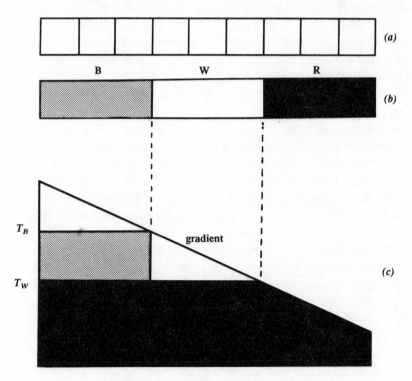

Figure 3.8. *The French Flag Problem*

part *(a)* of the figure we see a string of undifferentiated cells. The goal is to explain how this initially homogeneous string can differentiate into the pattern of blue, white, and red cells shown in part *(b)*, thereby mimicking the color pattern of the French flag.

Assume that the chemical substance (morphogen) whose concentration forms the coordinate information along the line of cells is distributed so that its source is at the left end of the line, while there is a sink at the right end. Then the morphogen will diffuse across the line moving from the source to the sink, where it is destroyed at a constant rate. This process produces a steady concentration drop across the line, which is graphically displayed in part *(c)* of the diagram. Under these conditions, each cell in the row has a particular morphogen concentration. It's now easy to see how we might produce regions of blue, white, and red cells. For instance, the presumed genetic program in each cell could contain an instruction of the following sort: "If the morphogen concentration is between T_B and T_W, produce proteins turning yourself into a white cell, while if the concentration is less than T_W, become a red cell; otherwise, become a blue cell." In practice, it might be rather simple to execute such a program. For example, a cellular enzyme might be active only between certain ranges of morphogen concentration. But what about things like regeneration?

In Figure 3.9 we see how Wolpert's scheme can be used if the original French flag pattern is cut midway through the white region. There are two possible ways to regenerate the flag: (1) by *remodeling,* in which missing parts are remodeled by the system, and (2) by *growth,* where the absent cells are replaced by cell division. Remodeling involves just a rescaling of the threshold levels using the same cells, while growth entails a change of thresholds but with new cells being created to replace those lost by excision. The regeneration of *Hydra,* a freshwater polyp, is an illustration of the first type of mechanism, while vertebrate limb generation is an example of the second. In either case, the missing parts are regenerated. Wolpert has emphasized the fact that it is not the profile of the gradient of the morphogen concentration itself that is important in this scheme, but rather what makes the magic work is the *interpretation* of this gradient by the cell. Thus, with the same type of coordinate system, different rules for interpretation built into the genetic program of the cells could give the French flag in one case, the Union Jack in another, and even the Stars and Stripes in a third.

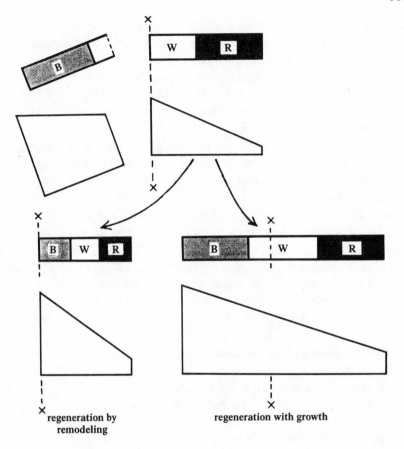

Figure 3.9. *Regeneration in the French flag model*

Perhaps the most characteristic feature of Wolpert's positional information idea is that the chemical concentration gradient set up by the morphogen to establish the spatial coordinate system is not affected if the morphogen itself participates in any of the chemical reactions going on within the cells. Thus there is a total separation between the specification of the spatial location information and its interpretation in terms of what should be happening at that location. This peculiar, and probably unrealistic, restriction is removed in a variant of the positional information idea termed *prepatterns*.

In the theory of prepatterns, the morphogen plays a more active role. Instead of just providing spatial information that each cell employs to decide its fate, the morphogen contributes directly to the formation of the pattern. The problem again is to offer a coherent mechanistic procedure whereby these more complicated chemical gradients could be set up within the developing tissue. Interestingly, the original idea for how this might be accomplished came not from the biological community, but from Alan Turing, a man far better known for his development of many of the ideas underlying modern computing machines.

Turing's life story was recently brought to the attention of the general public in the London and New York stage productions of *Breaking the Code,* a dramatization of Turing's tragically short life, especially his wartime work on cryptography and his later problems with the British authorities over his homosexuality. Following World War II, Turing devoted his energies to developing many of the principles underlying today's computers, including a proof that every type of computer in use today is abstractly equivalent to a simple device that he termed a universal computer, but that is now called a Turing machine in his honor. We'll take up these matters in some detail in this book's final chapter. For now, our interest lies more in Turing's work in developmental biology, specifically his demonstration of the feasibility of chemically based schemes for biological pattern generation.

A year or two before his death, Turing developed a set of mathematical equations whose solutions admit the possibility of a spatially inhomogeneous morphogen distribution arising from the interaction between the process of diffusion and the chemical reactions taking place within a group of cells. The motivation behind Turing's work was expressed by Hans Meinhardt, one of today's leaders in following up Turing's idea, when he stated that "in a developmental system a signalling and signal-receiving mechanism must exist which enables the cell to develop in a manner appropriate to its position. The necessity of such a signal system is easily demonstrated by the fact of regeneration."

A simple version of Turing's system involves letting two chemical substances having different diffusion rates interact with each other. One substance, termed the *activator,* stimulates its own production (*autocatalysis*) as well as the production of the other substance. The second substance, termed the *inhibitor,* acts to suppress production of the activator. Initially, there is a homogeneous concentration of both substances. To have an inhomogeneity develop, Turing needed three conditions:

- *Differential diffusion:* The inhibitor must diffuse more rapidly than the activator.
- *Autocatalysis:* There must be a strong, short-range, positive feedback on the production of the activator—i.e., the more activator there is, the more of it that's produced.
- *Lateral inhibition:* There must be a strong, long-range, negative feedback on the activator—i.e., over longer distances, the effect of the inhibitor should outweigh that of the activator.

Under these hypotheses, autocatalysis produces a local inhomogeneity while the lateral inhibition prevents the reaction from spreading like a brush fire. Figure 3.10 shows an example of the kind of patterns that can appear from such a system, where the bristlelike structure in the figure emerges as a result of random fluctuations in an initially homogeneous tissue. Here the local production of the activator enhances further activator production, while at the same time inhibitors produced in these same bristle centers diffuse outward to prevent further centers from forming nearby.

Another example of how prepatterns *might* explain an observed phenotypic feature arises in consideration of the bristle pattern on the abdomen of the bug *Onchopeltus*. The abdomen of this bug is divided into segments separated by an intersegmental membrane. To envision what this looks like, think of a piece of bamboo, where the ridges between segments correspond to the separating membrane. On each segment of *Onchopeltus* the bristles are uniformly distributed, all pointing in the direction toward the back end of the bug. But if part of an intersegmental membrane is missing, the bristles assume a quite dif-

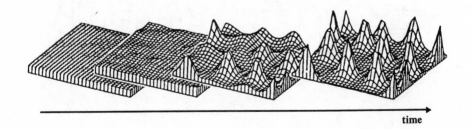

time

Figure 3.10. *A bristle pattern from a reaction-diffusion system*

ferent pattern: The bristles now arrange themselves in two vortices. The overall situation is shown in Figure 3.11, where the normal situation is shown in part *(a)*, while the bristle pattern with part of the membrane absent is displayed in part *(b)* of the figure. As part of his Ph.D. work at Cambridge University, Peter Lawrence offered an explanation for this behavior based on prepatterns.

Lawrence supposes that in each abdominal segment there is a gradient of some diffusible morphogen, which ranges from a high concentration at the front of the segment to a low concentration at the back. Since the membrane between segments does not allow diffusion, the high concentration at the front of one segment is maintained close to a low concentration at the back of the preceding segment. The

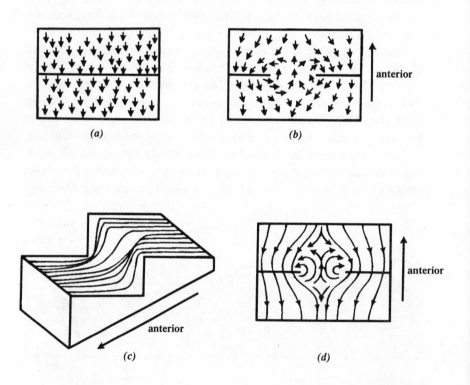

(a)   *(b)*

(c)   *(d)*

Figure 3.11. *Prepattern explanation for bristle pattern on* Onchopeltus

central hypothesis in Lawrence's work is that the bristles grow so as to point *down* the concentration gradient. This assumption results in the bristle pattern shown in part *(a)* of Figure 3.11. Now imagine that part of the intersegmental membrane is removed, allowing the supposed morphogen to diffuse from the rear segment to the forward one. This yields a concentration gradient like that shown in part *(c)* of the figure, which in turn leads to a morphogen flow pattern like that seen in part (d). If the bristles grow in such a manner that they point down the local concentration gradient, they will produce exactly the pair of vortices displayed in part *(b)* of the figure. While Lawrence's argument offers a theoretical explanation of the observed pattern, his experiments did not identify any material substance that was distributed in the manner required by his model.

Comparing the two procedures of pattern formation—Turing-type reaction-diffusion systems (prepatterns) in which the hypothesized pattern-causing agents (morphogens) play an active role, and Wolpert-style positional information where the morphogens are passive—we find that they give rather different predictions as to what kinds of patterns should be observed. Prepattern theory suggests that repeated structures should be very common, since they are easy to produce. Once a reaction-diffusion system has been set up, it's rather simple to alter the precise number and distribution of similar features. On the other hand, for the same feature to appear more than once in a region, different passive positional information must be interpreted to yield the same result. So if positional information, and not prepattern theory, is correct, it's hard to see why repeated patterns should be as common as they are. This is not to say that the reaction-diffusion systems don't have difficulties of their own. Not the least of the problems is the fact that such systems don't really explain morphogenesis at all, since spatial standing waves of morphogens are not equivalent to the actual shape change of cells or tissues.

But the greatest problem with both the Turing and Wolpert solutions to the pattern formation problem is that both theories predict that morphogens exist and should be spatially distributed in gradients or prepatterns in developing tissue. After more than thirty years of look-ing, there is not a single piece of incontrovertible evidence pointing to any specific chemical, electrical, or mechanical quantity performing this function. The strongest candidate discovered so far is the calcium concentration that seems to control the transitions between various stages of morphogenesis in the developing tissue of the filamentous plant *Acetabularia*. However, even here the transitions could be a result of properties of the plant's cytoskeleton and associated modulators of its state (e.g., calcium), and not due to any sort of morphogen. Thus, at present the idea of a morphogen directing pattern formation in embryos rests on about as solid a footing as the idea of a quark directing the formation of elementary particles in physics. Both are purely theoretical constructs that help focus our thinking about the problem at hand. But in neither case is there anything approaching conclusive experimental evidence supporting the construct's actual material existence.

In view of the obstacles to a chemically based theory of morphogens directing the formation of global patterns in embryos, the Nobel Prize–winning neuroscientist Gerald Edelman of Rockefeller University has suggested an alternate scheme involving surface interactions between cells. Edelman's contention is that the present location of a cell and its present activity must provide the information necessary for the cell to know what it is to do next. His strategy is to create a theory in which *all* the action is at the local level of small collectives of cells acting as a group on their immediate neighbors, a situation geneticist Richard Lewontin terms the "*perestroika* of the protoplasm."

The main claim of Edelman's scheme, which he calls *topobiology*, is that surface interactions of cells are mediated by molecules of a very particular type called *morphoregulatory* molecules. The heart of the topobiological thesis is that these molecules provide a sufficient basis for generation of form from the genetic program, i.e., for epigenesis. The morphoregulatory molecules turn on and off in cycles, thereby affecting the surface properties of the cells. This, in turn, causes the cells to cluster. Then, in some unspecified way, the surface interactions of cells with their neighbors turn on regulatory genes within the cells, resulting in the switching on and off of the genes responsible for cellular differentiation. Thus, at every stage it is the local interactions of cells and tissues that determine the future motion, division, differentiation, and even death of the cells.

With everything happening at the purely local level, how does an entire, integrated, globally patterned, functioning organism emerge? Edelman's answer is one that will brighten the day of every evolutionary biologist: natural selection! Topobiology asserts that only the developmental processes leading to a functioning organism have survived. In other words, the local anarchy gives the appearance of overall coordination only because it works; there is no overall controller making sure that each cell is playing its appointed role in some overall plan. Rather, only those cells whose program causes them to act so as to contribute to a functioning organism are given a ticket to ride into the next generation. While it's much too early to assess the ultimate viability of topobiology, Edelman has offered mechanists their last chance to include embryological development beneath their research umbrella.

Before closing the book on the mechanist view of development, it's worth spending a moment reconsidering the idea of a genetic program as a mechanist would think of the term, and comparing it with a computer program. Returning to Weismann's germ plasm/soma dichotomy, we can make the crude match-up between computers and organisms shown in Table 3.3.

Computer		Organism
input data	↔	amino acids in the cellular cytoplasm
program	↔	nucleotide pattern in the cellular DNA
output	↔	proteins determining cellular function
hardware	↔	cellular genetic translation machinery

Table 3.3. Organism/computer comparison

The mechanist thesis is that the fit between computer hardware and software on the one hand, and the hardware (cellular environment) and software (genetic programs) of an organism on the other, goes beyond mere surface similarity. Unfortunately, upon hearing such a claim, a neutral skeptic might raise an eyebrow over several empirical observations. For example, in a computer there is a virtually impassable barrier between hardware and software errors. So, for example, a software error like interchanging a plus and a minus can almost never be neutralized by a hardware fault like a blown capacitor or a surge in power. On the other hand, biological organisms frequently offset environmental perturbations with a corresponding genetic mutation. Furthermore, computer scientists learned long ago that it is virtually never possible to predict the future behavior of a computer from a mere inspection of its program. And, in fact, as we'll see in Chapter Six, even the seemingly simple problem of deciding whether a particular program will ever halt is, in general, unsolvable by inspection of the program alone, a result established by Alan Turing in 1936. So if the computer ↔ organism match-up is indeed a close fit, we can only conclude that it will never be possible to predict an organism's phenotypic properties like form and behavior from a knowledge of its genetic program. The relationship between the genotype and the phenotype is a highly nonlinear one, and as we've seen earlier this means that the primary behaviors and structures of interest are properties of the interaction between parts rather than being properties of the parts themselves. And these interactions necessarily disappear when the parts are studied independently.

Earlier we noted that the problem of development could be studied from either a bottom-up or a top-down point of view. The mechanist position presented thus far has focused on the bottom-up perspective. So before the organicists take the floor, let's turn the telescope around and have a quick look at some of the top-down explanations for why organisms take the form they do.

GOING ROUND IN CYLINDERS

Through one of those unplanned-for and unwanted sequences of events that far too often shape the course of a person's life, I have the misfortune to live on what is probably the only street in Vienna that has more foot traffic at three o'clock in the morning than at three o'clock in the afternoon. Recently, as a result of a late-night ruckus at one of the seemingly endless string of bars on our street, I was leaning out the window watching the police administer a well-deserved hassling to a couple of loud-mouthed drunks. Growing somewhat bored with the clownish antics of the drunks (and the police, too), I started looking around for more inspired entertainment. I soon spotted a large black sheep dog lying down in the middle of the street. While for all intents and purposes this dog looked dead to the world, it was still of marginally greater interest than either the police or the drunks. So I continued to watch to see if it would give any sign of life to indicate what it thought it was doing in the middle of a busy street at such an ungodly hour of the morning.

As I watched, the dog was joined by a tattered-looking tomcat of indeterminate color and disposition, no doubt out for a hot night on the town. The cat went over to the dog, sniffed it as a potential playmate or antagonist, and, receiving no response whatsoever, moved off down the street in search of more animated companionship. Later, as I turned my attention back to my own living room, a large moth flew in through the window and started putting on quite a show with its fluttering around inside the shade of my favorite reading lamp. Thinking later about these three animals—the dog, the cat, and the moth—I wondered just what it was about their physical appearances that caused me immediately to recognize each of these animals as being alive. It certainly wasn't their movement or lack of it, since the dog never so much as moved a muscle the whole time I was watching, while both the cat and the moth were moving about all over the place. And it wasn't sound either, as none of the animals uttered so much as a peep. Or at least nothing that could be heard above the din of the "music" blasting out from the clubs on the street below. Could there have been any unambiguous sign that would have immediately stamped these objects as "alive," while denying that label to the police car and to the cobblestones in the street?

Zoologist Stephen Wainwright has phrased my query in somewhat more compact and elegant terms: "Is there some single observation that can explain how all organisms are different from nonliving forms?" When stated in such bald fashion, the question seems to cry out for a resounding negative reply in view of the almost endless variety of life forms here on Earth. Nevertheless, Wainwright gives a surprisingly simple, and quite convincing, affirmative response: The bodies of multicellular plants and animals are cylindrical in shape. Can this really be true? Is cylindrical form a generally reliable indicator of life?

To address this point, let's first of all clarify what we mean by *cylindrical*. For purposes of our discussion, a cylinder is nothing more than a body that has a more or less round or elliptical cross section and a readily identifiable longitudinal axis. Familiar everyday examples include things like clarinets, pirates' spyglasses, cardboard mailing tubes, and rifle barrels.

Thinking about Wainwright's claim, obvious exceptions come to mind—cauliflower plants, stingrays, sponges, The Blob. Yet the exceptions really are exceptions, and the overwhelming majority of plants and animals truly do seem to be shaped like cylinders with numerous appendages. On the other hand, very few naturally occurring, nonliving objects take on cylindrical forms. Again there are exceptions: certain crystals, icicles, stalagmites, stalactites—and that's about it. So it does seem that a cylindrical shape is a good discriminator for separating living from nonliving objects. The immediate question then becomes: What's so special about a cylindrical shape?

Earlier we noted that every living organism is simultaneously the endpoint of two developmental pathways: ontogenesis, its developmental history as an *individual organism,* and phylogenesis. The second path, the *evolutionary history,* is the one that is of concern here, leading us to wonder about the following issues in regard to cylindrical shape:

* What functional abilities does cylindrical shape confer upon an organism? That is, what can cylindrical bodies do better than bodies of any other shape?
* Do the attributes of cylindrical body shape give species possessing this shape an evolutionary advantage? In other words, do such species get a selective leg up in the Darwinian race for survival and reproduction?
* In what manner did the cylindrical shape arise in the phylogenetic history of each species? And how does this shape emerge during the ontogenetic development of an individual?

While there's no room here to enter into details, let's at least take a few pages to gnaw around the edges of these tantalizing queries.

The form of an adult organism is basically the shape of the organism's mechanical support system, i.e., its skeletal system. Thus, it's reasonable to suppose that the shape will be strongly influenced, determined even, by mechanical considerations arising from the environment in which the organism must try to make its living. After some back-of-the-envelope calculations, it turns out that the most efficient use of materials in systems that have to reach out to identify friends, gather food, or fend off enemies occurs in cylindrical bodies. For example, if the organism moves through its environment, it will expend less energy in looking for food if it's cylindrical, since such shapes are streamlined. Moreover, for animals to move about on land or in the air, appendages supported by stiff cylindrical rods appear to be the best design for things like arms, legs, and wings. These elementary mechanical considerations suggest a host of functions that can be better performed by cylindrical bodies than by those of any other shape. But how did such shapes ever get started? After all, the original life forms on Earth were very likely just small, roughly spherical blobs. What features of cylindrical bodies caused these ancestral multicellular blobs to rearrange themselves into cylindrical form?

A partial answer to the origin of the blob-to-cylinder evolutionary path comes from considering the all-important body-mass-to-size ratio. It's an elementary fact of geometry and mechanics that bodies increase in mass (volume) as the cube of their radius, while the strength of a supporting cylindrical stem or leg (its cross-sectional area) increases only as the square of the radius. Therefore, if plants and animals are to grow larger, they cannot just get bigger in all directions uniformly. They must change shape. And, in fact, they must increase the radius of the cylindrical supporting parts at a rate faster than these same parts increase in length. Most likely, the first multicellular organisms were shapeless blobs that acquired a body axis and became soft, flexible, filamentous plants or worms. Then as these organisms tried to increase in size (body mass) to exploit their environment more efficiently, the cylindrical diameter increased disproportionately. Since the environment itself has preferred directions (e.g., gravity pulls downward and light comes from above), adaptations increasing bilaterality, streamlining, and locomotion would be favored. Such considerations ultimately led to the preponderance of cylindrical forms we see around us today.

But what about noncylindrical forms like sponges, corals, and heads of lettuce? Does their existence vitiate the mechanical arguments for cylindrical structure? Not really, since organisms like sponges and corals rely upon drag forces in the water for their dispersal, as well as meeting the flowing wind and water with the same profile in all directions. Basically, these organisms lead a pretty sedentary life. Thus, under such environmental circumstances, noncylindrical bodies have advantages that outweigh the mechanical disadvantages their shapes may confer. For instance, plate-shaped bodies like thin leaves are virtually all area. Consequently, they can increase in size almost without adding any mass. Such a shape is a strong competitor to a cylinder, and perhaps the cylinder won out only because it could outrun, outswim, and outfly the plates. On the other hand, a spherical form like The Blob increases its surface area as the square of its radius while increasing its mass as the cube. Consequently, such a form would be very inefficient if forced to compete with the more cost-effective cylinder (one of the many points that made *The Blob* sci-fi and not sci-fact). Since this idea of change of shape as a function of growth is rather universal, let's dig a little deeper into some of the relations that have been discovered linking growth and form.

*   *   *

In 1932 the biologist Julian Huxley, older brother of the novelist Aldous Huxley, looked into the way the process of development interacts with increasing spatial size and weight. His investigations involved monitoring the changes in size of bodily organs and relating these changes to each other and to changes in the size of the whole organism. Such relations often have the simple mathematical form $Y = aX^b$, where Y is the size of one part and X is the size of another part or the whole, a and b being constants that are to be determined for the particular parts involved. This kind of relation between the relative sizes of different body parts is termed an *allometric relation*, the parameter b being termed the *coefficient of allometry*. Note that if both X and Y grow in direct proportion, then $b = 1$ and the relation is called an *isometry*. Figure 3.12 shows such an allometric relationship between the head size and body size of the various worker groups in the ant species *Pheidole instabilis*.

It's amusing to note that a few years after Julian Huxley published

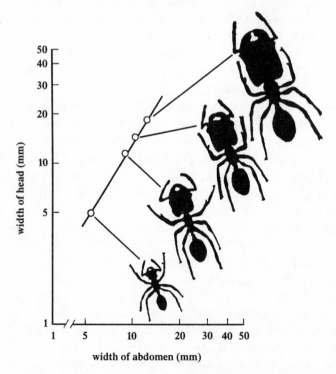

Figure 3.12. *An allometric relationship in an ant species*

his pathbreaking volume *Problems of Relative Growth* in 1932, his brother Aldous published the novel *After Many a Summer Dies the Swan*. This book ends with the hero, a scientist who has been hired to find an elixir of immortality, discovering the hideout of a British nobleman who two centuries earlier had carried out similar experiments on the differential rates of growth of human body parts. The scientist finds the old man still alive, but rather markedly changed in appearance—his experiments had transformed his body into that of a gorilla. As the scientist remarks, "It was the finest joke he had ever known."

This idea that species can evolve by changing the relative rates of growth of organs or body parts was systematically exploited by D'Arcy Thompson in his theory of biological transformations. But that's a story more properly told within the context of the organicist school of biological development. So let's finally part company with the mechanists and move over into the territory of the organicists, where the stories are all about whole organisms and morphogenetic fields rather than about genetic programs and individual cells.

THE FIELDS OF THE FORMS

In the Newtonian view of the world, the primary elements of explanation are material particles that move about and interact according to the dictates of mysterious, unexplained "forces." I doubt seriously that there's a self-respecting theoretical physicist alive today who clings to this vision of the hows and whys of worldly events, at least in the quantum and relativistic realms. Instead, today's upmarket, cutting-edge theoretician reserves primacy of explanatory position not for forces acting on particles, but for the equally mysterious concept of a *field*. In this world view, classical particles like protons, neutrons, and electrons are all thought of as being merely singularities of an as-yet-undiscovered, all-encompassing field, a field that physicists claim will unify the four known forces of nature—gravitational, electromagnetic, strong nuclear, and weak nuclear—bringing into harmony the theories of quantum mechanics and relativity. A tall order, but one that many of today's top theoreticians claim will be filled by the turn of the millennium.

Interestingly, while the notion of a field theory is all but taken for granted by modern physicists, for biologists the idea is still regarded with the sort of skepticism generally reserved for the campaign promises of politicians and the public pronouncements of economists. If one were to draw a comparison between biology and physics, it wouldn't be too far off the mark to claim that trying to explain embryological development in terms of genes and programs is akin to trying to explain electricity and gravity using Newtonian particles and forces. Happily, following the semimystical notions of Driesch and the vitalists with their entelechies, the idea of a physically real field governing development has come back into vogue in biology under the impetus of work by British biologists like C. H. Waddington and Brian Goodwin. But in many ways their work is a souped-up version of ideas first put forth by the group of nineteenth-century European biologists we spoke of earlier, the rational morphologists. So as a prelude to today's organicist school of thinking on problems of development, let's turn to a brief account of rational morphology.

In the nineteenth century, biologists like Geoffroy Saint-Hilaire in France and Richard Owen in England devoted their efforts to looking for empirical regularities in living organisms. The most important point in their program was to consider the individual organism as a systematic whole, and to regard the business of biology as the classification of the types of "wholes" that could occur. An example of the kind of regularity they were concerned with is the notion of a *typical form,* a concept defining what is common to a variety of different realizations of the same archetypal form. The idea was that a standard or quintessential form of something like a vertebrate limb could be understood in terms of basic generative principles capable of producing a wide range of limb forms, all transformable to each other under modifications of the limb-generating process. But it was the process that was important, not the kind of limb displayed by some particular species. Again in terms of physics, this idea is analogous to the fact that the different elliptical paths forming the orbits of the individual planets are all a consequence of the same inverse-square law of Newtonian motion. Thus, each path belongs to the same family of curves (technically known as the *conic sections*). The fundamental problem arising from such a view of organismic form is how to make explicit the nature of the internal relations that define the entire organism and, especially, how to identify the types of transformations an organism can undergo.

As we've already noted, a few years after the work of the rational morphologists, Hans Driesch also assumed that there are rules operating within organisms to constrain the forms that the organisms can assume. Driesch even thought of these rules as being manifested in some sort of field that would encompass the concepts of wholeness, self-regulation, and transformation. His idea was that these principles would then define the properties of tissues. But Driesch was unable to reconcile this field concept with the physics of his time, and ultimately abandoned all hope for physically based fields in biology. In particular, he failed to give his rules any kind of mathematical form, an omission that sounds the death knell in today's world of science for any purported theoretical framework for explaining anything.

But the light of rational morphology was kept burning in the window with the publication in 1917 of D'Arcy Thompson's pioneering volume *On Growth and Form*. In the concluding chapter of this monumental work, Thompson took the first steps toward putting the idea of biological transformations of form on a sound mathematical footing when he introduced coordinate systems to describe biological form. Using these coordinate grids, Thompson showed how different species could all be generated from a given "archetypal" species just by changing the coordinate system. The heart of Thompson's scheme is to superimpose a coordinate frame on an organ or the entire body of a member of some species. Then by continuously deforming the grid—i.e., by stretching and shrinking it in different ways—Thompson was able to transform the original entity into a related form. It was Thompson's hope that his theory would enable biologists to calculate from the features of a single species the relevant data pertaining to any other species that was sufficiently closely related. Figure 3.13 shows an example of how Thompson's scheme works to transform the porcupine fish *Diodon*, on the left, into the sunfish *Orthagoriscus mola*, on the right. Thompson's book gives many examples of a similar nature, although mechanists rightly note that at present there is no known cellular basis for such transformations; they are purely mathematical operations.

The rational morphologists, D'Arcy Thompson, and Driesch were all groping for what in hindsight looks to be the same thing—a field theory of biological form. What each of these investigators needed was some sort of organizing principle that would deal with form as a whole. So comes the notion of a morphogenetic field into biology, an idea originally proposed in the 1920s, but brought into modern biology by the work of Conrad H. Waddington in the early 1950s.

*   *   *

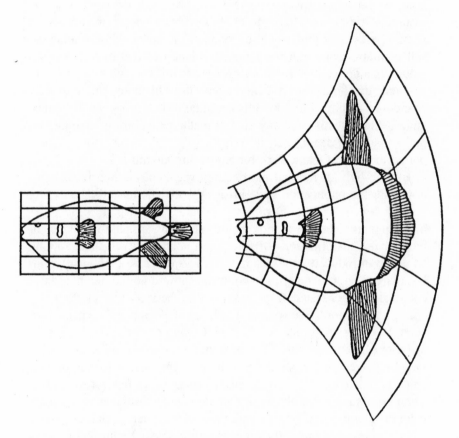

Figure 3.13. *A biological transformation involving fish*

Waddington considered himself to be philosophically a follower of Alfred North Whitehead, who, as well as being Bertrand Russell's mentor and collaborator on the *Principia Mathematica,* was also a staunch believer in a philosophy that took process as the generator of form. In 1952 Waddington revived the earlier ideas of Hans Spemann, Paul Weiss, and Alexander Gurwitsch on morphological fields, introducing the concept of a *chreod,* a kind of channel or groove in the morphogenetic field that defines a path to which a developing system returns after a disturbance. In dynamical systems terms, the final form of an organism can be regarded as a system's attractor. In this setting Waddington's chreod corresponds to the attractor's *domain of attrac-*

tion, the set of initial points that are eventually "sucked in" to the particular attractor. And, in fact, looking at things from such a system-theoretic perspective served to open the door to a full-scale mathematical attack on problems of development, some of which we'll consider in the next section.

The path from the rational morphologists and on to Waddington culminates today with the "structuralist" biology advocated by Brian Goodwin, Gerry Webster, and their followers in the United Kingdom. The starting point of their ideas is to assume that the organism itself is the fundamental biological entity, not the cell. Moreover, they assert that morphogenetic fields are every bit as real as the fields of physics, and that such fields are the self-organizing entities underlying biological form. In fact, they argue that such fields are coextensive with the organism. As Goodwin states: "The spatial organization of the whole derives from principles relating to global field behavior, together with constraints coming from the properties of the entities which are generated as parts."

But if such fields are to be taken seriously as the basis for a theoretical biology, they must be dressed up in suitable mathematical clothing in the same manner as the fields of physics are represented by designer items like Maxwell's equations of electromagnetism, Schrödinger's equation for the quantum wave function, Einstein's gravitational field equations, and all the other prestige labels in the world of theoretical physics. Goodwin claims that experimental work suggests that the field value at any point within the region of action of a morphogenetic field is the average of its values at equidistant neighboring points. Hearing these words, even an amateur mathematician would trot out Laplace's equation, which among other things describes the electric field potential inside a hollow metal sphere when we specify the electric potential on the sphere's surface. Can such a simple equation really describe developmental fields and, hence, biological form?

To address this foundational question, Goodwin looks at the problem of cleavage patterns in the developing embryo. Consider the first few steps of the radial cleavage pattern of the blastula as shown in Figure 3.14. By way of comparison, Figure 3.15 displays the geometry of the nodal lines of the first few solutions to Laplace's equation on a sphere, functions that are usually termed *spherical harmonics.* For Goodwin's claims, it's important to note that, in general, there are an infinite number of solutions to Laplace's equation, and the particular solution for a given situation has to be singled out by additional in-

Figure 3.14. *Radial cleavage pattern*

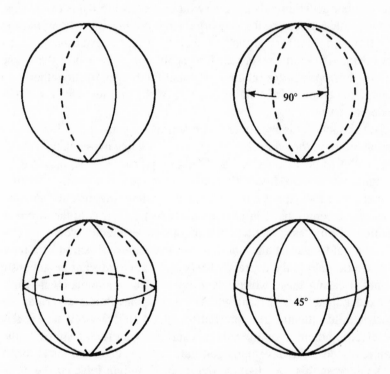

Figure 3.15. *The geometry of spherical harmonics*

formation that's usually supplied by prescribing the values the solution should have on the boundary of the spatial region of interest. Goodwin develops a convincing description of cleavage using an energy-minimization principle, leading to a mathematical formulation involving Laplace's equation. The details of this exercise can be found in the To Dig Deeper section of this book. What is important here is that

Goodwin is able to characterize the cleavage process during cellular development as being a series of transformations of the morphogenetic field described by the solutions to Laplace's equation.

An important side benefit of the approach to development via Laplace's equation is that this equation is the standard representative of an entire class of such field equations whose solutions are termed *harmonic functions*. These functions have the very desirable property that, like a hologram, they are reconstructible throughout their entire spatial domain of definition on the basis of information given about the values of the function in a small, local region of that domain. So if morphogenetic fields truly are describable by harmonic functions, then it's rather easy to see how the self-organizing process of reproduction, in which the whole is produced from a part, might come about by prescribing only local spatial information. This procedure would also make it easier to characterize processes like regeneration and regulation mathematically.

But where do the genes enter into such a setup? While there is an ever-increasing body of evidence to suggest that the genes are not the sole determinants of form, there is an even larger body of fact indicating that they do play a major role. In the organicist's world of morphogenetic fields, the genes act to define constraints that limit the forms that the organism can assume. We have already noted that, generally speaking, Laplace's equation possesses an infinite number of solutions. In an organicist biology, the genes play the role of a "super-selection rule," in much the same way that such rules are used in physics to single out physically realizable solutions of the analogous equations describing quantum fields. Thus, in this light the relation between genotype and phenotype is one of causal necessity, not sufficiency, since the gene products act only within the framework of the fields that generate the actual morphology. To adopt Goodwin's linguistic analogy, the genes determine the set of words from which a text can be constructed, while the morphogenetic field establishes the syntactic, semantic, and contextual constraints, i.e., the grammar.

The organicist theory sketched above suggests that the structure of the morphogenetic field is physically real in the same sense that electric and gravitational fields are real in physics, i.e., as timeless mathematical formulas. Recently, a radically different point of view has been proposed, suggesting that the field is far more "real" than even a physicist's reality. This theory of morphology, termed *formative causation*, asserts that the morphogenetic field results from the actual forms of previous organisms. Thus, the structure of the field depends upon what has happened in the past. Since the hypothesis of formative causation has been the focus of considerable attention in the scientific world of late, it's of much more than passing interest for us to look at it in more detail.

The British weekly *Nature* is probably the most respected, or at least influential, journal in print for the general scientific community. About half of each issue is taken up with job advertisements for cytologists and molecular biologists, together with communiqués from the trenches of science carrying titles like "Very High Frequency of Lymphoma Induction by a Chemical Carcinogen in *Pim*-1 Transgenic Mice" and "Interleukins 4 and 5 Control Expression of IL-2 Receptor on Murine B Cells Through Independent Induction of Its Two Chains." Isn't that interesting? But the other half of each issue is filled with book reviews, editorial statements, short accounts of scientific developments of current concern, and the kind of general news about the interaction between science and government that scientists of every stripe want and need to know about. Given *Nature's* lofty position and reputation in the scientific information-dissemination pecking order, many of its several hundred thousand readers were taken aback in 1981 when the magazine led off its September 24 issue with an editorial titled "A Book for Burning?" Given that free expression of ideas and theories, however speculative, is one of the foundations upon which the scientific ideology rests, what kind of book on science could have so outraged the editors of *Nature* as to provoke even the suggestion of an act that's as abhorrent to thinking beings everywhere as burning (or, at least, burying) a book?

Contrary to what one might imagine, the focal point of *Nature's* ire was not a treatise on spoon bending, creationism, tarot reading, or any of the other by-now-familiar calling cards of the pseudoscientist. In fact, the book under fire was written by respected biochemist Rupert Sheldrake, whose arguments in *A New Science of Life* are anything but woolly-headed fantasies about ancient astronauts, perpetual motion machines, or the disappearance of Judge Crater. Instead what Sheldrake offers is an approach to the problem of development that combines the old idea of a morphogenetic field with the radically new notion that such fields arise from the forms of previous organisms and, moreover, survive the death of the organism to influence in some fashion the forms of its progeny. To distinguish such form-causing fields from the energetic fields of physics, Sheldrake subtitles his book *The Hypothesis of Formative Causation,* invoking Aristotle's distinction between efficient cause by energy and formal cause by plan. Note here Sheldrake's careful use of the word *hypothesis.* Contrary to the assertions of many casual readers and critics, he has never claimed that formative causation is a *fact,* only that it is a possibility with the potential to explain many of the most puzzling features of morphogenesis. Let's look at this hypothesis and see if we can discover just what it is about it that generated such heated animosity among the editors (and some readers) of *Nature.*

The hypothesis of formative causation rests on the following premises:

I. Morphogenetic fields are physically real.
II. These fields shape and organize developing plants and animals, as well as stabilize the forms of adult organisms.
III. Each kind of cell, tissue, organ, and organism has its own kind of field.
IV. The morphogenetic field results from the actual forms of previous organisms.

Premises I and II are common to all organicist theories of form; it's Premises III and IV that raise the hackles of Sheldrake's critics.

The central idea of formative causation is that the developing embryo is "tuned in" to the morphogenetic fields of its species and becomes embedded within the pathways (chreods) that shape its development, just as the development of countless embryos before has been shaped. Figure 3.16 humorously illustrates the idea for a chicken. But in good Proustian fashion, Sheldrake's detractors want to know how these remembrances of forms past take place.

According to Sheldrake, the mechanism by which today's developing embryo gets in touch with its past is by a process he calls *morphic resonance.* The notion of resonance is well known in physics, taking place whenever any two oscillating bodies (like a radio antenna and the tuning circuit in your radio) reinforce each other's vibratory modes by having their respective frequencies match in the right way. But these kinds of resonances all involve a transfer of energy. Morphic resonance, on the other hand, takes place on the basis of similarity, and involves a nonenergetic transfer of information. Thus, it is a kind of action at a distance in time and space. Sheldrake claims that this field

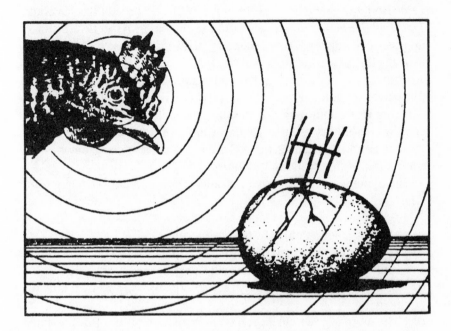

Figure 3.16. *A chicken embryo "tuning in" to its morphogenetic field*

of formative action is no less real than any other kind of resonant field, but that it is a kind of field currently unknown to physics—a field of information rather than one of matter or energy.

It's at this point that the hypothesis of formative causation starts getting iffy for the flinty-eyed community of mainline biologists, since one of the principal ground rules of scientific practice is Ockham's Razor, whereby hypotheses should not be introduced beyond the minimum number needed to explain the phenomenon under study. Since most biologists are dyed-in-the-wool mechanists at heart, an unknown and unmeasurable information field looks about as appealing to them as a trip to the dentist. And when Sheldrake adds that this invisible organizing principle of nature is not fixed, but evolves along with the system it organizes, then the fur really starts to fly.

Figure 3.17 gives a schematic illustration of how the hypothesis of formative causation works, as well as an indication of how it deals with the bugaboos of regeneration and regulation. Here we see the development of a complete system (two circles, a square, and a triangle) from a morphogenetic germ (the triangle) by following a normal chreod

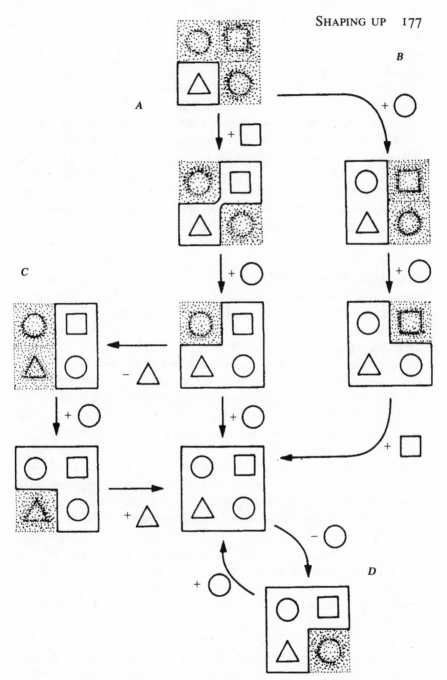

Figure 3.17. *Development from a morphogenetic germ*

in the vertical path downward beginning at *A*. An alternate chreod is shown at *B*, while the processes of regulation and regeneration are indicated by the pathways *C* and *D*, respectively. In all cases, the inherent virtual form within the morphogenetic field is shown by the shaded area. Note the role of the morphogenetic germ, which we might think of as the "seed" for the developing system. The remainder of the field contains the virtual form of the adult organism, which is brought to actuality only when all its material parts have taken up their right places, an activity guided, of course, by the field. At that time, the morphogenetic field and the actual form of the organism coincide.

Since Sheldrake's fields are assumed to be real, he draws no distinction between biological form and forms of any other kind. In fact, he claims that such fields underlie not only the forms of organisms but those of inorganic matter like crystals as well. Furthermore, Sheldrake claims that things like cognitive thought and behavior patterns are also governed by their own characteristic fields. In short, wherever information plays a role, fields of formative causation necessarily follow.

Recognizing that such a radical and sweeping proposal would need the most convincing empirical support before it could possibly hope to penetrate the conventional wisdom of science, Sheldrake proposed a number of experiments to test his ideas. While there's no room here to detail each of them, let me recount one such experiment that was the prizewinner in a contest sponsored by *Nature*'s spunkier weekly competition in the science information derby, the British magazine *New Scientist*. This test, suggested by Robert Gentle of Nottingham University, involves the memorization of nursery rhymes. Gentle submitted a Turkish nursery rhyme, in Turkish, along with a jumbled version that still rhymes. The argument is that if the hypothesis of formative causation is correct, then it should be easier for people who do not speak Turkish to learn the real rhyme, even though it seems no more comprehensible to them than the fake one. This is because millions of Turks have already learned the real rhyme in the past. Tests of a modified version of Gentle's ingenious proposal were carried out with Japanese rhymes and published in the September 12, 1983, issue of the *Brain/Mind Bulletin*. The results were that 62 percent of the people tested found the genuine nursery rhyme easier to learn, an outcome that was highly significant statistically. Other tests resulting in similar support for Sheldrake's hypothesis are reported in the references cited in the To Dig Deeper section. So it would appear that

Sheldrake's theory is at least a contender in the developmental biology sweepstakes. How strong a contender, no one can say at present.

On several occasions in our discussion of organicism we have mentioned Waddington's idea of a chreod to take into account temporal aspects of development. Let's close our all too brief review of the organicist claims with another radical approach to the problems of development, one that regards the emergence of form as nothing less than—catastrophic.

FORMAL CATASTROPHES

At the 1974 International Congress of Mathematicians in Vancouver, Canada, Christopher Zeeman gave one of the plenary lectures. His provocative title, "Levels of Structure in Catastrophe Theory Illustrated by Applications in the Social and Biological Sciences," coupled with the great curiosity of the mathematical community at this time about the ins and outs of catastrophe theory, ensured a standing-room-only audience. Zeeman, a great showman as well as a great mathematician, didn't disappoint his audience, as he vividly outlined how he and his colleagues had applied the theoretical ideas underpinning catastrophe theory to great advantage in numerous areas like animal aggression, economic growth, and prison riots. In fact, Zeeman's showmanship and dramatic claims in such a well-publicized forum have led many to date the beginning of the Sussman-led catastrophe-theory brouhaha discussed in Chapter One to this very lecture. One of Zeeman's examples on this historic occasion indicated how catastrophe theory could be employed to predict and explain certain important features of embryonic development. Since this example seems to have stood the test of time rather better than some of his other speculations, let's look at what he had in mind as a way of seeing catastrophe theory applied in the cause of developmental biology.

As we have observed, during the process of gastrulation an initially homogeneous layer of multicellular tissue differentiates into two types of cells—the ectoderm and mesoderm. During this process the frontier separating the two types of cells always forms to one side of its final position, and then moves through the tissue before stabilizing in its final location. This phenomenon can be thought of as a wave passing through the originally undifferentiated tissue, the wavefront slowing down and eventually stopping at the final position of the frontier separating the two cellular types. Zeeman's model uses catastrophe theory arguments to show how this behavior comes about and why it is the "typical," or generic, way for cellular tissue to differentiate.

In Zeeman's model, the dynamical behavior of the frontier separating the regions of the two cellular types moves in two waves, termed the primary and secondary waves. The distinction between the two types of waves arises from the presumed mechanism causing them. For the primary wave, the mechanism is assumed to depend upon both space and time, while the secondary wave's mechanism depends only upon time—i.e., it is a series of spatially local events, each occurring a fixed time after passage of the primary wave. To clarify this distinction, Zeeman suggests the metaphor of the spread of an infectious disease through a population. The primary wave corresponds to the contraction of the infection itself, while the secondary wave is the appearance of the actual physical symptoms of the disease. This is just like the situation with the radio wave, in which the wave itself is invisible and can be inferred only from the effect it has on something that *is* visible—your radio receiver. In our earlier terminology, we can think of the primary wave as being the spread of a morphogen whose action initiates the process of cellular differentiation. The secondary wave is the physically observed wave of differentiation itself. The catastrophe theory model shows how the existence of some sort of morphogenlike quantity is a mathematical necessity, assuming a small set of quite reasonable conditions. In addition, the mathematics then shows why the wave passes through the tissue in the "sidewinderlike" fashion that it does. Now let's look at these assumptions, as well as at how Zeeman manages to wave the magic wand of mathematics to turn catastrophes into forms.

Let's use E to represent the initial layer of undifferentiated cells, and assume that the process of gastrulation takes place over a finite time interval of length T. Zeeman's model then makes the following four *assumptions* about the developmental process:

1. *Homeostasis:* Each cell in the layer E is in a stable biochemical equilibrium, but it is an equilibrium that may change over time. What this means is that as time unfolds, the biochemical state of each cell may change. The cell will then rapidly move to a new equilibrium. The model assumes that these transient movements from equilibrium state to equilibrium state are very quick compared to the rate of change of the system's biochemical parameters.

2. *Continuity:* It is possible to represent the state of each cell by a smooth function on *E*. This requirement means that whenever possible neighboring cells will follow developmental paths that are very similar. Of course, this is not possible where a frontier stabilizes, so across the frontier the developmental paths of nearby cells will necessarily diverge.

3. *Differentiation:* Initially there is only one type of cell. But at the end of the time interval *T* there are two distinct types. Moreover, there is a discontinuous variation across the frontier separating the two types.

4. *Repeatability:* Development is a stable process. Consequently, a qualitatively similar development will occur if the initial conditions on *E* are disturbed only a little bit.

Under the preceding hypotheses, Zeeman shows that catastrophe theory's main mathematical result, the Thom Classification Theorem, implies the following behavior:

Developmental Theorem

A primary wave must exist. In other words, a frontier forms, moves and deepens, then slows up and stabilizes, and finally deepens further.

Figure 3.18 shows the entire developmental process in the model. For ease of drawing there is only a single spatial axis, the different spatial locations being denoted by s_0, s_1, . . . So, starting at some particular location like s_1 and following across in time, we are looking at the developmental history of a cell located at the point in the tissue whose spatial location is s_1. The figure shows clearly how from an initially homogenous layer of cells, the frontier, indicated by the heavy black line, between cell types *A* and *B* forms, originally at the space-time location labeled c_1. The frontier then moves along the indicated curve until it reaches the point c_2, where stabilization takes place and the frontier deepens.

As already noted, the existence of this primary wave is a necessary consequence of the assumptions plus the Thom Classification Theorem. The mathematics guarantees that something like a wave of morphogens passing through the tissue must exist. However, Zeeman cautions that these morphogens may not act like a classical organizer. We can expect to find some sort of chemical or physical gradient, but not necessarily a signal emanating from an organizing center. Never-

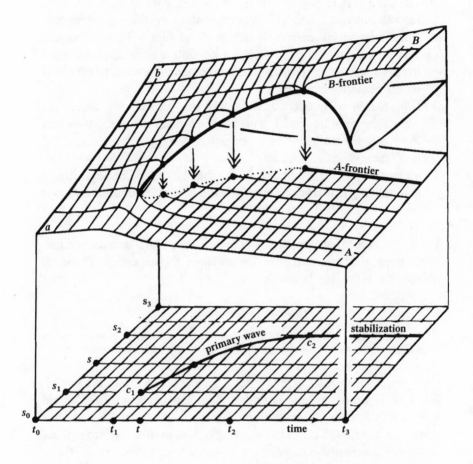

Figure 3.18. *Developmental paths of cells during differentiation*

theless, knowing that such a primary wave of morphogens exists, we can often think of various types of physical mechanisms that might account for it (like a reaction-diffusion process) and try to find them experimentally. Now let's return to the more general question of catastrophes and form.

Earlier we mentioned the British geneticist C. H. Waddington as one of the pioneers in bringing the idea of a morphogenetic field into modern developmental biology. In connection with his introduction of the idea of a chreod, or a canalized developmental pathway, Wadding-ton emphasized what he termed the *epigenetic landscape* as a geomet-rical way of visualizing the overall process of development. A stylized picture of such a landscape is given in Figure 3.19, showing Wad-dington's vision of development as being channeled into different val-leys, just like a ball rolling downhill.

Examination of the landscape, and its picture of a ball rolling down a valley, suggests the process of epigenesis as being tantamount to René Thom's vision of development in which the organism's final form is the attractor of some dynamical process. And, in fact, Thom's mathematical (and philosophical) views on using catastrophe theory to describe biological development were greatly influenced by Wadding-ton's work.

It turns out that in addition to the study of cellular differentiation, as in the Zeeman example just considered, the catastrophe theory frame-work described in Chapter One is especially convenient for studies of morphogenesis. The basic idea is to think of an organism's physical form at any moment as being the result of the interactions of a large number of variables—regulatory genes, chemical reactions involving proteins, environmental factors, space, and time. From what has gone before, it's reasonable to suppose that there are thousands, if not

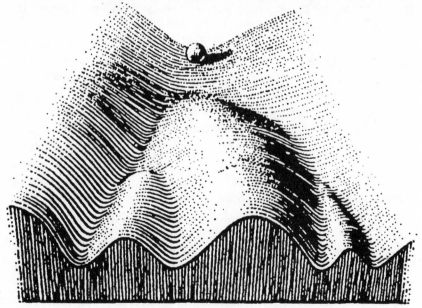

Figure 3.19. *An epigenetic landscape*

millions, of such quantities, all contributing to the developing form of an organism. Now assume that the resultant form is the attractor of a dynamical system, which as we know is some mathematical function of all these many variables. Furthermore, since we're interested in spatiotemporal structure, let's regard the three spatial directions and time as being parameters that we can vary for this dynamical process, letting all the other zillions of variables do their thing in the background. Insofar as change of shape is concerned, our interest is with those background variables displaying discontinuous changes (like the formation of the frontier in Zeeman's cellular differentiation example) as we move about in space and time by changing the four spatiotemporal parameters. In short, new tissues, organs, and forms emerge only at those locations in the parameter space (ordinary three-dimensional space and time) where the system's attractor undergoes a discontinuous shift from one attractor to another.

On the basis of quite general mathematical results, it can be shown that among the many variables in the background characterizing the organism's form, it's typical for only one, or at most two, of these variables at a time to exhibit discontinuous behavior as the parameters change. Catastrophe theory allows us to give a complete geometric characterization of the kinds of qualitatively new forms that can emerge in any small region of space and time as an organism follows its complete developmental pathway.

So if we accept the basic premise that overall development is ultimately determined by various chemical and physical interactions among the cells of a developing embryo, then to understand the emergence of form taking place in the arena of space and time we must consider four basic gradients: three in space and one in time. It is at the points of discontinuity in these gradients that new forms arise or, more properly, emerge. Thinking in Thom's terms, this means that we must look at a system involving four "tuning knobs," and ask what typical kinds of forms can appear as we twist the knobs. The celebrated Thom Classification Theorem of elementary catastrophe theory tells us that the only stable forms that can arise are the seven qualitatively distinct "catastrophes" listed in Table 3.4.

The names given in the second column of the table come from a combination of technical and geometric considerations involving the regions of parameter space where "catastrophes" happen. We have already seen the geometry of the cusp in Chapter One (page 67), but the complete geometric picture of some of these forms is a little hard

Parameters/ Morphological Variables	Name	Spatial Interpretation	Temporal Interpretations
1/1	fold	boundary; end	finish; begin
2/1	cusp	fault; pleat	break; unite
3/1	swallowtail	crack; corner	tear; stitch
4/1	butterfly	pocket; flake	give; receive
3/2	hyperbolic umbilic	crest of a wave	collapse; recover
3/2	elliptic umbilic	needle; hair	penetrate; fill
4/2	parabolic umbilic	mushroom; mouth	throw; open; close

Table 3.4. The seven elementary catastrophes

to portray within the space limitations of a volume like this. The main point is that the characteristic geometry of each catastrophe arises from the values of the morphological parameters at which discontinuous shifts take place in the attractor of the underlying dynamical system. Thus, the spatial and temporal interpretations of the catastrophes listed in the table come from viewing these mathematical discontinuities in ordinary three-dimensional space or in time. The interested reader should consult the references listed in the To Dig Deeper section for a complete account. However, just to get the flavor of why one of Thom's primary motivations for developing catastrophe theory was to create a mathematical language for developmental biology, the reader might like to look at Figure 3.20, showing side by side the process of sea urchin gastrulation and the unfolding of the elliptic umbilic catastrophe.

With this wildly abbreviated account of catastrophe theory and Thom's essentially Platonic view of morphogenesis, we have come to the end of our investigations into the ways living objects take the forms that they do. Figure 3.21 summarizes the positions of the competing schools.

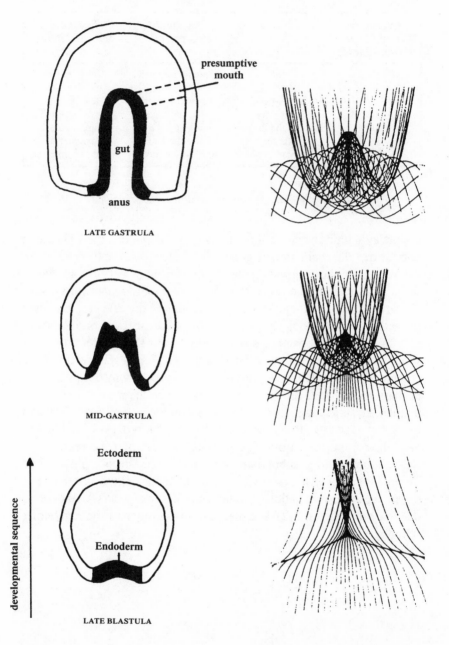

Figure 3.20. *Sea urchin gastrulation and the elliptic umbilic catastrophe*

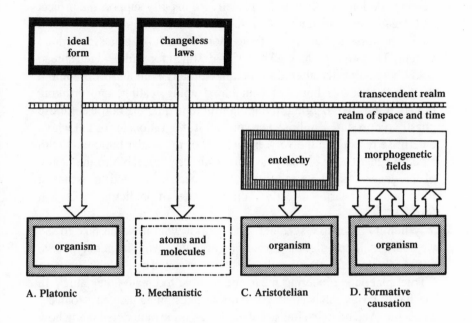

Figure 3.21. *Different theories of physical form*

MAKING THE GRADE

Prediction

Even in these days of mega- and beg-a-buck science, the announcement in January 1989 of the official launching of the so-called Human Genome Project was a special event and made front-page news just about everywhere. This project, which is estimated to take at least a decade and cost a cool $3 billion, has as its aim nothing less than the mapping of the entire human genetic code—those chemical instructions written into the DNA of each cell that mainline biologists believe constitute a complete set of rules for making a human being. Proponents argue that, by identifying the location and function of each of the hundred thousand or so human genes, the project will make it possible to pinpoint the genetic origins of maladies such as Huntington's chorea, Tay-Sachs disease, and sickle-cell anemia, ultimately allowing us to eliminate such debilitating diseases using the tools of genetic engineering. Perhaps so. But as for myself, I'd happily support the project and regard it as an unqualified success if the genetic cartographers would promise to identify nothing more than those genes governing weight. That way, perhaps, those of us destined for middle-aged spread could be genetically altered to remain eternally slim and trim without the need to devote hours of valuable sleeping, eating, and drinking time to things like jogging, pumping iron, and quaffing bottles of those ghastly diet sodas. But however you call it, the rationale for the whole enterprise rests upon the very explicit act of molecular biological faith asserting that every phenotypic trait is directly traceable to the action of the genes. As we've seen, this is the mechanist creed in its purest form, a belief bearing directly upon the matter of predicting biological form.

When it comes to a succinct statement of what it would take to say we could really predict the form of an organism from its genotype, we can hardly do better than invoke the criterion stated by Sydney Brenner: "True genetic engineering means being able to create a centaur." In mechanist terms, such a feat would involve designing the genes to make a centaur. And note that this is not merely an issue of understanding how to juggle the genes to place the man's heart and the horse's heart so they function. Much more is needed. In particular, creating such a beast would involve understanding all the processes of development, from the fertilized egg up through the final adult organism. Thus, a perfect grade for prediction, mechanist style, would necessarily entail at least two things: (1) the truth of the assumption that the genes are the master controllers of all the chemical reactions in the cell, and (2) knowledge of the exact developmental pathways by which the genes act to regulate every aspect of development, even assuming a fixed environment. Needless to say, our discussion here has shown just how far away we are from such a state of morphological bliss.

On the other hand, mechanists do understand the pathways between some genes and corresponding phenotypic traits, as with the congenital diseases mentioned a moment ago. And when it comes to form, it's almost true to say that we know how the genetic program determines the shape of a ribosome, the special-purpose enzyme that assembles amino acids into proteins within a cell. This results from following the path: DNA base sequence → amino acid sequence in proteins → three-dimensional shape of the proteins → assembly of proteins to determine the ribosome. But a ribosome is a far cry from a rhinoceros, and the argument stops with the ribosome because the shape of a rhino, unlike that of a ribosome, is independent of the shapes of its constituent molecules. In fact, the situation is even a bit worse than this, as recent work has shown that there cannot possibly be a one-to-one correspondence between a gene and the shape of the protein for which it codes. This is because there is often more than one possible three-dimensional structure that can form out of the sequence of amino acids coded for by the DNA bases composing the gene. Yet only one shape will work properly in the organism. So for mechanists there is a limited kind of predictability, but the limitations at present are very apparent and real, especially when it comes to the problem of form. Now what about predictability of form by organicists?

In all organicist theories of form, the central ingredient is the morphogenetic field that acts to guide the general developmental plan. In this view, the genes play the vital, but secondary, role of being selectors of the specific field that acts among the infinite spectrum of possibilities. In the language of physics, the genes set the boundary conditions that single out the one correct solution of the general field equations. Thus, to meet the Brenner test and create a centaur, an organicist would first have to know the general field equations for, say, a horse and a man. Then the organicist would somehow have to mix up a blend of these two sets of equations, suitably spiced with the right genes, so that a centaur emerged at the end of the developmental process. Again, none of the organicist theories we've looked at comes within even a faint whisper of being able to do anything remotely approaching these tasks.

The hope of the organicist is that if a mathematically based theory of the morphogenetic fields can be formulated, these fields will then serve as the foundation for a generative biology of form, i.e., one based upon the laws of form encapsulated in the mathematical representations of the field. But such a mathematical formalism is still a distant gleam in the organicist's eye, although the work of Goodwin, Thom, and a few others has taken us a faltering step or two down the road to such a theory. By the same token, the mechanist is also looking for a formulation of the genetic program in mathematical (read: lawful) terms, in order to understand the workings of each gene and the way the genes cooperate to direct the creation of the final organism. Again, a few stumbling steps down this road have been taken by Wolpert, Meinhardt, and Company, but the light is still very dim at the end of the tunnel. So putting all these remarks together, we work out the final grade as it pertains to prediction of biological form:

Term Grade—Prediction: D$^+$

Explanation

One of the great misnomers in science publishing was the title of Darwin's pathbreaking volume *On the Origin of Species*—a misnomer simply because the arguments Darwin presented have to do not with how common ancestors originate, but only with how their descendants may differ in a historical process, i.e., by natural selection. Thus the Darwinian claim is that organismic form is determined not by rational law but by historical accident. But if we believe that scientific explanation means explanation by law, then we're forced to conclude both that Darwinism does not offer a scientific explanation of form, and that the mechanists and organicists include something lawlike in their programs above and beyond the tenets of conventional Darwinism.

We have seen considerable evidence to the effect that mechanists do indeed believe in the idea of a lawful theory of development: the genetic program. So in order for the mechanists to be in a position to argue convincingly that they can explain the emergence of biological form, it would be necessary for the DNA base sequence *plus* the physico-chemical state of the fertilized egg *plus* the environment *plus* the laws of physics to give an accurate account of the following phenotypic traits:

1. The three-dimensional structure of all the proteins made by the organism
2. The properties of all these proteins
3. The organism's complete metabolic behavior
4. The nature and action of all the types of positional information the organism uses during its development
5. The structure of the organism's cells, tissues, organs, and form
6. The organism's instinctive behavior
7. The processes of regulation and regeneration

Mechanists are in a position to give *partial* answers to *some* of these points. But their explanatory tools, deeply rooted as they are in classical physics, may never begin to touch things like item 4 or item 6.

To turn to the organicists, the morphogenetic field idea does seem to contain at least the germ of a hope for explaining all of the items on the list. However—and this is a big however—without a much more detailed account of how these fields operate, and without a far better developed formal theory of such fields, and especially without some understanding of how the morphogenetic fields relate to the known energy fields of physics, the explanatory power of the morphogenetic field is in the same position as the explanatory power of the gravitational field before Newton and Einstein.

Despite the imposing tasks facing both the mechanists and the organicists, when it comes to explaining the processes of morphogenesis there can be little doubt that considerable progress has been made. Mechanists can convincingly employ the principles of mechanics to tell us why organisms look like cylinders and why ribosomes curl up the way they do. And organicists can tell us why sheets of cells twist in a particular manner during the course of gastrulation and why sea urchins shape up in one way and not in any other. So it's fair to say that both schools have some handle on the whys of biological form and how it emerges. With these facts in mind, we come to the final term grade for explanation:

Term Grade—Explanation: C⁻

The preceding chapters have focused on the natural sciences—the realms of the physicist and biologist. On the principle of equal time for all contending parties, let's now shift gears and spend the next two chapters examining the territory of the social scientist; in particular, our interest will be in the problems of predictability and explanation of human behavior. And since humans never display more ingenuity and more variety in their behavior than when they're engaged in trying to make a buck, our first port of call will be that most human of all institutions—the gambling den. Oops, sorry, I meant the stock market.

CHAPTER FOUR

MEANWHILE, OVER AT THE CASINO

Can We Predict/Explain the Behavior of Stock Market Prices?

Security markets are sophisticated but irrational betting parlors.
—JOHN MAYNARD KEYNES

Financial genius is a rising stock market.
—JOHN KENNETH GALBRAITH

Earnings momentum and visibility should continue to propel the [stock] market to new highs.
—Report by the brokerage house E. F. Hutton, October 19, 1987

When E. F. Hutton talks, people listen.
—Well-known television commercial

A BULL IN A BOWL

January 22, 1989, Super Sunday, the day on which football addicts the world over try either to recoup their losses or add the last bit of frosting to a cake that started baking in September, by placing their last-gasp bets on either the San Francisco 49ers or the Cincinnati Bengals in Super Bowl XXIII. In a heart-stopping storybook finish, 'Niner fans go wild watching their heroes eke out a narrow 20–16 victory, while Bengal supporters make their way out of Miami's Joe Robbie Stadium with the ritual grumble, "Wait 'til next year." First thing Monday morning I call my broker with a frantic order for a fistful of long-term call options on the market, convinced that 1989 will be a banner year for stocks. And, in fact, by the end of 1989 the Dow-Jones Industrial Average stood at 2753, a gain of over 500 points from its level on Friday before the game. What's the connection? Is it even remotely conceivable that the success or failure of Joe Montana's desperation pass in the closing moments of the game could have had any bearing on how stock prices would fluctuate on

Wall Street during 1989? Surprisingly, if you believe the record, maybe it does.

Some years ago, in a joking comment on the kinds of curious (and spurious?) correlations people find when they start mucking around in the stock market data, Robert Stovall of the 21st Advisers Fund published what is now termed the Super Bowl Indicator. Stovall's rule was simple: If the team that wins the Super Bowl originally belonged to the old National Football League before it merged with the American Football League, then the Dow will be up for the year and it's a time to run with the bulls; otherwise, it will be a year for losers and you should beware of bears coming out of hibernation. In the 23 years prior to the 1990 game, the Super Bowl Indicator has been right an astounding 21 times, a remarkable 91 percent success rate. No other market indicator has even begun to approach this level of reliability; hence, my bullish enthusiasm for index options on Super Monday. But you might argue (and probably rightly so) that these are just lucky coincidences. What about an indicator based on things that at least have some plausible relation to matters economic? OK, let's look at one.

A while back, the stock analyst Edson Gould advanced what has come to be termed the Three Steps and a Stumble Rule, which relates market fortunes to the Federal Reserve discount rate, the price the Fed charges the banks for their money. According to Gould's theory, after three successive increases in the discount rate, stock prices should tumble. Given the well-known economic reasons why stocks react negatively to rising interest rates (essentially because corporate costs go up, sending profits down), Gould's rule seems to make eminent economic sense. Since World War II there have been eight occasions when interest rates increased at least three successive times, but, contrary to the Three Steps and a Stumble Rule, in six of the eight cases the Dow-Jones Industrial Average *rose* over the following six months, giving the rule a bush-league batting average of only .250.

The story of these two indicators illustrates perfectly the two basic philosophies one can adopt in attempting to understand the mercurial meanderings of prices in speculative markets. The *fundamentalist* view of the world sees a price as only a reflection of an underlying value. The fundamentalist therefore claims that predictions of price movements should be anchored in an understanding of the way this value changes over time. Thus, companies like Chrysler or IBM own tangible assets like land, equipment, patents, and materials, and these assets are worth something. The sum total of these assets represents the true value of the company, which should be reflected in the price of a share of its stock. So, for a fundamentalist, since each share of stock represents ownership of a minuscule fraction of this underlying value, the price of that share should fluctuate as the underlying value changes. As a result, a fundamentalist spends his days poring over corporate earnings reports, interest rate movements, news of technological break-throughs, and the like, trying to relate them to a number representing what a share of the company's stock is "really" worth.

A *technician*, on the other hand, has a completely different philos-ophy toward price movements. The technician says that stock price fluctuations don't involve any notion of objective value at all. Rather, prices move according to the whims and fancies of the crowd, and successful investing relies upon estimating (i.e., guessing) how the investing public is going to behave in the future and trying to follow that trend today. Technicians employ a bewildering array of methods to divine the public's mood, some of them bizarre enough to make the Super Bowl Indicator look positively logical by comparison. My per-sonal favorite is the method used several decades ago by Frederick N. Goldsmith, who employed the pictures and dialogue in the popular cartoon strip of the time *Bringing Up Father* to predict the movement of the market. According to Goldsmith, when Jiggs, the hero of the strip, placed his hand in his right pocket, it was a signal to buy. Perhaps not so coincidentally, Goldsmith was later indicted for fraud and banished for life from securities trading—a right and proper fate for all technicians, according to many fundamentalists and academics. Nevertheless, technicians are, if anything, going even stronger today than in Goldsmith's time, what with their price charts, long and short waves, sunspots, Super Bowls, and all the other schemes they offer for guidance to the bewildered. The one thing uniting all technicians re-gardless of their methods is their belief in the irrelevance of intrinsic value as a basis for stock price fluctuations. This sentiment is exem-plified by technician John Magee, who works in an office with boarded-up windows so as not to be influenced by weather, and who won't even look at *The Wall Street Journal* until it's at least two weeks old, other than to get the price quotes.

On the basis of even such gross caricatures as these, it should be evident that fundamentalists and technicians are worlds apart when it comes to their views on what constitutes an explanation of market behavior. For a technician, an explanation (if the term even makes sense at all) of price movements must be based on the beliefs of the investing public, beliefs that then lead to price changes motivated by emotional, social, and psychological factors having little to do with so-called economic fundamentals. For a fundamentalist, explanation of price changes resides in deeper economic factors, with stock prices being determined in some not very well understood way by these more basic quantities. Of course, when it comes to prediction both parties agree on what it means to be able to predict the market—the use of some method or rule to write tomorrow's edition of *The Wall Street Journal* today. We'll take a more detailed look at these matters in a moment. But first let's pause to clarify just what we mean when we speak of the market being "up" or "down." Since the essence of change is price variation, if we're going to evaluate the ups and downs of technical and fundamental predictions and explanations, we're going to need some thermometer by which to measure the temperature of Wall Street.

More than seventeen hundred individual stocks are listed on the New York Stock Exchange. The American Exchange accounts for another few hundred, and the various regional exchanges and over-the-counter trading add tens of thousands more. Taken together, these stocks constitute what we generally term "the market." To get a snapshot of how this gigantic conglomeration of securities stands at any given moment, it's necessary somehow to aggregate this multitude of individual pieces of paper into a digestible indicator of the state of the market. Basically, there are three different approaches to constructing such an index. Let's quickly review the rationale for each of them.

• *Price-weighted indexes:* Here a representative sample of stocks is combined into a single number by measuring the contribution of each stock in the sample according to its price. Thus, such an index is formed by simply adding up the prices of the stocks in the sample, and then dividing the total by a fudge factor introduced to account for things like stock splits or the replacement of one stock in the sample by another. The best-known example of such an index is the Dow-Jones Industrial Average, computed by summing the prices of the stocks of thirty industrial giants like Eastman Kodak, General Motors, and Exxon, then adjusting by the current divisor. Despite the Dow's historical position as *the* arbiter of how the market is doing, the reader will have no difficulty in seeing the dubious nature of an index in which the importance of a stock is measured only by its price. Does it really make sense to think that General Motors selling at 92 is twice as important in assessing the state of the market as Exxon at 46? It does if you believe the DJIA.

• *Value-weighted indexes:* If you don't like price, why not try an index that weighs its components the same way the market does—by their market value? In this scheme of measurement, a stock's weight in the overall index is calculated by multiplying its current price by the number of shares outstanding. This number represents what the market thinks the company is worth, a figure that may or may not bear any relationship to the intrinsic value attributed to that company by the fundamentalist. Thus, the argument goes, if the market values IBM twice as highly as it does Ford, then it's probably true that movement in the price of IBM will somehow "swing" the market twice as much as a similar change in the price of Ford. The most familiar example of this sort of index is the Standard & Poor's 500 (S&P 500), a collection of four hundred industrial, twenty transportation, forty utilities, and forty financial issues representing well over half the market value of all common stocks traded in the United States. Such a broad, value-weighted index is generally conceded by experts to be the best measure of the experience of investors taken as a whole.

• *Equally weighted indexes:* For special purposes, such as the evaluation of a portfolio in which equal amounts of money have been placed in each security, another type of index has been developed. For such an equally weighted portfolio, it's useful to employ a measure in which all stocks count the same. We can construct this sort of market indicator by computing the average percentage change, up or down, in its component stocks. An example is the Value Line Index, a composite of about seventeen hundred stocks.

Most of our empirical investigations of technical and fundamental claims of market prediction will use the DJIA, primarily because it has the longest history, hence offers the largest database to test various theories of speculation. But the other indexes will also make their appearance from time to time as we wend our way through the barbed wire and minefields of the ongoing battle between the academics and the brokers. Now let's get back to our main themes: predicting and explaining the patterns of stock price movement.

*　　*　　*

Market indexes (any of them) are our key to understanding just what we mean when we say we are able to "predict" the market through the use of any trading scheme, be it fundamental or technical. And contrary to what your barber or golfing cronies probably assert, what market prediction *doesn't* mean is merely making a profit. Making a profit alone is far from sufficient proof that one is able to predict the market. To illustrate graphically how easy it is to turn a profit on the market, in June 1967 reporters at *Forbes* magazine threw twenty-eight darts at the stock listings in *The New York Times*. The magazine then invested $28,000—$1,000 in each of the dart-selected stocks. In 1984 this portfolio was worth $131,697.61, a gain of 370 percent and an annual rate of return of $9\frac{1}{2}$ percent—both far in excess of the increase in any of the market indexes over the same period. And this test was no fluke. Subsequent studies show that if portfolios are constructed randomly and then bought and sold at random times, over 75 percent of the portfolios turn a profit. So, tales of woe to the contrary, making money on Wall Street is literally as easy as throwing darts. Just tack the price quotes up on the wall and let fly. Then hold on and sail along with the generally growing economy. So the test of a prediction technique must be much more stringent than just buying stocks and freeloading off the fat of the land.

The real test separating the predictors from the pretenders lies in *consistently outperforming the market*. In other words, you can legitimately claim to be able to predict the market if, over a sufficiently long period of time, your trading scheme shows a rate of growth in excess of that displayed by one of the common market indexes like the DJIA or the S&P 500. Many prediction methods work fine—for a while. In fact, prediction methods seem a bit like academic research papers: For every paper there's some journal somewhere that will publish it. All the author need do is persevere by searching out more and more obscure, offbeat publications, and he'll eventually find his pearly gems dripping with printer's ink. And so it is also with stock market prediction schemes: For every scheme there appears to have been some time in the past during which that scheme would have brought its followers far-above-average returns. But the real name of the game is consistency, not mere profits. And this is the criterion by which we will judge the procedures developed by both the fundamentalists and the technicians in their attempts to show that the rainbow really does end on Wall Street.

On the explanation side of the house, the issues are somewhat more clear-cut. If we maintain that we have an explanatory model of price movements, then the variables used to explain the current price must be both measurable and available to us at the same time as the actual price we wish to explain. For example, we may say that the price of, say, Exxon today depends upon the current price of crude oil, the political situation in Libya, the price of substitutes like natural gas or coal, and the mood of Congress. If we could measure these factors precisely and knew the *exact* way (read: law) by which these quantities determine the price of Exxon stock, then we could claim we had an explanation for today's price. Nevertheless, even such virtually god-like knowledge as this might not be enough to predict the price movement in Exxon stock, since prices are also based upon expectations and changes in expectations. Thus, when it comes to explanation of stock prices, we are forced to evaluate claims on the degree to which they match up to the test of being able to account for observed price movements on the basis of general principles of investor behavior and movements in lower-level, more fundamental economic, political, and psychological indicators.

To anyone who's ever dropped by the visitors' gallery at the New York Stock Exchange, or even stopped in at a broker's office to check the tape, the shouting, the flashing video terminals, and the constantly ringing telephones in these monuments to Mammon hardly suggest an environment conducive to the contemplation of such essentially philosophical matters as explanation and prediction. So it's not surprising that our first stop on the way to understanding these rarefied aspects of market behavior is the cloistered world of the academic. But what is surprising is the time and place at which we begin our tour—turn-of-the-century Paris.

WALKING THE STREET—RANDOMLY

On March 29, 1900, in a dusty seminar room at the University of Paris, the renowned mathematician Henri Poincaré presided over an unusual doctoral dissertation defense. In Poincaré's words, "The topic is somewhat remote from those our candidates are in the habit of treating." And just what was that "remote" topic? It was a mathematical treatment of how prices for French government bonds and their options fluctuated on the Paris Bourse. The author of this dissertation, Louis Bachelier, received the insultingly low grade of *mention honorable,*

rather than the more usual *mention très honorable,* the level needed to
be taken seriously as a candidate for an academic post in France.
Perhaps the dissertation's title, "The Theory of Speculation," as well
as its frankly commercial character, had something to do with the
apathy with which the examiners viewed Bachelier's efforts. Who can
say? What we do know is that this pioneering work represented the
initial salvo fired by the academic community in its efforts to unlock
the secrets of speculative markets. And as an indicator of just how
visionary Bachelier's ideas really were, even today his conclusions
form the heart of the dominant paradigm as to how prices fluctuate in
such markets. So let's take a look at what Bachelier claimed on that
eventful Parisian afternoon nearly one hundred years ago.

To describe Bachelier's results, it's helpful to have a compact notation for security prices. Let's define the quantity P_t to be the stock
price at time t, where t can be taken in minutes, days, months, years,
or whatever other unit is appropriate for the study at hand. So if we
measure t in days, P_0 would be today's price, say the closing price on
the NYSE, while P_1 would be tomorrow's closing price, and so on.
Further, the daily *change* in price would be given by a new quantity
$C_{t,\,1}$, the difference between the price today and its level yesterday,
i.e., $C_{t,1} = P_{t+1} - P_t$. More generally, the price change over d time
units would be given by $C_{t,\,d} = P_{t+d} - P_t$. To fix these crucial
quantities, consider the following simple example. Suppose we take
the time unit to be days. Imagine that over one trading week (five
days), the daily closing price of Exxon stock from Monday to Friday
is 68, 70, $67\frac{1}{2}$, $68\frac{3}{4}$, and 70. Taking $t = 0$ to represent the beginning of
the period (Monday), we would then have $P_0 = 68, P_1 = 70, P_2 =
67\frac{1}{2}, P_3 = 68\frac{3}{4}, P_4 = 70$. Furthermore, the crucial price change quan-
tities would then be given by $C_{0,\,1} = P_1 - P_0 = 70 - 68 = 2$,
$C_{2,\,1} = P_2 - P_1 = 67\frac{1}{2} - 70 = -2\frac{1}{2}$, and so on. Since what everyone
is really interested in is price changes, Bachelier rightly focused his
mathematical artillery on the changes, not the absolute prices themselves. Moreover, for technical reasons, Bachelier used the changes in
the *logarithms* of the prices rather than the absolute changes discussed
above. Thus, the quantities of mathematical interest, both for Bachelier and for us, are the differences $\log P_{t+d} - \log P_t$, which we can
compactly denote as $L_{t,\,d}$. Here, of course, the parameter d represents
the time period over which the difference is taken. With this notation
in hand, we can finally describe Bachelier's findings.

Suppose we fix a moment of time and call it t^*. Now let's look at the series of price changes over several time periods by varying the time-period parameter d. That is, we look at the sequence of numbers $S_{t*} = \{L_{t*, 1}, L_{t*, 2}, \ldots\}$. This sequence is just the time series of price changes from the starting time $t*$ expressed on a logarithmic scale. Bachelier expressed his conclusions in terms of these time series. Briefly, he claimed the following properties held for any such series of observations taken on price fluctuations in a speculative market:

• *Independence:* The quantities $L_{t*, d}$ and $L_{t*, d'}$ are statistically independent for any two different time intervals d' and d. In short, the price differences taken over any particular time period give no information about the differences over any other time period.

• *Stationarity:* The time series of price changes obeys the same probability law regardless of the starting time—i.e, the series of numbers S_t and S_{t*} are what statisticians call identically distributed for any choices t and $t*$ of the starting time, $t \neq t*$.

• *Normality:* The probability law that each time series follows is the normal, or Gaussian, distribution with mean zero. In other words, regardless of the choice of starting time $t*$, the series of numbers S_{t*} distributes itself according to the familiar bell-shaped curve of the normal distribution with its peak at zero.

Since these properties are crucial to an evaluation of stock market prediction and explanation schemes, let's add a few amplifying remarks as to what they mean in everyday language. But before doing so, let me pause to emphasize the point that Bachelier did not *prove* that price changes on speculative markets must obey these properties. Rather, he constructed a mathematical *model* for such price changes, then argued that his model would best fit the observations if the market behavior really did adhere to these statistical precepts. Thus what we have from Bachelier is more like a "speculation on speculation" than an airtight mathematical theorem. The reader should try to keep this point in mind as we proceed. For now, let's give Bachelier the benefit of the doubt and look at the implications of his claims.

First of all, independence. If price changes between time $t*$ and any other moments of time are independent, then the implication is clear: No amount of information about past price changes will be of any help in predicting future movements. In short, no statistical wizardry or massaging of past price data will be of the slightest assistance in deciding whether AT&T is going to move up or down tomorrow, next week, or next year. Thus, the independence assumption, if true, would deal a death blow to any technical analysis based upon price data alone.

Next, stationarity. The stationarity hypothesis says that regardless of when we start taking observations, i.e., the initial time t^*, the time series of price changes obeys the same probability law. In short, there is no preferred moment of time when it comes to price variation on speculative markets. For the investor there are at least two implications that follow from this assumption. One is that any time is as good as any other to begin taking data upon which to base investment decisions. The second is that the market price-setting mechanism, whatever *that* may be, remains the same through all time periods. Thus, if the stationarity hypothesis is true, statements often seen in the popular financial press about structural change in the market due to computers, faxes, communication satellites, and all the other marvels of modern technology are sheer nonsense. If the price change law really is stationary, then these toys of the technologist have no effect whatsoever on the way prices are set. Of course, they may do wild and wondrous things to the speed at which information is processed and transactions take place. But they don't influence the basic market mechanisms one whit.

Finally, normality. The outcomes of many stochastic phenomena in nature and life distribute themselves according to the familiar bell-shaped curve, the highly unlikely outcomes (both good and bad) being represented by the "tails" of the curve, while the more likely outcomes cluster near the center. Bachelier's claim was that speculative price variation is just such a phenomenon. As the conventional wisdom has it, a price change represents the aggregate response to innumerable small, lower-level actions on the part of investors. By summing these unpredictable microscopic behaviors, we arrive at the price change. Using this line of reasoning, Bachelier thought it was reasonable to assume that the Central Limit Theorem of probability theory would apply to these price fluctuations. This theorem states (roughly) that, regardless of the probability law governing the microscopic behavior of a set of independent individual units, the behavior of an aggregate of such units always follows the bell-shaped curve of the normal distribution. Thus emerged Bachelier's conclusion that price changes are normally distributed.

In this stock market context, the most germane properties of the normal distribution are its symmetry and finite variance. The symmetry property implies that negative price swings of a given amount are as likely to occur as positive fluctuations of the same magnitude. Moreover, the larger these swings (positive or negative), the less likely they become. The finite variance property means that, in effect, very large fluctuations are so unlikely as to be impossible for all practical purposes. Bachelier also stated that the Gaussian distribution according to which price changes move has zero mean. What this means to the investor is that the expected, or most likely, change of price is no change at all! Thus, if we are forced into a guessing game in which the goal is to predict tomorrow's price of Polaroid, then the best we can do in the absence of additional information is to say that it will be the same as today's price. In short, the expected, or most likely, price change is zero. We'll come back to all these points with a vengeance in later sections. For now, let's discuss the way in which Bachelier's pioneering insights have been enshrined in the lexicon of modern finance.

In the rarefied world of the mathematician, a time series of price changes satisfying Bachelier's three postulates is termed a *Gaussian random walk*. Why call such fluctuations a random walk? The terminology comes from envisioning the path a drunkard might follow on the way home from a late-night bender at the corner pub. Suppose we designate the pub corner as ''ground zero,'' and assume that the drunkard lives on the same street as the pub, so that it's necessary only to move along this single street in order for her to find her way home. Let the drunkard's direction of movement at each instant be determined by flipping a coin. So, if heads appears she staggers to the right, while if tails turns up the lurch is to the left. Making the usual assumptions that the result of each flip of this coin is independent of any other flip and that the same coin is used to determine the path home each time the drunkard leaves the pub, we reproduce the independence and stationarity assumptions for stock price changes introduced by Bachelier.

In the simple case of the drunkard, there are only two possibilities for movement—one step down the street, left or right. This corresponds to the case of a stock price change in which prices can move only up or down by a fixed amount. The Gaussian assumption comes into play when we add the condition that price changes are more than a simple up-or-down affair—many different levels of change are possible. To accommodate these various levels, Bachelier assumed they were distributed according to the Gaussian probability law. In the 1960s finance professors dubbed the movement of price changes *á la* Bachelier *the random walk hypothesis*. In short, the hypothesis is that every time series of price change data has Bachelier's independence, stationarity, and normality properties.

Bachelier's claims about the statistical independence of price changes over different time periods would definitely send any sort of technical analysis based upon price data alone into a fatal tailspin. But there still remains the fundamental problem of the fundamentalists. And this is not to mention the question marks following the holy trinity of statistical conclusions constituting Bachelier's overall thesis as well as his "thesis." As usual in life, fundamentals come first.

In late summer 1967, just a couple of months after the famous *Forbes* magazine dart-throwing portfolio-selection experiment, Senator Thomas McIntyre of New Hampshire was participating in Senate Banking Committee hearings on the management of mutual funds. The thrust of McIntyre's inquiry was to question the extraordinarily high fees being charged by fund managers for the so-called investment services they performed for their clients. One of the witnesses before the committee was Nobel-winning economist Paul Samuelson, who stated categorically that there was no kind of publicly available information, price data or otherwise, that would enable fund managers to outperform the market.

Senator McIntyre, like most politicians, fancied himself a practical, no-nonsense type of guy. So, while listening with great interest to Samuelson's theoretically oriented reasons for why a randomly selected portfolio would yield results as good as or better than those of the funds, the senator did a little dart-throwing of his own. The outcome of his experiment showed that a hypothetical $10,000 investment ten years earlier in the senator's dart-selected portfolio would have been worth a cool $25,300 by the time of the hearings—a rate of growth far in excess of even the most growth-oriented mutual fund. This was definitely bad news for the fund managers' attempts to justify their outrageously high fees on the grounds that they brought special expertise to the stock selection process. And, in fact, after this debacle the fund managers made no real effort to rebut Samuelson's testimony—although *The New York Times* reported that a couple of them did offer the senator a job!

The McIntyre incident vividly illustrates what has come to be termed *the efficient market hypothesis* (EMH). In everyday terms, the EMH is the claim that all information available is already reflected in the price of the stock. In the finance literature, the EMH and the Bachelier claims are lumped together and collectively labeled random walk theories (RWT), which come in three different flavors:

- *The weak RWT:* No technical analysis trading system based on price data alone can ever outperform the market. This weak version of the RWT is just Bachelier's claim that you can't create information about tomorrow's prices from looking at what happened in the past.

- *The semistrong RWT:* No trading scheme based on any publicly available information will be able to outperform the market. According to the semistrong RWT, not only are technical analysts useless, fundamentalists are too! But note that the semistrong theory applies only to *publicly available* information of the sort you see in *The Wall Street Journal* or that comes from scanning corporate earnings reports and listening to governmental agency pronouncements. The semistrong RWT constitutes what we earlier termed the efficient market hypothesis: All publicly available information has already been taken into account in setting the current price of the stock. But perhaps there's still hope for a winning portfolio selection strategy by employing so-called insider sources of information. For this case we have:

- *The strong RWT:* No trading scheme based upon *any* information sources whatsoever can outperform the market. Thus, the strong version says that no matter where you get your information, it will prove useless over the long haul in obtaining better-than-market-average investment results.

The perceptive reader will have already noticed that there's something inherently paradoxical about the EMH. On the one hand, the EMH says that it's useless to gather information; it will do you no good at all in the development of a trading strategy that will outperform the market. On the other hand, the EMH says that all available information has already been factored into the price of the stock. But how can this happen if no one gathers information? The fact is, it can't. Therefore, in order for the EMH to be valid, there must be a sufficiently large number of traders who don't believe it! So it can only be true if you don't think it's true—a stock market version of the famous Liar's Paradox ("All Cretans are liars. I am a Cretan. I'm lying").

So here we have the main pillars [...] [...]ifically based attacks on the stock market are founded: the random wa[...] [...] the efficient market hypothesis. Both of these ideas come with a no[...] of built-in assumptions, either explicit, like Bachelier's statistical properties, or implicit, like the EMH's inherent assumptions about the pricing mechanism and rationality on the part of investors.

But if the EMH is even approximately true, then it should be impossible to make consistently better-than-average returns. Yet the empirical evidence clearly indicates otherwise; Wall Street is filled with market operators who do just that. How can we reconcile this fact with the EMH theory? According to the academic finance establishment, these above-average returns can be obtained only by accepting above-average risks. In short, the investor who achieves such returns is merely being compensated for a willingness to shoulder a level of risk higher than the market norm. Not so, say members of the vocal opposition. They say that there are so many stock market anomalies and just plain inconsistencies having nothing to do with risk premiums that it's necessary to look at the very idea of the EMH with a jaundiced eye. So to adjudicate this debate, let's turn to a consideration of these matters, and try to see if there might really be loopholes that we can slip through to actually construct an effective prediction/explanation scheme for beating the market. The first item on our agenda is to examine the standard risk-premium arguments.

LOOKING FOR A BETA WAY

In the March 1952 issue of the *Journal of Finance,* an article appeared that would forever alter the way investors think about risk when assembling their portfolios. In fact, this seminal work by Harry Markowitz provided the mechanism by which today's crop of junk-bond junkies have been able to finance the multibillion-dollar takeover bids that seem to have been the commonly accepted way of getting rich quick over the past decade. What Markowitz's mathematical treatment showed was that by mixing together a collection of risky stocks, one could actually assemble a portfolio whose overall risk was lower than that of any of its components—and without reducing the portfolio's total rate of return! To see how Markowitz created this silk purse from a collection of sows' ears, let's take a look at what we mean by risk in the investment context.

In everyday parlance, a "risky venture" is one whose outcome is highly uncertain. In other words, the greater the uncertainty, the greater the risk. But what is uncertainty? In the investment setting, uncertainty is simply the variability in possible returns. To illustrate the idea, consider the situation shown in Figure 4.1. Here we see plotted the frequency of monthly percentage returns from a hypothetical investment over a long period of time. The dashed line indicates the probability distribution of monthly rates of return for this investment. The way this curve spreads out away from its peak near 1 percent represents a measure of the uncertainty in the return, hence a measure of the riskiness of the investment.

Recalling our discussion from Chapter One, we see that this measure of risk is nothing more than the *standard deviation* of the distribution of returns. Thus, for the two investments depicted in Figure 4.2, each having the same average monthly return of 1 percent, we conclude that Investment 1 is far less risky than the alternative. This is because the spread of possible returns away from the mean for Investment 1 is much more tightly clustered than that of Investment 2. Consequently, we obtain the same average return from Investment 1 as

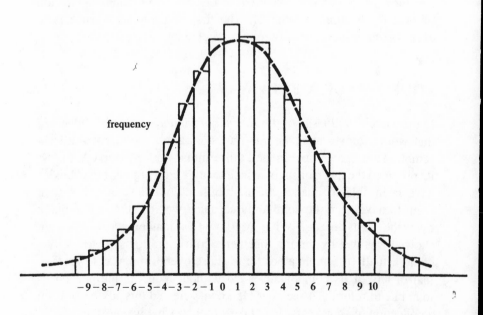

Figure 4.1. *Monthly percentage returns*

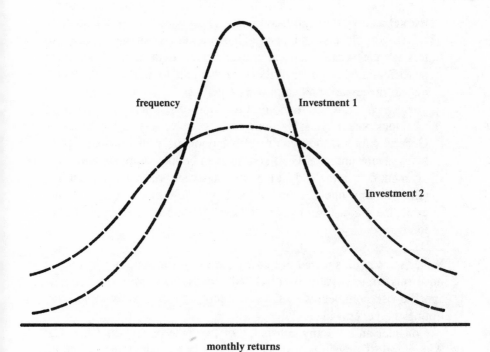

Figure 4.2. *Monthly returns from two alternative investments.*

from Investment 2, but with a smaller variation; hence, our return is more certain, thus less risky.

Not surprisingly, research shows that actual returns from stocks do not follow the perfectly symmetrical distributions shown in this figure. Furthermore, since no one objects to pleasant surprises, the only kind of risk the investor really cares about is the kind that involves uncertainty in the negative direction, i.e., losses. Nevertheless, actual patterns of returns are symmetrical enough that the standard deviation is still useful in providing us with some measure of insight into the behavior to be expected from different investments. With this idea of risk in mind, let's get back to portfolio selection and Markowitz's pioneering idea.

To understand the Markowitz theory, we first have to realize that the overall riskiness of any investment is a combination of two quite different components:

• *Market risk:* This is the kind of risk that is associated with the market as a whole, and has nothing to do with the specific stock in which you place your money. Thus market risk involves such factors as interest rate changes, unemployment data, rumors of war (or peace), and other things of this type that tend to influence all stocks, but not necessarily all in the *same* way.

• *Specific risk:* Here we find the kind of risk that's particular to the stock under consideration. For example, if you buy stock in General Motors, then you're also buying risks like gasoline price hikes, labor unrest at GM, shortages in copper supplies, bad management decisions, and all the other nasty surprises that can cut into GM's bottom line. Generally speaking, these kinds of risks do not affect the market as a whole, and are confined to a particular firm or industry.

What Markowitz showed is that by carefully selecting a portfolio of uncorrelated, or negatively correlated, stocks, it's possible to eliminate specific risk completely. Let's take a look at a simple example illustrating the general idea.

Consider an economy consisting of two enterprises: the Good Car Automobile Company and Speedy Wheels Bicycles, Inc. In times when oil prices are low, people prefer riding to pedaling so the sales and profits of Good Car soar—and so does its stock. But when problems flare up in the Middle East and the price of gasoline goes through the roof, bicycles come back into vogue and Speedy stock becomes a high-flier on the local exchange. Suppose the following table represents the rates of return per year for the two firms under the two sets of conditions:

	Good Car	Speedy
Low oil prices	50%	−25%
High oil prices	−25%	50%

Table 4.1. Annual rates of return for Good Car and Speedy

Let's assume that, on the average, half the years see high oil prices and half see low prices—i.e., the probability of seeing a high or a low oil price is $\frac{1}{2}$ for each year. Then an investor who buys Good Car stock would find that half the time the investment earned a 50 percent annual rate of return, while the other half of the time it lost 25 percent. Thus, the overall expected annual rate of return on Good Car is $\frac{1}{2}$ (50 percent) + $\frac{1}{2}$ (-25 percent) = $12\frac{1}{2}$ percent. Since the situations for Good Car and Speedy are perfectly symmetrical, another investor who bought Speedy instead of Good Car would also see an average $12\frac{1}{2}$ percent annual rate of return. But observe that investing in either of these stocks would be rather risky since the results are quite variable, and it's more than plausible that high or low oil prices could persist for several years—as we witnessed in the mid-1970s.

Now consider an investor who decides to buy stock in *both* companies. Suppose this individual purchases equal amounts of stock in Good Car and in Speedy. Note here that to maintain parity with the investor who put money into only one of the firms, this kind of investment would require twice as large a capital outlay as that of the single-firm investor. What kind of return does this shrewd operator receive? Well, in years of high oil prices, the return is 50 percent from Speedy and -25 percent from Good Car, or a net return of 25 percent on each dollar invested. These returns are exactly reversed in years of low prices for oil. Therefore, since each situation occurs half the time, the overall return is 25 percent, *regardless of what the oil price turns out to be*. But remember that twice as much money was put on the line, so the total *rate* of return on each dollar invested is only half this amount, or $12\frac{1}{2}$ percent of the total. So this investor receives the same average annual rate of return ($12\frac{1}{2}$ percent) as the investor who buys stock only in Speedy or in Good Car. Yet he has no risk whatsoever! By including both stocks in the portfolio, the investor has eliminated all risk without sacrificing anything by way of return. This is the essence of Markowitz's idea: *diversification*. And Markowitz showed that, by carefully diversifying the portfolio, the overall firm-specific risk could be reduced to zero.

It's clear, I think, that what makes the above diversification trick work is the fact that the fortunes of Speedy and Good Car are diametrically opposed: good times for one automatically means bad times for the other. This is exactly what we meant when we spoke earlier about the stocks in the portfolio being negatively correlated. The essence of diversification doesn't lie just in buying shares in more and more companies. For example, adding shares of the Try-A-Lemon car rental firm would do nothing toward reducing risk, since car rental companies would be subject to the same adverse impacts of high oil prices as the car manufacturers. In fact, filling up a portfolio with such *positively correlated* stocks would magnify risk rather than reduce it. Hence, the essence of proper risk management lies in creating a portfolio of negatively correlated, or at least uncorrelated, stocks.

Since diversification, or what is now termed *portfolio theory,* tells us that specific risk can be totally eliminated in a properly constructed portfolio, the only risk that we can hope to be compensated for assuming is risk associated with the market as a whole, i.e., the risk imposed simply by being in the market at all. So the question now becomes: Given a particular stock, how do we measure its market risk? That is, how sensitive is the particular stock's price to overall movements in the market? This is the real risk associated with holding the stock. And, according to the conventional financial wisdom, this is the only place where we can hope to look for better-than-market-average rates of return. To investigate this question, we have to dig in to one of the central concepts proposed for explaining the way stock prices are determined, the so-called *Capital Assets Pricing Model* (CAPM).

Suppose your aunt Polly from Peoria dies leaving you her dogs and cats, as well as an unexpected bequest of $10,000. Now this is not a sum to change your life, but it's certainly enough to be taken seriously as the nucleus of a nest egg to provide for your kindergarten-age daughter's college education. So your interest is in putting this money to work at hard labor for her without putting it at too great a risk. The task, as always, lies in balancing these two conflicting goals. After a bit of perusing the do-it-yourself finance literature, you talk to a broker who pushes the idea of a drawerful of Amalgamated Uranium Explorations shares as the solution to the problem of financing your daughter's fling with academia. But being a fiscal conservative, you also consult your banker, who assures you that doing anything other than placing the money in totally risk-free, long-term certificates of deposit constitutes negligence of a kind that ought to give nightmares to any decent, self-respecting parent. Putting these two conversations together, you come away with only one bit of real information: the idea that the key to your investment dilemma lies in assessing the "risk" of the AUE stock. So what to do?

Let's assume you're basically risk averse, yet willing to accept some modest level of risk for greater-than-average returns. The job at hand then is to determine some measure of how risky AUE is relative to the market as a whole. Suppose you go back and dig out your high-school algebra books and try to express a relationship between the net return for AUE versus the net return on a market portfolio (say the S&P 500) over some period of time. Here by *net return* we mean the rate of return on the stock minus the risk-free rate you could get by dumping Aunt Polly's bequest straight into CDs. Suppose, further, that you recall at least enough of your algebra to write a linear relation between the AUE return and the market return. You would then end up with an expression that looked like this:

$$Y = a + bX + e$$

where

Y = the net return from AUE over some period
X = the net return from the S&P 500 for the same period
e = an "error" variable, representing random fluctuations in return
a = a number representing AUE's general tendency to perform better or worse than the market, apart from returns attributable to market risk
b = a multiplier relating the return on AUE to the S&P 500 return

But now you recall the various random-walk theories and the EMH from your tour through the literature of finance. As a result, you conclude that the expected value of the error term e is zero (in accordance with the weak RWT), and that a must also be zero (by appeal to the EMH). Hence, you conclude that the volatility of AUE vis-à-vis the market as a whole comes solely from the multiplier b or, as it's termed in the world of finance, *beta*.

If you had gone through this simple exercise, you would have re-created what is, in essence, the CAPM. It's of particular importance to note the manner in which both the weak RWT and semistrong RWT (the EMH) were invoked in the derivation in order to eliminate the error term e and the drift term a, leaving us with only beta. Since the "beta way" has been so actively publicized and represents the very core of conventional thinking about possibilities for beating the market, let's look at it from another perspective.

Consider the ratio

$$\frac{\text{rate of return on AUE} \; - \; \text{risk-free rate}}{\text{return from S\&P 500} \; - \; \text{risk-free rate}}$$

This ratio equals some number, which we'll call β. Clearly, if the rate of return on AUE is the same as the rate from the market as a whole (the S&P 500 rate), then $\beta = 1$. But if AUE's rate is greater than that of the S&P 500, then we will see a value of β greater than 1. And β will be less than 1 if the AUE return lags behind that of the market. After a little thought, we conclude that this ratio β is identical to the beta obtained via the linear analysis carried out earlier.

But beta is not given as an intrinsic property of any stock; it must be computed from past price information. The usual manner of calculating beta involves comparing the price behavior of the stock with the behavior of the market over many time periods, then calculating the *average* relationship. So in real life beta is only a tendency, not a rule. The CAPM says that returns from any stock will be related to beta, i.e., to the market risk of the stock, not to its specific risk. However, the manner of computing beta suggests that it is not a very reliable measure of an *individual* stock's overall riskiness. The standard deviation of returns is still usually a better estimator of this kind of riskiness. The real value of beta resides in its ability to measure the amount of riskiness that the stock contributes to a diversified portfolio (one in which specific risk has been eliminated). Thus, beta represents the riskiness of a portfolio, and it is this risk that you hope to get a reward for accepting. And, in fact, according to the mainline financial gurus, this is the *only* reward that you can hope to receive above and beyond just riding along with the general market trend.

But as always in life, academic theories and practical reality fail to coincide, and there are reasons to be bearish on beta. As an initial foray into the realm of the avant-garde financial analysts, let's look at a couple of the indictments that have been leveled against beta.

- *Zero beta:* Portfolios with zero betas should yield a rate of return exactly equal to the risk-free rate. In practice this doesn't happen, and we find that the zero-beta rate exceeds the risk-free rate. This means that the market is rewarding something other than the beta measure of risk. Some, like Fisher Black, argue that this discrepancy is due to uncertainties about inflation. But the matter is still far from settled.
- *High beta:* It turns out that high-beta portfolios don't achieve returns as high as would be suggested by their level of beta. Thus the additional risk associated with such portfolios is only partially rewarded by the market. Moreover, such portfolios achieve higher

rates of return only in the long run; in the short run, they simply exaggerate the market trend.

• *Instability:* If we were to plot the best straight-line fit to measure the relationship between market returns and returns from our portfolio, the slope of this line would exactly equal the quantity beta. Simple mathematical arguments show that this slope is notoriously sensitive to the empirical data used to generate the best straight-line fit. Thus, values of beta computed from past price data can vary wildly, depending upon the accuracy of the data.

Since the terminology of financial markets has been coming rather fast and heavy, before the technicians and fundamentalists really start to battle it out, on the next page there is a short glossary of terms that the reader can use as a reference point as we wend our way through the theories and arguments that follow.

The CAPM and beta represented the distilled wisdom of the academic finance community up until a decade or so ago. But the kinds of problems just noted about beta, coupled with a host of other market anomalies, suggested to financial analysts that there was something inherently incomplete (or just plain wrong) about the picture of the market created by the various forms of the RWT and the CAPM. So let's take a look at some of the things that both radical fundamentalists and technicians have been saying recently about the likelihood of beating the market.

THE INFOMANIACS

Somewhere in the bowels of Broadway, the manuscript of a play bearing the title *Bull Market* is making its rounds from producer to producer looking for its moment in the spotlight. Aside from its somewhat offbeat subject matter, centered on wheeling and dealing in the pits and on the street, this play is probably indistinguishable from thousands of others aspiring to the roar of the greasepaint. Indistinguishable, that is, except for its author. This particular playwright was no neophyte Sam Shepard or Neil Simon struggling for recognition in some dingy, cold-water, East Village walk-up. Quite the contrary. The creator of *Bull Market* was probably more successful in dealing with the real-life aspects of his play's topic than almost any other playwright I can think of. You see, this hopeful man-about-Broadway was none

Beta   A measure of the sensitivity of the rates of return on a stock or portfolio compared with the rates of return on the market as a whole

Capital Assets Pricing Model (CAPM)   A mathematical model explaining how stocks should be priced, based on their relative riskiness in comparison with the return on risk-free assets

Diversification   The purchase of a group of stocks whose returns are uncorrelated in an attempt to eliminate specific risk

Efficient market hypothesis (EMH)   The hypothesis that the market price of a stock reflects all publicly available information and adjusts instantly to any new information; often used as an alternate name for the semistrong random-walk theory

Fundamental analysis   Analysis of stock value grounded in basic factors such as corporate earnings, management quality, research and development, and the like

Market risk   Risk caused by factors affecting the prices of virtually all stocks, although in different proportions; sometimes called *systematic risk*

Semistrong random-walk theory   The hypothesis that no publicly available information is of any value in forecasting future prices

Specific risk   Risk that is specific to an industry or firm; sometimes called *unsystematic risk*

Stock index   An aggregated measure of the state of stock prices in the market taken as a whole; examples include the Dow-Jones Industrial Average (DJIA) and the Standard & Poor's 500 (S&P 500)

Strong random-walk theory   The hypothesis that no information of any kind, public or private, is of any value in forecasting future prices

Technical analysis   The study of relationships among stock market variables such as price levels, trading volume, and price movements in order to gain insight into the future price movements of a stock

Weak random-walk theory   The hypothesis that past stock prices are of no value in forecasting future prices because all price information merely reflects responses to information coming into the market at random

other than the late Arnold Bernhard, founder of *The Value Line Investment Survey,* which is probably the most successful living counterexample to the cherished efficient-market hypothesis.

Following his graduation from Williams College as a Phi Beta Kappa with a degree in English, Bernhard began writing theater criticism for *Time* magazine and the *New York Post* back in the Roaring Twenties. But he was soon attracted to the market, taking a position as an account executive with Moody's Investors Service. Unfortunately, he got caught in the middle of a lawsuit between Moody's and one of its major clients. So instead of trading on the street, Bernhard was out on the street—and this in 1931 just as the Depression was getting into full swing. Luckily, some of his customers stuck by him, asking that he continue to manage their money. This led to a fifteen-year career as a successful investment counselor.

Shortly after the Second World War, Bernhard started *The Value Line Investment Survey,* a newsletter in which he attempted to formalize his conviction that there had to be some way of establishing a stock's intrinsic value. His ultimate weapon, the cross-sectional analysis, was incorporated into the *Survey* in April 1965, and to this day forms the heart of the formulas used to obtain the Value Line rankings. Let's pause for a moment to look at the general principles that the Value Line staff uses in arriving at its estimate of a stock's value.

As noted, the key ingredient in the Value Line rating scheme is cross-sectional analysis: the comparison of one stock against all others at a point in time, rather than against its own individual performance over time. Once this cross-sectional analysis has been carried out, the top one hundred stocks of the seventeen hundred or so that Value Line ranks are labeled Group 1: the *primo* picks. The remaining stocks are then assigned to one or another of four lower categories. While the ranking scheme itself is company confidential, the basic components are well known: 50 percent of a stock's rating is determined by *relative earnings* and *relative price,* i.e., earnings and price over the last twelve months, divided by average earnings and price of all Value Line stocks over the same period. Another 25 percent of the rating is attributable to *earnings momentum,* the year-to-year change in quarterly earnings per share compared to that of all Value Line stocks. Finally, the remaining 25 percent is given by the *earnings surprise,* a factor added or subtracted in accordance with the extent to which the stock's quarterly earnings exceed or fall short of the Value Line analysts' projections.

These components are recomputed weekly and published in *The Value Line Investment Survey*. Figure 4.3 shows how the various Value Line groups have fared over the period from April 1965 to December 1989. Here we see that if an investor had juggled a portfolio so that it never contained anything but Group 1 stocks, the gain would have been a whopping 17,459 percent, not counting dividends, transaction costs, or taxes. This represents a compounded annual rate of nearly 23 percent. If we compare this rate of return with the market over this same period, we find that the DJIA grew 202 percent, or at an annual compounded rate of just under 3 percent! And this is not a phenomenon confined to the American markets. Value Line has found that pretty much the same formula works as well in Tokyo as in New York. The only exception is that the weight assigned to price momentum is neg-

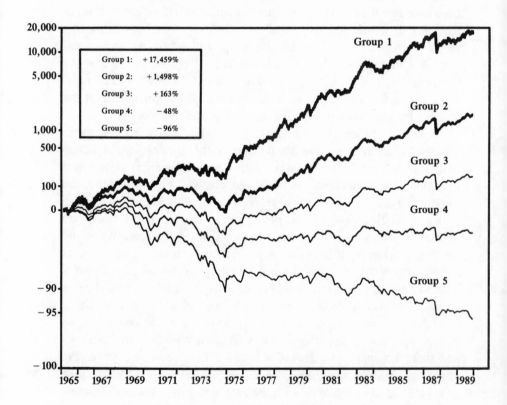

Figure 4.3. *The Value Line results from April 1965 to December 1989*

ative instead of positive, reflecting the fact that the Japanese tend to buy on weakness rather than on strength.

With this kind of record, no one can doubt that a strategy of investing in the Value Line Group 1 stocks constitutes a method for vastly outperforming the market. In fact, it's rather easy to show that it's not even necessary to form a portfolio including all one hundred Group 1 securities. A collection of about fifteen of them would be sufficiently diversified to duplicate the overall performance of the Group 1 collection. Moreover, when we look at the data that goes into making up the Value Line rankings, we see that it involves only things like corporate earnings, stock price history, and other publicly available information. This fact is a direct contradiction to the semistrong random-walk theory (the EMH), which states that no such publicly available information can form the basis for a strategy that will consistently outperform the market. We'll come back a bit later and look at the arguments given by the academics for how one might reconcile the EMH with the Value Line results. But first let's look at a couple of other anomalies that throw the conventional wisdom about beating the market into doubt.

Probably the most common standard of a stock's value is its price-to-earnings ratio (P/E), i.e., its price divided by its annual earnings per share. If the EMH is true, then there should be no difference whatsoever in rates of return attributable to P/Es, since both prices and earnings are publicly available information. Studies have repeatedly shown that this is just not the case. One of the first such studies was carried out by Sanjoy Basu in 1977 on stocks from the New York Stock Exchange over the period April 1957–March 1971. In his study, Basu constructed several different portfolios based upon P/E ratios, with Portfolio A having the highest P/E and Portfolio E the lowest. Moreover, to eliminate any possible bias resulting from the inclusion of companies that lost money (with a consequent negative or even infinite P/E), Basu also considered a Portfolio A*, which was the same as Portfolio A but with the money-losing firms removed. The results of his study are displayed in Table 4.2.

In the table, the term *excess return* is used to represent the difference between total return and the risk-free rate of return available at the time (U.S. Treasury bills). The conclusion of the Basu study is evident: High P/E stocks are clearly associated with lower returns than those obtained from low P/Es, the difference between the two being about 7 percent a year. Moreover, this difference cannot be explained by

Portfolios	A	A*	B	C	D	E
Median P/E	35.8	30.5	19.1	15.0	12.8	9.8
Average annual rate of return	9.3%	9.5%	9.3%	11.7%	13.6%	16.3%
Excess return	5.6%	5.8%	5.6%	8.0%	9.9%	12.6%
Beta	1.11	1.06	1.04	0.97	0.94	0.99

Table 4.2. Performance by P/E on the NYSE, April 1957–March 1971

risk, as the low P/E portfolios had even lower risk factors (lower betas) than the portfolios of high P/E stocks. Thus, we can only conclude that investors seem to overvalue the chances of high P/E issues systematically, while at the same time exaggerating the weaknesses of the low P/E performers. In short, there is a systematic bias of exactly the kind that the EMH says cannot exist. Just to show that the "low P/E" strategy is not an isolated singularity when it comes to EMH-threatening market anomalies, let's take a look at another well-chronicled example—the case of small companies.

About ten years ago, Rolf Banz and Marc Reinganum of the University of Chicago began to investigate the hypothesis that the stock of small companies does better than that of larger ones. In this study company size was measured by market capitalization, i.e., the market price per share times the number of shares outstanding. To test this idea, Reinganum, in a famous study published in 1983, took all the stocks traded on the NYSE and the AMEX, grading them by size into ten portfolios. He did this at the beginning of each year from 1963 to 1980. Table 4.3 shows the return obtained over the period for each of these portfolios, where the return is calculated by averaging the return from each portfolio for each year.

Portfolio	P1	P2	P3	P4	P5
Average return	32.77%	23.51%	22.98%	20.24%	19.08%
Portfolio	P6	P7	P8	P9	P10
Average return	18.30%	15.64%	14.24%	13.00%	9.47%

Table 4.3. Reinganum's small-firm effect study, 1983

The size effect displayed in this study is startling: The returns from the smallest firms (Portfolio P1) were almost triple those of the largest companies on the exchanges (Portfolio P10). We note also that the relation between size and return is perfectly consistent: When we move from a smaller to a larger capitalization group, the returns decline. It's of some interest to note that the difference in levels of capitalization between the largest and smallest firms was substantial. The average capitalization for the largest P10 firms was around $1 billion, while the average at the other end for the P1 companies was a meager $5 million. Nevertheless, the size effect persists throughout the entire range of capitalizations, so even investors who don't want to fool around with nickel-and-dime companies can still profit from assembling a portfolio from one of the larger-capitalization groups. While we'll come back later to the arguments of those who pooh-pooh the small-firm effect, it's worth noting here that the small-stock portfolios did have a higher beta (greater risk) than those of the large firms, suggesting that at least some of the effect is just the familiar risk premium considered earlier.

These anomalies—Value Line, low P/E, small firms—are all based upon fundamental data involving prices, earnings, capitalization, and so on. And each of them casts a very long and dark shadow over that talisman of the mainline academic, the efficient market hypothesis. While these anomalies give succor to the fundamentalists, they are far from being the only inconsistencies that have been observed in the market. Now let's turn the floor over to the technicians and give them the opportunity to show you a few of the more puzzling anomalies to be seen from their side of the street.

WHERE HAVE ALL THE GURUS GONE?

Each year, the Financial Traders Association sponsors a tournament in which traders compete with monitored portfolios in different categories (stocks, options, and others) over a period of several months. In 1984 the Options Division of the tournament was won by Robert Prechter, who increased the value of his portfolio by 444.4 percent in four months! To gain some perspective on the magnitude of this achievement, consider that the second-highest gain in this category was only 84 percent, and over 80 percent of the competitors actually *lost* money. Prechter, a former drummer in a rock band and a man who holds a psychology degree from Yale, described his victory with characteristic modesty when he stated that ''there are people who hate the idea that anyone can be successful at predicting the market. I just try to avoid them. But sometimes you walk out on the dusty streets at noon, and there's some guy standing there with his guns.''

Given his margin of victory, as well as his previous record as a Wall Street pundit, Prechter had his fifteen minutes as a celebrity during the bull-market price runup prior to the Black Monday crash of October 19, 1987. During that time he was busy issuing regular guru-like pronouncements on the state of the market to his avid followers from a rural redoubt somewhere in the wilds of Georgia. But what exactly is the method that Prechter espouses when he claims to be able to predict market movements? Interestingly enough, Prechter's method is nothing new. In fact, it's an idea that's been around for fifty years or so, having been resurrected by the insight and promotional genius of Prechter under the rubric of the *Elliott Wave Theory*. Let's take a look at how it works.

Ralph N. Elliott was a Los Angeles accountant who lost part of his savings on Wall Street in 1929. In frail health and out of work during the Depression, Elliott had plenty of free time to wonder where his money had gone when the market crashed on Black Tuesday. He became convinced that there is a repetitive pattern that market indexes like the DJIA go through, and that an understanding of these cycles would enable the alert investor to see things like October 1929 (and 1987) coming and get out of their way. Of course, to say that the Dow moves in cycles is not really saying much. What we need to know is the *kind* of cycle that the market goes through. And it is just this sort of information that Elliott Wave Theory advocates claim their brand of medicine provides.

While there's no room here for us to enter into a detailed analysis of the Elliott theory, the basic idea is rather simple to describe. The fundamental pattern upon which the entire Elliott edifice rests is shown in Figure 4.4. Here we see a sequence of up and down price movements, constituting a complete cycle of eight waves. The reader can think of these waves as being the ups and downs of a market indicator like the DJIA. Waves 1, 3, and 5 are called *impulse* waves, while Waves 2 and 4 are termed *corrective* waves. Thus, one complete Elliott cycle consists of eight waves divided into two distinct phases: Numbered phases are in the direction of the main trend, while lettered phases move against the trend.

Elliott found that, following completion of the above cycle, a sim-

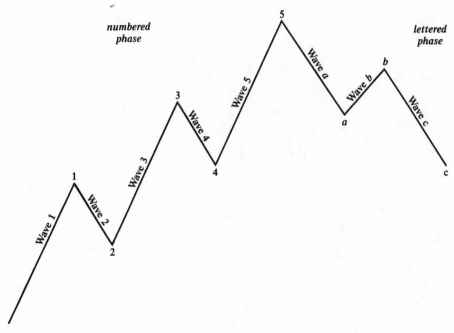

Figure 4.4. *The basic Elliott wave pattern*

ilar but higher-level cycle began: another five-wave up pattern followed by another down pattern of three waves correcting the up pattern. The overall pattern is shown in Figure 4.5, while Figure 4.6 carries the idea through one entire market cycle. Figure 4.5 shows that each of the numbered and lettered phases is actually a wave itself, but of one degree higher than its component waves. Incidentally, the numbers shown in figure 4.6 for the bull and bear cycles are the number of cycle waves, primary waves, intermediate waves, and so on present in the overall movement.

Prechter has summarized the basic tenets of Elliott wave formation as follows:

1. Action is followed by reaction.
2. Impulse waves subdivide into five waves of lower degree, while corrective waves subdivide into three waves of lower degree.
3. A complete cycle consists of an eight-wave movement (five up and

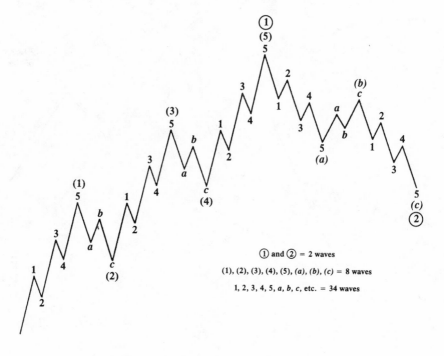

Figure 4.5. *A major Elliott wave pattern*

three down), which then becomes two subdivisions of the wave of next higher degree.

4. The time frame does not enter into the pattern, i.e., the waves may be stretched or compressed without losing the underlying pattern.

How many cycles, subcycles, and sub-subcycles are there? According to Elliott, there are at least nine identifiable cycles beginning with the Grand Supercycle at the top and going on down to the most microscopic Sub-Minuette cycle at the bottom. The complete market cycle shown in Figure 4.6 is the third cycle from the top in this classification, being just a subcycle of both the Grand Supercycle and the Supercycle.

The diagram in Figure 4.7 shows how the Elliott Wave Theory works in practice. Here the various cycles and subcycles are marked for the DJIA over the period 1919–1978. To close out our brief tour of Elliottland, the reader might be interested to know that Prechter

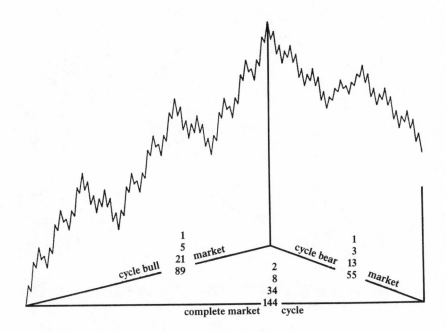

Figure 4.6. *A complete market cycle*

claimed in 1985 that the Cycle Wave V bull market shown in Figure 4.7 will peak with the DJIA near 3686. More recently, he and his collaborator A. J. Frost have revised this estimate downward to 3250, at which point they see the DJIA heading south in a catastrophic bear market lasting until 1993 or 1994. So the good news is that with the Dow currently at only 2365 (in autumn 1990), there's still lots of room left for Elliott fans to make a market killing. The bad news, however, is that following this peak, Elliott Wave Theory predicts a prolonged bear market the like of which will make Black Monday and Tuesday look like White Christmas. But the Elliott Wave Theory is not the only technical finery that's been proposed as a counter to the EMH and RWT. Let's look at some ideas in which, unlike the Elliott theory, timing is the central ingredient.

The traditional chartist methods against which the weak RWT argues involve plotting stock prices or indexes as a time series of data.

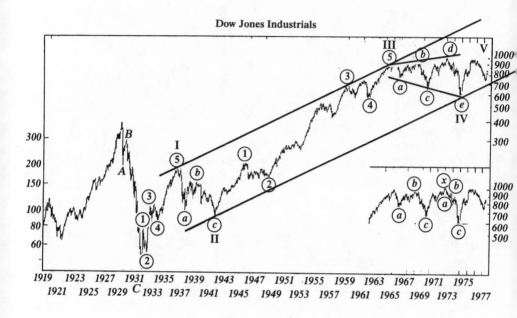

Figure 4.7. *The DJIA and Elliott from 1919 onward*

The chartist then looks for characteristic patterns in these plots. Some typical patterns of the kind that such technical analysts look for are displayed in Figure 4.8. In these patterns, the ends of the vertical bars represent the high and low levels of the price during the period covered by the bar, typically a daily or weekly time-frame. While conventional technical analysts are convinced that the road to market riches is buried in the meanderings of such patterns, as Burton Malkiel, former dean of the Yale School of Organization and Management, notes, "I have never seen a successful technician yet."

To underscore his point, Malkiel tells the story of an experiment he conducted with some of his students. The experiment involved a hy-

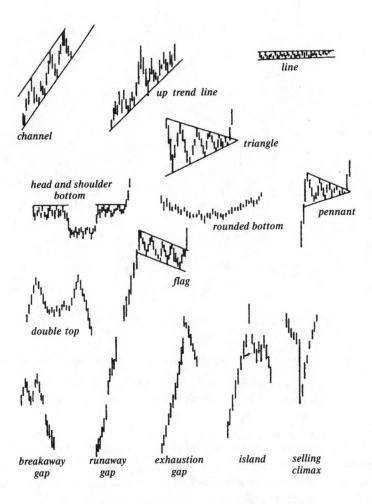

Figure 4.8. *Typical chartist patterns*

pothetical stock that initially sold for $50 per share. To construct a time series for the stock's price changes, Malkiel told the students to flip a fair coin. Heads would send the stock's closing price up half a point, while tails would send it down by the same amount. An actual chart resulting from this experiment is shown in Figure 4.9. Following the experiment, Malkiel showed this "chart" to a technician friend, who insisted on knowing the name of the company, frantically stating, "We've got to buy immediately. This pattern's a classic." But even

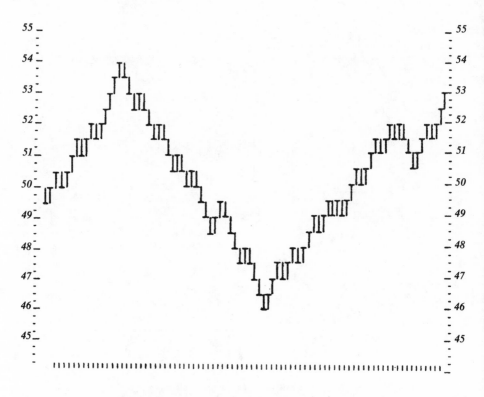

Figure 4.9. *A hypothetical stock price "chart"*

though there's not a shred of evidence to support these traditional charting methods, there are a variety of other time-based patterns associated with market behavior that are not so easy to dismiss. Let's look at a couple of them.

One of the most successful technical strategies for beating the market is the so-called *January Barometer*. This strategy is based upon a very simple principle: As January goes, so goes the market for the rest of the year. In other words, if the market is up for January, then it will be up for the year as well. Between 1950 and 1985, this technical indicator was right an astounding thirty-one of thirty-six times—nearly a 90 percent success rate. Even the Super Bowl Indicator has to respect this "January effect."

In an attempt to make sense out of why January should be so important in presaging what the market will do in the coming year, Yale Hirsch looked at the market performance all the way back to the turn of the century. He discovered the following remarkable fact: Prior to 1934, the January Barometer worked only an anemic nineteen times out of thirty-three. But following 1933, all the way up to 1985 when the study ended, the success rate was a phenomenal forty out of fifty. Digging just a bit deeper, Hirsch offered a very plausible explanation for the dramatic change: The "lame-duck amendment" to the Constitution enacted in 1933. Prior to this amendment, the Congress elected in November didn't actually take office until December of the following year, more than one year after its election. As a result of the amendment, legislators now take office only a few weeks after their election, with the result that we now see many significant events affecting the economy squeezed into the month of January.

Another kind of technical trading scheme that has paid above-average dividends to its followers has been the so-called *Monthly Effect*. This indicator shows that the average return for stocks is positive only on days *immediately before and during* the first half of the calendar month, and is essentially zero for days during the last half of the month. As evidence, consider that during the period 1963–1981 *all* of the market's cumulative gain occurred just before and during the first halves of months, with the second halves contributing absolutely nothing to the advance. The effect is graphically depicted in Figure 4.10 using the value-weighted S&P 500 index over the given period. Subsequent studies have shown that this effect is real and cannot be attributed to biases like the January effect or the concentration of dividend payments in the first or last half of the month.

It turns out that there are many such technical indicators like the January Barometer and the Monthly Effect—all based on trading schemes involving certain days of the week, parts of the year, political changes, and the like—each of which seems to outperform the market averages! Putting this kind of empirical evidence from the technicians together with that presented earlier by the fundamentalists, it's hard to avoid the conclusion that there's something dramatically wrong with the EMH and its built-in assertion that above-average performance can be achieved only by taking above-average risks. So let's take a harder look at the assumptions underlying the EMH in order to see where the weak links in the chain might be hiding.

The basic premises upon which EMH is based can be summarized concisely in the following four principles:

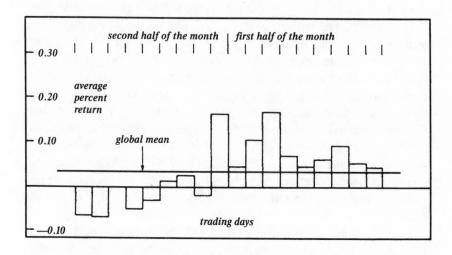

Figure 4.10. *The Monthly Effect over the period 1963–1981*

1. Information is processed without error or misinterpretation.
2. Information is processed instantaneously.
3. All information relevant to stock prices is taken into account.
4. Investors act rationally.

Let's take a skeptic's-eye view of each of these assumptions.

• *Error-free processing:* In an assessment of the performance of major institutional pension funds during the period 1966–1975, *Fortune* magazine found that these funds would have been worth at least $13 billion more if their managers had done only as well as the S&P 500 over the same period. In short, a buy-and-hold strategy would have enriched the contributors to these funds far in excess of what they received by way of results from the "professional management" supplied by their fund's caretakers. This result is flatly impossible to reconcile with the EMH, particularly its assumption regarding error-free information processing.

• *Instantaneous processing:* One of the market anomalies we didn't discuss earlier involves the so-called Sweet SUEs, standardized unexpected corporate earnings. Basically, this works in the following way: The analyst uses various statistical tricks to extrapolate past earnings trends into the future. These extrapolations are then compared with actual earnings to see if the earnings are unexpected. The unexpected earnings are then adjusted (standardized) to account for volatility patterns in that stock's earning history. In general, the stock of a firm showing a high SUE tends to shoot upward for obvious reasons. Studies show that the process of market adjustment to SUEs is not quite what the EMH predicts, as the revaluation process of the stock goes on far longer than the EMH claims it should. This observation is prima facie evidence that information doesn't get around in the market nearly as fast as the EMH says it must.

• *Every bit of relevant information is included:* Each of the anomalies we've considered puts the lie to this assumption, since the very existence of systematic methods for outperforming the market implies that the market is rewarding something that's not contained in the actual information processed. Thus it's manifestly evident from this ever-growing list of anomalies that all relevant information is not included in the market's assessment of a given stock's chances.

• *Investors act rationally:* Without a doubt, this assumption is the weakest link in the whole EMH chain. What does it mean for an investor to act rationally? The commonsense answer involves things like collecting and processing information in an unbiased fashion and making decisions independent of the decisions of others, as well as considering the relative returns and risks from alternative investments and choosing among them accordingly. The observational evidence shows time and again that investors just don't act rationally, regardless of what the professors say. If this is indeed the case, then you might well ask: Why do economists and professors of finance persist in using this outmoded concept of human behavior as a cornerstone of their theories? The short answer is that, without this kind of assumption, it's impossible to produce any definite theoretical, i.e., academic, model "explaining" the way stock prices are set. The long answer cuts right to the heart of what we mean by an *explanation* of stock price fluctuations. So without further ado, let's move on to a much more detailed look at this matter of rationality and the market.

NOT SO GREAT EXPECTATIONS

Item: In the Ford Foundation's annual report for 1966, foundation president McGeorge Bundy chided the portfolio managers of university endowment funds, saying that over the long run excessive caution had cost the universities much more than excessive risk taking. In a check of the Ford Foundation's own investments over the decade preceding Bundy's admonition, *Fortune* magazine found that the foundation's portfolio gained 35 percent as opposed to a 63 percent gain for the DJIA over the same period.

Item: At the Third Annual Institutional Investor Conference in New York in 1970, the moneymen voted overwhelmingly for National Student Marketing as the most promising stock for the coming year. Within five months the price of NSM fell by over 95 percent.

Item: In a 1973 survey, *Institutional Investor* magazine asked 160 portfolio managers from around the country to pick their five "best buys" for the coming year. Although several hundred stocks were mentioned, the top ten received strong support from most of the group. During the next year, the top ten lost 40.4 percent versus a drop of only 17.4 percent in the S&P 500 over the same period.

What each of these sad stories has in common (and the list could be multiplied several hundredfold) is the convergence of the investment community on a course of action that turned out to be markedly, even disastrously, wrong. These sorry episodes set out in the strongest possible terms the kind of irrational behavior displayed by presumably sober, responsible, shrewd financial operators entrusted with the fortunes, pensions, and livelihoods of those whose assets are under their control. The investment adviser David Dreman has called the kind of mass psychology responsible for these fiascos "groupthink," and it forms the basis for a good bit of what's wrong with the hallowed efficient-market hypothesis. But to see why irrationality of this sort deals such a damaging blow to the EMH, we must dig a bit deeper into a few of the technical foundations supporting the notion of market efficiency. To do this, let's go back about thirty years to the School of Industrial Management at what is now Carnegie-Mellon University in Pittsburgh.

Herbert Simon is an economist, computer scientist, and psychologist at CMU, and a man who was awarded the Nobel Prize in Economics for his pioneering work in developing many of the concepts underlying what is now known as management science. In the late 1950s Simon was deeply concerned with the issue of decisionmaking, in particular the amount of information that a decisionmaker could effectively assimilate during the process of arriving at a course of action. As a result of these deliberations, Simon came to the concept of *bounded rationality,* which stresses that an individual has only limited computational abilities when it comes to making a decision. Simon assumed that economic agents can never make truly optimal decisions because they are inherently limited in the amount of information that they can process prior to having to make a decision. So for Simon, all decisions, economic or otherwise, generally lead to a nonoptimal "satisficing" kind of behavior.

At the very same time he was developing these ideas of satisficing behavior, Simon was also collaborating with his CMU colleague John Muth on a book about inventory management. But quite independently of this collaborative venture, Muth was himself working on a theory of the behavior of economic agents that would directly contradict the ideas of Simon. While Simon was arguing that economic models put too much emphasis on rational (i.e., optimizing) behavior on the part of the economic actors, Muth claimed just the opposite. According to Muth, existing economic models did not assume *enough* rational behavior. This view led to Muth's developing the idea that has now come to be known as *rational expectations.*

The basic thrust of rational expectations is the observation that all economic decisions are taken not only on the basis of past information, but also on the decisionmaker's expectations for the future. Muth's aim was somehow to bring together these subjectively determined estimates of the future with the expected outcomes arising from the presumed objectively determined, but unknown, probability distributions actually governing the possible outcomes. Before we see how Muth went about establishing this connection and what it means for the EMH, let's look at the rational expectations idea itself in a bit more detail.

Consider an economic system of some kind, e.g., the stock market, a national economy, an open peasant market, or whatever. Let's suppose this system behaves in some stochastic fashion that can be described only in a probabilistic sense. In other words, we can assign only probabilities, not certainties, as to what the system will be doing next. But we do grant that the probability distribution governing these doings definitely exists and is fixed—i.e., there is a true, *objective* law that governs the way the economic system behaves. Now let's imagine we have an economic agent who interacts with the system—an individual investor in the stock market, for instance. This investor does not know the true probability distribution for the system dynamics. As a consequence, the investor must form his or her own private, *subjective* estimate of what the market is going to be doing next. Suppose our investor is interested in the future behavior of some market variable, e.g., tomorrow's DJIA. Using the subjectively determined probability law for the market, the investor estimates the DJIA. The market itself, using its objective probabilistic law of behavior, moves to the new, *true* value of the DJIA. The rational expectations hypothesis states that, *on the average,*

the subjective estimate of the DJIA = the true value of the DJIA

Let's illustrate this hypothesis of rationality with a simple example due to Steven Sheffrin.

Suppose we have a wheat farmer who faces the dilemma of how much wheat to plant. The farmer knows that the sale price of the wheat at harvest time will depend upon many factors. But in order to decide today how much wheat to plant, our farmer must estimate the price that will prevail in the autumn when it comes time to sell the harvest. Thus he assumes that there is a true, but unknown, probability law governing how prices will be set on the wheat market. This is the law that governs the outcome of uncertain things like the weather, the success of the Russian grain harvest, and government subsidy policies, as well as the planting decisions made by other farmers. And it is exactly these unknown quantities that will ultimately determine the actual price of wheat in the fall. Not being privy to this real law of the wheat market price-setting mechanism, our farmer has to create his own subjective probability distribution based upon his own insight and information. He then uses this subjective probability law to make an estimate of what the wheat price will turn out to be. How does he process the information available in order to do this?

If the farmer is a believer in rational expectations, he asks himself the following question: What price can I expect that will make everyone correct, on average, if we all anticipate that price? He then makes his planting decision on the basis of this estimate of the price. So the farmer's estimate of the price is rational if his anticipated price leads to an actual price that will, on the average, coincide with his expectation. Thus the farmer's rational expectation will diverge from the true price level only because of some unpredictable uncertainty in the wheat price-setting mechanism.

Since the idea of rational expectations is so central to an understanding of the EMH, let's express it more formally in the language of elementary probability theory. Suppose we call I_t the information available at time period t, and let's imagine we want to form an expectation (best estimate) of the value of some random quantity X like the wheat price at the next time period $t+1$, i.e., we want to estimate the quantity X_{t+1}. Since the information I_t is available, the estimate of any rational person will, of course, reflect (be conditioned on) the actual content of this information set. So let's denote our conditional expectation of the value of X_{t+1} by $E[X_{t+1} \mid I_t]$. We can now think of this conditional expectation as nothing more than our forecast of the random variable X_{t+1}, and write the forecast error as

$$\text{forecast error} = e_{t+1} = X_{t+1} - E[X_{t+1} \mid I_t]$$

There are two important properties of the above forecast error e_{t+1}. The first is simply that the conditional expectation of the forecast error is zero. This follows from the obvious fact that at time t we know what forecast we made (it's part of the information set I_t), so that the conditional expectation is just the forecast itself, which is known with certainty. Expressed mathematically, $E[e_{t+1} \mid I_t] = 0$. But forecasts should not just have an expected error of zero. They should also be uncorrelated with any information available to the decisionmaker at the time the forecast is made. If this were not the case, then whatever correlation exists could be incorporated into the forecast, thus improving the estimate. Note that this does *not* mean that the forecast is independent of the available information, which would be nonsense, but rather that there is no systematic bias in the forecast attributable to the way the information is processed. This point is subtle, but shows the difference between correlation and independence.

The rational expectations hypothesis connects the foregoing conditional expectations of the system variables (like X) generated by using the true probability distributions (buried in the expectation operator $E[\ .\ ]$, with subjective estimates of those same variables made by the economic agents interacting with the system. If we let $X_{t+1}^{\exp}$ denote this subjectively derived estimate, then we can express the entire rational expectations idea compactly in the following equation in which the agent's guestimate appears on the left side of the equation, while the true conditional estimate is on the right:

$$\{\text{subjective expectation} = X_{t+1}^{\text{exp}}\} = \{E[X_{t+1} \mid I_t] = \text{true conditional expectation}\}$$

While there have been several aguments put forward for why the rational expectations idea may rest on shaky ground, I'll resist the temptation to go into them here and instead move on now to the main order of business—showing that the efficient market hypothesis is nothing more than the rational expectations assumption in disguise.

Before jumping in and tackling the semistrong random-walk theory (the EMH), let's first show how the idea of rational expectations addresses the weak RWT. Recall that the weak RWT states that price changes follow a random (i.e., unpredictable) pattern, and that no amount of information on prices alone will allow development of a trading scheme that's better than just buy and hold. In other words, if there were a pattern in the price changes, technicians would discover the pattern and act on it. So if a stock was going to go up $10 tomorrow, it would go up $10 today.

Thinking of this argument in terms of conditional expectations, we can rephrase the weak random-walk theory as follows:

today's price = the conditional expectation of tomorrow's price

Therefore, the change in price between today and tomorrow is analogous to a forecast error. Mathematical properties of forecast errors then ensure that the error (i.e., the price change) is uncorrelated with any available price information. This is just another way of saying that past price information is of no help in predicting future price changes, i.e., the weak RWT. With the weak RWT settled, now let's move up to consideration of the semistrong RWT from the point of view of rational expectations.

The basic assumption underlying market efficiency is that financial markets use the true conditional probability distribution in determining prices. What does this assumption actually mean in everyday terms? Basically, it says that there is a definite probability distribution governing the future price of a security, and that this distribution reflects all the available information. As it stands, this hypothesis is untestable. In order to test it, we need to make some specific assumptions about the two main components of the hypothesis: (1) the information set, and (2) the price determination procedure.

As for assumptions about the information set (what we earlier denoted I_t), the assumptions are those with which we are already familiar:

- *Weak:* I_t consists solely of past price data.
- *Semistrong:* I_t is past prices plus any other publicly available information.
- *Strong:* I_t includes information held only by a subset of the market.

When it comes to assumptions regarding price-setting mechanisms, the fun really begins since there are in principle an endless variety of schemes that one could dream up. However, the finance literature has focused on three schemes that combine the virtues of on-the-street plausibility with mathematical tractability.

Since the one thing that both the brokers and the professors seem to be able to agree on is that stock prices ultimately depend on some concept of value, let's follow the custom and agree to measure price by return on our investment. In other words, we agree that we're willing to pay a higher price for an asset from which we expect to receive a greater rate of return on the money invested. For stocks, the conventional wisdom suggests that this return is essentially determined by the anticipated future flow of dividends versus the current selling price. Let's use the symbol Z_t to represent the return from purchasing a particular stock at time t, while E, as always, denotes the expectation operation. With this idea in mind, now let's turn to a consideration of some price-setting procedures.

- *Positive expected returns, $E[Z_t] > 0$:* Under this price-setting assumption, strategies based on short selling or trading will always be dominated by the strategy of buy and hold. *Short selling* means selling a stock you don't own in the hope that the price will go down and you can then buy it for delivery later at a lower price. This strategy is tantamount to betting that the expected return will be negative (the price will fall), while *not holding,* i.e., trading, is giving up sure gains, and is thus irrational. Consequently, we can reject the joint hypothesis of positive expected returns and EMH if there is a market-outperforming strategy that involves either short selling or not holding. We have already seen several strategies of this sort, so it appears rather likely that either the EMH or the idea of positive expected returns (or both) is seriously off the track.

• *Constant expected returns, $E[Z_t]$ = a constant:* In this situation of constant returns, any correlation in the past history of returns is an indicator of market inefficiency. Why? Simply because theoretical properties of conditional expectations imply that the difference between expected returns and actual returns is uncorrelated with past information; if it were not, then it would be possible to use this correlation to improve the returns, contradicting the constant returns hypothesis.

Several studies have been carried out to test the joint hypothesis of constant returns and EMH, meeting with varying degrees of success. The essence of all these tests is to look for significant autocorrelations in the returns from various types of securities like stocks, bonds, T-bills, and so forth. In some of these markets the tests appeared to support the joint EMH/constant returns hypothesis, while there are substantial deviations for other types of securities. Of considerable interest for us is the fact that in those studies in which deviations appeared, the authors almost without exception retained the EMH half of the hypothesis, arguing that the deviations were attributable to the assumption of constant returns. If nothing else, these studies show the tenacity with which academics cling to the concept of market efficiency.

• *CAPM:* We have already looked at this kind of asset-pricing scheme in some detail, so it suffices here just to observe that the CAPM implies that, in an efficient market, fluctuations in returns that are not correlated with the market can be diversified away. Furthermore, the market pays no premium for accepting such diversifiable risk. It's important to note that the rational expectations hypothesis plays a central role in most tests of the joint EMH/CAPM hypothesis. The majority of statements of the theory are couched in terms of individuals' beliefs about the mean and standard deviation of stock returns. So to test the model it's necessary to identify these subjective beliefs. The assumption of rational expectations solves this problem by the neat trick of equating the subjective beliefs with the actual means and standard deviations of the stocks over the period under study.

The traditional tests of EMH outlined above have for the most part tended to support the idea of market efficiency. However, as noted above, there is a kind of psychological barrier that mainline academics find hard to breach when evaluating the joint EMH/pricing scheme hypothesis. A good illustration of this is given in a 1978 study conducted by Ray Ball of the Value Line anomaly vis-à-vis the EMH/CAPM hypothesis. In his conclusions, Ball argued that the evidence of market inefficiency from the Value Line data is more likely an indictment of the CAPM than an indicator of market inefficiency. So here again we see an unwillingness to give up the EMH if there is even the faintest possibility that the anomaly can be argued away on other grounds. But these tests have all been based on traditional ideas of rational expectations founded upon properties of conditioned probability distributions. Let's close this discussion of market efficiency by relating some of the more recent work attacking the EMH on the basis of "volatility."

The volatility tests rest upon the very simple premise that forecasts based on conditional expectations should have lower volatility (have lower variances) than the actual observed results. To see why, consider the following simple experiment. Suppose we are called upon to forecast the output of a computer that has been programmed to produce a random number at each time period. Let's suppose that the program calls for the machine to select the number from a normal distribution having mean 0 and variance $V > 0$. Further, suppose that the drawing for each period is from this same distribution and that the drawings are independent. From the symmetry and unimodality properties of the normal distribution, it's evident that the best forecast for each period is to predict that the number drawn will be 0. Thus, since every forecast predicts that the number 0 will turn up, the variance in the sequence of optimal forecasts is zero. But the variance in the actual outcomes is V, which is greater than zero, thus exceeding the variance in the forecasts.

Since we have already seen that stock price changes are essentially forecasts, the above argument implies that if the EMH is true, the variance in prices should be lower (less volatile) than the variations in the price that someone with perfect foresight would pay for a stock (the price based upon the stock's future stream of dividends). However, just the opposite seems to be true: The actual price variation far exceeds the variance of the actual properly discounted stream of future dividends—a clear violation of the principle that forecasts should be less volatile than the variables that are to be forecasted. This phenomenon has been observed in many markets, and while a number of explanations have been offered that retain the EMH, none of them is especially convincing.

So we bring to a close our whirlwind tour of rationality and the EMH with the tentative conclusion that what's needed is either to inject some weaker version of rationality into models of the market, or to substantially soup up the pricing schemes. At present the finance journals are mostly filled with papers on the latter; the actual practitioners of finance are employing the former each and every business day. One hopes that someday soon the two communities will smoke the peace pipe on neutral ground somewhere in the middle. The newly emergent science of system complexity could be a venue for reconciling these radically different views of the market. So let's wrap up our consideration of market prediction and explanation with a look at how system thinking might bring about some kind of rapprochement.

CLARITY IN CHAOS

Beyond any shadow of a doubt, the greatest native-born American physicist of the nineteenth century was Josiah Willard Gibbs, who, together with Ludwig Boltzmann in Vienna, was responsible for developing the foundations of what we now call statistical mechanics. Gibbs spent most of his career as a professor at Yale, teaching in an era when the academic life was still a vocation rather than a business proposition. The Yale administrators, happy to exploit their faculty in any manner they could get away with (not unlike many university administrators nowadays), refused to pay Gibbs even one penny for his teaching and research for more than ten years. Finally, a recruitment effort by John Hopkins forced their hand. But despite this too-little, too-late display of generosity, Gibbs probably didn't receive more than a grand total of $20,000 in salary for his thirty-two years on the Yale faculty. Yet he died in 1903 with an estate valued at more than $110,000. And it didn't come from fat consulting fees or juicy calculus-textbook royalties either.

It seems that Gibbs was a lifelong player of the market, amassing what for the time was a considerable portfolio. Rumor had it that he was fond of dispensing hot tips on the market to his barber, butcher, and other New Haven tradesmen. But this was also an era when professors were considered as otherworldly as the clergy, and Gibbs's tips were uniformly dismissed as the aimless mutterings of an absent-minded professor. However, there was one student who did take Gibbs seriously, becoming the only Ph.D. candidate Gibbs ever guided to a degree in experimental physics. Oddly enough, the student, Irving Fisher, was actually more interested in economics than in physics, and for his thesis constructed an elaborate hydraulic model of the American economy involving a complicated arrangement of pipes, valves, and connectors. By opening and closing appropriate valves in this Rube Goldbergian device, Fisher could determine the interrelated effects of changes in different parts of the economy. Fisher later went on to become one of America's premier economists, his name destined to live in infamy for his ill-timed comment of October 15, 1929, that "stocks are now at what looks like a permanent high plateau," made exactly two weeks before Black Tuesday!

The case of Gibbs's love affair with Wall Street is just one example of the fascination that financial markets seem to have held for physicists and mathematicians throughout the ages. Perhaps the lure is the vast amount of data available, or maybe the attraction is that the seemingly closed system of trading looks like the closest approximation we'll ever find to a perfectly competitive market. Perhaps it's just basic human greed. Whatever it is, the observational evidence shows that whenever there's a new methodological development by mathematicians or theoretical physicists, one of the first things these keepers of the abstract processes consider is how their new toy might be used to beat the market. So it's not surprising to see some of the practitioners of the still-developing theory of chaos looking to the market as a testing ground for their very novel mathematical notions. In this section we'll find out how these exciting ideas match up to the test of the market. But first, let's look at another somewhat more classically based attack on the conventional wisdom of the RWT, but one that is in many ways still quite modern in spirit.

Benoit Mandelbrot of the IBM Research Laboratories is a man who seems to have been everywhere (Harvard, Yale, Princeton Institute for Advanced Study, École Polytechnique, MIT, Geneva . . .) and done just about everything (mathematics, engineering, physiology, economics . . .). In recent years, his name and face have been seen regularly in the scientific and popular press as he was proclaimed the "father of fractals," those wild-looking, colorful, mysterious geometrical forms that publishers have developed a fondness for using to decorate the dust jackets of otherwise dull, dusty tomes trying to pass as works of pop science. Since Mandelbrot's fame is bound up with his geometric work on fractals, what often escapes attention is his past interest in the stock market. More than twenty years ago he disputed the weak random-walk conclusions of Bachelier, suggesting a crucial modification that has been almost completely ignored by the Brahmins of the academic finance community. Interestingly, this work is closely related in spirit to the ideas of self-similarity underlying fractal geometry. Let's look at what Mandelbrot had in mind.

Recall that Bachelier's main assertions were that the changes in the logarithms of stock prices are independent, and that the probability distribution characterizing these changes is both stationary and Gaussian. Mandelbrot focused his attention upon the Gaussian assumption, noting that actual stock price variations display fluctuations that are just too large to be associated with a normally distributed random variable. The problem is that the normal distribution has only a *finite* variance. We saw earlier that the variance describes the way the price changes spread out around the average, or expected, change. Thus, Bachelier's Gaussian distribution, with its finite variance, implied that extremely large negative or positive fluctuations in prices would be so unlikely as to be for all practical purposes impossible. In short, the "tails" of the normal distribution, which measure the likelihood of extremely large fluctuations, are too small for such radical price swings to occur often enough to jibe with the data, at least over any reasonable time-frame. Yet as even the neophyte investor knows, the only interesting price swings are the big ones. And without an adequate supply of booms and busts, the market would soon lose its attraction for most participants. But in Bachelier's world, the kind of price changes that investors dream about (or have nightmares over) would be so infrequent as to make the floor of the New York Stock Exchange resemble the somnambulant atmosphere that one might associate with the exchange in Pyongyang or Tirana. Enter Mandelbrot.

Following the discovery of Bachelier's work by the finance community in the late 1950s, a number of investigators tried to account for the extremes of price changes by using various statistical maneuvers and mathematical contortions that preserved the Gaussian assumption. Probably the most common such scheme was to drop the stationarity assumption and claim instead that the actual probability law governing the market itself changes from time to time. The cause of this change was usually left unspecified, although it was presumably due to changes in the overall economic system within which the markets are embedded. Mandelbrot said, in effect, let's not throw out the baby with the bathwater. For him, dropping the stationarity assumption was much too dramatic a move just to explain extreme tail events. Moreover, the Gaussian assumption, despite its inadequacies when it comes to accounting for extreme fluctuations, serves rather well as a description for the majority of price shifts. So, he argued, let's keep stationarity and look for a probability law that's similar to the Gaussian but with an *infinite*, rather than finite, variance.

As it turned out, Mandelbrot didn't have far to look in order to find the kind of probability distribution he was seeking. In fact, he found an entire family of them—the so-called *Lévy stable laws*. This family of probability distributions is characterized by a single parameter D, which ranges between 0 and 2. Every number in this range, and there are an uncountable number of them, corresponds to a different probability distribution in this family. Our old friend the Gaussian distribution, for example, is the head of the family, having the "name" $D = 2$. Equally important is the fact that the Gaussian is the *only* member of the family that has a finite variance; for all values of $D < 2$, the corresponding probability distribution has an infinite variance. Roughly speaking, what this means is that random quantities that distribute their values in accordance with such a distribution have a nonnegligible chance of displaying very large negative or positive values. Needless to say, these were exactly the kinds of probability laws that Mandelbrot wanted—similar to the Gaussian, but with infinite variance. And the Lévy stable laws offered an uncountable number of candidates to play with in the search for a probabilistic rule that would describe market price fluctuations, especially the large ones. So what did Mandelbrot discover?

Figure 4.11 shows three different price-fluctuation curves, together with the distribution corresponding to the member of the Lévy stable law family having the name $D = 1.7$. In the figure, the two curves labeled 1*a* and 2*a* are for daily cotton price changes in New York during the period 1900–1905. The curves 1*b* and 2*b* are also daily changes in the cotton price on various exchanges for 1944–1958, while the curves 1*c* and 2*c* are for monthly cotton price changes in New York on the fifteenth of each month for the years 1880–1940. Since the plots are on double logarthmic scales, which may be unfamiliar to the reader, let's spell out exactly what they say.

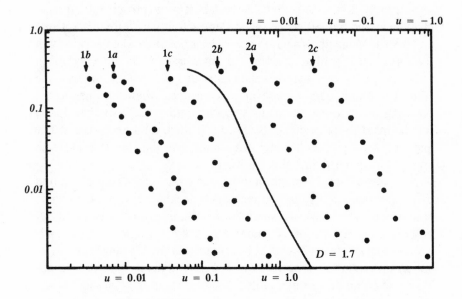

Figure 4.11. *Cotton price fluctuations and the Lévy stable law*

If we let Z_t represent the cotton price on day t, then curve 1*a* plots the *frequency* with which the quantity $\log Z_{t+1}$ changed by more than an amount u from its close on the previous day. That is, curve 1*a* plots the quantity

$$\text{frequency } [\log Z_{t + 1 \text{ day}} - \log Z_t] > u$$

Here the u values for the curves labeled 1 are taken from the lower edge of the figure, while the values for the curves labeled 2 are read from the upper edge. Just as curve 1*a* measures relative price changes greater than u (price increases), curve 1*b* measures price decreases, i.e., daily changes less than $-u$. A similar interpretation holds for curves 2*a*, 2*b*, 3*a*, and 3*b*.

In order to appreciate the implications of Figure 4.11, we can do no better than to listen to Mandelbrot himself:

. . . the distribution based on a record of daily price changes over a period of five years of average economic variability extrapolated to monthly price changes goes right through the data from the various recessions, the depression, and so forth. It accounts for all the most extreme events of nearly a century in the history of an essential and most volatile commodity. I do not believe there is any other comparably successful prediction in economics. It warrants being explored further.

Indeed it does! But time and space forbid our doing so here, so we must refer the interested reader to the To Dig Deeper section in this book for the juicy details, as well as for the expected counterarguments from Mandelbrot's detractors. Let's now move from the descriptive, but inherently static, explanatory ideas of Mandelbrot to the current rage aimed at actually predicting the ups and downs of the market by rejecting probabilistic concepts altogether. To this end, we cross over into the territory of those modern-day explorers of the unknown, the connoisseurs of chaos.

In earlier chapters we have already given ample evidence to support the surprising assertion that the observed output of a dynamical process can be generated by a fixed, purely deterministic rule, yet be indistinguishable on the basis of any standard statistical test from a completely random process. Of course, we have also seen that it *is* possible to separate the completely random from the knowable, but only by use of the ideas of strange attractors and all the other magical incantations of the modern dynamical system theorist. Since a time series of stock price data represents the quintessential example of observed output coming from some deeper underlying generative mechanism (the market), what could be more natural than to ask if these system-theoretic gadgets can shed any light on the issue of whether or not the market price-generating mechanism is inherently random? In other words, is a probabilistic law of price fluctuation the best we can hope for? Or do the observed price data support the hypothesis of an underlying market mechanism that is at rock bottom deterministic? System theorists with a penchant for playing the market and economists with a flair for system thinking both claim that their methods offer us a means for answering this question. So let's close our books on the behavior of speculative markets by listening to what these avant-garde thinkers have to say about the intrinsic randomness of speculative markets.

The best way to see what's at issue is to look at a toy version of price setting in a speculative market. For this, consider the logistic map, which is a purely deterministic rule for generating a sequence of numbers that are observationally indistinguishable from a perfectly random sequence. This rule consists of the simple requirement that the next number in the sequence be formed from the previous number and its square. More precisely, the logistic rule is $x_{t+1} = ax_t(1 - x_t)$, $t = 0$, 1, . . . , where the parameter a is required to lie between 0 and 4 in order to ensure that, starting with a number between 0 and 1, every number generated stays in this same range. Chaos theorists have discovered that if a value of the multiplier a larger than about 3.82 is chosen, the numbers produced by the above rule are completely random as far as any conventional statistical test can tell, for almost every choice of the starting number x_0.

Suppose, for the sake of argument, that we have a speculative market in which the price P_t of a security at time t is given by the following rule: $P_{t+1} = P_t + x_t - \frac{1}{2}$. In words, the underlying market pricing mechanism is just the rule: Tomorrow's price equals today's price plus a *deterministic* fluctuation given by whatever the logistic rule serves up, minus a fixed fudge factor of $\frac{1}{2}$ (thrown in so that price variations from period to period always lie between $\pm\frac{1}{2}$). Of course, we have no knowledge of the market mechanism (the logistic rule above) and are given only the series of numbers $\{P_0, P_1, P_2, . . .\}$ as the time trajectory of prices for the security. So on the basis of this data, the task is to determine whether the market for the security is efficient. In other words, does knowledge of past prices help in any way to predict the movement of future prices? If it does, then the market is not efficient.

The rational expectations hypothesis asserts that properly anticipated prices fluctuate randomly—i.e., past price changes can be of no help in predicting future price variations. Of course, if you *do* know how the price data were generated, then future prices are completely predictable: Given the state of the price-generating mechanism at time t, you can predict the state of time $t + 1$ with perfect accuracy. But if you don't know the mechanism, then it's necessary to resort to standard statistical means to test whether or not the price data are consistent with market efficiency. Actually carrying out such tests on the above data, you will find that our toy market is indeed efficient. Clearly, it's possible to make a lot of money in an "efficient market" like this one! Why? Simply because if there really is a deterministic rule like the simple logistic law above underpinning security prices, then we can use our knowledge of the existence of that rule to predict future prices with better-than-random accuracy, by definition. On the other hand, if the mechanism is truly random, then we can't. Let's briefly look at two of the tests the system theorists have devised to distinguish between these two fundamentally different cases.

Since we have already gone into some detail on the ideas underlying chaotic dynamics in Chapters One and Two, let's just briefly summarize the main points here. The central concept upon which all else hinges is that of the *attractor* for the system. Roughly speaking, this is the set of points characterizing the long-term behavior of the process. In general, the more complicated the attractor set, the more complex the system dynamics, with the most complicated kinds of attractors being associated with chaotic motion. These are the so-called *strange attractors*.

For the classical attractors, fixed points and limit cycles, the geometric dimension of the attractor is much smaller than the dimension of the state manifold M. For instance, M could have a very high dimension, yet a point attractor still has the geometric dimension of a point, namely, 0. Similarly, a closed curve attractor like a limit cycle is a one-dimensional curve, irrespective of the dimension of M. On the other hand, when we look at something like the "bowl-of-spaghetti" attractor shown in Figure 1.10 (page 73), it's hard to avoid the feeling that the dimension of such an object is certainly greater than that of a curve or a point. Yet it is clearly not as large as the dimension of the state manifold M itself. This intuitive feeling can be formalized for strange attractors, leading to different tests for measuring the level of chaotic behavior displayed by the system. Let's briefly sketch the basics of two of these measures—the *correlation dimension* and the *K-entropy*.

The idea underlying the correlation dimension is to consider the correlation of a set of points sampled from a trajectory that has been moving on the attractor for a long time. It's important to note here that the correlation dimension is *not* equal to the geometric dimension of the attractor. The reason is that the geometric dimension doesn't take into account the dynamics of the system on the attractor; every point on the attractor, no matter how infrequently visited, is counted equally in computing the geometric dimension. But it's usually not the case that all points are visited equally often. Thus, since the correlation dimension weights the points on the attractor according to how frequently they are visited, it is usually seen as a better measure of what's going on with the attractor than the geometric dimension. It turns out that if the correlation dimension is much greater than 1 and is not an integer, then that's an indication that the system's attractor is strange and the dynamics are chaotic. Now let's shift our perspective from geometry to information.

Suppose our starting points x_0 and x'_0 are indistinguishably close to one another. From the arguments given for the Circle-10 system in Chapter One, we know that as time goes by the two trajectories from these starting points will diverge if the system's behavior is chaotic, since a key sign of chaotic behavior is sensitivity to initial conditions. Thus, two trajectories that are indistinguishable at the outset become distinguishable; that is, there has been a creation of information. The average rate at which the trajectories become distinguishable is the mean rate of information creation, or what in technical terms is called the *Kolmogorov entropy*. This entropy, usually written as K, is directly related to the rate at which the two trajectories are separating in various directions. Clearly, if the trajectories do not diverge at all, we must have $K = 0$, while for a chaotic path we have $K > 0$, but finite. For a totally random path, e.g., when the state manifold M itself is the attractor, the Kolmogorov entropy is infinite.

The procedure for uncovering hidden chaos in stock price data is now clear: Look at the time history of prices and calculate the correlation dimension and the K-entropy. If the correlation dimension is high and/or the K-entropy is positive and finite, then there is a very good chance that the price data are being generated by a deterministic mechanism whose output just looks random. And for economic data even more refined tests have been developed. Let's briefly sketch one of them.

William Brock of the University of Wisconsin is one of the leaders of the "chaotic" school of economic theorists. Brock and his colleague W. Denchert have observed that peculiar features of certain types of economic time series may "fool" the usual chaos tests described above. Consequently, they suggest a more sensitive test that exploits a peculiar feature of chaotic systems—invariance to coordinate transformations. In simple terms, what this means is that if we start with a time series of stock prices that comes from a chaotic process and change the scale by which we measure the prices—for example, by expressing them in Italian lira instead of U.S. dollars (technically, a *linear* change of variable)—then the original price data and the transformed data will have the same correlation dimension and the same K-entropy. In short, these quantities are independent of the coordinate system used to label the prices. This basic fact forms the heart of Brock's *residual test* for chaos.

The essence of the Brock-Denchert test is to compare the correlation dimension and K-entropy for both the original data and the differences between the output of a linear model of the data and the actual data. If the stock price data did indeed come from a chaotic process, then the correlation dimension and/or the K-entropy should not differ between these two time series. Otherwise, the hypothesis of an underlying deterministic chaotic law of motion is suspect. With all of this mathematical machinery in hand, let's finally see what it has to say about market mechanisms and prices.

In a 1986 study of American stock prices, José Scheinkman and Blake LeBaron considered a weekly index of prices, finding a correlation dimension of around 6. Their results were consistent with the belief that there is a deterministic mechanism underlying price variations. In fact, they state the stronger conclusion that "the data is not incompatible with a theory where most variation would come from nonlinearities [i.e., chaos] as opposed to randomness and is not compatible with a theory that predicts that the returns are generated by independent random variables." A number of other studies have arrived at similar conclusions. So let's conclude this abbreviated tour of market chaos by reporting on the work of Murray Frank and Thanasis Stengos using a time series of actual price data, not for stocks but for gold.

Denote the rate of return on day t by the quantity r_t. The efficient market hypothesis asserts that this rate of return is completely independent of the rate in any preceding period. The simplest test of this hypothesis is to assume that r_t depends only on the previous day's rate r_{t-1}. Under this assumption, we have the relation $r_t = a + br_{t-1} + u_t$, where a and b are constants, and u_t is a term introduced to account for the error in assuming this relationship between r_t and r_{t-1} to be the linear one above. If the gold market is indeed efficient, we must have $a = b = 0$, i.e., today's return is unrelated either to yesterday's return ($b = 0$) or to any systematic bias effect ($a = 0$). Using actual gold price data, Frank and Stengos applied standard statistical methods to test this hypothesis and found that indeed a and b were both zero to within the statistical uncertainty of the tests and the accuracy of the data. So by following standard methodology we would be led to conclude that the gold market is indeed efficient. But not so fast!

The preceding picture changes dramatically when the techniques of dynamical system theory are applied to the same data. In estimating the correlation dimension for the system, Frank and Stengos found a value of about 6.3, quite sufficient to suggest deterministic chaos in this situation. Furthermore, when they used Brock's residual test on the data they could discern no appreciable difference between the correlation dimension of the original data and that of the residuals, another finerprint of chaos. Finally, they calculated the K-entropy as $K = 0.15 \pm 0.07$, again strongly indicative of underlying chaos.

These empirical tests show the substantial gains possible by thinking of financial time-series data in modern dynamical system terms. The standard methods of econometrics, which emphasize statistical techniques, were unable to detect any structure in the gold price data. By way of contrast, the correlation dimension and K-entropy estimates strongly suggest that there is structure lurking in the data, and that there may well be a deterministic mechanism residing at the heart of the price-setting procedures in the gold market.

But why should we care about knowing whether the economic data are generated by random or deterministic means? After all, you might well argue that even if the underlying rule is deterministic, it's too deeply hidden for us to have even a ghost of a chance of ever discovering what it really is. So, as with statistical mechanics vis-à-vis classical particle mechanics, here it may be more useful and computationally convenient just to carry on with the fiction of a probabilistic law of economic behavior. There are at least two responses to this argument.

First of all, there would be definite implications for government economic policy if we knew with assurance that the data came from a deterministic rather than a stochastic mechanism. If it could be established that macroeconomic fluctuations in things like unemployment rates and the balance of payments are generated by deterministic mechanisms, then this would imply that the fluctuations are inherently part of the system and don't arise as a result of outside "shocks." To use the kind of terms that economists and other obfuscators love to employ, they would be endogenous, not exogenous. In this case, good arguments could be made for strong government stabilization policies. On the other hand, if the fluctuations really are due to perturbations arising outside the system, then government stabilization policies are at best useless, and at worst harmful.

The second response is more along the lines of the aesthetics of model building. If we know that the economic time series are in reality the observed output of a deterministic mechanism, then we can cling to the hope of being able to internalize (endogenize) the error terms in our models. In short, knowing that the real dynamics are chaotic, modelers will be much less cavalier about throwing in a random error term in a feeble attempt to bury the sins of their modeling omissions.

We've finally come to the end of our methods for making it big in the market. Let's now assess where we stand on the issues of prediction and explanation of the caprices of speculative markets.

MAKING THE GRADE

Prediction

When it comes to capturing the essence of prediction in the market, we can probably do no better than to listen to the words of that Bloomsbury regular, Cambridge don, and general man-about-the-world John Maynard Keynes, who stated that "most people are largely concerned not with making superior long-term forecasts of the probable yield of an investment over its whole life, but with foreseeing changes in the conventional basis of valuation a short time ahead of the general public." How true! As far as the typical investor is concerned, prediction means exactly this kind of short-term, beat-the-crowd anticipation of tomorrow's prices. So what standards should we apply in awarding a grade for the predictability of speculative markets?

At one end of the spectrum, perfect prediction of the *summa cum laude* variety would consist of a scheme by which we could produce tomorrow's closing stock price quotations today. Moving away from this level of prognosticative satori, we come to the still-imposing but nevertheless more realistic goal of beating the market. We have spoken of this level of predictive power before. It consists of employing some forecasting method that is capable of consistently outperforming some market indicator like the S&P 500 over a substantial period of time. Prediction at this level would certainly merit a better-than-average grade. Next on the scale come prediction schemes that merely turn a profit. Since even mindless random-number generators and dart throwers can turn a profit the majority of the time, a prediction method that just makes money is basically run of the mill and deserves at best a low pass. Needless to say, prediction methods that lose money are fated for summer school and a trip back to the beginning of the chapter to take the course over again. With these criteria in mind, we can now assess the problem of market prediction.

There are no As in this class. Even the best of the predictive methods we've examined don't come close to printing out tomorrow's *Wall Street Journal* for our investing pleasure today. However, many of the methods centering upon classes of stocks or overall market timing—the Value Line Indicator, small firms, low P/Es—do indeed show every sign of being able to outperform the market averages consistently. This is not to say, however, that academics haven't found ways to suggest that perhaps these methods are really cribbing from the paper of our star pupil, Market Risk. For example, some claim that the small-firm effect is really attributable not to the performance of small firms in general, but to spectacular performances by just a few small firms. In turn, the implication then becomes that this group of stocks taken as a whole is somewhat riskier than the overall market portfolio. Thus, the critics argue, the small-firm effect is really just market risk premium in disguise. Similar complaints have been leveled at the Value Line Indicator, claiming that because Value Line rates over seventeen hundred stocks, it necessarily includes many small firms that are not included in market indexes like the S&P 500.

But whether it's risk premium in disguise or genuine market inefficiency, it's difficult to argue with success. And the above-average records of these market anomalies have persisted for so long and in so many places that even the professors have to bow to the facts: It *is* possible to beat the market systematically! On the other hand, there appear to be no known methods for beating the market that involve just a single stock; all successful prediction schemes seem to rely upon what we might term *the financial law of large numbers:* For success, you must form a portfolio consisting of a collection of certain *types* of securities. Faced with these hard facts, not speculations, we come to our verdict on prediction:

Term Grade—Prediction: C⁺

Explanation

To put it simply, in the context of speculative markets, explanation = mechanism. Since the distilled essence of market behavior comes down to the dynamics of prices, what this elementary equation tells us is that we can legitimately claim to be able to explain market behavior if we can produce a convincing mechanism by which investors behave and prices are set. Our deliberations in this chapter have shown that the conventional wisdom on this score can also be encapsulated in a simple equation:

$$\text{mechanism} = \text{rational expectations} + \text{a pricing scheme}$$

As we've seen, the hallowed efficient-market hypothesis assumes rational behavior on the part of all market participants, while various pricing schemes like positive expected returns, CAPM, and all their analytical relatives account for the assignment of return, hence prices. Unfortunately, we've also seen a lot of evidence suggesting that there's something highly suspicious about this kind of "explanation" of the market.

To get a feel for the sort of rearguard action waged by the true believers of the EMH fairy tale, let's listen to EMH devotee and Nobel laureate Milton Friedman: "The value of the model [conventional EMH + pricing] lies in its predictive and explanatory power and the model cannot be judged by reference to the realism of its underlying assumptions." Going back a few hundred years, this very statement would have served equally well to describe the Ptolemaic model of planetary motion or the phlogiston theory of combustion. And, in fact, since Friedman made this eyebrow-raising remark, both the predictive and the explanatory power of the conventional wisdom have sunk lower than snake hips. So I think it's safe to say that as far as explanation goes, the EMH-based ideas flunk the course. But what about alternatives?

At present, the most interesting possibility for a genuine explanatory mechanism underlying price fluctuation seems to be the work involving deterministic chaos. It's especially revealing to note that the standard statistical tests upon which the claims for the validity of the EMH rest appear to be incapable of identifying deeper structure in economic time series. Yet as has been demonstrated time and again on actual data, the methods of dynamical system theory point to a deterministic rule governing the price generation process. But these methods and ideas are still in their infancy, and it's much too early to speak with any authority as to whether or not they will banish the EMH to that scientific graveyard where lie the skeletons of other "explanatory" mechanisms that don't explain. We'll just have to wait and see. So putting all these observations together, we come to a final grade for explanation of the market as

Term Grade—Explanation: D

Stock markets reflect one of the most universal of all human traits—greed. Now let's turn our analytical instruments of prediction and explanation to the study of another—aggression in the form of organized warfare.

CHAPTER FIVE

A NICE LITTLE WAR

Can We Predict/Explain the Outbreak of War?

While you may not be interested in war, war is interested in you.
—LEON TROTSKY

Any theory of the causes of war in general or any war in particular that is not inherently eclectic and comprehensive is bound for that very reason to be wrong.
—BERNARD BRODIE

War should be the only study of a prince. He should consider peace only as a breathing time which gives him leisure to contrive, and furnishes an ability to execute, military plans.
—NICCOLÒ MACHIAVELLI

CLEOPATRA'S NOSE AND THE WICKEDNESS OF HEGEL

Directly across Ocean Avenue from the pier in Santa Monica, California, lies a complex of orange-and-cream-colored buildings done in a style that might charitably be termed Mid–Twentieth Century Government Bland. In sharp contrast to the nondescript exterior of these structures, life inside their walls can only be described as Twenty-first Century Avant-garde. The reason? Simple. This modest complex, looking more like the offices of a small insurance company or, perhaps, a slightly down-at-the-heels medical center, is in actuality the home of the internationally renowned RAND Corporation, the role model of "think tanks" or, as they're now called, QUANGOs (quasi-nongovernmental organizations) the world over. Through a lucky turn of events, I found myself employed in this heady intellectual environment in the late 1960s as a researcher trying to finance simultaneously a family and the pursuit of a doctoral degree in mathematics at the University of Southern California.

RAND's public profile derives principally from its work in military systems analysis, particularly strategic thinking on the use of nuclear weapons, as well as more recent work in a variety of national-security and public-policy areas. However, my own chores were centered on far less controversial, life-threatening, and publicly visible activities, mainly the development of mathematical methods for solving certain classes of differential and integral equations of interest to applied mathematicians, physicists, and engineers. Nevertheless, working in such an environment offered ample opportunity to the curious for listening to the leading thinkers of the day expounding their views at in-house seminars on things like the most cost-effective way to bomb Moscow back into the Stone Age and what the Muscovites might try to do about it.

I recall one such RAND seminar at which the speaker advanced a theory regarding the outbreak of warfare. While the details are by now a bit hazy, the talk's central claim was to the effect that the transition from harsh words and threats to bombs and bullets is always a chancy affair, almost totally dependent on the capricious whims of a particular national leader. To those of the tide-in-the-affairs-of-men school of historical thought, putting forth a thesis of this kind is tantamount to waving a red flag in front of a charging bull, and the cries of outrage, the posturing, and the ranting and raving (i.e., the discussion) following the seminar were hot and heavy indeed. Since the antipodal claims of chance versus necessity as the driving force behind historical events lie at the heart of whether we can predict and/or explain the outbreak of warfare, it will be of interest for us here if I try to reconstruct a bit of the flavor of the discussion following that RAND seminar.

To protect the innocent and the just plain naïve, let me label the seminar speaker Dr. Chance, reflecting his epousal of the theory that historical events, including the outbreak of war, are driven by the whimsy of leaders and can be neither predicted nor understood, at least not in the sense that those terms are being used in this book. The opposing view, which incidentally represented the consensus of the attendees at the seminar, will be presented by Professor Fate. His thesis is that the actual outbreak of war is almost inevitable, provided certain broad sociopolitical, economic, and technological patterns are present. In this view, the actions of individual leaders play a role in initiating war only to the extent of determining the fine details, such as the *exact* time and place of the conflict. Let's listen for a moment to a bit of the interchange between our two antagonists.

FATE: Now if I understand your position correctly, you are asserting that whether or not war occurs is fundamentally just a matter of chance or accidental factors, such as a leader's having a headache or a message's being garbled. Could you give an example or two to illustrate your point?

CHANCE: I'm glad you asked that question. You've expressed my position exactly, and the history books are full of examples supporting it. For instance, when bearded King Louis VII of France was married to Eleanor, daughter of a French duke, he received a dowry of two provinces in southern France. Upon coming home from the Crusades, Louis shaved off his beard. Eleanor said he looked ugly without it, and when he refused to grow the whiskers back again, she divorced him and married King Henry II of England. She then demanded return of her dowry. When Louis refused, Henry declared war to regain the provinces by force. This "War of the Whiskers" started in 1152 and raged on for 301 years until peace was declared in 1453, following the Battle of Rouen. So here's an example of over three centuries of warfare initiated by the chance shaving-off of a beard. And if you're looking for something closer to home, what about the recent (1969) half-hour war between Honduras and El Salvador, sparked off by El Salvador's 3–0 victory over Honduras in the World Cup soccer playoffs?

F: All very interesting to be sure, but I'm afraid I don't find it very convincing. In fact, Honduras and El Salvador were already at each other's throats over a border dispute. So I think one could convincingly argue that the result of the soccer game was only an excuse, and that some sort of hostilities were imminent in any case. Don't you have any stronger evidence?

C: Allow me to call your attention to one of the major wars of recorded history, the Thirty Years' War in Europe, a conflict that lasted from 1618 to 1648 or thereabouts. This war, which resulted in the establishment of the European nation-state system, started on May 23, 1618, when angry Protestant nobles opposing the militantly Catholic King Ferdinand of Bohemia, stormed Ferdinand's castle in Prague and hurled two royal councillors from the window. History records that they survived the seventy-foot fall by landing in a pile of horse manure. This chance survival of the councillors in the so-called Defenestration of Prague led to the Thirty Years' War. You can't get much closer to a chance outbreak of war than this.

F: Surely you're joking. You can't seriously think that if those councillors hadn't been thrown from the window of Hradčany Castle there would have been no Thirty Years' War. What about the turmoil and strife that Europe was undergoing at the time, things like the decline of Spain, the political and religious forces pulling apart the Holy Roman Empire, and the fading of the Habsburgs' dream of European hegemony? Surely these social, political, and cultural forces would have led to armed conflict sooner or later, quite independently of a couple of councillors of a minor monarch being thrown into a pile of horse manure.

C: Of course these sociopolitical and cultural factors enter into play. I'm only saying that without the chance event, the unpredictable occurrences of life, things may take an entirely different course—including warfare's *not* breaking out. But since you've been asking me for examples, let me turn the tables and ask you to give me some for-instances supporting your own resolutely deterministic view of war.

F: With pleasure. Let's move into the twentieth century and consider what's probably the most thoroughly studied war of all time: World War I. An "accidental theorist" like you would probably argue that the war wouldn't have started without the assassination of Archduke Franz Ferdinand in Sarajevo on June 28, 1914. But I think most historians would say that the war was an almost inevitable outgrowth of several much deeper factors: the desire of France to recover Alsace-Lorraine, the

European system of alliances, Austria's aspiration to dominate the Balkans, the German Kaiser's aims and ambitions, even the activities of the munitions makers and the international bankers. Any one of these fundamental factors seems more likely to have precipitated World War I than the archduke's assassination.

C: I see that you include the Kaiser's ambitions on your list of determinants. If this is indeed a significant cause of the war, don't you think it's more a matter of chance than design that such a kaiser happened to be sitting on the throne in Germany? If a kaiser with a less acquisitive makeup had been in place, maybe the war wouldn't have started.

F: I'm sorry, but I *don't* think another kaiser would have made one iota of difference. The actual Kaiser's ambitions were just one of many such factors, all of which taken together spelled war. The chance mental makeup of the Kaiser certainly played *some* role. But it was the overall pattern of politics and life at the time that dragged the world into war, not the personal quirks of a quirky kaiser. So the *underlying* causes of World War I were inherent in the structure of the international system, even if the *proximate* cause may well have been the archduke's assassination. But I suppose we could go on debating this chance-versus-necessity issue indefinitely. . . .

Indeed they could. So let's try to summarize the diametrically opposed visions of Chance and Fate as to how armed hostilities come jumping out of the closet. To give these competing positions labels, let's call Chance's arguments the *Cleopatra's Nose* theory of the outbreak of war, commemorating Mark Antony's well-known infatuation with the temptress of the Nile. As the history books and Hollywood tell it, Antony's chance glandular obsession led him to abandon his naval forces at a crucial juncture in their battle at Actium with the Roman Emperor Octavian in 31 B.C., leading to a crushing defeat and centuries of Roman hegemony. By way of contrast, we can term Professor Fate's deterministic theory of the emergence of war *The Wickedness of Hegel,* reflecting the German philosopher's lifelong antipathy to the idea of explaining human actions in causal terms, thus denying human free will. Here are the main sales pitches for both positions.

- *Cleopatra's Nose:* The events that really shake things up, historically speaking, including those responsible for the outbreak of war, are random, inherently chance occurrences. A typical example is an event like Leon Trotsky's falling victim to a bad cold following a duck-hunting excursion, putting him out of action at a crucial moment in his power struggle with Stalin. According to those admiring the cut of Cleopatra's jib, it's just this sort of caprice that turns the tide of events and accounts for revolutions, economic collapses, and all the other discontinuities of history—including the outbreak of war.
- *The Wickedness of Hegel:* Big events don't just "happen." Historical discontinuities like the outbreak of war have causes, and could not have happened differently unless something in the causes had also been different. In this view, the nightmare quality of events of the sort found in Kafka's novels lies in the fact that nothing that happens has any apparent cause, or at least any cause that can be discerned. Thus, in the context of warfare, events like Trotsky's illness or Cleopatra's charms are just accidents of history and do not belong to any rational analysis of the onset of fighting. In short, there are genuine laws of history involving broadly based properties of states like their economic, social, military, and political strength, and it's to these laws that we must turn in attempting to understand and predict when and where warfare will break out.

It's evident, I think, that our antagonists Chance and Fate would argue for radically different positions on the matters of predicting and/or explaining how wars come about. Chance would undoubtedly say that predicting a war is flatly impossible, since to do so would involve predicting the occurrence of what is by definition an unpredictable event. He would further claim that such chance occurrences, should they happen at a time and place when competing forces are delicately balanced, can tilt the scales of history and spark off a chain of events that may lead to a totally different world. Thus, in Chance's world there is neither prediction nor explanation of war in any of the senses we've been discussing in this volume.

On the other side of the seminar room, Fate claims that prediction is in principle possible, at least in a statistical sense. Furthermore, he makes the stronger claim that the explanations or causes of war are very plain for all to see, residing in sociopolitical and military factors that have remained unchanged for millennia. Thus, in Fate's deterministic view of the world, the only obstacles to the accurate prediction and explanation of wars are practical, not theoretical, clustering about the twin barriers of insufficient data and inadequate understanding of human behavioral patterns. In the opinion of those sharing Fate's convictions, these barriers will gradually melt away with time, ultimately allowing us to understand the outbreak of warfare as one of the fruits of an increased understanding of human nature.

Clearly, both Chance and Fate are caricatures. I have drawn their respective positions in broad strokes, using only the brightest colors for the sake of making evident the dichotomy between the chance and necessity schools of armed conflict. The sections that follow will fill in many of the subtler shades of each line of argument. But before taking up the palette and fleshing out the details, let's pause for a few moments to dig a little deeper into what we mean here when we speak of war, causes of war, and crises.

CASUS BELLI

Early in the morning of October 16, 1962, National Security Adviser McGeorge Bundy brought President John F. Kennedy incontrovertible evidence that Soviet offensive missiles were being installed in Cuba. This news set in motion the best-chronicled and most carefully scrutinized thirteen days in modern American history, a crisis that in today's world of fumble-fingered decisionmakers and shadowy, seemingly unanswerable terrorist attacks stands as probably the highwater mark of America's worldwide prestige. While the details of the Cuban missile crisis are too well known to merit repeating here, what's important for our purpose is to note that the crisis situation brought on by this daring Soviet ploy is a quintessential example of the circumstances under which wars begin. Armed hostilities don't start as a bolt out of the blue. Rather, they are the result of what Winston Churchill called a ''bolt out of the grey,'' arising as the culmination of a crisis situation. But not all crises are created equal; there are many types, some of which are more likely to lead to war than others. So let's run through a brief taxonomy of crisis in an attempt to separate the bark from the bite.

According to international relations expert Ned Lebow, there are three qualitatively distinct types of crises:

- *Justification of Hostilities:* The purpose of this type of crisis is to provide an excuse for war. A typical example is the August 2, 1964, Gulf of Tonkin incident, which involved a reported attack by North Vietnamese boats on two U.S. destroyers. The Johnson administration used this ambiguous event as a lever to pry open the door to active American intervention in Vietnam. The distinguishing feature of this type of crisis is that the leaders have already made a decision for war before the crisis happens. Consequently, as far as influencing the outbreak of war is concerned, a Justification-of-Hostilities crisis really doesn't have too much of an effect since the decision for war has already been taken.

- *Spin-off:* The sinking of the British pleasure liner *Lusitania* by a German U-boat in 1915 is representative of this kind of crisis. The *Lusitania* incident resulted in the loss of 128 American lives, and generated strong anti-German feeling in the United States despite the fact that the Germans had warned passengers not to travel on British vessels. Spin-off crises like this come about when the actions of one party in a conflict provoke a confrontation with a third party. In the *Lusitania* crisis we had one party to the European war (Germany) antagonizing a neutral party (the United States) by an action directed against a country with which it was already at war (Britain). This action ultimately led to the U.S. entry into the war, thereby broadening it into World War I. Like the Justification-of-Hostilities type of crisis, a Spin-off crisis has a minimal influence on the outbreak of war for the simple reason that neither party to the crisis really wants a confrontation with the other.

- *Brinkmanship:* By far the most common type of crisis in the modern world comes about when one state knowingly challenges an important commitment of another in the hope that the challenger can force the other state to back away from its commitment. Such crises, originally termed *brinkmanship* by John Foster Dulles, are dangerous indeed, as each party expects the other to back off. In such a highly charged setting, a miscalculation in the assessment of the other side's resolve can easily lead to the outbreak of war. The October 1962 Cuban missile confrontation and the U.S.-Iraq faceoff over the 1990 Iraqi invasion of Kuwait are perfect examples of Brinkmanship crises.

Looking at a list of crises of all types, you don't need much in the way of deep insight to recognize that there are a handful of features characterizing crisis situations. If the following circumstances prevail, then you're in a crisis: (1) high stakes, (2) short decision time, (3) a high level of uncertainty, and (4) few apparent options. A few years ago, to emphasize some of these points graphically, Charles Hermann drew the "crisis cube" shown in Figure 5.1. Hermann regarded each of the eight corners of the cube as being a different type of "situation." The closer a situation is to the lower left-hand corner of the cube, where there is high threat (stakes), short decision time, and low awareness (high surprise), the closer the situation is to being a crisis. We'll return to Hermann's basic idea in a later section, showing how it's been dressed up in modern geometric language to serve as a means for predicting the outbreak of war. But since one man's war is another man's border skirmish, before proceeding further with our consideration of the outbreak of "war" let's take a couple of pages to spell out just what we're thinking about here when we use that term.

In his monumental two-volume 1942 treatise *A Study of War,*

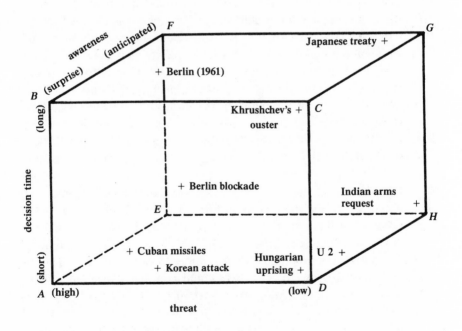

Figure 5.1. *Hermann's crisis cube*

Quincy Wright offers the definition: "War is a state of law and a form of conflict involving a high degree of legal equality, or hostility, and of violence in the relations of organized human groups." Just the sort of definition that one might expect from a professor of international law, who argued forcefully against both the U.S. naval blockade of Cuba in 1962 and the American involvement in Vietnam as being violations of international covenants. But, frankly speaking, Wright's definition is a bit dry for my taste and, moreover, would include hostile actions like the joint U.S.-Colombian efforts against the Medellín drug cartel under the rubric *war*. Interesting and important as such armed actions are, if we're to make any sense out of the ideas of prediction and explanation in the context of war, we need to restrict Quincy Wright's usage of the term severely.

An even more general definition of war was offered by the nineteenth-century German military strategist Karl von Clausewitz, when he wrote that "war is an act of violence intended to compel our opponent to fulfill our will." In this well-known statement, as well as in his other works, Clausewitz wrote as if war is something that's given, and our job is to discover what it really is. But despite the visceral appeal of Clausewitz's definition, it also leaves open the possibility of labeling too many conflicts as wars. For example, by Clausewitz's definition a barroom brawl arising out of the amorous attentions of one gent to another man's lady would qualify as a war. We need a view of war that's far more restrictive than this if we're to have even the faintest prayer of being able to speak *scientifically* about its onset. As in most matters of the intellect, the inspiration for our concept of what constitutes a war can be traced back to ancient Greece. So let's leave Clausewitz and Quincy Wright, shifting our attention back a couple of thousand years to happenings on the Peloponnesian peninsula.

With the statement "What made war inevitable was the growth of Athenian power and the fear this caused in Sparta," the Greek historian Thucydides was the first to advance the idea that the force driving international relations is the differential rate of growth in power among states. In his eight-volume *History of the Peloponnesian War*, Thucydides created a theory of what we would now term *hegemonic war*. Hegemonic war differs from other types of war in several ways:

1. It is caused by broad changes in political, economic, cultural, technological, and strategic situations.

2. The behavior of states is largely dictated by their strategic interactions within a system of states.
3. The war threatens, and ultimately transforms, the whole international system.

Thucydides' concept of war delimits both Quincy Wright's legalistic definition and Clausewitz's militaristic one, replacing them with the notion of a hegemonic war, which is the kind of war we'll usually have in mind during the course of this chapter. If you're wondering just what types of wars fit into this category, think about struggles like the aforementioned Thirty Years' War or World War I (but don't think of World War II, for reasons we'll get to a bit later). With these matters settled, let's direct our attention to a more detailed consideration of what it could mean to speak of a *cause* of war.

By now, the reader might be thinking that talking about the causes of a war can be a pretty slippery business. And so it can, as shown by the following list of proffered "causes" of the First World War.

Some Proposed Causes of World War I	
Russian and German mobilization	The Austrian ultimatum to Serbia
The Sarajevo assassination	The German Kaiser's ambitions
France's desire to recover Alsace-Lorraine	The international bankers
Austria's desire to dominate the Balkans	The European system of alliances
Colonial rivalries	The inadequate European political order
The activity of the munitions makers	
Nationalistic sentiments	Commercial policies
The tendency of nations to expand	The concept of sovereignty
An unequal distribution of resources	The struggle for existence
The value of war as an instrument of policy	The law of diminishing returns
	Enthnocentrism

Far better than any esoteric, theoretical argument, these so-called causes of the First World War give ample support to the claim that there are many notions about causation when it comes to the outbreak of war. So in formulating a coherent picture of the degree to which the tools of science can be brought to bear on predicting and explaining the emergence of war, we'll have to distinguish carefully among the various concepts of causation.

At the first level of causation, we have already had occasion to consider the difference between the *proximate* and the *underlying* causes of war. The former are the events, issues, or crises that actually trigger a war. Things on the above list like the Sarajevo assassination and the Russian and German mobilization fall into this category. At the other end of the scale are the underlying causes, those long-term factors contributing to hostility and tension between states. Most analysts would probably assign the majority of the items offered as causes of World War I to this group. And for historians like Thucydides, these are the causes that really count. And for us, too, these are the causes that count, if for no other reason than that it's hard to imagine constructing any sort of "laws" of the outbreak of warfare involving the essentially random proximate causes. If we're to ascertain any patterns in the outbreak of war, they're going to have to be found in the underlying, not the proximate, causes.

To ease our burden of analyzing causal factors in warfare, it's convenient to subdivide the category of underlying cause into three types: scientific, historical, and practical. In outline, the characteristics of these types can be described as follows:

- *Scientific:* Such causes center about specific events that can be combined into general concepts or ideas leading to a rule or law expressing the likelihood of war. Some of the more common scientific causes of war include: (1) the difficulty of maintaining a stable political and military balance of power within the international system of states, (2) the problems in utilizing international law to make it an effective instrument for the just settlement of international disputes, and (3) the obstacles to be overcome in making peace a more important symbol in world public opinion than other symbols, like nationalistic or religious fervor, that may favor war. Basically, in the scientific view war breaks out because humanity has failed to establish the conditions for peace.

- *Historical:* As a general *modus operandi,* historians tend to try to explain a particular war by drawing upon events, circumstances, and conditions that preceded the war, and that can be related to it by practical, political, economic, and legal conditions coming from unchanging aspects of human nature. Basically, explanation by historical causes amounts to a classification of the causes of a particular war in a particular period of history. In actuality, as noted by Oxford's Michael Howard, historians are more interested in the causes of peace than of war. As Howard remarks, the fascination with peace is a bit like Dr. Samuel Johnson's wonder at women preaching: It's not that it is done so imperfectly, but that it is, under the circumstances, ever done at all. So it is with peace, too, as is firmly attested by the surprising fact that in the entire history of the United States, there have been only twenty years when the Navy or the Army has not been engaged in active, "hot" operations on some days, somewhere.

Oversimplifying a bit, we can summarize the historians' position on the cause of war as simply a matter of power—in Howard's words, "the perceptions by statesmen of the growth of hostile power and the fears for the restriction, if not the extinction, of their own." From ancient times to the seventeenth century, power was the physical control of territory. Beginning in the seventeenth century, the *effectiveness* with which one could control territory became an equally important factor in the power equation. By the early twentieth century, under the influence of the transportation revolution (mainly the railroads), power was measured by growth of communication and population. Finally, in today's world the dominant element in the international power calculus is technology. So if your interest is in understanding war, concentrate on indicators of power. Or so say the historians, at any rate.

It's interesting to note that at a general level there's not really much difference between historical and scientific cause, since historians use words like *ideology, policy,* and *law* to stand for universal concepts that may be seen in varying degrees at all times. The main point of departure from the scientific view is that the scientists try to relate these general concepts by means of mathematical relations and/or computational models. The historians, on the other hand, are generally content to try to draw these notions together with verbal arguments expressed in somewhat vaguer terms than scientists generally care to entertain.

• *Practical:* In the view of practical men of affairs, war arises from human nature taking its natural course. Hence, wars arise as a result of states finding themselves in situations where they feel they must fight or cease to exist; when people want something like territory, money, or power; or when people fight for ideological reasons, to name but a few of the many kinds of practical causes.

Reflecting upon these different types of underlying causes of war, Quincy Wright observed that all of them are generalizations about

(1) *material forces* in the state system (balance of power, political factors), (2) *rational influences* (international law, national interests), (3) *social institutions* (ideology, international organizations), and (4) *reactions of personalities* (public opinion, psychological and emotional factors). Thus, the overall picture that emerges is one of war coming about from a constellation of politico-technological, rational, ideological, and economic conditions.

The preceding ideas are all rather general, even abstract, notions about causation as it pertains to armed hostilities. This is fine as far as it goes. But if we're looking to apply the techniques and principles of scientific investigation to the problem of predicting the outbreak of war, we need some actual data upon which to test our general theories. So let's close this background section with a list of observations, or "data points," serving as empirically based generalizations about the conditions under which real wars break out.

In a recently published study of war in the modern world, the diplomat, politician, author, and Oxford fellow Evan Luard has noted the following general features of warfare in our time:

A. *The great majority of wars involve single states on either side.*
   Implication: Alliances may or may not deter wars, but they don't tend to participate in them. Thus, the two world wars of this century are exceptions, not the general rule.
B. *Most wars, especially after 1945, seem to arise out of specific incidents or disputes.*
   Implication: Not many wars are the result of deliberate policies of aggression or aggrandizement by governments.
C. *Many internal conflicts involve external intervention.*
   Implication: There is a basic change of motivation among states, from the desire to have direct physical control over another's territory to wanting indirect political control over it.
D. *There have been an increasing number of limited conflicts over frontiers.*
   Implication: Nations are more inclined to go to war over issues of their borders, no matter how small the intrinsic value of the territory, than over matters of trade, tariffs, or investment that are of far more importance to their basic interests.
E. *Balance-of-power systems have not been successful in securing peace.*

Implication: States do not seem to be decisively influenced by power-balance considerations in reaching the decision to go to war.

F. *External wars are more often undertaken to restore a status quo previously disturbed than to change it.*
Implication: Modern wars tend to arise out of the security apprehensions of countries concerning the areas immediately adjacent to their borders.

There are far more guidelines of this sort, not only in Luard's work, but also in many other volumes focusing on empirical investigations of war, ancient and modern. Nevertheless, this list suffices for our needs and reveals at least a few of the highlights. The motivated reader is invited to consult the To Dig Deeper section at the end of this book for a more complete account. With the preliminaries finally out of the way, let's turn the floor over to the Professor Fates of the world, inviting them to argue the case for the existence of discernible patterns in the underlying causes of war.

A TIDE IN THE AFFAIRS OF NATIONS

In early 1939 an odd research paper arrived at the offices of an influential American political science journal, along with a transmittal note from the author urging the editors to publish the paper quickly as its appearance could help avert the outbreak of an impending war. Not only did the editors fail to expedite the paper, they rejected it summarily as, I strongly suspect from my own duties as the editor of a journal, the work of a misguided crank, a wild-eyed fanatic, or most likely both. But the line between genius and insanity is, as they say, a very fine one. And it turned out that this paper was indeed the work of, if not genius, then at least a very unusual and far-ranging mind. In fact, the paper represented the first step toward a truly scientific approach to the study of the outbreak of war.

In his charming little volume *A Mathematician's Apology*, G. H. Hardy remarks that "it is a tiny minority who can do anything *really* well, and the number of men who can do two things well is negligible." I tend to disagree with Hardy's claim, at least if taken literally, since I can think of many things that I do extremely well, e.g., napping on the sofa after lunch, listening to music, reading science fiction and thriller novels, and being on sabbatical leave, to name but a few. But I suppose I'll have to concede Hardy's point when it comes to being able to do things that the rest of the world values. And Hardy's observation is of special interest for us here, as the author of the aforementioned paper was none other than Lewis F. Richardson, the very same Lewis F. Richardson we met in Chapter Two as the author of the first treatise on the use of numerical methods for weather forecasting.

Richardson's thesis about the outbreak of war was based upon the reasonable assumption that states would not go to war unless they were suitably armed. Thus, he argued, the underlying cause of the outbreak of war resides in a runaway arms race. In this view, when the armaments expenditures reach sufficiently high levels, warfare is imminent. From this hypothetical starting point, Richardson developed a model of how armaments levels change as a function of perceived threats, past grievances, trade, and similar factors. Putting empirical data into his model, in 1939 Richardson came to the conclusion that the world was on the brink of war; hence, the note of urgency in his transmittal letter to the editors of the journal.

Observe that Richardson's theory is based on the idea that there are some fundamental indicators of a state's power (arms levels or defense expenditures, in Richardson's case), and that the outbreak of war can be both predicted and explained by relations among these indicators. But Richardson's indicators of power occupy a position somewhere between being underlying and proximate causes of war, and more basic indicators have been proposed. So let's take some time to consider these foundational indicators before returning to Richardson's model.

In one of his patented multiple-character performances in the 1959 spoof *The Mouse That Roared,* Peter Sellers played the duke of Grand Fenwick, a small, bankrupt country that to the Austrian eye looks suspiciously like the Principality of Liechtenstein (with the notable difference that Liechtenstein is very far from being bankrupt). The film's story line involves the duke's scheme to have his country declare war on the United States, lose, and then get rehabilitated, thereby replenishing the national treasury with a Marshall Plan–like infusion of U.S. taxpayers' dollars. The only problem is that Grand Fenwick forgets to lose!

In the context of current geopolitical thinking, Grand Fenwick represents a textbook example of a country that is totally unequipped to initiate a war with anyone. Power is the name of the war game, and modern conventional wisdom has it that a nation's power rests upon three pillars: population, resources, and technology. Needless to say, of the three, Grand Fenwick had very little of any. Since population, resources, and technology play such an overriding role in determining the ability of a country to go to war, let's look a bit more carefully at how each of these factors enters into the calculus of war.

- *Population:* Wars are fought with people. If you don't have enough of them, or if they're not of fighting age, then you're in trouble when it comes to putting together a credible fighting force. Thus the size, rate of change, composition, distribution, and mobility of a state's population play a central role in assessing its war-making capabilities.
- *Resources:* People alone are not enough to put together a good war machine; a nation also needs things like raw materials and manufacturing facilities, as well as the human skills to use them for military ends. In short, you need resources.
- *Technology:* The key to modern warfare lies in the efficient conversion of resources into military tools. This means not only the ability to produce effective fighting equipment like tanks, airplanes, guns, and bombs, but also the means for rapid and efficient processing of information with computers and modern communication systems. Taken together, these requirements for waging modern war effectively imply that a nation must have a highly developed technological base.

So these are the master variables underlying war: population, resources, and technology. In a detailed consideration of the relation between these variables and the outbreak of war, Nazli Choucri and Robert North have put forward the proposition that the roots of war are to be found in population growth, which, when combined with the other master variables, affects a nation's disposition toward conflict, as well as its intent and ability to wage war successfully. Their claim is that things like population growth, advancement in technology, rising societal demands, increase in military capability, and the like generate demands, constrain capabilities, and contribute to the attitude of other nations toward a state.

According to Choucri and North, changes in the master variables are seldom the proximate cause of war. Thus, the outbreak of conflict is rarely, if ever, explained directly by the master variables alone. But the master variables set the parameters within which the "accidents" so beloved by the Dr. Chances of the world can ignite a conflict. So let's consider some of the different master-variable profiles states may display, with an eye toward identifying those that are likely to encourage a state to go to war. The possible profiles are outlined in Table 5.1, where the symbol + represents a high level of the master variable, while − signifies a low level.

Master Variables				
Popu- lation	Tech- nology	Re- sources	Examples	Profile
+	+	+	U.S., U.S.S.R.	necessity for outward-oriented activities—military, diplomatic, economic
+	−	−	India	little chance for international behavior
−	−	+	Kuwait, Brunei	entirely dependent on the outside world
−	+	−	Israel, Singapore	foreign policy aimed at obtaining access to resources
−	−	−	Chad, Niger	completely survival oriented
+	+	−	Japan	major goal is to assure access to resources
−	+	+	Sweden, Canada	high levels of trade and diplomacy
+	−	+	China	oriented toward technology imports

Table 5.1. Master variables and state profiles

Consideration of these master-variable profiles strongly suggests that the roots of violence are defined by a nation's need to expand beyond established boundaries in order to satisfy the demands of a growing population. Thus, for example, the needs of countries like Japan and Israel that are constrained by lack of resources can result in activities that may well lead to conflict. But in today's world, the only realistic candidates for instigating what we've termed a hegemonic war are countries that rank near the top of the master-variable list in at least two of the three variables, especially in the all-important area of technology. Keeping this fact in mind, let's consider some master-variable-based theories of how wars break out.

To summarize the situation thus far, we have seen that, when it comes to making war, power is what it's all about. Moreover, power is, in some yet-to-be-defined way, directly related to the master variables just considered. Taking these observations as axiomatic, fundamentalists like Professor Fate argue that to understand the outbreak of war we have to be able to give convincing answers to these basic questions:

A. In what way *exactly* do the master variables determine a state's power?
B. Are there certain patterns of power distribution in the international system that are particularly conducive to the outbreak of armed conflict?
C. If there are indeed such "warlike" patterns, which states are the most likely candidates for initiating the conflict?

Let's first look at Questions B and C, leaving the power measurement issue for later.

Consideration of the power allocation structure and its change among the nations of the world, as well as its implications for war, leads to a plethora of different theories, all of which can be conveniently subsumed under the label *power distribution models.* While there are almost as many ideas about different power distributions and their relation to war as there are investigators, to keep matters within reasonable bounds we'll consider here only what look to be the three leading contenders: Balance of Power, Collective Security, and Power Transition.

  • *Balance of Power:* Such theories assert that when power is more or less equally distributed among great powers or major alliances, then peace will ensue. Conversely, when large asymmetries in the power balance take place, the probability of war increases significantly. Thus the Balance-of-Power theories are based on three major premises: (1) equal power among states or alliances is conducive to peace, (2) an imbalance of power leads to war, and (3) the most likely aggressor will be the most powerful party.

  Those adhering to the Balance-of-Power thesis claim that the political actions of nations are motivated by a desire to enhance their power. In this regard, the assertion is also made that the major mechanism sustaining the balance of power is the making and breaking of alliances.

From a system-theoretic perspective, such an international system is inherently homeostatic; that is, the model assumes that the strongest uncommitted player in the system will always step in on the weaker side and redress whatever imbalance arises. Underlying this assumption is the deeper hypothesis that such a balancer would want to increase its own power by attacking one coalition with the help of another.

Since it's hard to accept both the idea that a nation really acts so as to maximize its power and the view that an equal distribution of power keeps the peace, let's turn to the next candidate.

• *Collective Security:* In this view of geopolitics, the key phrase is "All against one." The idea is that the global power distribution should be highly lopsided, assuming that all members of the international community will act against any aggressor. The two tenets upon which Collective Security theories rest are (1) a highly unbalanced distribution of power (with defenders collectively much stronger than any aggressor) will sustain the peace, and (2) a more or less equal distribution of power will lead to war.

Key assumptions underlying the Collective Security models of international relations are that when a serious dispute breaks out, the identity of the aggressor will be known to everyone (compare problems in identifying the aggressor in the terrorist attacks of recent years), and that all nations will be equally interested in preventing aggression and hence can be expected to organize their activities to that end.

In both Balance-of-Power and Collective Security theories, alliances are the major method by which the necessary imbalance of power between the aggressor and the defenders is to be achieved. Thus, these models assume that states will form and withdraw from alliances with the deliberate goal of creating and/or sustaining a pronounced imbalance in the respective power of the competing coalitions. Note, however, that in contrast to the Balance-of-Power theories, in the Collective Security picture the commitment to resist aggression is made a priori, the necessary coalition then following automatically as the need arises. Many scholars and international relations experts find these assumptions at least as hard to swallow as those associated with the Balance-of-Power theories, leading to our third class of models.

• *Power Transition:* In this view, the source of war lies in the differences in the levels and rates of growth of the power possessed by states in the international system. The decision to go to war arises from a nation's dissatisfaction with its position in the system, and a desire to rewrite the rules dictating the relations among nation-states.

Part of the claim of the Power Transition school is that alliances are not a realistic method of preventing threatening changes in the distribution of world power. Basically, the fundamental evolution of power distribution is set and cannot be manipulated; in the long run, alliances cannot alter secular trends.

Since dissatisfaction with one's lot in life is what drives the Power Transition theory, it's the tension in the relationship between the dominant power and the challenger that is most likely to start a major war. The theory says that the attacker will be the weaker party. In the most popular Power Transition version of the scenario for war, there is a period during which both dominant and challenging nations are approximately equal in power. The ruling elites on both sides see that the challenger will soon pass the dominant power, and they all regard this as a threatening state of affairs. The Power Transition model states that any attempt to hasten this passage leads the faster-growing nation to attack.

Before turning to the vexing Question A, involving how we could actually measure power and test these theories, let's first summarize the basic points of each in Table 5.2.

How would one go about testing these theories? And which of the three competing theories makes the best match with reality? These were the overarching questions that A. Organski and J. Kugler (denoted henceforth O&K) addressed in their 1980 study *The War Ledger*. And it was at this point of testing against the real world that O&K came up against the bugaboo of how to translate the master variables into a measure of power.

As we've seen, the master variables encompass many aspects of a nation's life—economic, political, technological, military, demographic—and each of them reflects a different aspect of power. In their study, O&K simplified the problem several orders of magnitude by arguing that, in one way or another, all of these aspects of power

	Balance of Power	Collective Security	Power Transition
Power distribution	equal	lopsided	slightly lopsided
Dominant power versus coalition	equal	weaker	slightly stronger
Goals of elites	increase power	prevent aggression	no general rule
Power redistribution method	alliances	alliances	nation's own socioeconomic and political development

Table 5.2. Power distribution theories

ultimately come down to hard cash: If you don't have it, then you can't muster a war machine worthy of even honorable mention in the international power game. So in the O&K study, power = gross national product (GNP). But you might argue that GNP doesn't even begin to measure the ability of the political system to do its job of mobilizing resources. O&K are sensitive to this criticism, conceding that GNP is far from being perfectly correlated with anyone's vague, yet intuitive, notion of power. Nevertheless, they choose GNP on the pragmatic grounds that: (1) there are more reliable data available on GNP than on competing indicators of power, (2) using GNP is more parsimonious than trying to amalgamate a cluster of other indicators, and (3) it is theoretically attractive since, as wise men say, money is the root of all evil—including warfare.

As to their choice of powers and contenders, O&K regard the dominant power as being the nation having the highest GNP. The contenders are any country whose GNP is at least 80 percent of that of the dominant power. And if no country meets this test, then the contenders are the three strongest nations. Thus, in the current international system the dominant power is the United States, the contenders being the U.S.S.R., France, Germany, and Japan.

In keeping with our restriction on types of wars, the O&K study looked only at the outbreak of hegemonic war during the period 1860–1975. During this time-frame, four major wars were identified: (1) the Franco-Prussian War of 1870–1871, (2) the Russo-Japanese War of 1904–1905, (3) World War I, and (4) World War II. Note that the inclusion of World War II in the study goes against our earlier admonition to ignore it as a hegemonic war. The reason we differ from the choice of the O&K study is that by our earlier criteria for a hegemonic war, World War II fails to qualify as it was really just the continuation of World War I, which ended without settling the hegemonic struggle between Europe and the United States that emerged during the course of the war.

Using the GNP measure of power, together with an array of sophisticated statistical hypothesis-testing procedures to examine the claims of the competing power-distribution models, O&K come to these conclusions in their study of the outbreak of hegemonic wars:

1. Power distributions are not a predictor of the coming of war; both equal and unequal shares of power between adversaries are associated with war.
2. Great-power wars occur if the balance of power isn't stable, i.e., if one power is overtaking the other.
3. If a conflict breaks out among the contenders, it does so only if one of them is in the process of passing another.

The overall conclusion O&K draw is that major powers fight whether they are weaker, stronger, or equal in power to their opponent. On the other hand, contenders fight only if the weaker is overtaking the stronger. Now what do these results tell us about the competing models?

Looking at the Balance-of-Power model, the O&K study renders an unambiguous verdict: The conceptions underpinning the Balance-of-Power model are completely wrong. The mechanism making for major wars is the difference in the rates of growth of the great powers. And of special importance is the difference in the rates of power growth between the dominant nation and the leading contender. It is the leap-frogging of the challenger that destabilizes the system, particularly if the passage is rapid. This destabilization between the "elephants" of the international system then acts as a magnet to attract all the major powers into the war. And it is only at this point that alliances become a consideration in generating war.

The O&K study suggests strongly that it is the difference in the rates of change of power (i.e., GNP) that is ultimately responsible for the outbreak of war. And in this scenario it is the leading challenger that will be the aggressor. If such a picture is even approximately correct, the astute hedger in international relations futures might want to go long with a few call options on the Pacific Rim countries, especially

Japan and China, as logical candidates for starting the next hegemonic war.

Conclusions similar to those of O&K have been obtained by zoologist Paul Colinvaux, who looked at the outbreak of war from an ecological perspective. Colinvaux's work focused on the hypothesis that wars between civilized states arise as an emergent property of individuals' seeking to better their socioeconomic "niches." Let's spend a few moments looking at some of the details of his theory.

Arguing by analogy with conflict in the animal world, Colinvaux's niche theory of war is based upon the following conditions that he claims are necessary for a population to initiate a conflict:

- *A rising standard of living:* The population is relatively rich and getting richer.
- *Fighting for liberty:* Aggressive armies fight for booty to support a way of life; their leaders talk about fighting for "liberty." The apparent contradiction is resolved by recognizing that the struggle is really for the "freedom" to expand individual niche space.
- *A rising population:* An increasing standard of living generates confidence in the future, leading people to have more children. It should be noted that this is not the same thing as the Third World "population bomb." In our situation the population is already living well and is getting used to the idea of living better. Thus the real pressure here is on the niche space of those in political power.
- *Population relatively advanced in technology:* Much effort has already been devoted to increasing niche space by methods less costly than an aggressive war. Such a country will have already expanded its resources by means of advanced techniques of agriculture, industry, and government.
- *Existence of a suitable victim:* For initiation of an aggressive war, the ideal victim is a country that is technologically backward by the standards of the aggressor, but with territory and resources that the aggressor can exploit to increase its standard of living.
- *Apparent military superiority:* The aggressor must *think* that it possesses superior military strength to overcome its intended victim.

From these requirements for aggression, Colinvaux draws the profile of an attacking nation as one that (a) is relatively rich and getting richer, (b) has both a rising population and rising aspirations, (c) is composed of people who think of themselves as being free, and (d) has a sense of technical superiority to other nations, a feeling coming from recent successes in applying technical fixes and symbolized by advanced weapons.

So what kind of countries in today's world present themselves as likely candidates for initiating a major war of aggression? Looking at the above profile, we see that such a country must be rich, free, ambitious, literate, skilled in trade and commerce, but dependent on the living space of other lands for the wealth and freedom of a large population. These factors strongly suggest either a great island country (e.g., Japan, Taiwan) or a geographically isolated power (Israel or South Africa?) as being the most evident candidates for starting World War III.

It's fairly clear that Colinvaux's world will soon be a very dangerous place, since the world is filled with countries that fit his profile of a potential aggressor. The real problem is finding a suitable victim. On the positive side of the ledger, the ecological hypothesis predicts that there can be no war of aggression involving an attack of one superpower on another. Such a war would be irrational. Therefore, Colinvaux concludes that neither the United States nor the U.S.S.R. will be of much interest to future military historians.

The observant reader will have seen that the Niche Space theory of war provides an ecological underpinning to the Power Transition model of O&K. The O&K theory claims that the aggressor in a hegemonic war will be the challenger that's in the process of passing the dominant power. O&K measure the strength of the challenger simply by its GNP. The Niche Space theory gives far more detailed information about the profile of such a challenger. Not only is the challenger relatively rich, but it possesses the many other characteristics noted above. The only point of conflict between the Power Transition and the Niche Space theories is the identity of the victim. In the O&K version, the victim is the current dominant power; the Niche Space theory argues that the victim is much more likely to be a state of lesser power. But the culprit in both cases remains the same: a fortunate nation wanting to become even more fortunate.

Both the O&K study and the Colinvaux ecologically based theory come down strongly on the side of the Power Transition theory of conflict. On the equal-time principle, let's return to Richardson's pioneering paper for some arguments favoring the Balance-of-Power view of the outbreak of war.

*　　*　　*

Suppose you were an empirical-data-minded sort of person living in Europe in the early part of this century. If you were interested in the forces at work pushing countries into war, it might have occurred to you that warfare means armaments, and that a pronounced increase in arms levels could be a not-so-distant early warning signal of war. Following this line of reasoning, you might then go to the data and plot the annual rate of increase in arms expenditures for the combined forces of the major European powers (later to become the Central Powers and the Allies during World War I). If you carried out this exercise for the period 1909–1913, your digging around in the data would yield a set of points representing the annual increase in arms expenditures for each year. After a bit of staring at these points, you would probably soon realize that all four points lie very close to the same straight line. Drawing this line, you'd end up with a plot looking something like that shown in Figure 5.2.

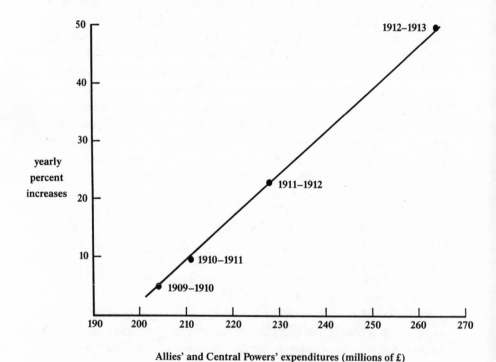

Figure 5.2. *The arms race of 1909–1913*

For the resolutely empirically minded, this would end the matter. But not so for an empirically minded scholar with theoretical leanings like Lewis F. Richardson. Such a person would never be satisfied with a mere plot of the data; what a theoretician would demand is a deeper relation to explain why the data appear to fall on a straight line. And out of such considerations was born Richardson's fundamental paper on the origins of war mentioned earlier.

In developing his theory of conflict, Richardson took armaments levels—i.e., defense expenditures—as his basic measure of a state's power. His model for the outbreak of war is based upon three premises, which for simplicity we will describe here only in terms of a two-power—i.e., bipolar—world (extensions to the multipolar case can be found in the references cited in To Dig Deeper). For Richardson, the rate of change of a nation's armaments level (a) increases in direct proportion to the perceived threat (level of arms) posed by its opponent, (b) decreases in direct proportion to the state's own perceived security, and (c) increases by the level of residual hostility the state feels toward its opponent, i.e., the "grievance factor" remaining from past conflicts.

To translate these principles into a formal model, suppose there are two countries Xeno and Yon having armaments levels x and y, respectively. To see how the factors threat, security, and grievance each contribute to the rate of change of the arms levels of Xeno and Yon, let's go to Xeno and be a fly on the wall, eavesdropping at a meeting of Xeno's Cabinet Ministers as they consider the annual budget. The participants are Xeno's Ministers of Defense, Commerce, and the Treasury, the meeting being chaired by Treasury.

TREASURY: As always, I see you've both submitted budgets far in excess of what our dwindling tax revenues can support. So before deciding how much should be trimmed from each of your requests, I'd like to hear your arguments justifying these outlandish sums. Why don't you tell me the arguments for guns first. Then I'll listen to the case for butter.

DEFENSE: I don't think it's necessary to tell either of you about the increasingly belligerent behavior of Yon. Everyone knows about last month's border incursion up north, and intelligence reports indicate that Yon is gearing up for a full-scale offensive later next year. Our agents also report that Yon's leaders are stepping up their rate of arms production in preparation for this attack. In light of these signs, I regard Yon's threat as very real, very dangerous, and very immediate. And my budgetary request is the bare-bones minimum that will give us a fighting chance, literally, to boost our own rate of weapons production to meet this threat.

T: Yes, we can all see that Yon's saber rattling and outright provocations do appear very threatening. Nevertheless, it seems to me that our own current rate of arms production is already quite high, and I personally feel secure enough in our current ability to destroy Yon ten times over. Why do we need to build up to a still higher level? Don't you think that increasing our rate of armaments production will just result in Yon's seeing us as a greater threat? This might then send both our countries into an arms race that could easily spiral out of control.

D: In the defense game, it's advantage that counts—not absolute numbers. So if Yon can destroy us twenty times over and we can destroy them only ten times, then they have a two-to-one advantage and we'll be forced into dealing with them from a position of weakness rather than strength. The President and the people won't accept this—and neither will I!

T: What's the position of Commerce on all this?

COMMERCE: I think Defense overstates the case. OK, so we've had a couple of recent border skirmishes with Yon. But by comparison with the economic and cultural ties between us and Yon, these border incidents are nothing. You both know that after the War of '97 our relations with Yon were at an all-time low, and there was a lot of residual hostility on their part from the way our soldiers treated them during the occupation. Since then we've worked hard to overcome those not entirely unjustified grievances, particularly by strengthening our mutual economic ties. Personally, I feel we're succeeding very well in this, and I wouldn't like to see the process jeopardized by the kind of overreaction that Defense is suggesting. Frankly, if I were President Hither of Yon and saw us taking the kind of actions Defense is proposing, I'd start getting very nervous and might well start building up my own military machine again.

T: So you feel perfectly secure with our current rate of arms production, and think we can do better by pumping resources into further development of trade and cultural ties than by building more weapons.

C: Precisely.

T: All right. Let me make sure I've gotten the drift of this discussion. Defense, you're saying that threatening indications from Yon suggest a military buildup on their part, possibly in preparation for an attack. So we should increase our own rate of arms production, both to discourage Yon and to be ready in case they do attack. On the other hand, Commerce, you argue that we're already perfectly secure with our current arms program, and that we'd do better to invest our resources in furthering economic and cultural ties as a way of reducing the friction remaining in our relationship with Yon over past hostilities. Does that about sum things up?

D: Right.

C: Exactly.

T: OK. Give me a week to read and digest your reports. Then let's meet to settle the matter. Shall we say next Wednesday at ten o'clock?

Before Wednesday's showdown, Treasury ponders how she should balance out the seemingly very reasonable, but mutually contradictory, arguments made by Defense and Commerce. Somehow, her task is to juggle the three factors—the threat posed by Yon, the security from Xeno's own rate of arms production, and Yon's residual grievance—and come up with a division of the ever-shrinking budgetary pie that will respect the concerns of both Defense and Commerce. Being a bit of a closet mathematician as well as a power broker, Treasury decomposes the problem into its constituent parts, and makes these arguments to herself for each component:

Threat: Defense sees Yon's arms level y as a threat, with the greater the level of y, the greater the threat. Therefore, he thinks we should increase our own rate of arms production in proportion to the magnitude of the threat, which he identifies with Yon's arms level y. Suppose I let the number a be a measure of the *increased* threat felt by Defense if Yon were to make a unit increase in its arms level y. Then, the greater the threat Defense sees from an arms buildup in Yon, the greater will be the value of a. Under these circumstances, I can translate Defense's arguments into symbolic form by saying that, everything else being equal, we should increase our own rate of arms production by an amount ay. Unfortunately, everything else isn't equal, and I still have to account for matters of security and grievance.

Security: Suppose I use our own level of arms x as a measure of Commerce's perceived sense of security. Then, following the arguments of Commerce, the larger x is, the less compelled we should feel to step up our rate of arms production. So if I let the number m represent the level of security we feel from each unit level of increase in our own weapons stockpile, I can symbolically represent Commerce's sense of perceived security by the quantity $-mx$. Here, of course, I have to use the minus sign, since as our own arms level increases, our *rate* of arms production must decrease. Now how can I account for this nebulous grievance factor?

Grievance: Suppose I use the number g to measure the amount of grievance that Yon feels toward us from the past. A positive value of g means that there is still some residual hostility, a situation that would contribute to Defense's claim that we should increase our rate of arms production. On the other hand, a negative value of g acts to support Commerce's contention that we need to reduce our rate of arms buildup. The well-known theoretician Lewis F. Richardson interpreted such negative values of the grievance factor in terms of international trade levels, just like Commerce, and he felt that the more interdependent two countries are on the basis of trade, the less residual hostility they would feel toward each other from past altercations. Now let me see if I can pull all these threads together and come up with a fair assessment of where to draw the line between Defense and Commerce.

Following this line of reasoning, Treasury sees that each piece of her budgetary puzzle makes its own contribution toward the matter of how Xeno should adjust its own rate of armaments production, depending on the values of the threat, security, and grievance parameters a, m, and g. To arrive at what the actual rate of change should be, Treasury simply combines all three by adding them together. As a result, Xeno's arms level will change at a rate of $ay - mx + g$. In other words, the actual level of weapons will move up or down by this amount in one time unit (for example, one year).

Moving across the border, we can introduce analogous parameters b, n, and h to represent the threat, security, and grievance coefficients, respectively, as seen by Treasury's opposite number in Yon. A word-for-word repetition of the preceding argument then leads to the conclusion that the change of Yon's armaments level in a unit of time will be $bx - ny + h$. The interrelationship between these two rates of arms level change constitutes the distilled essence of Richardson's model. Now let's see what it all has to do with the outbreak of war.

What Richardson was looking for was a level of arms for Xeno and Yon at which the rate of change, i.e., arms buildup, for each country is zero. In short, he sought a balance of power. The Richardson argument is that if such a balance-of-power equilibrium point exists and is stable (that is, if it persists as an equilibrium point to which the arms levels return when the level of armaments moves away from this balance point a little bit), then war will not break out. On the other hand, Richardson thought that if such a balance-of-power point either did not exist or was unstable, then a runaway arms race would ensue, ultimately leading to an outbreak of hostilities. So let's examine both the question of the existence of such an equilibrium level of arms and the conditions under which such a balance of power will be stable.

Since the rate of change of Xeno's arms level is given by the expression $ay - mx + g$, for Xeno's production to level off this rate of change must be zero, i.e., $ay - mx + g = 0$. Similarly, for Yon's armaments industry to enter the no-growth mode, we must have $bx - ny + h = 0$. Thus we conclude that for both countries' rates of arms production to remain unchanged, thus allowing the arms race to grind to a halt, these two equations must be satisfied simultaneously for some values of x and y. And it's exactly those levels of arms that constitute a balance-of-power point. Let's consider the situation geometrically.

If we let the arms levels x and y of Xeno and Yon be the coordinates of a point in the x-y plane, then in this space of possible arms levels the pair of equations $ay - mx + g = 0$ and

$bx - ny + h = 0$ show up as two straight lines whose orientations are determined by the specific values of the coefficients a, b, m, n, g, and h. Figure 5.3 shows a typical pair of such lines. From this picture it's evident that the levels of armaments at which the arms race stops will occur at the point where the two lines intersect, denoted by (x^*, y^*).

This figure makes it clear that a balance-of-power point exists at the intersection of the two lines characterizing zero rates of armaments growth for both Xeno and Yon. Elementary geometry tells us that there can be (a) an infinite number of such points (the lines are coincident, i.e., they lie on top of each other), (b) no points of intersection (the lines are parallel), or (c) a single point of intersection like that shown in the figure. Only the last case is "typical" (that is, cannot be changed by a small perturbation of some of the parameters a, b, m, n, g, and

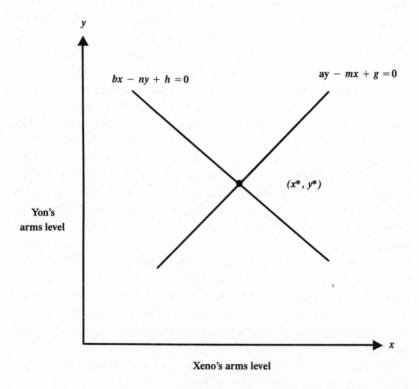

Figure 5.3. *A Richardson-type arms race*

h); hence, a single balance-of-power point is what we expect to find in a Richardson-type model. But will such an equilibrium level of arms be stable? In other words, if Xeno and Yon find their weapons stockpiles at such a level, and the leaders of one country or the other decide to change their level, will the system tend to return to the balance-of-power levels? Or will such a departure from the equilibrium point send the two states spiraling into an out-of-control arms race?

Arguing first on intuitive grounds, we would expect that if the overall perceived threat in the system exceeds the security, then the equilibrium will be unstable. Why? Simply because threat is what drives the countries to increase their arms levels, while security induces them to lower the rate of arms production. So if the threat felt by one country is sufficiently great to overcome the security felt by the other, we might expect an arms race to develop. But how could we measure the total level of threat in the two-state system?

Since the parameters a and b measure the threat levels felt by Xeno and Yon, an obvious candidate for the overall threat level in the system is to combine these two numbers in some manner. It turns out that the product ab is the kind of combination needed for analyzing the stability of the balance-of-power point. Similarly, the overall security in the system can be measured by the product mn. But, as is often the case, intuition alone doesn't tell the whole story, and we need to turn to the mathematics to fill in the details.

By means of analytic arguments, it can be shown that the balance-of-power point is stable if and only if $ab < mn$ and $m + n > 0$. Thus, as we conjectured above on intuitive grounds, stability depends on the security outweighing the threat. But we also need the second condition involving the security terms alone. This condition says that if the security felt by one party is more than outweighed by the insecurity felt by the other, then the balance-of-power point will not be stable. So if the overall feeling of security in the system is great enough, there will be no arms race. This much seems pretty obvious. But where do the grievance factors come into the picture?

What may not be so immediately evident is that the grievance factors g and h play no role at all in assessing the system's stability. The grievance terms come into the picture in determining the exact levels (x^*, y^*) of arms constituting the balance-of-power point. But when it comes to deciding whether this level is stable, mathematics says we can ignore the grievance factors entirely.

At this point it's relevant to recall Clausewitz's idea that the essence of war is "an act of violence intended to compel our opponent to fulfill our will." This statement leads logically to the conclusion that escalation is inevitable. In short, according to Clausewitz the balance-of-power point is always unstable, and an arms race leading to war is what we can inevitably expect. We saw earlier that Richardson's model fit the arms race preceding World War I. But is this grim conclusion really the general case? Is it always borne out by the actual historical record? Let's go to the data and try to find out.

We started this exposition of Richardson's model of arms buildups with the graph of the joint expenditures of the European powers prior to the First World War. A mathematical consequence of Richardson's equations is that the combined arms levels of Xeno and Yon, the quantity $x + y$, should follow a straight line when measured in terms of percentage increases per year. The empirical data shown earlier in Figure 5.2 for the combined arms expenditures for the Allies and Central Powers gave strong testimony to the utility of Richardson's model for the pre–World War I era. In an effort to test the model against more recent arms races, we show the 1945–1960 defense expenditures for the United States and the U.S.S.R. in Figure 5.4.

Besides the actual data shown by the circles (U.S.) and crosses (U.S.S.R.), Figure 5.4 also shows the expenditure curves for both superpowers. These curves were obtained by finding the best fit to the actual data of the threat, security, and grievance coefficients in a Richardson model. Then letting x represent U.S.S.R. arms expenditures and y those of the United States, the best-fit model was employed to calculate the dynamical evolution of the expenditures. Using the empirical data in this way, the best estimates for the threat parameters turned out to be $a = 0$, $b = 4.1$, while the security parameters were $m = 0.45$, $n = 0.8$. Finally, the grievance coefficients came out to be $g = 21$, $h = -142$. These estimates have several interesting implications:

1. The U.S.S.R. arms buildup is driven by the grievance factor g, since the parameter a measuring the perceived threat from the United States is zero.
2. The United States reacts strongly to a Soviet arms buildup, since the American perceived threat factor b is relatively large. However, the United States is otherwise favorably disposed to the U.S.S.R., as indicated by the high negative grievance factor h.
3. The system balance-of-power point is stable, since the overall

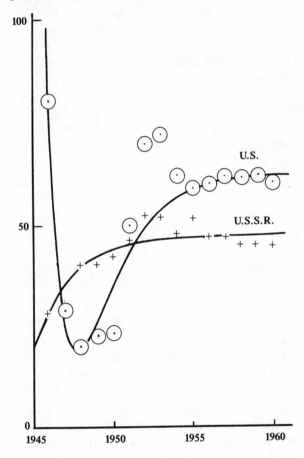

Figure 5.4. *Postwar U.S. and U.S.S.R. arms expenditures (in billions of 1970 dollars)*

threat in the system ($ab = 0$) is less than the overall security ($mn = 0.36$) and the total security $m + n = 0.8 + 0.45 = 1.25$ is positive.

It's of considerable interest to contrast these superpower results with those of the other major arms race of modern times, between the Arabs and Israelis. Letting x represent Arab (Egypt, Syria, Jordan, and Iraq) expenditures since 1949, while letting y denote the corresponding Israeli defense outlay, another curve-fitting exercise yields the parameter estimates for threat as $a = b = 0$, while the security terms turn out to be $m = -0.22$, $n = -0.11$. The grievance factors are $g = 0.005$, $h = 0$. The implications of this model are quite surprising, considering the realities of the situation:

1. Since the threat parameters are both zero, there is no perceived threat by either party; the Arab and Israeli arms buildups are two totally separate growth processes driven entirely by internal apprehensions about security.
2. Further reinforcing the foregoing point, the grievance factors are either zero or negligible for both the Arabs and the Israelis. (Recall that Richardson defines *grievance* in terms of levels of trade, i.e., cooperative interaction, and not necessarily in the usual sense of resentment or the harboring of ill will.)
3. The equilibrium expenditure level at $x^* = 0.022$, $y^* = 0$ is unstable since, although the system threat level ($ab = 0$) is less than the security level ($mn = [-0.22][-0.11] = 0.0242$), the overall security in the system is negative ($m + n = -0.33$).

These results at best only partially support the Balance-of-Power theory and, in fact, many other studies using Richardson's model seem to point to fundamental gaps in the model's contact with geopolitical and military reality. References to some of these analyses can be found in the To Dig Deeper section for this chapter.

Let's now leave Richardson and turn to our last spokesman for the "fundamentalist" view of war. The final issue before the house will be to determine whether the recent profound changes in the global system, such as the rise of international trade and the emergence of international organizations, present any new factors influencing the elements of power politics underlying the theories we've considered to now.

In the traditional Clausewitzian view of international relations, war is a calculated choice of governments based upon states acting so as to enhance their interests (i.e., power). In this essentially economic view of behavior, constraints on the choice of war exist as the costs of action against which the decisionmakers must balance benefits. But the sweeping changes wrought in the international system by developments in transportation, communication, and information processing cast doubt on this cozy "rational actor" interpretation of the decision to go to war.

In a recent study of the effects of structural change in the international system on the decision for war, William Domke investigated three basic questions:

A. Does the degree of political openness and competition in the society affect the likelihood of a national government's going to war?
B. Does the level of international trade in a national economy influence the chances of a state's starting a war?
C. Does participation in international organizations have any bearing on the probability that a state will instigate a conflict?

To get a scientific handle on these matters, Domke first reformulated each question as a hypothesis. For example, Question A was stated as Hypothesis A: "The greater the level of political openness and competition in a society, the less likely a national government is to decide for war." He then applied standard techniques of statistical hypothesis testing to a historical database consisting of 217 national decisions for war in 61 interstate wars during the period 1815–1986.

After a detailed analysis of the data, Domke came to the following conclusions:

A. Domestic political structure does not seem to be directly related to decisions for war, as both authoritarian and democratic regimes initiate hostilities with about equal likelihood.
B. There is a strong negative correlation between exports as a share of GNP and decisions for war.
C. Participation in limited-membership international organizations is weakly correlated negatively with the starting of wars.

In summary, the structure of the international system does constitute an important determinant of the foreign policy actions of governments; ergo, power politics by itself is not enough to understand why states choose to go to war.

On this note we wrap up the case for Professor Fate and his view of the outbreak of war as being determined by a tide in the affairs of nations. Now let's call Dr. Chance and his followers to the podium, giving them the opportunity to argue that while broad, general notions such as power are important, it is small groups of individuals that start wars, not vague, general concepts and trends.

EYEBALL TO EYEBALL

```
YOU HAVE IGNITED A NUCLEAR WAR.

AND NO, THERE IS NO ANIMATED DISPLAY
OF A MUSHROOM CLOUD WITH PARTS
OF BODIES FLYING THROUGH THE AIR.

WE DO NOT REWARD FAILURE.
```

And so ends another titanic struggle between the forces of good and evil—at least in the microworld of the personal-computer geopolitical game *Balance of Power*. For anyone infected with the germ of the idea that war is the outcome of inexorable historical trends operating outside the acts of individual decisionmakers, my remedy is a few hours' worth of interaction with this fascinating and sophisticated computer simulation. Acting the role of the American or the Soviet President, you'll face the daunting task of trying to enhance your country's international prestige in the face of a spectrum of provocations and confounding, competing actions by "the enemy." Through a variety of decisions—making treaties, sending military matériel and forces, giving economic aid—in *Balance of Power* your goal is to acquire lots of powerful friends, while at the same time trying to avoid letting crises escalate to DefCon 1, the highest level of defensive readiness, characterized by the above-cited pronouncement of Armageddon. Of course, your opponent (or the computer) is doing his or her best to thwart your efforts and acquire a complementary set of allies, while also skating as close as possible to the thin ice of nuclear disaster. Provided both parties manage to avoid falling into the abyss, the prestige points are totaled at the end of eight simulation years, the winner presumably inheriting the Earth—at least till the next game.

So how does an aspiring George Bush or Mikhail Gorbachev succeed in winning the struggle for global influence in *Balance of Power*? What are the key ingredients in winning friends and influencing people without touching off World War III? According to the game's designer, Chris Crawford, "Most players are too impatient and adventurous. . . . You cannot win by playing cowboy. You must be circumspect. You must learn the skills of the diplomat. . . . There can be only small victories—or total defeat." This is about as clear a statement as I can find that statesmanship and political acumen count in the international arena, and that the outbreak of war is tantamount to a leader's failure to achieve his country's goals without resorting to force. But *Balance of Power,* along with its many close relatives living in the memory banks of computers at the Pentagon, the RAND Corporation, and other QUANGOs around the world, is just an imitation of life. Or is it? Do the scenarios and decisionmaking environments built into these simulations really mirror a world in which the actions of individual leaders and their advisers are the real determinants of war? Dr. Chance thinks they do, and so do a lot of other contemporary thinkers and strategists absorbed with matters of international security. To set their overall position into a familiar framework, let's return to the fateful thirteen days of October 1962 and the Cuban missile crisis.

In his memoir of the Cuban crisis, Robert F. Kennedy repeatedly emphasizes the role of individual idiosyncrasies and prejudices on the part of the members of Exec Comm (the group of advisers to President John F. Kennedy), as they pondered their recommendations about how to remove the Soviet missiles from Cuba. Some Exec Comm members argued their position in a consistent, rational, basically cost-benefit-analysis fashion right from the start. Others, especially some of the military, clung to the knee-jerk recommendation of an air strike, seemingly without ever considering seriously any other course of action. And still others vacillated between the air strike, a naval blockade, or even no action at all, apparently on the basis of nothing more than gut feel and the emotions of the moment. And superimposed over each of these individual modes of decisionmaking was the ever present atmosphere of "group think," which ultimately and insidiously shaped all the participants' views of the actions they finally recommended to the President.

For students of both international relations and decisionmaking, two of the most important lessons to emerge from this example of real-life decisionmaking under stress and uncertainty are that (1) the personalities, characters, and psychologies of individual leaders and their advisers can indeed spell the difference between the outbreak of war and the preservation of peace, and (2) every decisionmaker operates on the basis of a conceptual model, or paradigm, of the decisionmaking process, a model that has the most dramatic consequences for the spectrum of possible actions that are even considered in arriving at a recommendation.

Some years after the Cuban crisis, Graham Allison of Harvard University examined in great detail the Exec Comm deliberations in an effort to pinpoint the types of decisionmaking paradigms employed by the committee's members. Allison identified at least three qualitatively distinct models:

• *Rational Actor:* This is the paradigm by which most strategic analysts look at problems of policy. Such decisionmakers conceptualize a problem in terms of the following kinds of questions: What is the problem? What are the alternatives? What are the strategic costs and benefits associated with each alternative course of action? What are the domestic and international constraints? In such a view, the government is thought of as being much like an individual choosing from among the various delicacies on offer at a Chinese restaurant. And just as at the restaurant, where the Peking duck is succulent and crispy but gives you heartburn at three o'clock in the morning, so it is with governmental choices as well. Each possible action carries with it a benefit and a cost, the final choice being made rationally by weighing up the net benefit from among the alternative courses of action.

Rational Actor is by far the most popular decisionmaking paradigm among the academically inclined analysts of policy, especially those coming from a scientific background. But severe practical difficulties arise when the action to be explained is not the behavior of an individual but rather the decision of a large organization, not to mention a government. By personifying nations, the analyst neglects critical aspects of behavior in which organizational factors are the driving force. In addition, such a view of decisionmaking omits consideration of the many personality types among the individual national leaders whose positions and power bases may give them very different perceptions and preferences on the issue at hand. These facts lead to Allison's two alternative paradigms.

• *Organizational Process:* By way of contrast to the Rational Actor paradigm, Organizational Process minimizes the role of the individual as decisionmaker, regarding government action as the output of an organization composed of many actors, fractionated power, and parochial priorities. Basically, in the Organizational

Process paradigm, decisions are the outcomes of bureaucratic procedures and processes. The overall problem is decomposed and parceled out to the various components of the bureaucracy, the final action being largely determined by present standard operating procedures (SOPs) and programs, as well as by long-term organizational goals. In short, there is no such thing as a single decisionmaker; ultimately, action is an emergent property of a collection of decentralized bureaucratic units, each of which acts according to its own limited priorities and procedures.

Again returning to the Cuban missile crisis for an example of the Organizational Process model in action, one of the Soviet negotiating ploys to end the crisis was to call for the withdrawal of U.S. Jupiter missiles from Turkey and Italy in exchange for removal of the Soviet missiles from Cuba. As Murphy's Law would have it, President Kennedy had repeatedly ordered the State Department many months earlier to negotiate with the Turks and the Italians for the removal of these missiles on the grounds that they were both a provocation to the Russians and technologically obsolete. Despite these instructions, bureaucratic entrenchment and Foggy Bottom SOPs combined to ignore the President's wishes, opening up the opportunity for Khrushchev to use the Jupiters as a card to play in this deadly poker game.

• *Governmental Politics:* "It's all politics" is the catchphrase for this paradigm. In contrast to decisions arising from the rational deliberation of a single agent ("the government") or from the actions of a "bureaucratic machine," the Governmental Politics perspective regards decisions as the outcome of political horse trading. What players are involved and what positions do they hold? Where are foul-ups likely? How do job pressures, past decisions, and personalities affect the players? What deadlines will force the issue to resolution? These are the kinds of questions characterizing the Governmental Politics model of decisionmaking. In short, the view is that governmental action is the result of bargaining. Typical illustrations of this kind of decisionmaking appear in the newspaper every day, as congressmen trade favors and votes in the time-honored traditions of legislative back scratching and pork-barrel projects seemingly built into the SOPs of governments everywhere.

In order to put these three decisionmaking paradigms into perspective, Table 5.3 displays the basic characteristics of each.

	Rational Actor	*Organizational Process*	*Governmental Politics*
Unit of analysis	"individual" choice	organizational output	political bargain
Organizing concept	rational actor	bureaucracy	players and positions
Inference pattern	rational choice	SOPs and programs	bargaining
View of Cuban crisis	Why is a blockade the optimal action?	How did bureaucratic output lead to a blockade?	Why was a blockade the political result?

Table 5.3. Decisionmaking paradigms

Unfortunately, from the kind of formal modeling perspective we've been emphasizing here for explaining the outbreak of war, neither the Organizational Process nor the Governmental Politics paradigm has been as well developed by the scholarly community as the Rational Actor model. Therefore, for the most part we'll have to confine our attention to considering the Rational Actor perspective as a candidate for the Dr. Chance school of thought on how individuals, not history, bring us to war. But the reader should be cautioned that in real-world decision making leading to choices for war, the other paradigms are very likely of equal importance, if not dominant.

For fans of the cult hero and movie idol James Dean, one of the great scenes in cinema history takes place in the 1955 film *Rebel Without a Cause* when Dean and his antagonist Buzz face each other in a "chicken race." For those who didn't see the film (or spend their youth in western America in the 1950s), the race involves two cars driving straight toward each other (or, as in the film, driving on parallel paths toward the edge of a cliff). The first driver to lose his nerve and veer off (or bail out of his car) is the "chicken," and is so reviled thereafter by his peer group. From the perspective of adults, especially parents, this kind of game seems like an especially dangerous way of settling teenagers' pecking-order disputes—at least at the level of individuals. Nevertheless, it can be rather convincingly argued that the abstract principles underlying a chicken race are identical to those governing many of the games that superpowers play. Let's have a quick look at why.

For the last forty years, mutual deterrence has been the pillar on which U.S. and Soviet military relations rest. The fundamental premise is that each country wants to make the choice of aggression so unattractive to the other through the threat of retaliation that they will both be deterred from starting a "hot war." Structurally, when they play the game of Deterrence, the superpowers are in fact often playing the game of Chicken. The reason is that if the threatener is forced to carry out its threat, then it will do as much damage to itself as to its opponent. In short, any crisis situation involves both countries driving head-on at each other with the U.S. and Soviet Presidents at the respective wheels, the speed of approach being proportional to the magnitude of the crisis.

Political scientist and game theorist Steven Brams has examined the Deterrence game, looking for strategies that a rational actor would employ to increase both the effectiveness and the credibility of his threat to respond to a provocation. What Brams discovered is that the optimal strategies seem to involve employing threats that are both probabilistic and robust. What this means is that the threatener should maintain a level of uncertainty in regard to his readiness to respond to an aggressive move by the other side. Robustness is a technical property of a probabilistic strategy that ensures the stability of the situation over a wide range of circumstances. Brams emphasizes the point that perilous games like Chicken are not cast in concrete but are subject to manipulation—i.e., they can be changed to be made more benign and less unstable. An excellent real-world example of this kind of game-theoretic analysis occurred with the 1973 U.S. alert decision arising from the Arab-Israeli Yom Kippur War.

On October 25, 1973, President Nixon ordered U.S. military forces put on a worldwide "precautionary alert," making what amounted to a nuclear threat. This action was prompted by the threat of the Soviet Union to intervene in the Yom Kippur War. Here are the circumstances leading up to this dramatic decision: Armed with Soviet weapons, Egypt and Syria made a coordinated surprise attack against Israel on October 6 during the Jewish Yom Kippur holiday. Initially, the attack was a success and Israel suffered heavy losses. However, a week later Israel launched a counteroffensive under the promise of a large supply of American weaponry and, as the counteroffensive went forward, the Arab forces were pushed backward. On October 22 the U.N. Security Council called for a cease-fire, but as fighting continued President

Nixon received a note from Soviet leader Leonid Brezhnev accusing Israel of violating the cease-fire agreement. Brezhnev's note went on to warn that if the United States didn't rein in the Israelis, the Soviets would "be faced with the necessity urgently to consider the question of taking appropriate steps unilaterally"—i.e., intervening directly with troops supporting the Arabs. At this point Nixon called the world-wide U.S. troop alert, warning Brezhnev of "incalculable consequences" if the Russians intervened. At the same time, Nixon also sent an ultimatum to the Israelis demanding that they let the Egyptian Third Army, which was surrounded by Israeli troops, be resupplied with nonmilitary equipment, food, and water. On October 25 the Security Council passed a resolution establishing an emergency U.N. policing action, at which point Nixon canceled the alert and the crisis abated.

From a game-theoretic perspective, it has been argued on the grounds of the international situation at the time that the actions and probable consequences facing the superpowers on October 24 were as depicted in Table 5.4. Here the pair of numbers after each entry represent the *perceived* payoffs to the United States and to the Soviets for the corresponding outcome, where 4 is associated with the most desirable outcome, 1 with the least preferable. The first number in each pair is the measure of desirability to the United States, while the second represents the Soviet level of preference. Thus, for example, if both sides were to choose their conciliatory option resulting in outcome A, then they would each receive 3 "payoff units." Analogous remarks apply for the other possible outcomes.

The particular numerical values of the preferences are irrelevant; what's important is the *preference ordering* that the two countries perceived for the possible outcomes. The numbers shown in the table have been chosen to reflect what political scientists and international relations experts now see as the two countries' preferences at the time of the alert decision crisis. In this connection, it's important to note that outcome D is not a nuclear war, but only the *possibility* of such a holocaust. So, while it's hard to see how anyone could prefer nuclear devastation to any other alternative, it's certainly defensible to argue that the possibility of a nuclear exchange might be preferable to the massive loss of face (or territory) involved in giving in to certain types of demands.

It's easy to see that from Nixon's point of view the best action was to try to frustrate the Soviet initiative, since the United States would have then received 4 units of payoff if the Russians chose diplomacy

		U.S.S.R.	
		Seek diplomatic solution	Intervene in war
United States	Cooperate with Soviet initiative	A. *Compromise*: Egyptian Third Army resupplied; cease-fire of October 22 re-established; political resolution of Middle East conflict attempted (3, 3)	C. *Soviet victory*: possible joint Soviet-American peacekeeping force; Soviet military presence in Middle East reintroduced (1, 4)
	Frustrate Soviet initiative	B. *Israeli victory*: possible occupation of Egypt, Syria, and Jordan (4, 1)	D. *Superpower confrontation*: possible nuclear war (2, 2)

Table 5.4. U.S. and Soviet alternatives and payoffs
for the 1973 alert crisis

and 2 units if they didn't. In either case, the corresponding payoff was greater than if Nixon opted for cooperation. A similar argument shows that the Russian strategy of intervention uniformly dominated the diplomacy alternative. Therefore, if both Nixon and Brezhnev had been rational actors operating according to the preference ordering given here, the outcome would have been a superpower confrontation and the possibility of a nuclear war. Note the crucial fact that this outcome would have given each country only 2 points, far less desirable than the 3 points they would have each received by doing what in actual fact they did do, i.e., cooperate.

As the preferences are given in Table 5.4, this game is typical of what's called the *Prisoner's Dilemma,* a class of games closely related to Chicken. The terminology *Prisoner's Dilemma* reflects the following prototypical situation: There are two prisoners being held on suspicion of having jointly committed a crime. The police don't have enough evidence to convict them on a major charge, although they have plenty of evidence to put each away separately for a variety of lesser offenses. The police interrogate the prisoners one at a time, offering each the same deal: If the prisoner will "defect" from his partner and confess to the police, thereby turning state's evidence against his pal, while the partner "cooperates" with the defector by remaining silent, then the police will arrange for the judge to give a lenient sentence of one year to the prisoner who confesses. At the same time the judge will throw the book at the prisoner who remains silent, giving him the maximum four-year sentence. But if they both confess, they'll each receive a three-year sentence on a lesser charge. Finally, if they cooperate with each other and remain silent, then they'll each receive a two-year sentence on even further reduced charges.

By thinking through the choices of the two prisoners, the reader will quickly conclude that the individually selfish and rational thing to do is for each prisoner to defect to the police and confess. But if they both take this route, they'll each get a three-year sentence, one more year than they would have received if they had cooperated with each other and remained silent. Thus, the dilemma: How to balance out actions that are individually rational but collectively suboptimal? This is the Prisoner's Dilemma. And this is also the dilemma presented by a payoff structure like that given in Table 5.4 for the alert decision.

As noted, in the real-world alert decision situation both the Soviets and the Americans chose the diplomatic path, actions that are difficult to understand in the context of the payoffs shown in the table. It seems that either both Nixon and Brezhnev forsook their rational choices, or that the concept of what constitutes a rational choice needs to be refined. Steven Brams opts for the latter alternative, arguing that the rational choice is not so obvious if the rules of the game change.

To press home his point, Brams introduces the distinction between short-term stable outcomes, or what he terms *myopic equilibria,* and long-term stable outcomes. A myopic equilibrium is an outcome that neither player stands to improve upon by changing his decision unilaterally. By way of contrast, a long-term, or *nonmyopic,* equilibrium is an outcome such that in deciding whether to depart from it, a player considers not only the immediate effect of his actions but also the consequences of the other player's probable response, his own counterresponse, and so on. Consequently, in this setup Brams has changed the rules of the game so that there is now a *sequence* of choices instead of just a single round of play. In deciding what action to take on each round, the players now take into account not only the immediate payoff, but future payoffs as well.

Brams uses the notions of myopic and nonmyopic equilibria to analyze the superpower arms race with a Prisoner's Dilemma preference structure under two assumptions: (1) each side possesses an ability to detect what the other side is doing with a specified probability p, and (2) each side pursues a TIT-FOR-TAT strategy. What this means is that each side cooperates on the first round of play. Thereafter, each country chooses the action taken by the other on the preceding round. This kind of "copycat strategy" displays the properties that it is nice (not the first to defect), provocable (defections are immediately punished), and forgiving (punishment, i.e., noncooperation, stops as soon as the opponent starts cooperating again). Under these assumptions, Brams's analysis leads to the following conclusions about arms races:

1. Conditional cooperation will benefit both parties if p, the probability of detecting an arms control violation, is large enough.
2. Developments that increase the costs of a continuing arms race do more to encourage conditional cooperation than developments that increase the benefits of an arms control agreement.
3. Very probably, the best way to make an arms race more expensive is to invest heavily in research and development.
4. To promote movement toward an arms control agreement, it's in the interests of both the United States and the Soviet Union not only to improve their own detection capabilities, but also to help improve the detection capabilities of the opposition—subject to the proviso that neither side gives away so much information that a preemptive first strike by the other looks attractive.

These game-theoretic results showing how a rational decisionmaker would behave in trying to come to an arms control agreement emphasize the crucial role of probabilistic factors in setting the parameters of the decisionmaking environment. In the arms control context, the stochastic factor is the probability p that an arms control violation will be detected by the other side. Uncertainty considerations such as these are part and parcel of most decisionmaking environments, forming the heart of the subject known in the world of mathematics as statistical decision theory. To understand what science can tell us about war, it's important for us to examine how ideas from this field have been employed to shed light on how it is that individual leaders come to a decision for war (or anything else).

Scanning a recent issue of the *International Herald Tribune*'s sports page for the latest baseball scores, my eye was captured by an article telling of Oregon's becoming the next state after Nevada to legalize betting on pro football games. As a born and bred Oregonian and a longtime believer in my home state's self-image as a place that's always just a bit ahead of its time, I found my territorial chauvinism greatly reinforced at this latest example supporting my natal prejudice. An extra fillip was added by the fact that the Oregon betting law was enacted over the ingenuous and absolutely hilarious, ostrichlike opposition of the National Football League Commissioner, who had lobbied the Oregon legislators on the ground that legalizing betting on pro football might compromise the integrity of the game. Can a savvy businessman like the Commissioner really believe that people are that stupid? Can he really be unaware of the billions of dollars bet every season both with illegal bookies and in the legal betting parlors of Nevada? It's remotely plausible, I suppose, but certainly not the way a prudent man would bet (if you'll pardon the pun).

With my thoughts turned by this story to gambling and Oregon, it was but a short associative-memory leap away to an equally pleasurable moment or two of reflection on a youth misspent at the Oregon greyhound and horse tracks, at poker games in friends' cellars, in contributions to office football and World Series betting pools, and, in general, to the pursuit of a variety of related activities all designed to put as much distance as possible between me and an honest day's work. But rather early on in my relentless pursuit of parlays, daily doubles, pointspreads, teasers, and all the other things "investors" need to know about to avoid a gambler's ruin, I came to the not-so-profound realization that successful betting (i.e., decisionmaking) ultimately rests on the relation between the payoffs and the "true odds," whatever that term may mean. Later I discovered that the academic community had dressed up these rather obvious street smarts, studying the relation between payoffs and odds under the rubric *expected utility theory* (EUT). And since decisionmaking is what it's all about in both the sports and the international arenas, let's go out to the horse track and look at the application of the core concepts of EUT to the problem of which of the glue-factory candidates presented for our approval should be supported with our investing capital. Then we'll turn our attention to how these same ideas apply to the far weightier question of the decision for war.

To illustrate the basic ideas of EUT, suppose we're at the track pondering our bets on the first race. For the sake of definiteness and compactness of exposition, assume that only three horses are entered in the race: Alpha, Beta, and Gamma, or A, B, and G for short. Now it's well known in gambling circles that every self-respecting horse player does his handicapping prior to leaving home for the track. So let's assume we're serious, scientifically oriented bettors, whose analysis suggests that the chances of A, B, or G's winning the race are 25 percent, 33⅓ percent, and 41⅔ percent, or ¼, ⅓, and 5⁄12, respectively. For us, these figures are the *true "odds,"* or the *probability*, of each horse's winning the race.

Once we get to the track and the betting starts, the toteboard regularly updates the *track odds* on each horse, odds that tell us what the payoff will be for each horse if it actually does romp home ahead of the pack. These odds reflect nothing more than the relative amounts of money bet on each horse. Note that the track odds may or may not be consistent with the true odds that the individual horseplayer calculates on the basis of past performance, track conditions, astrological incantations, hunches, and whatever other kind of divine inspiration horseplayers rely upon. The track odds are merely these many independent sets of perceived true odds, weighted according to the amount of money each player feels his analysis is worth. In short, the track odds represent the overall degree to which the players are willing to put their money where their analysis is, so to speak. Let's suppose that the track odds on A, B, and G are 6 to 1, 5 to 2, and 10 to 1, respectively. What this means is that for a $2 bet on Beta, the bettor would receive a return of $7 if Beta were to win the race (a $5 profit for being right, plus the original $2 investment). The same $2 bet would yield returns of $14 on Alpha and $22 on Gamma, should Beta lose out to one of these other competitors. So how should the savvy player lay down his cash?

From our discussions on probability theory and expected value in the opening chapter, we can easily calculate the *expected return* from an investment on any of the three horses. For example, the expected return for a bet on Alpha is just the amount of money we receive if Alpha wins the race, multiplied by the probability that Alpha does win, minus the amount of money we lose if Alpha loses the race, times the likelihood of Alpha's not winning. Using our true odds for the probability of each horse's success and the track odds for the payoff, we see that the expected returns from investing in each of the horses are:

$$\text{expected return from Alpha} = \$14 \times (\tfrac{1}{4}) - \$2 \times (\tfrac{3}{4}) = \$2$$
$$\text{expected return from Beta} = \$7 \times (\tfrac{1}{3}) - \$2 \times (\tfrac{2}{3}) = \$1$$
$$\text{expected return from Gamma} = \$22 \times (\tfrac{5}{12}) - \$2 \times (\tfrac{7}{12}) = \$8$$

In its crudest form, EUT argues that the prudent investor should make the bet that maximizes expected return. If we adopt this approach at our fictitious track, Gamma is the clear choice, having an expected return four times greater than its nearest competitor. Of course, what makes Gamma so attractive in this example is the great discrepancy between what we think are the true odds for Gamma, and what the other bettors think as evidenced by their making Beta the betting favorite. It's deviations like this that horseplayers live for (and die from).

Examination of this setup shows that there are three crucial aspects that go into making the decision problem amenable to analysis by EUT arguments: (1) a set of actions and associated possible outcomes that the decisionmaker has to choose among (a bet on Alpha, Beta, or Gamma to win the race), (2) a payoff associated with the possible outcomes (the track odds), and (3) a probability distribution associating a likelihood of occurrence with each outcome (the horseplayer's perceived true odds). With these ideas in hand, let's see how they're used to get an analytical handle on the decisionmaking process in international affairs.

As just noted, we need a set of possible actions and outcomes, a payoff structure for the outcomes, and an estimate of the likelihood of each outcome in order to employ the methods of EUT for selecting rational courses of action. Unfortunately, in the world of *Realpolitik*, as opposed to the equally sordid world of the track, none of these three elements is generally available with any degree of clarity and/or simplicity. Usually the total set of actions that a decisionmaker has available is far from clear, the "payoff" associated with each possible outcome is almost never assessed in something as easy to measure as money, and the outcomes resulting from any course of action are often uncertain to the degree that it's difficult even to assign a probability distribution to them with any degree of confidence.

The second obstacle, how to count the payoff, is especially tricky, as witnessed by the fact that analysts have even given a less suggestive name to the benefit obtained from a given outcome, calling it *utility* rather than *payoff* or *return*. This nomenclature recognizes explicitly that in many cases, especially in the political world, the reward structure is not money but something far more difficult to quantify—yet no less real. In an introductory account of this sort we can afford just to blithely ignore these difficulties, referring the reader to the voluminous literature on the problems and possible solutions, a smattering of which is cited in the To Dig Deeper section for this chapter. So henceforth we will assume that the set of actions and possible outcomes, the set of utilities, and the set of likelihoods are all available as the result of preliminary analysis of whatever problem we happen to be dealing with. Now let's get back to politics and war.

In a series of very provocative and enlightening papers and books, Bruce Bueno de Mesquita has applied the above concepts and ideas in an attempt to show how EUT can bridge the seemingly unbridgeable gap between our earlier Balance-of-Power and Collective Security theories of international power configurations. The way Bueno de Mesquita goes about carrying out his program yields valuable insight into the role of the rational actor in bringing a nation to the brink of war.

In his exploitation of EUT in the cause of war and peace, Bueno de Mesquita makes these assumptions:

1. Decisionmakers rank-order their alternatives in terms of their utilities, which are the intensities of their preferences.
2. The ordering of alternatives is transitive, i.e., if X is preferred to Y and Y to Z, then X is preferred to Z. So, for example, if JFK had preferred a naval blockade to an air strike and an air strike to doing nothing in the Cuban missile crisis, then his alternatives would be transitive if he also would have preferred the blockade to doing nothing. (It should be mentioned that transitivity is by no means routinely satisfied in the majority of situations. The psychology literature contains many everyday cases in which decisionmakers are seen to have a preference ordering that is not transitive. The reader should consult the references in To Dig Deeper for examples.)
3. Decisionmakers act rationally—i.e., they always select the action that yields the largest expected utility. Note that this does *not* mean that decisionmakers explicitly go through the kind of calculation given above to obtain expected utilities at the horse track. Rather, the assumption is only that decisionmakers act *as if* they had made such a calculation. Just as with transitivity, rationality is also an ideal that is often violated in practice as, for instance, in the decisions by Brezhnev and Nixon in the 1973 alert crisis.

With these simple hypotheses in hand, we can return to two of the competing schools of thought on international power—Balance of Power and Collective Security.

Let's first recall the basic elements of the competing theories. Balance of Power says that alliances are nonideological, power seeking, and short-lived, imbalances in the coalitions tending to produce war. Collective Security argues just the opposite, claiming that alliances are long-lived and ideological, with imbalances producing peace.

To use EUT, let's return to the 1973 alert crisis and consider the possible outcomes arising from the actions of Nixon and Brezhnev, shown earlier in Table 5.4 (page 297). We'll assume that the actions available to each leader are either to escalate or to negotiate, corresponding to the actions given by a different set of labels in Table 5.4. Let's label the possible outcomes WAR, INTERVENTION, and PEACE. The combinations of actions leading to the various outcomes are as shown in Table 5.5, where the quantities $P_{U.S.}$ and $P_{U.S.S.R.}$ represent the probabilities that the United States and the Soviet Union, respectively, decide to escalate. Note that the decision by one side to escalate is made independently of what the other side does. Thus, the events {U.S. escalates} and {U.S.S.R. escalates} are statistically independent. As a result of the discussion in Chapter One, this means that the probability of *both* countries' escalating is just equal to the product $P_{U.S.} \times P_{U.S.S.R.}$. The probabilities for all the possible outcomes are shown in the table, and are computed from $P_{U.S.}$ and $P_{U.S.S.R.}$ as indicated, using the independence condition just noted.

	U.S.S.R. escalates $P_{U.S.S.R.}$	*U.S.S.R. negotiates* $1 - P_{U.S.S.R.}$
U.S. escalates $P_{U.S.}$	WAR $P_{U.S.} \times P_{U.S.S.R.}$	INTERVENTION $P_{U.S.} \times (1 - P_{U.S.S.R.})$
U.S. negotiates $1 - P_{U.S.}$	INTERVENTION $(1 - P_{U.S.}) \times P_{U.S.S.R.}$	PEACE $(1 - P_{U.S.}) \times (1 - P_{U.S.S.R.})$

Table 5.5. Alert crisis outcomes and their probabilities

On the principle that any violence is the absence of peace, we also have the derivative outcome VIOLENCE, representing either WAR or INTERVENTION. Symbolically, the likelihood of VIOLENCE is simply the probability of WAR plus the probability of INTERVENTION. To calculate this quantity, it's simpler just to say as above that VIOLENCE is the absence of PEACE, and represent its likelihood as

$$\text{Prob(VIOLENCE)} = 1 - \text{Prob(PEACE)}$$
$$= 1 - [(1 - P_{U.S.}) \times (1 - P_{U.S.S.R.})]$$

To see how this line of reasoning makes contact with both the Balance-of-Power and the Collective Security theories of international stability, consider Figure 5.5. The curves in the figure represent the utility of escalation for the United States and the U.S.S.R., where utility is measured here by the countries' respective likelihoods of choosing to escalate rather than negotiate, given how each sees its respective advantage vis-à-vis the other.

Points A and B in the figure are both power transition points at which one hegemonic power is passing the other. Yet we can easily see that the likelihood of war is high at point A and low at point B. Balance-of-Power theorists tend to focus on point B or the transition region D,

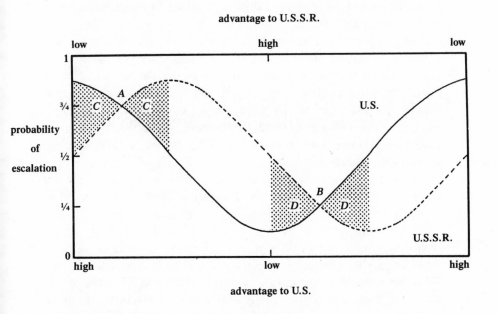

Figure 5.5. *Expected utility theory and the likelihood of war*

assuming that decisionmakers are risk averse. Collective Security advocates take just the opposite stance, concentrating upon the transition point A and the shadow zone C, assuming decisionmakers to be risk takers. In the one case, Balance-of-Power theorists ignore conditions under which the balance of power implies war (point A) or imbalance implies peace (region D). The Collective Security theories overlook the complementary point B and region C, where balanced expectations lead to peace. Expected utility theory encompasses both possibilities by allowing for the fact that decisionmakers vary in their attitudes toward risk.

From the EUT perspective, it's easy to see how a leader could rationally initiate a war even if chances of success are small. All that's needed is for the leader to care enough about policy objectives, i.e., attach a large enough utility to the outcome of a successful war, that the gain outweighs the small chance of success. The devoted horseplayer will recognize this line of reasoning as the same argument that justifies placing money on a 50-to-1 long shot at the track. A good example of this kind of decisionmaking in the international arena took place during the Napoleonic Wars, when Napoleon was at odds with his adviser Talleyrand, who realized that Napoleon was overextending himself. As history records, Napoleon refused to make any concessions to his ambitions, eventually losing everything.

The final message from the EUT view of war is that power by itself is neither necessary nor sufficient for a rational leader to choose to go to war. Other factors enter into play, things like degree of risk aversion, perceived utilities, and subjectively felt probabilities of outcomes. To test some of the theoretical predictions based on EUT, Bueno de Mesquita examined thirty-seven wars, finding that the Balance-of-Power theory correctly predicted the outbreak of war and its initiator in twenty-five cases. However, EUT was correct in thirty-one of the thirty-seven cases. The six extra successes for EUT are highly significant statistically, representing a difference that could be expected to occur by chance less than one time in a hundred.

To this point in our deliberations the focus has been more on explanation than on prediction of war, although the outbreak of war is an issue where the boundary between the two is even fuzzier than usual. With this imbalance in mind, let's complete our consideration of predicting and explaining war by discussing two relatively recent methodological approaches to the question, ideas whose focus this time is primarily on prediction.

WARGASMS AS CHAOSTROPHES

In 1960 the RAND Corporation researcher Herman Kahn published a book that so outraged certain left-leaning defenders of the American ideal on Capitol Hill that federal funding for RAND's research program was temporarily jeopardized. This work, suggestively titled *On Thermonuclear War* in allusion to Clausewitz's classic account *On War,* was described by *Scientific American* reviewer James R. Newman as "a moral tract on mass murder: how to plan it, how to commit it, how to get away with it, how to justify it." To his many critics, Kahn replied that "people who don't like it will say, 'unsound, but creative.' People who do like it will say, 'creative, but unsound,' " the sort of rejoinder that every author should keep close at hand as a convenient bludgeon for administering justice to hostile reviewers of all persuasions. But regardless of how one feels about the book, its publication date is as good a moment as any to mark the moment of birth of what has subsequently come to be called the science of "futurology." And Kahn himself, prior to his death in 1983, served as by far the most publicly visible advocate of the notion that predicting the future, especially the relations among nations, was a scientifically feasible task.

In his many lectures on how nuclear wars might arise, be fought, and end, Kahn regularly provoked his audience by offering a $1,000 reward to anyone who could devise a plausible scenario for the outbreak of nuclear war between the United States and the U.S.S.R. As Kahn set himself up as the sole judge, jury, and paymaster as to what kind of scenario would be "plausible," it's no surprise to learn that the prize was never awarded. But his challenge draws attention to the idea of a scenario, a hypothetical view of the world situation over a particular period of time, usually rather limited. And oddly enough, given his formal training as a quantitatively oriented physicist, Kahn used the essentially qualitative notion of a scenario to form the heart of his way of speculating about the future—especially the outbreak of nuclear war.

The general approach pioneered by Kahn, and subsequently refined by his many followers in the world of futurology, is to look for the likely outcomes of any crisis by creating a context and a script for the crisis situation. The analyst then examines the results of alternative courses of action by the decisionmakers, actions circumscribed by the social, economic, military, and political parameters specified by the scenario. Basically this is the approach followed, for instance, in the computer simulation *Balance of Power* described earlier. The game designer creates a plausible world, i.e., a scenario, to which the leaders of the two superpowers must react in their efforts to win friends and influence people. It's amusing to speculate as to whether any of these computer-generated scenarios would qualify for the $1,000 prize if Kahn were alive today. I strongly suspect not, despite the scenarios' looking all too real, not only to geopolitical duffers like myself but also to many professional wargamers and analysts.

Despite their fascination as vehicles for entertaining and eliciting Strangelovian visions of the "megadeaths" and "wargasms" that so offended Kahn's detractors, prediction by scenario alone is not quite what we have in mind here when we speak of predicting the outbreak of war. As we've emphasized many times throughout the book, our concerns are with prediction methods having their basis in scientific law, as opposed to intuitive methods based principally on subjective judgment, or even highly informed personal opinion. Thus, even though many of the predictions arising from scenario-oriented studies of war, including those in *Balance of Power,* are based on formulas derived from sophisticated statistical massaging of large amounts of socioeconomic, political, and military data, what we seek are prediction schemes more firmly anchored in the long-term behavioral properties of the kinds of dynamical systems that have been regularly employed in the preceding chapters. So with this idea in mind, let's examine a couple of different ways that the tools and techniques of modern dynamical system theory might serve this end.

In earlier chapters we have seen the use of René Thom's theory of catastrophes in elucidating the dynamical properties of the processes of biological development like gastrulation in sea urchins. Here we'll follow a path laid down by Robert Holt and his colleagues at the University of Minnesota, who used the same mathematical machinery in a different way to construct a catastrophe-theoretic model for predicting the outbreak of major wars, including the two world wars of this century.

Recall that the theory of catastrophes tells us about the qualitatively different ways that the observed behavior of a system can change in response to changes in the system's parameters. Of special concern is the identification of those values of the parameters from which small departures can result in large, discontinuous jumps in the behavioral variables. Under rather mild technical conditions, catastrophe theory enables us to classify the typical, or generic, way such discontinuous, or catastrophic, changes can occur when the number of parameters is small (five or less, for example) and the number of behavioral outputs under consideration is no greater than two. As the outbreak of many types of wars can be seen as just such a discontinuous shift in the behavior of nation states, one in which small changes in various aspects of the international system (e.g., making or breaking an alliance, an assassination, or the imposition of a trade embargo) can unleash the dogs of war, the use of catastrophe theory to model the process of going to war seemed a natural step to Holt and his collaborators. It's instructive to have a look at how they proceeded and what they learned.

Since their study was designed to address conflict at the global level, Holt and Company took the observed behavioral variable of the international system to be the level of conflict present in the system. They measured this quantity by the rate of casualties. With this interpretation, the level of conflict can range from total peace to total war, positive values representing war and negative values peace. The midpoint on this continuum is the transition point from peace to war. The positive values can be easily understood as casualties per month, but it's hard to give a good physical interpretation to negative values. About the best we can say is that the more negative the level of conflict, the greater the overall goodwill that nations have toward each other. As we saw earlier, Lewis Richardson and several others have associated negative conflict with the level of international trade, but not without running into a variety of difficulties. So for now we'll agree with the Holt team's view of the matter and just say that negative conflict can range from a fragile to a stable peace and leave it at that.

In a previous section we spoke of Charles Hermann's crisis cube as a geometrical representation of various sorts of tension-filled situations. Hermann chose three variables—threat, available decision time, and surprise—as the key variables whose interrelations dictate the character of a situation, including its likelihood for developing into an intense crisis, i.e., war. The Holt study retains two of Hermann's parameters, decision time and level of threat, but drops surprise in favor of two other independent quantities: coalition opportunities and the level of unsatisfied demand in the system. Let's take a moment to look at all of these variables in somewhat more detail.

• *Level of unsatisfied demand:* This parameter measures the demands that nation states place on each other that cannot be satisfied simultaneously. Within the international system, each state is assumed to be pursuing goals involving things like enhancing its wealth, security, power, and prestige. Usually these demands cannot be satisfied for all players at the same time, giving rise to the parameter termed *unsatisfied systemic demand.* This quantity reflects two important aspects of the international system: (a) the aggregation of national aspirations, and (b) the capacity of the international system to accommodate these aspirations. It's plausible to assume that the level of conflict in the system is a monotonic, although not necessarily linear, function of unsatisfied demand— i.e., the greater the unsatisfied demand, the greater the level of international conflict.

• *Coalition opportunities:* Here we define a coalition in broad terms to be any cooperative agreement among states, such as an alliance, a trade agreement, or membership in an international organization. This interpretation allows us to account for the notion of *polarization* in the international system. As the coalition factor increases, the Holt study takes this to mean that the opportunities for cooperative agreements decrease—i.e., the international system becomes more tightly bound into a set of alliances, thereby reducing the degrees of freedom available within which the players can maneuver. Depending upon the values of the other variables in the system, the level of opportunities available for cooperative agreements can either increase or decrease the level of conflict. We'll see examples of both situations in a moment.

• *Violence potential:* Reflecting the fact that you can't fight wars without weapons, regardless of the unsatisfied demand or the tightness of the coalition structure, violence potential measures the level of military forces and weapons present in the system. The assumption is that there is some "natural" or "appropriate" level of arms in the international system at any moment, with positive or negative levels of violence potential representing deviations from this standard. The effect of violence potential on international conflict is to amplify whatever conflict arises due to unsatisfied systemic demand. Thus, violence potential is effectively what Hermann termed the "threat" in the system.

• *Relative response time:* The idea of response time involves two considerations: (a) communication technology, and (b) the decisionmaking time involved in generating a response to a message. But since communication technology is essentially constant in any given crisis situation, the dominant factor is the capability of the decision-making process for deciding upon a course of action. As we've already seen in the context of the Cuban missile crisis, this capability depends greatly on sociopsychological factors like bureaucratic SOPs, individual psychologies, political bargaining, and the like. It's also important to note that the relative response time reflects the importance of the perceptions and responses of the decisionmakers in the system during the period of the crisis situation. Observe that it's the *relative* response time that's important here, not the absolute time needed to come up with a decision. This means that the governing consideration is how fast the decisionmaking machinery can be mobilized relative to the rate of change of the other parameters affecting the situation.

In keeping with catastrophe theory conventions, as well as to ease our exposition of how the Holt group's model can account for the outbreak of different sorts of wars, let's give the foregoing quantities symbolic names. We'll denote the observed behavior *level of international violence* by x, while letting the parameters be labeled a_1 = unsatisfied systemic demand, a_2 = coalition opportunities, a_3 = violence potential, and a_4 = response time. Since we have four parameters and a single behavioral response, the reader will recall from the discussion of the Thom Classification Theorem for elementary catastrophes in Chapter Three (page 181) that the generic geometry governing situations with one response variable and four parameters is the so-called butterfly catastrophe. This geometry is depicted in Figure 5.6, where the behavioral variable x is plotted against the first two parameters, the remaining parameters a_3 and a_4 being held fixed in the background.

The points on the convoluted surface lying above the a_1-a_2 plane in Figure 5.6 are the equilibrium levels of international violence for the corresponding levels of the parameters a_1 and a_2. The terminology *butterfly catastrophe* for this situation is explained by looking at the way the folds in this surface of violence equilibria project down onto the a_1-a_2-parameter plane. The picture also makes it clear how a combination of changes in unsatisfied demand and coalition opportunities can result in any of the types of situations inscribed on the output response surface.

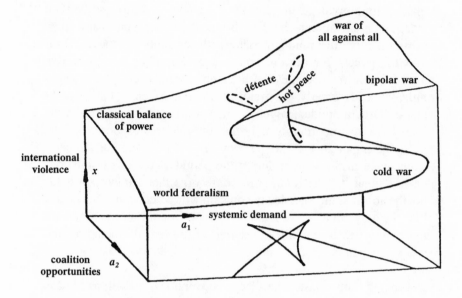

Figure 5.6. *The butterfly catastrophe and the classification of wars*

For example, a steady increase in a_1, keeping a_2 fixed, could lead to a slow, steady transition from a classical balance of power to a Hobbesian war of all against all if the change in unsatisfied demand passes behind the butterfly region in the parameter plane. On the other hand, if the fixed level of coalition opportunity is great enough to force the a_1 transition to take place by passing *through* the butterfly region, then there will be a sudden, discontinuous jump from a balance-of-power situation to a hot peace or even a bipolar war. The reader can easily imagine the many other possibilities presented by the geometry of Figure 5.6. The main point is that it's the complicated interaction of all four parameters that determines whether there will be a smooth or a discontinuous change from war to peace—and back again. Before leaving this figure to consider a real war, let's discuss for a moment the roles of the suppressed quantities a_3 and a_4.

What's especially important about the butterfly geometry is the "pocket of compromise" in the level of international violence, represented by the values of the parameters lying at the center of the butterfly region. It's just these combinations of a_1 and a_2 that can lead to the détente situation shown in the figure. However, the remaining parameters, violence potential (a_3) and response time (a_4), play a crucial role in generating this possibility. It can be shown that if the response time is negative (i.e., the pressure for a decision is much greater than normal), then the pocket of compromise disappears entirely. Thus, if options are to be kept open for a diplomatic resolution of the crisis, the center of the butterfly region should be made as large as possible. This means trying to ensure that there's a lot of time available for decisionmakers to act. As regards the parameter a_3, its role is to bias the relative sizes of the two butterfly wings: Large values of a_3 increase the size of the wing corresponding to war; small values shrink the war wing and enlarge the possibilities for peace.

Using the variables and nomenclature of this generic war model, Holt and his co-workers examined both World War I and World War II. Their results predicting the outbreak of World War I are shown in Figure 5.7. Those for the Second World War are analogous, and can be found in the paper cited in the To Dig Deeper section. In summary, for World War I the time paths of the governing parameters were as follows: After the turn of the century, the degree of polarization (a_2) and the violence potential (a_3) both began to increase, while the unsatisfied systemic demand (a_1) changed only marginally from its value in the 1890s. After 1909 the unsatisfied demand and the response time (a_4) began to increase. The unsatisfied demand continued to increase through 1914, but the response time began to get very short, thereby removing the pocket of compromise. The outbreak of the war itself then occurred as the level of international conflict jumped from the lower to the upper sheet of the response manifold.

While there are many additional aspects of the outbreak of war that we could account for by employing catastrophe theory as a modeling and prediction vehicle, I think these examples, brief as they are, convey the essential ideas. Now let's shift our attention to how the theory of chaotic processes has also been used to shed light on the questions of why, how, and when leaders send their troops into battle.

With the announcement on March 23, 1983, of a ''comprehensive and intensive effort'' to create a space defense system, President Ronald Reagan committed the United States to a multibillion-dollar investment in an idea that many thought to be the height of fiscal folly, if not just plain irresponsibly dangerous. While the objections of the scientific community emphasized the many technical obstacles in the path of making Reagan's ''Stars Wars'' Strategic Defense Initiative

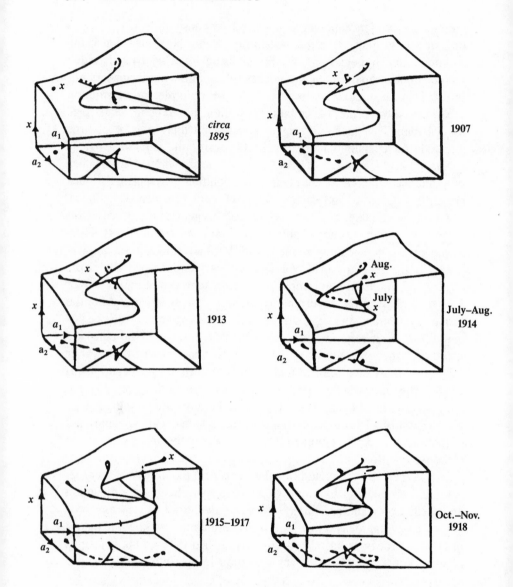

Figure 5.7. *Catastrophe theory explanation for the outbreak of World War I*

(SDI) system workable, other opponents vociferously argued that a system that worked would be even *worse* than one that didn't. Their argument was that a functioning SDI system would so upset the delicate balance of power between the United States and the U.S.S.R. that the most dire consequences might result—including the possibility of a preemptive Soviet nuclear strike. Proponents of the system, like Edward Teller, counter with the claim that a working SDI system will drive the evolution of the superpower arms race into a defensive mode in which the development and deployment of offensive weapons will no longer be an attractive option. Let's turn to the mathematics for some insight into the relative validities of these competing positions.

The idea of a nuclear war arising out of a working SDI system follows exactly the line of reasoning originally pioneered by Richardson in which the outbreak of war comes about as the result of an arms race that's gone out of control, i.e., is unstable. The reader will recall that Richardson's model was developed around a pair of linear equations representing the perceived threat and security felt by the competing powers. On theoretical grounds, it can be shown that linear models like Richardson's cannot display the kind of chaotic behavior that has characterized so many of the phenomena dealt with in this book. Recently, Alvin Saperstein and Gottfried Mayer-Kress have extended Richardson's idea by developing a nonlinear model that describes the implications of an SDI system for the stability properties of the current superpower arms race. Let's look at a few of the highlights of their investigation.

In their simplified SDI model, Saperstein and Mayer-Kress assume that each country's strategic arms system consists of three elements: (1) offensive intercontinental ballistic missiles (ICBMs), (2) satellite-launched weapons (ABMs) that can destroy the ICBMs, and (3) weapons capable of attacking the satellites (ASATs). Thus, the model ignores things like the possibility of a satellite's attacking another satellite or of an ICBM's attacking a satellite or a satellite-killer missile. Also ignored are other components of strategic nuclear war such as submarine-launched missiles, cruise missiles, bombers, ground-launched anti-ICBM missiles, anti-aircraft missiles, and so forth. Thus, the dynamical equations constituting the model consist of equations describing only how fast the numbers of ICBMs, ABMs, and ASATs are changing for each country.

In developing the nonlinear relations linking the buildups of ICBMs, satellites, and satellite killers, Saperstein and Mayer-Kress make use of a variety of conventions and assumptions in the defense community as to the effectiveness of an ICBM warhead in producing damage, the effectiveness of the satellites in destroying ICBMs, target "hardness," costs, and several other factors. Consequently, there are a number of different "scenarios" possible with their model, one for each set of numbers chosen for these parameters. The benchmark scenario assumes that both sides begin with an equal number of ICBMs and no satellites. The arms buildup of ICBMs using the model under these conditions is shown in Figure 5.8, with the buildup of ABMs and ASATs also monotonically increasing. The error bars shown denote the maximal and minimal values of ICBM levels in one hundred thousand simulation runs, where there was a 50 percent random perturbation of the buildup parameters at each time step.

To examine the effect of an SDI system on the standard scenario, let's increase both the offensive and the defensive weapons production rates. For definiteness, assume that the U.S. defense rate is increased by a factor of ten (introduction of SDI), while the Soviet offensive

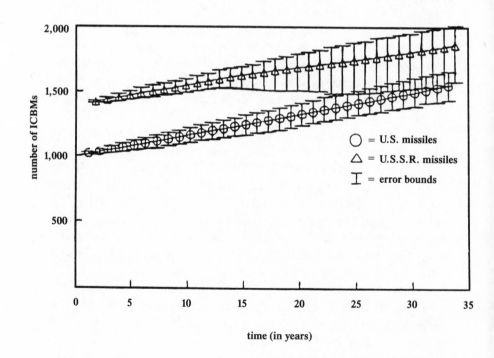

Figure 5.8. *The standard scenario ICBM buildup*

production rate is also increased by the same factor (build more ICBMs). In this case the model predicts that there will be a great increase in Soviet ICBMs and ASATs, a small decrease in U.S. ICBMs, and a collapse to zero of U.S. ASATs. The result is that the Soviet Union gains a clear lead in the offensive race, but the U.S. has a five-to-one lead in the defensive weapons race.

Finally, suppose there is a symmetrical tenfold increase in both offensive and defensive weapons production rates—i.e., both countries increase each side of their arsenals by a factor of ten by building both ICBMs and SDIs. Figure 5.9 shows that in this case a transition to a defensive mode finally takes place. There is a collapse to zero of Soviet ICBMs, accompanied by a decrease in U.S. ICBMs. But note that the noise fluctuations represented by the error bars marking the upper and lower bounds for the model uncertainty are much greater than the average levels themselves. Thus, the prediction of a U.S. advantage cannot really be believed; the outcome is basically chaotic. This transition to chaos as a result of a strongly accelerated arms buildup is the

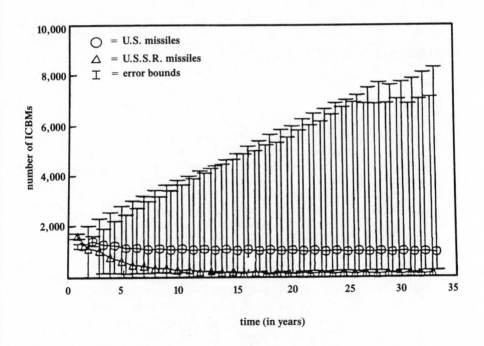

Figure 5.9. *ICBM buildup with SDI included*

souped-up, contemporary version of the loss of stability and consequent outbreak of war seen earlier in Richardson's model.

To summarize the conclusions of the Saperstein-Mayer-Kress exercise, for most plausible scenarios the introduction of an SDI system leads to an extension of the offensive arms race (increases in ICBMs) rather than to a defense-dominated arms posture. But if either the number of warheads per ICBM is limited to much smaller levels than at present, or the accuracy of offensive weapons is reduced, then a defense-dominated strategy is possible. Finally, when economic and risk variables are included in the model, both of these quantities tend to increase with introduction of an SDI system. So, to the degree that this simplified model bears any resemblance to reality, the mathematical verdict on SDI is a pretty definite thumbs down—even if the system could be made to work.

Having now run the gauntlet of historical inevitability, great men, games, catastrophes, master variables, balances and imbalances of power, and chaos, let's try to pull all the threads together and come to some conclusions about the ability of science to predict and explain the outbreak of armed hostilities.

MAKING THE GRADE

Prediction

FÁTIMA, Portugal, October 13, 1917—Our Lady of the Rosary today predicted the outbreak of a great world war to the ten-year-old shepherd girl Lucia de Jesus dos Santos and her younger cousins Francisco and Jacinta Marto. The Lady, who confirmed her identity as the Blessed Virgin Mary to the children, warned: "When you see the night lit up by a great, unknown light, know that it is a sign that God gives you of punishment of the world by another war, famine, and persecution of the Holy Church and of the Holy Father." The Virgin Mary went on to tell the children that the threatened war would come "within the next pontificate," if mankind did not change its ways.

MUNICH, September 30, 1938—British Prime Minister Neville Chamberlain and French Premier Édouard Daladier today signed a pact with the German leader Adolf Hitler, enjoining the Prague regime to cede to the Third Reich all districts of Bohemia and Moravia having more than half their population of German origin. Many observers feel that the British and French governments' action in acceding to Hitler's demands by signing the pact was taken in order to stave off the outbreak of total war in Europe. Reflecting this sentiment, upon his return to London Chamberlain stated that "I believe it is peace for our time."

This pair of fictitious news flashes report two widely publicized predictions about the outbreak of World War II—one correct, at least in broad outline, the other infamously wrong. But both made on the basis of wishes, hopes, faith, and divine inspiration, all methods probably forever beyond the bounds of what we would today consider to be science. So in trying to come to a judgment on the ability of modern science to forecast the outbreak of wars like World War II, let's review what distinguishes a scientific prediction method for war from these alternative kinds of inspired guesswork.

In general terms, it's easy to state the requirement for a scientific method of predicting war: a method firmly anchored in laws governing the behavior of nations during periods of crisis. In short, a perfect prediction scheme for the outbreak of war would be something like a machine with two lamps—say, red and green—and a big input hopper. Into the hopper we shovel all the data available about the current international crisis situation, the psychology of individual leaders, each nation's economic, military, and sociocultural resources, and whatever other information seems pertinent. We also give this "War Machine" a particular time in the future. The machine's task is then to tell us with certainty if war will break out by the specified time. Having fed in the data, we flip on the power switch and the War Machine starts churning through this mass of numbers and impressions, eventually lighting up one of the two lamps—red for war, green for peace. This is the economy-version War Machine. An upmarket model would have a pair of lamps for each pair of countries, lighting up red or green to indicate whether the particular pair of nations would be at each other's throats within the specified time-frame. In essence, the machine's program or procedure for arriving at its decision as to which light to turn on constitutes the embodiment of a perfect scientific prediction method for war, just as long as whatever procedure the machine employs can be unambiguously specified as a repeatable process (i.e., an algorithm) for digesting the data. Our question then reduces to asking how the prediction schemes discussed above match up to the workings of the War Machine.

On balance, the match-up is only so-so. The methods we have examined to predict war—game theory, expected utility theory, catas-

320 Searching for certainty

trophe theory, chaos—all give some insight into when a hot war might flare up. In favor of each of these "machines" as a tool for encapsulating laws of human behavior is the fact that these formal methods all give definite prescriptions for processing the data, prescriptions that are repeatable by any interested party. In short, the method itself is independent of vague, personal opinions or subjective judgments. In this sense, the inner workings of each of our prediction machines are completely objective and well defined.

On the other hand, all of the prediction schemes we have discussed need input data; no data, no prediction. And it's at this point that science and the prediction of war start to part company. The problem is well stated by the computer acronym GIGO: "garbage in, garbage out." None of the scientifically based prediction schemes can create information out of thin air. The best any such prediction method can do is to make explicit what is already implicit in the original data. Thus, for example, if an individual leader's state of mind is a crucial factor in determining war or peace in a given crisis and the input data omit this factor, then the machine will probably fail in its prediction. And even if the data do include all relevant variables, if their measured levels are inaccurate and/or incomplete, the machine will also fail in its duty. These kinds of problems surface in various ways in the physical sciences, but really come to the fore when we pass over to considering social phenomena. So until we have better ways of getting a quantitative handle on things like Richardson's grievance coefficients, the utilities leaders attach to events like naval blockades and air strikes, and the level of variables like "polarization" in catastrophe models, we will be limited to half-baked and half-hearted methods for predicting war. With these considerations in mind, we come to our grade for prediction as:

Term Grade—Prediction C⁻

Explanation

One day in the early 1950s Peter George, a British Royal Air Force pilot, was sitting in the ready room of his base waiting with his bored colleagues for the end of their shift. To kill time, they started stacking empty coffee cups on the table. Jet fighters nearby, tuning up for practice sorties, began rattling the cups and saucers with the roar of their engines and one of the cups in the stack, unnoticed until it was too late, suddenly fell off the table and shattered on the floor. This event prompted one of the pilots to remark, "You know, that's how World War III is going to start."

George picked up on this casual comment, expanding upon the idea of an accidental nuclear war in his 1958 novel *Red Alert*. This book, on which Stanley Kubrick loosely based the screenplay for his classic film *Dr. Strangelove, or: How I Learned to Stop Worrying and Love the Bomb*, tells the story of a deranged Strategic Air Command base commander who orders his bombers to attack the U.S.S.R. All the planes are shot down except one. That single bomber gets through the Soviet air defenses and delivers its load of megatonnage on Moscow. The American President is then forced to sacrifice New York in exchange in order to prevent an all-out war. And so goes one popular explanation for the outbreak of a superpower nuclear exchange: temporary insanity or accident. As an interesting aside, George later became involved in some rather heated litigation over what he saw as the plagiaristic use of his story's ending in the 1962 book *Fail-Safe* by Eugene Burdick and Harvey Wheeler, which was later made into the popular film of the same title starring Henry Fonda.

Insane base commanders and silicon chip failures in NORAD computers come under the general category of "great men" (or "great things") explanations of war. At a slightly more fundamental level, others offering explanations for the outbreak of a nuclear exchange run the spectrum from hawks ("weakness and Munich-style appeasement") to owls ("loss of control à la World War I") and on to doves ("Pearl Harbor–like provocations"). Some kind of at least remotely plausible scenario can be generated for each of these types of explanations, even if one might be forced to a Kubrick-style dark satire to bring home the point. Nevertheless, just as with prediction, our concerns here are with scientifically based explanatory schemes, and the great-men theories just don't seem to have a solid enough basis in scientific law to be considered suitable candidates. Again, what we seek are convincing, mathematically structured relations and models enabling us in some sense to explain why nations end up settling their disputes by going to war instead of going to the negotiating table.

As our earlier discussion showed, there are only a handful of scientific explanatory approaches for the outbreak of war—all of them variants of the Professor Fate school of fundamentalist thinking. At the heart of each of our candidate schemes for explaining war is the idea of power. We heard the competing claims of the Balance of Power, Collective Security, and Power Transition theorists as to how various configurations of power do or do not lead to war. And we also saw how the expected utility school offered some hope for reconciling at least some of the competing claims.

A striking aspect of our examination of explanation schemes for war is the recognition of how very few genuinely distinct types of crisis situations leading to war there are. For example, certain types of power transitions offer reasonably convincing explanations for the outbreak of a wide variety of wars, ranging from the Napoleonic Wars to World War I. The universally valid geometrical picture of the outbreak of war given by our butterfly catastrophe model in Figure 5.6 underscores the point. So, putting all these observations together, we seem to be in at least fair shape when it comes to being able to offer scientifically defensible schemes for explaining how any given war came about. With this happy state of affairs established, the grade for explanation of war works out to be:

Term Grade—Explanation: B

Pursuit of wealth on the floor of the stock exchange and armed hostility on the battlefield are doubtlessly two of mankind's most primitive passions, equaled perhaps only by the fear of attorneys. Plumbing the depths of mathematical worlds in search of universal truths gives the appearance of being just the opposite: an activity dealing with ideal objects and abstract concepts seemingly very far removed from the mundane, emotion-charged affairs of money, territory, or power. And, in fact, most people would probably feel comfortable with the idea that if there's anything we can really be certain about, it's the truth or falsity of mathematical statements. In short, the claim would be that mathematics offers the last, best hope for us to lift completely the veil of uncertainty. So as our final stop in quest of *something* that can be known for sure, let's examine this ambitious claim.

CHAPTER SIX

PROOF OR CONSEQUENCES

Can We Predict/Explain the True Statements of Arithmetic?

In mathematics there are no true controversies.
—Karl Friedrich Gauss

What is laid down, ordered, factual is never enough to embrace the whole truth.
—Boris Pasternak

What is truth?
—Pontius Pilate

LET THEM EAT *SACHERTORTE*

Demel's *Konditorei* is unquestionably Vienna's most famous pastry shop, celebrated by tourists and locals alike for its sinfully rich *Malakofftorte, Apfelstrudel,* and *Cremeschnitte,* all of which are served up smothered in that sine qua non of Viennese cuisine—vast expanses of whipped cream. It's one of the small ironies of life that on my thrice-weekly trek through Heldenplatz and the grounds of the Hofburg Palace to the John Harris Fitness Center for my regular workout, the route takes me right by Demel's display window. Of course, while one side of my brain is ogling the goodies in the window, the other side is reminding me of exactly why it is that I'm heading this direction in the first place, moving toward another hour or two of grappling with stationary bikes, Nautilus machines, and all the other instruments of the modern torturer's art—the not so commonly accepted price to be paid for those who vacuum up more than their allotted share of Demel's luscious creations.

Not long ago, while I was again confronting these caloric temptations, I thought about what a boon to humanity it would be if someone were to invent a Chocolate Cake Machine (CCM) so that any of us, anywhere, could produce these goodies in the comfort of our own homes. What I had in mind was some sort of device, the basics of which are shown in Figure 6.1. To operate the CCM, we shovel eggs, milk, flour, chocolate, and all the other raw materials that might be needed for a cake into one end, along with a recipe for making, say, the famous *Sachertorte*. The CCM would then proceed to process the ingredients in accordance with the instructions given by the recipe, eventually serving up the called-for *Sachertorte* at the machine's output slot. Of course, a sensible person would say that any decent pastry chef is a living embodiment of my CCM. But in the spirit of today's computer-oriented, high-tech culture, it's of more than passing interest to consider whether the entire process could be mechanized to the extent that it would be possible to build a CCM whose savory collations were indistinguishable from the chocolate cakes of the world's greatest patisseries. Let's think for a minute about what such an ideal CCM should be like.

First of all, we want the CCM to be *reliable*. This means that when we feed in the ingredients and the recipe for something we are ready to label "chocolate cake," the CCM should produce chocolate cakes and nothing else. Of course, we need to have some criteria for what constitutes a chocolate cake, and it's not the business of the CCM to establish these criteria. However, once we have agreed upon a test for

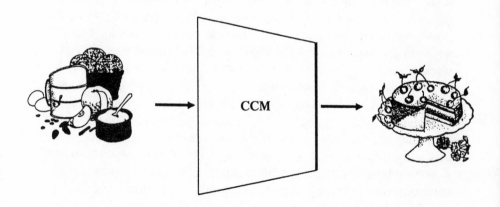

Figure 6.1. *A Chocolate Cake Machine*

what does and what doesn't qualify as chocolate cake, the CCM should faithfully adhere to the criteria; otherwise, it's not a CCM, but some other kind of cooking machine, right? Let me embroider upon this point of reliability for a moment.

At first hearing you might ask: What's the harm in the CCM's producing some other kind of cake besides chocolate cake? Why insist on the reliability property as defined above? The answer is that, by our convention and definition, in the cake world the only "true statements" are chocolate cakes and no others. Therefore, since our interest is in having a machine that tells the truth and nothing but the truth, we are forced into demanding that the CCM produce nothing but chocolate cakes. We can see the point more clearly if we generalize the situation and think in terms of a Universal Cooking Machine instead of a CCM. The UCM is capable of producing any edible item, and in this more general world the true statements consist of anything and everything fit for human consumption. I think it's pretty obvious that we definitely don't want the UCM serving up inedible, or possibly even poisonous, items like "strychnine stew" or "cobblestone cobbler." Following the same line of reasoning, we don't want a Chocolate Cake Machine that serves up "false statements" like peanut butter cream cake or strawberry shortcake. But reliability is only one half of what's needed for a good CCM.

If our contraption is to be a state-of-the-art, upmarket, yuppies-only CCM, then it should be possible to make any conceivable type of chocolate cake with it. So any object satisfying the chocolate cake test should be producible by the CCM. In short, if it's chocolate cake, the CCM can make it. Let's call this the *totality* property.

To my palate, these two properties—reliability and totality—form the basis for the kind of machine I dream of having in my kitchen, ready for service at all times. Such a CCM would produce every possible type of chocolate cake—and only chocolate cake. But is such a CCM just an adolescent fantasy? Or can a sufficiently clever and motivated engineer with a sweet tooth duplicate Demel's chocolate cake chef in a machine, at least in principle? While on the surface it may seem far removed from any deep philosophical or epistemological considerations about life, the universe, or anything else, the question of the constructibility of a reliable and total CCM captures completely one of the most basic questions of philosophy and science: Is it possible to prove every truth? Or, put another way, is there any difference between a statement's being true and its being provable? From the viewpoint of this book, this question amounts to asking about the degree to which we can provide a set of rules, or scientific laws, enabling us to predict and/or explain observed phenomena. Our goal here is to show that the answer to this question ultimately reduces to the seemingly much simpler question: Can we build a CCM? To get a better feel for what's involved in answering this foundational question, let's examine the issue in a bit more detail.

The essence of perfect prediction and explanation is getting at The Truth. In particular, since the scientist's way of fencing off what's true from what's false is via the medium of the various laws of nature, the route to perfect prediction and explanation—scientific style—is through a set of rules that single out the actual state of affairs from the possible in any given context. And if these rules are to be reliable, i.e., perfect, they should never give self-contradictory or false predictions and/or explanations. In particular, to say we have a reliable scientific law characterizing something like tomorrow's weather is tantamount to saying we can *prove* that tomorrow's weather will be just what we say it will be—i.e., every true assertion about tomorrow's weather can be generated by a law governing the factors that go into making up the weather. Since this relationship between what's true and what can be proved has haunted all of our deliberations throughout the book, let me elaborate a bit further on the general theme within the simple chocolate-cake context before going on to discuss the entire matter in broader terms.

At those moments when I'm passing Demel's window and entering into my customary salivatory fit over the thought of sinking my teeth into one of their delectable creations, my world consists solely of cakes—period. And if my particular interest in that world centers upon a generous slice of *Sachertorte* smothered in whipped cream, then choc-olate cake is the only brand of truth I recognize in this universe of cakes. So, in this cake context, the totality of all "statements" that can be made consists of a description of every conceivable type of cake. Some of these statements pass the test for being a chocolate cake and, hence, are "true." A description of any kind of cake failing the test is relegated to the set of statements I label "false." Thus, for example, I call the state-ments *"Sachertorte," "Parisercremetorte,"* and *"Schwarzwälder-kirschtorte"* true, while labeling the assertions *"Malakofftorte"* and *"Mohntorte"* false. It's evident that this cake world is like one of Plato's worlds of ideal forms, in that its objects exist beyond the realm of space and time, and are related to each other by sharing the abstract quality "cake." For me, the true statements in this world consist of those elements passing the chocolate cake test. Some of these truths, like *"Sachertorte,"* have actually been produced and may even be on display in Demel's window. But most have never appeared on the menu or in the window of any *Konditorei,* Viennese or otherwise. Consequently, the true statements of this cake universe consist of the totality of *all possible* chocolate cakes—real or only imagined.

Suppose now that you tell me that the statement *"Sachertorte"* is a true assertion in the cake world—i.e., a *Sachertorte* satisfies our agreed-upon test for chocolate cakehood. If I'm feeling particularly testy that day, I may reply: "I don't believe you. Prove it." How would you go about convincing me of the correctness of your claim? What means would you employ to demonstrate to a doubting Thomas like me that *"Sachertorte"* is a genuine truth of the cake world, meeting up to the stringent requirements of the chocolate cake test? I'm sure you see the obvious answer: Just write down a recipe for *Sachertorte,* feed it into the CCM, and actually produce a real cake satisfying the criteria for chocolate cake. So in the cake world, as in the rest of life, the proof is in the eating—literally! A statement (i.e., a cake) is provable (i.e., is a genuine chocolate cake) if and only if there is a recipe that can be followed by the CCM for actually making that cake. But note carefully that, for a cake to be provable, it's not necessary to actually *implement* the recipe with the CCM. It suffices just to provide the recipe and show that if you did feed it into the CCM, the result would indeed be something satisfying the chocolate cake test. In other words, provability means that there is a rule that could be followed to actually produce the cake. Thus, for the universe of cakes we have

truths = all conceivable cakes satisfying the chocolate cake test
proofs = all recipes for actually making chocolate cakes with the CCM

Now comes the Big Question: Is there a recipe for every conceivable chocolate cake? Or, equivalently, is every true statement provable? What we're asking here is whether there are honest-to-god chocolate cakes in the Platonic universe of cakes for which no recipe can ever be given. Or can every object satisfying the chocolate cake test actually be produced by following a set of instructions? Looked at from the perspective of the CCM, the question reduces to: Is there any theoretical barrier to the construction of a reliable and total CCM?

Most pastry chefs, amateur or otherwise, would probably answer that if you can imagine it, you can not only make it, you can also write down the recipe so that anyone else can make it, too. Interestingly enough, until 1931 not only pastry chefs but just about everybody else would have agreed with this claim. But believing and knowing are radically different matters, and in that fateful year the Viennese logician Kurt Gödel showed conclusively that what's true and what's provable are just not the same thing at all—and not only in the restricted universe of cakes. Gödel's remarkable result, which many (myself included) regard as the most profound and far-ranging philosophical result of this century, applies to the far broader universe of general, everyday events.

Stripped to its bare essentials, what Gödel's Theorem accomplished was to shatter forever the belief that there is no difference between truth and proof. The theorem's punchline is that there is an eternally unbridgeable gap between what's true (and can even be seen to be true) within a given logical framework or system and what we can actually prove by logical means using that same system. So, despite the best efforts of an army of chefs, the "cake bibles" are forever doomed to an existence in the shadow world of incompleteness; there will always exist chocolate cakes that can be demonstrably seen to be bona fide chocolate cakes, yet whose recipes can never be written. My mission in this chapter is to show not only how this astonishing fact could be so, but also to indicate how Gödel's result eliminates once and for all the hope of ever attaining perfect scientific prediction and explanation of anything.

From the way one would go about following a recipe and baking a chocolate cake, it's fairly easy to see that the operation of the CCM doesn't differ in any essential way from the operation of a typical computer. The CCM takes some basic ingredients and processes them in accordance with the instructions given in a recipe, eventually producing a cake. The computer also has a "recipe," its program, which is a set of instructions for how to process "raw ingredients" (the input data) into a finished product (the output, or result). In general terms, the only real difference between the two lies in the fact that the CCM is a very special-purpose type of computer—one that produces only chocolate cakes—whereas the output of a general-purpose digital computer is numbers. But we'll soon see that in a very definite sense this means that the output of a computer can really represent anything: a van Gogh painting, a telephone bill, a dictionary, or anything else that's humanly describable. A good part of our path to Gödel's Theorem and beyond will take us through the reasons why we can make such a sweeping claim, and why, insofar as matters of truth and proof are concerned, what's provable = what's computable. So another way of stating Gödel's result is just to say that not everything that's dreamed of in our philosophies can be obtained as the result of carrying out a computation. With this Shakespearean dictum in mind, let's start our journey by digging a little deeper into what we actually mean when we speak about carrying out a computation.

TURING AROUND

Several of the computer programs I have on my system (including the graphics program with which I prepared many of the figures in this book) have the feature that when you set them to work on some time-consuming task, a small hourglass-shaped icon appears on the screen telling you not to panic; the machine hasn't packed it in, but is only churning away on the data for the problem at hand and you'll just have to wait for it to finish. A few days ago a friend of mine asked me to convert a complicated picture file for him from one graphics language format to another, using one of the handy-for-all-occasions conversion programs that every computer nut cherishes. As we were putting this program through its paces, the hourglass appeared on the screen and my friend peered closely at it to see if he could notice any "electronic sand" falling through the glass.

Not being very computer-savvy, my friend quite reasonably supposed that the program's designers had thoughtfully provided the hourglass icon to tell users how long it would take for their job to finish. Regrettably, I had to inform him that I had both good news and bad: The bad news was that, in general, there's no way to predict how long it will take for a particular program to process a particular set of input data; the good news was that he had unwittingly stumbled across one of the deepest questions in all of theoretical computer science, the so-called *Halting Problem*. And, moreover, this very definite problem involving computers and programs is completely equivalent to the apparently much deeper issues surrounding the relationship between truth and proof. For the beginning of that story, which ultimately led to the development of today's fast-paced computer industry, we have to travel back to Cambridge University about half a century ago.

In 1935 the same Alan Turing we met in Chapter Three in connection with chemical models of cellular development was an undergraduate student at Cambridge, sitting in on a set of lectures being given by the mathematical logician M.H.A. Newman. During the course Turing was introduced to Hilbert's *Entscheidungsproblem* (Decision Problem), which is the logician's equivalent to the Halting Problem. The essence of both problems is to ask whether or not there exists an effective procedure for determining in advance if a certain conclusion follows logically from a given set of assumptions. The central difficulty Turing had in trying to come to grips with this query was that there was no clear-cut notion of what was to count as an *effective procedure*. Despite the fact that humans had been calculating for thousands of years, in 1935 there was still no good answer to the question: What is a computation? Turing set out to overcome this difficulty. To do so he had to invent a theoretical gadget that ended up serving as the keystone in the arch of the modern theory of computation.

As it eventually turned out, Turing's primary task was to figure out how to replace the intuitive idea of an "effective process" by some notion that could be formally expressed within a well-defined mathematical framework. What he came up with is what we now call an *algorithm*, an idea he modeled on the steps a human being actually goes through when carrying out a computation. In essence, Turing saw an algorithm as a rote process or set of rules that tells one how to proceed under any given set of circumstances. Let's return to the problem of making a cake to illustrate the basic idea.

Standing in front of me at this moment is a copy of the recipe for chocolate hazelnut cake, which I've taken from the first volume of *The Silver Palate Cookbook*. The authors modestly describe it as "the best chocolate cake in the universe." If I had the CCM at hand, I might be tempted to gather together all the ingredients, plug this recipe in to the CCM, and actually put this temerarious claim to the test. To see what the CCM would be called upon to do, here's a flavor (no pun intended) of what the recipe is like:

1. Beat egg yolks and sugar together until mixture is thick and pale yellow.
2. Meanwhile, in the top part of a double boiler set over simmering water, melt the chocolate with the butter, whisking constantly until smooth; cool slightly.

⋮

10. Decorate the top of the cake with 8 whole hazelnuts. Refrigerate the cake for at least 1 hour before cutting and serving.

These steps, which the CCM would have to execute faithfully, are a perfect example of an algorithm: a rigidly prescribed and unvarying set of operations leading from the original input data (the raw ingredients of the cake) to the final result. One and only one operation is specified at each step, and there is no interpretation of the intermediate results or any skipping of steps (although for the sake of brevity I have compressed several substeps into one numbered statement here). So we see that what's involved in following the *Silver Palate* dictates for chocolate hazelnut cake is just a boring, basically mechanical, repetition of the various operations of stirring, blending, boiling, mixing, and so forth.

This blind following of a set of rules is the distilled essence of what constitutes an algorithm. To reflect the mechanical nature of what's involved in carrying out the steps of an algorithm, Turing invented a hypothetical kind of computer now called a *Turing machine*. He then used the properties of this machine in order to formalize his attack on the Decision Problem. Here's how.

A Turing machine consists of two components: (1) an infinitely long tape ruled off into squares that can each contain one of a finite set of symbols, and (2) a scanning head that can read, write, and erase symbols from the squares on the tape. Since it involves no loss of generality, for the most part I'll assume here that the symbols are just the two elements 0 and 1. For future reference, it's important to note that we're not thinking here of the symbols 0 and 1 as being the *numbers* zero and one, but only the numerals that represent these numbers. And, in fact, we could have just as easily chosen any other two recognizably distinct symbols like the Roman numerals I and II, the letters X and Y, or even the more abstract symbols ★ and ✦. However, for a variety of reasons, both historical and practical, it's convenient to adhere to the usual convention and use 0 and 1. The general setup for a Turing machine is shown in Figure 6.2.

The behavior of the Turing machine is governed by an algorithm, which is manifested in what we now call a *program*. The program is composed of a finite number of instructions, each of which is selected from the following set of possibilities:

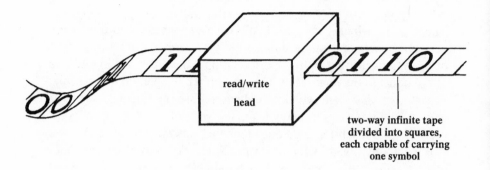

Figure 6.2. *A Turing machine*

PRINT 0
PRINT 1
GO LEFT ONE SQUARE
GO RIGHT ONE SQUARE
GO TO STEP *i* IF THE CURRENT SQUARE CONTAINS 0
GO TO STEP *i* IF THE CURRENT SQUARE CONTAINS 1
STOP

That's it. From just these seven simple instructions we can compose what are called *Turing-Post programs*. These programs tell the machine what kind of computation it should carry out. The operation of the Turing machine is simplicity itself. We first feed in a tape containing a certain pattern of 0s and 1s (the input data). The machine then begins by placing the scanning head at some agreed-upon starting square. Thereafter, the actions taken by the machine are completely governed by the instructions contained in its program. But rather than continuing to speak in these abstract terms, it's simpler just to run through an example in order to get the gist of how such a device operates.

Suppose the initial tape configuration consists of a string of 1s with a 0 at each end like this:

$\cdots$	0	*1*	1	1	1	1	1	1	1	1	0	$\cdots$

Here, and in all the other examples of this chapter, the boldface entry indicates the square where the scanning head is currently located. For this example, let's assume that we want the Turing machine to change the terminating 0s into 1s and then stop, thus increasing the length of the block of 1s by two. Here is a program that accomplishes this task:

1. GO RIGHT ONE SQUARE
2. GO TO STEP 1 IF THE CURRENT SQUARE CONTAINS A 1
3. PRINT 1
4. GO LEFT ONE SQUARE
5. GO TO STEP 4 IF THE CURRENT SQUARE CONTAINS A 1
6. PRINT 1
7. STOP

By tracing through the steps of this simple program, we find that the scanning head moves right until it finds the first 0, which it replaces with a 1. The head then moves left until it finds a 0, replacing that with a 1, whereupon it stops.

On the face of things, you might speculate that the Turing machine, with its very limited menu of symbols and instructions, couldn't really do very much by way of serious computation. Well, from small acorns great oak trees can grow. And so it is with primitive computers, too. In fact, Turing showed that *anything* that *any* computer can compute can be calculated using a Turing machine. Let's just accept this astonishing statement as a fact for the moment. We'll see why it's true later. For now, let me try to make good on my earlier, equally astonishing claim that the output of a computer can in actual point of fact represent anything that can be humanly described.

Suppose, purely hypothetically and for the sake of argument, that I decide to go on a diet, thereby foregoing the pleasures of the *Konditorei*—at least for a little while. Nevertheless, I might still want to amuse myself by creating some "virtual cakes" that I could at least drool over when they appear on my computer screen, even if I can't sample them in material form. One way to go about conjuring up these virtual goodies, at least in principle, is just to represent the ingredients for some kind of cake *in symbols*. I could then process these symbols in accordance with a recipe, thereby creating a string of new symbols representing things like "beaten egg whites," "creamed butter," "sifted flour," and the like, the last symbol in line being a virtual representation of whatever real-world cake made of matter and batter the recipe specifies. So in this world of virtual cakes, there are no material eggs, milk, flour, and all the rest, but only their symbolic representations, or what we might think of as "informational versions" of these objects. In fact, this is just exactly the situation in Figure 6.1 (page 324), where what's shown on the page are not real cake ingredients at all, but only *pictures* (i.e., symbols) of these ingredients.

In light of these considerations, it's clear that if we had a good coding scheme for symbolically representing the raw ingredients, the intermediate products, and the final cake, together with a way of translating the instructions of the recipe into rules for manipulating these symbols, then there would be no essential difference between a real-world *Sachertorte* and its symbol-world counterpart (other than the not so trivial difference that you can eat as much of the virtual cake as you want, safe forever from the clutches of Mr. John Harris and his merry band of fitness freaks).

With the foregoing ideas in mind, one can see that the success of the whole venture hinges upon being able to symbolize, i.e., code, every element and action of the real world using a coding scheme that something as simple as a Turing machine can understand. But a Turing machine really understands only strings of 0s and 1s. Therefore, we need a code whose elements are, not surprisingly, strings of 0s and 1s. After much experimentation, the computer industry has now settled on a standard coding scheme of this type. It's something called the *extended ASCII* (as-key) code and it works as follows:

Suppose we take the Turing machine tape and mark off the squares in groups of eight. In computer lingo each square of the tape is called a *bit*, and each such block of eight cells is termed a *byte*. Since there are eight bits to a byte, and each square can contain either the symbol 0 or 1, there are a total of $2 \times 2 \times 2 \times 2 \times 2 \times 2 \times 2 \times 2 = 2^8 = 256$ possible byte patterns. The ASCII coding scheme uses these 256 distinct combinations of 0 and 1 to code the letters of the English alphabet, punctuation marks, and other special symbols we use in written communication. The table below shows a few examples.

Symbol	ASCII Code
E	01000101
G	01000111
2	00110010
S	01010011
⊔ (blank space)	00100000

Using these ASCII codes for the various letters and the space, we see that the cake ingredient "2 EGGS" can be symbolized in ASCII form as

$$2 \sqcup EGGS = 00110010|00100000|01000101|01000111|01000111|01010011$$

While this coding procedure is more than a little bit tedious and confusing for human consumption, it's just the ticket for Turing machines—and every other type of computer. So it's clear how, by use of the ASCII code, we could write down all the ingredients of our cake on some suitably long segment of the Turing machine tape. And, in fact, we could employ a similarly long stretch of the tape to express absolutely anything else that's describable in the English language. But you ain't seen nothin' yet!

Being able to code the input data in a standard form is certainly convenient, as it gives us a standardized symbolic language that we can use to tell a Turing machine about anything in the real world that can be communicated between two human beings by means of language. But ingredients for a cake are just passive elements. To make something happen we need to act upon these symbols in some way, transforming them into new symbols—expressed in the same code. The action elements are the job of the instructions given in the cake's recipe, or program, for processing the ingredients. The perceptive reader will by now have recognized the absolutely central point that the program itself can also be symbolized using the very same ASCII code used for the input data. This follows from the evident fact that, just like the input data, the program is also written in the English language. So, just as we can code all the ingredients of our cake in some long ASCII byte string, we can also code the recipe for the cake in a similar string. A large part of Turing's genius lay in recognizing the overriding importance of this rather evident fact: As far as the coding scheme is concerned, there is no essential difference between the program and the data that the program operates upon. But let me defer detailed consideration of this point for a moment, pausing here for a short historical and notational digression that will be of considerable use to us later.

When he originally developed the idea of a Turing machine in the mid-1930s, Alan Turing didn't conceive of the machine's program as being written in the Turing-Post language given earlier. In particular, he envisioned that the machine's scanning head would not only be capable of reading and writing symbols to and from the tape, but also that the head could be in any of a finite number of internal "states." The particular action taken at any step would then be determined both by what symbol was read from the tape and by what state the head happened to currently be in. This is similar to the situation you might face after a call from your banker telling you that the royalty check you received from your publisher just bounced. If you're in a good mood, you might just shrug it off and ask your agent to look into the matter. On the other hand, if you're in a bad mood, you might get out your shotgun and head directly for the publisher's premises. Thus, your action would depend not only on what actually happened, but also on what kind of mood, i.e., state of mind, you're in. The scanning head's internal state can be thought of as being its mood or "state of mind." Thinking in these terms, Turing envisioned a computing machine being something like what's shown in Figure 6.3 (for a machine capable of being in one of twelve possible internal states A–L).

Using the idea of an internal state turns out to be convenient for at least two reasons: (1) it enables us to eliminate the two branching statements "GO TO STEP *i* IF . . ." from the Turing-Post program repertoire, replacing them with the single idea of an internal state, and (2) it shortens dramatically the amount of space required to describe completely the action of any given Turing machine program, since we can now compactly write the whole thing in a short table instead of having to list what might well be a very long program. Let me illustrate both of these points with a couple of concrete examples.

Suppose we have a Turing machine with three internal states A, B, and C. Assume we want to use this machine to carry out the addition of two whole numbers. For definiteness, let's adopt the convention that a string of *n* consecutive 1s on the tape represents the number *n*. Then the program shown in Table 6.1 serves to add any two whole numbers using this three-state Turing machine.

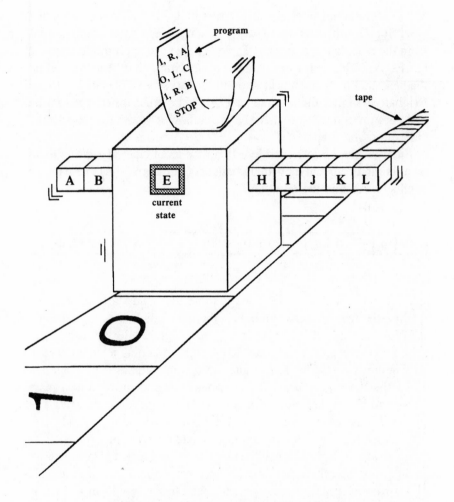

Figure 6.3. *A twelve-state Turing machine*

	Symbol Read	
State	1	0
A	1, R, A	1, R, B
B	1, R, B	0, L, C
C	0, STOP	STOP

Table 6.1. A Turing machine program for addition

The reader should interpret the entries in Table 6.1 in the following way: Suppose the scanning head is in state A and reads the symbol 1 from the tape. The program in Table 6.1 says the appropriate action is (1, R, A). This expression is Turing-machine shorthand for telling the head that it should "print 1 on the square, move one square to the R(ight), and enter the internal state A." The other instructions in the table are interpreted similarly. Let's see how it works for the specific case of adding 2 and 5.

First we place two 1s and five 1s on the input tape, separating them by a 0 to indicate that they are two distinct numbers. Thus the machine begins by reading the input tape

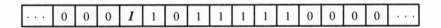

For the sake of definiteness, we assume the head starts in state A, reading the first nonzero symbol on the left, which is again indicated in boldface. Since this symbol is a 1, the program tells the machine to print a 1 on the square and move to the right, retaining its internal state A. The head is still in state A and the current symbol read is again a 1, so the machine repeats the previous step and moves one square further to the right. Now, for a change, the head reads a 0. The program tells the machine to print a 1, move to the right, and enter state B. I'll leave it to the reader to complete the remaining steps of the program, verifying that when the machine finally halts the tape ends up looking just like the input tape above, except that the 0 separating 2 and 5 has been eliminated—i.e., the tape has seven 1s in a row, as required. Adventuresome readers might like to consider the action of the six-state Turing machine having three possible tape symbols 0, 1, and 2, whose program is given in Table 6.2. Assume the input tape is

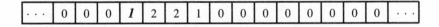

and that, as is our convention, the scanning head starts in state A at the boldface entry marked on the tape. The answer is given in the To Dig Deeper section.

State	Symbol Read		
	0	1	2
A	Print YES, STOP	0, R, B	0, R, C
B	0, L, D	1, R, B	2, R, B
C	0, L, E	1, R, C	2, R, C
D	STOP	0, L, F	0, Print NO, STOP
E	STOP	0, Print NO, STOP	0, L, F
F	0, R, A	1, L, F	2, L, F

Table 6.2. A Turing machine program for ??

With these technical ideas in hand, let's look a bit deeper into the revolutionary implications of Turing's ideas about algorithms and computing.

Modern computing machines, even home computers like the one I'm using to write this book, look vastly more complicated and powerful in their calculational power than a Turing machine with its handful of internal states and very circumscribed repertoire of scanning-head actions. So despite the fact that Turing postulated an unbounded storage capacity for his machine (the infinitely long tape), I think most people would believe at first glance that a modern computing system like that shown in Figure 6.4, with its hundreds of millions of storage cells and elaborate programs, can easily outdistance "Turing's Tortoise" in raw computing capability. Surprise! A big part of Turing's story was to show that *any* algorithm, i.e., program, executable on *any* computing machine can be carried out on a Turing machine.

When my editor read the preceding paragraph in a draft version of this chapter, her reaction to Turing's remarkable result was probably typical of that of most nonscientists. She wrote, "I can't picture how people using this [a Turing machine] are arriving at more than the most elementary solutions to mathematical problems. How do they *know* all these earthshaking conclusions you say Turing has arrived at are so? . . . You couldn't compute the first thousand decimals of pi with a Turing machine, could you?" Strangely enough, Maria, when it comes to computing, there really is a Santa Claus. And his name is Alan Turing.

Not only did Turing show that the primitive-looking infinite-tape-

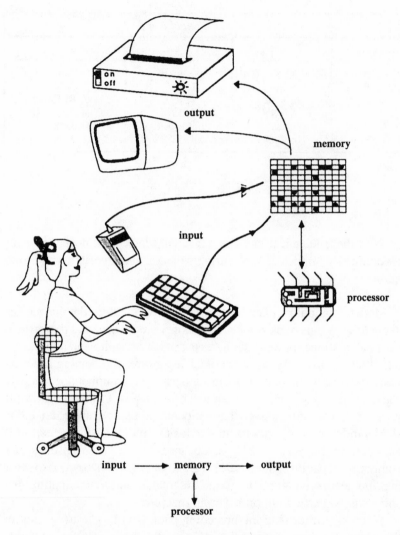

Figure 6.4. *A typical modern computing system*

and-scanning-head setup is capable of computing anything that can be computed, but that there exists a particular version of his machine, termed a *universal Turing machine* (UTM), that can do the job of every other possible Turing machine. Of course, a modern electronic computer is not *structurally* constituted out of a long strip of paper or magnetic tape and a scanning head. But material composition is basically irrelevant here. What's theoretically important is information.

And when it comes to information processing, every computer known to humankind is *functionally* identical to the UTM. This means that from an information-processing point of view, the operations any computer performs are mirrored with complete fidelity by those of an appropriately programmed UTM. Consequently, except for the computational *speed,* which definitely is hardware dependent, there's no difference at all between computing on a Cray Y-MP, your personal computer, or a UTM—anything one of them can compute, so can the others, because they all operate in accordance with exactly the same underlying principles of symbol manipulation.

As to how we know Turing's conclusions are true, a complete and proper answer would take us rather deeper into the labyrinth of mathematical logic and the theory of computation than I'd care to go here. Nevertheless, at least a glimmering of why this kind of result should be so can be gleaned from considering the ASCII coding scheme discussed earlier. If, as is indeed the case, every practical, real-life, day-to-day computer codes its input data and program into byte strings in accordance with the ASCII code, operating upon these strings to produce new strings that are eventually decoded into the machine's output, then there really is no difference between this kind of processing of strings of 0s and 1s on a real computer and the kind of processing carried out by a Turing machine. Of course, the real-world computer transforms the strings at a far faster rate than would be possible if we were to do it using a linear tape and a scanning head. But by replacing the tape with high-speed electronic memory chips and replacing the scanning head with electrical or even optical circuitry, the functional operations of the UTM can be matched in a perfect one-to-one fashion with those of any computer. To complete the overall picture, let me spend just another moment or two looking a little harder at how this UTM really works.

To specify his UTM, Turing realized that not only the input data on the tape, but also the program could be coded by a series of 0s and 1s. The ASCII coding scheme is now the standard way for doing this. However, an even simpler way would be to code the programming statements constituting the Turing-Post language using the scheme shown in Table 6.3. Consequently, the program itself can be regarded as another kind of input data, and can be written onto the input tape along with the data it is to operate on. With this key insight at hand, Turing constructed a program that could simulate the action of any

Turing-Post statement	Code
PRINT 0	000
PRINT 1	001
GO RIGHT ONE SQUARE	010
GO LEFT ONE SQUARE	011
GO TO STEP i IF THE CURRENT SQUARE CONTAINS 0	10$\underbrace{100 \ldots 0}_{i \text{ repetitions}}$1
GO TO STEP i IF THE CURRENT SQUARE CONTAINS 1	11$\underbrace{011 \ldots 1}_{i \text{ repetitions}}$0
STOP	100

Table 6.3. A coding scheme for the Turing-Post language

other program $\mathcal{P}$ when given $\mathcal{P}$ as part of its input—i.e., he created a UTM. The way the UTM operates is simplicity itself.

Suppose we have a particular Turing machine with program $\mathcal{P}$. Since a Turing machine is completely determined by its program, all we need do is feed the program $\mathcal{P}$ into the UTM, along with the input data that $\mathcal{P}$ is supposed to process. Thereafter the program of the UTM will cause the UTM to simulate the action of $\mathcal{P}$ on the data—i.e., there will be no recognizable difference between running the program $\mathcal{P}$ on the original machine or having the UTM pretend it *is* the Turing machine defined by the program $\mathcal{P}$.

If we think in terms of the virtual Chocolate Cake Machine considered earlier as being analogous to a particular Turing machine for making symbolic chocolate cakes, then the UTM corresponds to a Universal Cooking Machine capable of cooking anything that can be cooked (except, of course, the account books). So, for instance, if we want the UCM to make a *Sachertorte* for us, thereby mimicking the actions of the CCM, all we need do is first feed in the program describing the CCM, followed by the program and the ingredients for *Sachertorte*. The UCM will first process the CCM program in accordance with its own *fixed* program. This processing in effect gives the UCM the instruction: "Pretend you are a CCM." Thereafter, the program and the ingredients for the *Sachertorte* will be processed by the UCM in exactly the same way as they would have been processed on our original CCM.

One of the most profound contributions of Turing's work on the theory of computation was to recognize not only that such a UTM should be possible, but also how one would actually construct the fixed program for the UTM that enables it to simulate the behavior of any other kind of Turing machine and, hence, any possible type of computer.

The reader will recognize the fact of the existence of a UTM as the real source of the utility and power of modern computers: They can masquerade as anything. Even a primitive personal computer can become a master-level chess opponent, a spelling checker, an artist, a postman, or a bookkeeper. It's the machine's ability to play this essentially unlimited variety of roles that accounts for the modern computer industry. And it's all ultimately traceable to Turing's idea of the UTM. Whenever I get depressed about my notorious inability ever to guess right about the turn of worldly events, I like to think about this capacity of computers to mimic just about anything, and recall a remark made by Howard Aitkin, Harvard professor and pioneer in the development of computer algorithms for solving scientific problems. As late as 1956 Aitken stated:

> If it should turn out that the basic logics of a machine designed for the numerical solution of differential equations coincide with the logics of a machine intended to make bills for a department store, I would regard this as the most amazing coincidence that I have ever encountered.

Ah, fair Harvard. I wonder if Aitken ever encountered any professors of government or politics on his strolls through Harvard Yard!

Turing's work finally put the idea of a computation on a solid scientific footing, enabling us to pass from the vague, intuitive idea of an effective process to the precise, well-defined notion of a program. In fact, Turing's work, along with that of the American logician Alonzo Church, forms the basis for what has come to be called

The Turing-Church Thesis

Every effective process is implementable by running a suitable program on a UTM.

The universal Turing machine also gives us a tool for identifying just what is and what isn't actually computable. Roughly speaking, Turing discovered that anything that can be described by following a set of rules is computable. Of course, this means that just about anything that can be communicated in language is computable, since languages have a set of rules, i.e., a grammar and syntax, according to which valid expressions are formed. At first glance, this might suggest that anything and everything is computable. Not so! To see why, let's retreat from the murky, slippery world of everyday language, misunderstandings, and communication gaps, taking refuge for a while in the far more culturally independent and far less cluttered world of pure number.

By definition, a number is *computable* if and only if it can be obtained as the output of a UTM. Turing's pioneering 1936 paper in which he introduced the idea of a Turing machine considered the question of whether or not every real number is computable. While my editor may find it incredible that a Turing machine could crank out the decimal digits of π, I suspect she wouldn't blink even once if I told her that a modern computer is capable of computing any number that she might care to specify. After all, that's what computers are for, isn't it, to compute numbers? If we're clever enough, can't we find a program that will produce every possible number? The surprising fact is that almost every number is *not* computable. We'll see the full reason why in the next section. The short reason is that in order to compute a number, you have to be able to write a program that will produce it. But this means that you have to be able to describe the number, at least implicitly, with a finite number of statements. As we'll soon see, almost all numbers, like almost all chocolate cakes, are "indescribably delicious," hence uncomputable. But we'll get to that story in a moment. For now, let's just have a little fun with Turing machines and look at an example of one such uncomputable quantity.

Suppose you're given an *n*-state Turing machine and an input tape filled entirely with 0s. The challenge is to write a program for this machine obeying the following rules: (1) the program must eventually halt, and (2) the program should print as many 1s as possible on the tape before it stops. It's clear that the number of 1s that can be printed depends only on *n*, the number of internal states available to the machine's scanning head. Equally clear is the fact that if $n = 1$, the maximum number of 1s that can be printed is only one, a result that follows immediately from the requirement that the program isn't allowed to run forever. If $n = 2$, it can be shown that the maximum number of 1s that can be printed before the machine halts is four. Programs that print a maximal number of 1s before halting are called *n-state Busy Beavers*. Table 6.4 gives the program for a three-state

Busy Beaver, while Figure 6.5 shows how this program can print six 1s on the tape before stopping where, as before, the position of the tape-scanning head is shown in boldface.

	Symbol Read	
State	0	1
A	1, R, B	1, L, C
B	1, L, A	1, R, B
C	1, L, B	1, STOP

Table 6.4. A three-state Busy Beaver

STATE										TAPE
A	0	0	0	0	**0**	0	0	0	0	
B	0	0	0	0	1	**0**	0	0	0	
A	0	0	0	0	**1**	1	0	0	0	
C	0	0	0	**0**	1	1	0	0	0	
B	0	0	**0**	1	1	1	0	0	0	
A	0	**0**	1	1	1	1	0	0	0	
B	0	1	**1**	1	1	1	0	0	0	
B	0	1	1	**1**	1	1	0	0	0	
B	0	1	1	1	**1**	1	0	0	0	
B	0	1	1	1	1	**1**	0	0	0	
B	0	1	1	1	1	1	**0**	0	0	
A	0	1	1	1	1	**1**	1	0	0	
C	0	1	1	1	**1**	1	1	0	0	
STOP	0	1	1	1	1	1	1	0	0	

Figure 6.5. *The action of a three-state Busy Beaver*

Now for our uncomputable function. Define the quantity $BB(n)$ = the number of 1s written by an n-state Busy Beaver. Thus, the Busy Beaver function $BB(n)$ is the maximal number of 1s that any halting program can write on the tape of an n-state Turing machine, or, equivalently, $BB(n)$ is the largest number computable with an n-state Turing machine. We have just seen that the first few values of this function are $BB(1) = 1$, $BB(2) = 4$, and $BB(3) = 6$. From these results for small values of n, you might think that the function $BB(n)$ doesn't have any particularly interesting properties as n gets larger. Hah! Just as you can't judge a book by its cover (or title), you can't judge a function from its behavior for just a few values of its argument. In fact, it's been shown that

$$BB(12) \geq 6 \times 4096^{4096^{4096^{4096^{4096^{\cdots^{4096^4}}}}}}$$

where the number 4096 appears 166 times in the dotted region! So in trying to calculate the value of $BB(12)$, we quickly reach the point where it becomes impossible to distinguish between the finite and the infinite. It turns out that for large enough values of the number of states n, the quantity $BB(n)$ exceeds that of any computable function for that same argument n. In other words, the Busy Beaver function $BB(n)$ is uncomputable. So for a concrete example of an effectively uncomputable number, just take a Turing machine with a large number of internal states n, and consider the number $BB(n) + 1$. This quantity is uncomputable by any n-state Turing machine. So as we let n become larger and larger, $BB(n) + 1$ gets closer and closer to a truly uncomputable number. Now let's get back to Turing's resolution of the Decision Problem.

Turing's machine-theoretic version of Hilbert's Decision Problem is the same question that bothered my friend when he saw the hourglass icon appear on my computer screen: "Will this #$@?★! program $ever$ stop?" In the language of logic and computing, the question is known as

The Halting Problem

Is there a general algorithm for determining if a program will halt?

Put more precisely, the Halting Problem asks if there exists a single program that will process any other program P and a set of input data

I, outputting a YES if the program P eventually halts when given the data set I, and outputting a NO if it doesn't. Of course, for some programs and some data sets such an algorithm certainly does exist. For example, most cake recipes contain an explicit instruction saying, in effect, "Stop now, the cake is finished." But the Halting Problem asks a much stronger question: Does there exist a *single* algorithm that will give the correct answer in *all* cases?

To see that the question is far from trivial, imagine we had a program that read the Turing machine tape and stopped when it came to the first 1—i.e., the program said, in essence, "Keep reading until you come to a 1, then stop." In this case, the input data I consisting entirely of 1s would result in the program's stopping after the first step. On the other hand, if the input data were all 0s, then the program would never stop. Of course, in this case it's clear by inspection whether or not the program will halt when processing the data set I: the program eventually stops if I contains even a single 1; otherwise the program runs forever. So here's an example of a halting rule that works for any data set I processed by this especially primitive program. Unfortunately, most real computer programs are vastly more complicated than this, and it's far from clear by simple inspection of the program what kinds of quantities will be computed as the program goes about its business. After all, if we knew what the program was going to compute at each step, we wouldn't have to run the program, would we? Moreover, the stopping rule for real programs is almost always an implicit rule of the foregoing sort, saying something like: "If such and such a quantity satisfying this or that condition appears, stop; otherwise keep computing." The essence of the Halting Problem is to ask if there exists any "effective process" that can be applied to the program and its input data to tell *in advance* whether or not the program's stopping condition will ever be satisfied.

Turing settled the matter once and for all in the negative with his 1936 result that given a program P and an input data set I, there is no way in general to say if P will ever finish processing the data I. We'll see later that Turing's solution to the Halting Problem also solves Hilbert's Decision Problem, which applies to logical systems instead of computer programs. In addition, Turing's result gives us our first look at Gödel's landmark result on the limitations of machines and rules for getting at the truth—even in the limited realm of numbers.

Gödel's Theorem—Turing Machine Version

No computer program can ever generate
all the true statements of arithmetic.

(Terminological note: In everyday language, the word *arithmetic* is generally used to mean addition, multiplication, and the other kinds of operations with numbers we all learned in grammar school, basically the third leg of "'readin', writin', and 'rithmetic.'" In the mathematical world, the term has a somewhat broader meaning. In this world, *arithmetic* refers to *all* relations and properties of the natural numbers 1, 2, 3, . . . So, in addition to the simple facts and operations we know from elementary school, arithmetic for the mathematician also encompasses statements like "The sum of two odd numbers is even," "The set of prime numbers (numbers divisible only by 1 and themselves) is infinite," and "Every even number is the sum of two primes (Goldbach's Conjecture)." It's in this more general mathematician's sense that I will employ the term *arithmetic* in all that follows.)

Since the ASCII coding scheme shows us that anything that can be described in any rule-based language can be obtained as the result of carrying out a computation on a UTM, it's somewhat disquieting to realize that there exist uncomputable quantities, even within what looks like a very restricted realm, that of the whole numbers. Following this train of thought, we might be led to think that if *computable* means "rule governed," then *uncomputable* means "not governed by rules," i.e., complex, patternless, or even, in the vernacular, random. The systematic exploration of this circle of ideas has recently shed much new light not only on Gödel's results, but on the limitations of logical systems and rational thought in general.

THE IMPORTANCE OF BEING ARBITRARY

The replacement of the Earth by the Sun as the center of heavenly motions is widely (and rightly) seen as one of the great scientific paradigm shifts of all time. But what is often misunderstood is the reason why this Copernican "revolution" eventually carried the day with the scientific community. The commonly held view is that Copernicus's heliocentric model vanquished the competition, especially the geocentric view of

Ptolemy, because it gave better predictions of the positions of the celestial bodies. In actual fact, the predictions of the Copernican model
were a little *worse* than those obtained using the complicated series of
epicycles and other curves constituting the Ptolemaic scheme, at least to
within the accuracy available using the measuring instruments of the
time. No, the real selling point of the Copernican model was that it was
much *simpler* than the competition, yet still gave a reasonably good account of the observational evidence.

The Copernican revolution is a good case study in how to wield
Ockham's Razor to slit the throat of the competition: When in doubt,
take the simplest theory that accounts for the facts. The problem is that
it's not always easy to agree on what's "simple." The notion of
simplicity, like truth, beauty, and effective process, is an intuitive one,
calling for a more objective characterization, i.e., formalization, before we can ever hope to agree about the relative complexities of
different theories.

Basically, simplicity = economy of description. To illustrate this
claim, suppose you wanted to put a new tile floor in your bathroom and
were considering the two tile patterns shown in Figure 6.6. If you were
trying to describe the candidate patterns over the telephone to a friend,

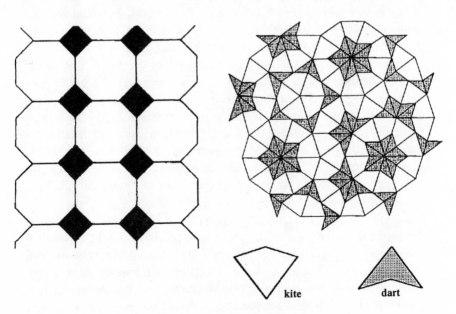

Figure 6.6. *Two floor tilings*

the chances are you'd have little difficulty conveying a clear picture of the first pattern using a very compact description. For example, you might say, "Alternating columns of large white octagons and small black diamonds." To write down this description, I had to use 69 keystrokes on my computer keyboard (including spaces and punctuation). Moreover, the same description works to describe the pattern regardless of how large your bathroom happens to be. And with a little thought it would probably be possible to create a good description using even fewer keystrokes. On the other hand, despite the fact that the second pattern also tiles the floor completely using two primitive figures (in this case, the kite and the dart), just like the first pattern, it seems hard to find a short description that accurately describes what the overall pattern really looks like. The problem is that while there seems to be some kind of structure in this "Penrose tiling," it's just not very easy to capture it in a condensed, easy-to-express way. Thus, the Penrose tiling seems intuitively more complex, or complicated, than the first pattern. So here we see the essence of complexity: Complex objects necessitate long descriptions.

But we have already seen that anything that can be expressed in language can be coded in a string of binary digits. So we can apply the same ideas about complexity to these binary strings, saying that a string is complex if it requires a long description. For instance, the sequence 01010101010101010101, consisting of ten repetitions of the pair 01, looks simple, since we can compactly describe it as "01 repeated ten times." And, in fact, the length of the description would hardly change at all if the sequence were composed of a billion or a trillion such pairs. So for such a well-patterned sequence, the description is far shorter than the length of the sequence itself. By way of contrast, the string 00110110110010001011, which is of exactly the same length as the first one, seems complicated, having no readily identifiable pattern. Its shortest description appears to be just the sequence itself, written out digit by digit. Thus we intuitively feel it's complex while regarding the first sequence as simple.

In 1964 Ray Solomonoff, a researcher at the Zator Corporation, published a pioneering article in which he presented a scheme to measure objectively the complexity of a scientific theory. He based his idea on the premise that a theory for a particular phenomenon must encapsulate somehow the available observational data characterizing that phenomenon. With this idea in mind, Solomonoff proposed to identify a theory with a Turing machine program that, given a description of the experimental setup as input, would produce the empirical observations as the output. Solomonoff argued that the complexity of a theory could be taken to be the "size" of the shortest such program, measured perhaps by the number of keystrokes needed to type the program or, what effectively amounts to the same thing, the number of bits or bytes needed to express the program in ASCII code.

By use of this definition of the complexity of a scientific theory, Solomonoff was anticipating an observation made later by the computer scientist Gregory Chaitin and by the mathematician and philosopher René Thom, who both noted that the point of a scientific theory is to reduce the arbitrariness in the observational data. Thus, a good theory is one that somehow compresses the data, enabling us to describe compactly what's known about the phenomena of concern. On the other hand, if a program (read: theory) reproducing the observational data is not appreciably shorter than the actual data itself, then the theory is basically useless, since we could just as well account for the observations by simply writing them down directly. But we don't need a theory to do that. So if the *shortest possible* program that reproduces a set of observations is no shorter than a mere listing of the observations themselves, then we're justified in calling the observations "random" in the sense that there are no compact laws, or rules, by which the observations can be either predicted or explained, i.e., generated.

Since this idea lies at the heart of the modern theory of algorithmic complexity, let me try to hammer home the point using our Chocolate Cake Machine scenario. The universe of possible observations is our old Platonic friend consisting of all possible chocolate cakes. Consequently, the experimental circumstances are just the ingredients needed to make any kind of chocolate cake. Now suppose we make an observation in this universe, our measuring (i.e., tasting) apparatus recording something satisfying the description of a *Sachertorte*. Thus, the observational data of this experiment is just a description of everything needed to pick out a *Sachertorte* from among the myriad other inhabitants of the chocolate cake world. To write down such a description involves using a certain number of words and punctuation marks and, hence, has some length.

Now let's imagine we want to create a "theory" of the observational evidence—i.e., we want a theory of *Sachertorte*. What this means is that we want to write a program—a recipe—that can be processed by the CCM, and that will single out *Sachertorte* from the universe of chocolate cakes. So, in accordance with the dictates above, the theory will reduce the arbitrariness of what we might have observed in the universe of chocolate cakes by specifying a procedure for making a cake whose description will be in exact agreement with what in fact we have actually observed, i.e., with the description characterizing *Sachertorte*.

If our recipe is to be a good theory of *Sachertorte,* it must be able to identify a *Sachertorte* from among all chocolate cakes, and it must do so in a more efficient manner than by merely listing all the features characterizing a *Sachertorte.* Even from a practical cookery point of view, any recipe that only lists descriptive characteristics of *Sachertorte*—for instance, that it has a layer of chocolate sponge cake, that the cake is covered with glazed chocolate icing, and that the cake and the icing are separated by apricot jam—would be pretty useless. Clearly, we would prefer to have a recipe for actually making the cake. In fact, ideally we would like to have the simplest possible such recipe, since that recipe would presumably involve the least work in the kitchen. The length of this simplest possible recipe for making a cake whose description agrees with that of *Sachertorte* is what we call the *complexity* of *Sachertorte.*

To anyone who's ever tried baking something from the chocolate cake universe, it should be clear from these arguments that some cakes are just more complex than others. And in perfect harmony with this idea of cake complexity, I think most chefs would agree that a chocolate cupcake and a *Sachertorte* are of quite different levels of complexity: The shortest possible recipe for cupcakes is far shorter than the shortest recipe for a *Sachertorte.* And probably both of these kinds of chocolate cakes have complexity less than that of the chocolate hazelnut cake I spoke of earlier.

But we began this discussion of simplicity and complexity by arguing that simplicity and complexity are both directly related to pattern and structure. Therefore, it's reasonable to say that if something is complex, then it is relatively unstructured, or, more prosaically, it's without pattern. Following this line of thought leads immediately to the question: What about randomness? Does randomness correspond in any meaningful sense to a complete lack of structure? Since we already know that everything describable can ultimately be coded by a number, let's leave the world of chocolate cake and go back to look at this question in the universal universe of abstract numbers.

*   *   *

At about the same time Solomonoff was developing his ideas about the complexity of scientific theories, Gregory Chaitin was enrolled in a computer-programming course being given at Columbia University for bright high-school students. At each lecture the professor would assign the class an exercise requiring writing a program to solve it. The students then competed among themselves to see who could write the shortest program solving the assigned problem. While this spirit of competition undoubtedly added some spice to what were otherwise probably pretty dull programming exercises, Chaitin reports that no one in the class could even begin to think of how to actually prove that the weekly winner's program was really the shortest possible.

Even after the course ended Chaitin continued pondering this shortest-program puzzle, eventually seeing how to relate it to a different question: How can we measure the complexity of a number? Is there any way that we can objectively claim π is more complex than, say, $\sqrt{2}$ or 759? Chaitin's answer to this question ultimately led him to one of the most surprising and startling mathematical results of recent times.

In 1965 Chaitin, now an undergraduate at the City University of New York, arrived independently at the same bright idea as Solomonoff: Define the complexity of a number to be the length of the shortest program for a universal Turing machine that will cause the machine to print out the number. Using this idea, Chaitin came up with the following complexity-based definition of a random number: A number is *random* if the shortest program for calculating the number is not appreciably shorter in length than the number itself. Or, expressing it another way, we can say a number is random if it is maximally complex. Here, of course, we take the length of a number or program to be the number of binary digits needed to write down that number or program. With this definition, a number such as $\pi = 3.14159265\ldots$ is not random, since arbitrarily many digits of π can be generated using any of a number of known programs that are of fixed length. Nevertheless, an infinitely long number like π is certainly more complex than a simple number of finite length like 47, since we can always use a program like "PRINT 47" to generate the latter quantity. And this shortest program for 47 is quite a bit shorter than the shortest program that will successively crank out the digits of π.

So if something as complicated looking as π isn't random, do random numbers really exist? Or does Chaitin's definition define an empty set? The surprising fact is that almost *all* numbers are random! To see why, think about what it means for a number to be nonrandom. By definition, a number is nonrandom if it can be produced by a computer program whose length is significantly shorter than the length of the number itself. Suppose we consider all numbers having length n, i.e., all binary strings of n digits. Since each of the n digits can be either 0 or 1, there are a total of 2^n numbers of length n. Let's compute the fraction of these numbers having complexity less than, say, $n - 5$. That is, we're looking for all numbers of length n that can be produced by a computer program that can be coded in no more than $n - 5$ bits.

Since our interest is in all computer programs that can be coded in no more than $n - 5$ bits, we could actually list each one of these programs. So, for example, there is one program of length zero (the empty program consisting of no instructions), two programs of length 1 (the single-element strings 0 and 1), four programs of length 2 (the strings 00, 01, 10, and 11) and, in general, 2^k programs of length k. Counting all possibilities, there is a total of $1 + 2 + 4 + \ldots + 2^{n-5} = 2^{n-4} - 1$ such programs having length $n - 5$ or less. Consequently, there are at most this many numbers of length n whose complexity is less than or equal to $n - 5$, since at best each of these programs can produce an output corresponding to an actual number of length n. But we have seen that there is a total of 2^n numbers of length n. Therefore, the proportion of these numbers having complexity no greater than $n - 5$ is at most $(2^{n-4} - 1)/2^n \le \frac{1}{16}$.

So we see that no more than one number in sixteen can be described by a program that's at least five bits shorter than the number itself. Similarly, no more than one number in five hundred can be produced by a program ten or more bits shorter than the number's length—i.e., its complexity is ten or more units away from being random. Using this kind of argument and letting $n \to \infty$, we can fairly easily prove that the set of real numbers having less than maximal complexity forms an infinitesimally small subset of the set of all numbers. In short, almost every real number is random, since there exists no program that produces the number that is shorter than the trivial program that just prints the number itself. Now let's look at this shortest-program business in a little more depth.

The starting point for Chaitin's remarkable results is the seemingly innocent query: "What is the smallest number that cannot be expressed in words?" This statement seems to pick out a definite number. Let's call it $\mathcal{U}$ for "unnameable." But thinking about things for a moment, we see that there appears to be something fishy about this labeling. On the one hand, we seem to have just described the number $\mathcal{U}$ in words. But $\mathcal{U}$ is supposed to be the first number that *cannot* be described in words! This paradox seems to have originally been suggested to Bertrand Russell by a certain Mr. G. G. Berry, a Cambridge University librarian.

Just as Alan Turing had to formalize the intuitive notion of an effective process, the Berry Paradox contains its own unformalizable notion, the concept of denotation between the terms in its statement and numbers. In arriving at his results on randomness, complexity, and the limitations of rule-based knowledge, part of Chaitin's insight was to see that the way around this obstacle was to shift attention to the phrase: "the smallest number not computable by a program of complexity n." This phrase *can* be formalized, specifying a certain computer program for searching out such a number. What Chaitin discovered was that no program of complexity n can ever produce a number having complexity greater than n. Therefore, the program of complexity n can never halt by outputting the number specified by Chaitin's phrase. This fact constitutes an algorithmic complexity version of the unsolvability of the Halting Problem.

More generally, this result shows that even though there clearly exist numbers of all levels of complexity, it's impossible to prove this fact. That is, given any computer program, there always exist numbers having complexity greater than that program can generate. In Chaitin's words, "A ten-pound theory can no more generate a twenty-pound theorem than a one-hundred-pound pregnant woman can birth a two-hundred-pound child." Speaking somewhat informally, Chaitin's Theorem says that no program can calculate a number more complex than itself. In the cake world, we could loosely interpret Chaitin's Theorem as saying that you can't make *Sachertorte* from the recipe for chocolate cupcakes. The cupcake recipe is just too simple to generate anything more complicated than cupcakes. Or, equivalently, the operations needed to make a *Sachertorte* are too complex to be carried out with the limited repertoire of steps and actions specified in the recipe for cupcakes.

The implication of Chaitin's Theorem is that, for sufficiently large numbers N, it cannot be proved that a particular string has complexity greater than N. Or, what is the same thing, there exists a level N such that no number whose binary string is of length greater than N can be proved to be random. Nevertheless, we know that almost every number is random. We just can't prove that any *given* number is random. Here's a quick proof of this surprising and important fact.

Let's take an arbitrary, but fixed, number n. By the arguments above, the likelihood is overwhelmingly high that this arbitrarily se-lected number is random. Suppose we want to prove that n is indeed "typical" in this sense. So let's assume there did exist a program $\mathcal{P}$ that checks that n can be generated only by a program longer than $\mathcal{P}$. As long as we select our number n to be sufficiently large, the existence of such a program $\mathcal{P}$ would constitute a way of proving that n is random. Let's show why no such program $\mathcal{P}$ can possibly exist.

First of all, we use $\mathcal{P}$ to generate all programs of length 1, length 2, and so on. Some of these programs will actually be proofs that the number n cannot be generated by programs as short as $\mathcal{P}$. But for these proofs we could have the program $\mathcal{P}$ print out the number n, in effect generating it. Thus $\mathcal{P}$ will have generated a number that it is too short to generate. This contradiction leads us to conclude that no such program $\mathcal{P}$ exists. Consequently, it's impossible to prove that our arbi-trarily selected number n is random—despite the fact that almost all numbers really are random.

The essence of the difficulty in proving that any particular number is random lies in the fact that each digit in a random number carries positive information, since it cannot be predicted from its predeces-sors. Thus, an infinite random sequence contains more information than all our finite human systems of logic put together. But since almost all real numbers consist of an infinite, nonrepeating sequence of digits, we find that almost all numbers are in fact random. Neverthe-less, verifying the randomness of any particular such sequence lies beyond the powers of logical proof. Looking at the problem in another way, in order to write down an "arbitrarily long" patternless se-quence, we need to give a general rule for each element of the se-quence. But then this rule is shorter than suitably large sections of the sequence, so the sequence can't really be random after all! Chaitin's Theorem also gives us another perspective on Gödel:

Gödel's Theorem—Complexity Version

There exist numbers having complexity so great
that no computer program can generate them.

Chaitin's Theorem says that if we have some program, there always exists a finite number t such that t is the most complex number our program can generate. Nevertheless, we can clearly see that numbers having complexity greater than t exist. To construct the binary string for one, simply toss a coin a bit more than t times, writing down a 1 when a head turns up and a 0 for tails.

It's not only thought-provoking, but of central importance to the theme of this book, to consider the degree to which Chaitin's result imposes limitations on our ability to find or create scientific theories, i.e., laws, compressing our observations of natural and human phenomena. Suppose $\mathcal{K}$ represents our best present-day knowledge about mathematics, physics, chemistry, and all the other sciences, while $\mathcal{M}$ denotes a UTM whose reasoning powers equal those of the smartest and cleverest of human beings. Then we can estimate the number t in Chaitin's Theorem as

$$t = \text{complexity } \mathcal{K} + \text{complexity } \mathcal{M} + 1 \text{ million}$$

where the last term is thrown in to account for the overhead in the program of the machine $\mathcal{M}$. To estimate the complexities of $\mathcal{K}$ and $\mathcal{M}$, the logician and science-fiction writer Rudy Rucker has offered the following argument. First of all, suppose that the knowledge in around 1,000 books suffices for $\mathcal{K}$. Since an average-sized book like this one takes around 8 million bits (= 1 million bytes) to express in ASCII code, the total complexity of $\mathcal{K}$ comes to a number in the neighborhood of $1,000 \times 8$ million $= 8$ billion. This is as good an estimate as any for the complexity of $\mathcal{K}$. As to $\mathcal{M}$, using a similar argument Rucker suggests that it should be possible to characterize everything that we need to know about the UTM with the information contained in another 1,000 average-sized books. If so, then the complexity of $\mathcal{M}$ also amounts to about 8 billion. Thus we conclude that t is certainly less than 16 billion.

The bottom line then is that if any worldly phenomenon generates observational data having complexity greater than around 16 billion, no such machine $\mathcal{M}$ (read: human) will be able to prove that there is some short program (i.e., theory) explaining that phenomenon. Thus, recalling René Thom's idea of scientific theories as arbitrariness-reducing tools, Chaitin's work says that our scientific theories are basically powerless to say anything about phenomena whose complexity is much greater than 16 billion. But note that Chaitin's Theorem also says that the machine will never tell us that there does *not* exist a simple explanation for these phenomena, either. Rather, it says that if this "simple" explanation exists, we will never understand it—it's too complex for us! Complexity 16 billion represents the outer limits to the powers of human reasoning; beyond that we enter the "twilight zone," where reason and systematic analysis give way to intuition, insight, feelings, hunches, and just plain dumb luck.

The theorems of Turing and Chaitin have shown that there are fundamental, irremovable limitations on our ability to generate truths from rules, i.e., programs. For the sake of exposition, up to now I've spoken mainly about how these limitations arise within the context of computation. Some readers might hold to the view that limitations on the generation of knowledge by computers are one thing, but that limitations on the powers of the human mind to get at the scheme of things by logical analysis are something else again. Such a belief would be based on the argument that it may be possible to arrive at "truth" using logical arguments that transcend the capabilities of a Turing machine, i.e., that the human mind can *systematically* generate truths that cannot be obtained as the result of running a UTM program. Historically, in fact, all the arguments I've presented so far were originally formulated within the context of logic and mathematics, and were quite far removed from the ideas of programs and computation that were developed somewhat later on. So to stamp out once and for all the idea that logical reasoning and computation are somehow different, let's set our computers aside and spend a section or two tracing the path between truth and proof as it was originally followed—through the world of mathematics.

THE LIMITS TO PROOF

Roma, Venezia, Milano, Firenze, Napoli—*de rigueur* ports of call on the "See Italy in Five Days" package tours. And that's as it should be for Cousin Katy from Kankakee on her once-in-a-lifetime pilgrimage to the land of Benetton, the Mafia, and Leonardo. But those jaded travelers looking for just a bit more than the obligatory churches, statues, and museums will have none of the blandishments of the tour operators, heading instead for the exit as the train pulls into the Bologna station midway between Venice and Florence. Yes, I said Bologna. For besides being regarded by many gourmets as the eating capital of Italy, a sort of Italian counterpart to the French culinary mecca of Lyons, Bologna is also the focal point of the Italian exotic-sports-car industry, with the Lamborghini, Ferrari, Maserati, and de Tomaso factories all located within a few miles of beautiful (really!) downtown Bologna. And as if this were not enough, Bologna also claims the distinction of having the world's oldest university. And it was at this venerable site during the 1928 International Congress of Mathematicians that the famed German mathematician David Hilbert threw down a challenge that would ultimately change forever the way we think about the relationship between what's logically provable and what's actually true.

At stake in Hilbert's 1928 address was the foundational issue of whether or not it's possible to prove every true mathematical statement. What Hilbert was looking for was a kind of Truth Machine capable of settling every possible mathematical statement. Just feed the statement in at one end, turn the crank, and out the other end pops the answer: TRUE or FALSE. Ideally, in this setup the original statement would be either a true mathematical fact and, hence, logically deducible from the given assumptions and thus a theorem, or it would be false and, consequently, not a theorem, i.e., its negation would be a theorem. In short, Hilbert's Truth Machine would give a complete account of every mathematical assertion. In his Bologna talk Hilbert laid down the requirements for such a Truth Machine, or what's more pedantically termed an *axiomatic,* or *formal, logical system,* along with the conviction that his "Program" would ultimately yield a complete axiomatization of all of mathematics.

With this challenge to the mathematical world, Hilbert was reemphasizing a different aspect of another problem he posed at an earlier ICM gathering in Paris in 1900. Since unsolved problems are the lifeblood of any field of intellectual activity, to mark the turn of the century Hilbert listed twenty-three problems whose resolution he felt was of crucial importance for the development of mathematics. The second problem on this list involved proving that mathematical reasoning is reliable. In other words, by following the rules of mathematical reasoning, it should not be possible to arrive at mutually contradictory statements; a proposition and its negation should not both be theorems. Of course, this self-consistency requirement is a necessary condition for any axiomatic system of the sort Hilbert had in mind to work, since if the system is inconsistent it's possible to prove any assertion TRUE or FALSE as we wish, hardly a secure basis for reliable knowledge.

As an amusing illustration of the crucial importance of self-

consistency, Bertrand Russell once gave the following "proof" that if
$2 + 2 = 5$, then he was the Pope. Here's Russell's argument: If we
admit that $2 + 2 = 5$, then we can subtract 2 from each side of the
equation, giving us $2 = 3$. Transposing, we have $3 = 2$, and sub-
tracting 1 from each side of this equation gives us $2 = 1$. Thus, since
the Pope and Russell are two people and $2 = 1$, then the Pope and
Russell are one. Hence, Russell is the Pope! This is about as good an
argument as any for why an inconsistent logical system is basically
useless as far as getting at the truth goes.

But why was Hilbert even concerned in the slightest about such
matters? After all, mathematicians had been using successfully the
very methods that worried Hilbert at least since the time of Euclid.
Why get worried now? Was $2 + 2$ all of a sudden going to become
4.007? Or was the sum of the angles of a triangle going to turn out to
differ from 180 degrees? Actually, it was exactly this question about
triangles that served as one of the sparks that ultimately touched off
Hilbert's concern. In the early part of the nineteenth century the ge-
ometers János Bolyai and Nikolai Lobachevski had shown independently, and quite contrary to popular belief and everyday intuition, that
there were other perfectly consistent ways of mathematically talking
about things like points and lines besides the way of Euclid. And in
these "noneuclidean geometries," the sum of the angles of what passes
for a "triangle" could be less than 180 degrees (hyperbolic geometry)
or greater than 180 degrees (elliptic geometry). So despite its unques-
tioned utility in the physical world, Euclid's geometry turns out to be
no more or less "true" than its competitors, at least in the universe of
mathematical objects. And, in fact, even in the physical world these
noneuclidean geometries come into their own when we start considering objects on a cosmological scale. For example, on the basis of
current observations of the distribution of matter in the universe, it's
beginning to look more and more likely that the large-scale structure of
the universe obeys the geometry of Bolyai and Lobachevski in which,
given a fixed line and a point not on that line, we can draw an infinite
number of lines through the point, all of which are parallel to the given
line. This is in stark contrast to the world of Euclid, in which only a
single such parallel line may be drawn.

Alternate geometries call into question the relationship between
mathematical objects and the external world, since by definition the
universe is the real world, while points, parallel lines, and triangles

seem to have a far less tangible existence, living as much in the mind as in the universe of material objects and everyday events. But far more troubling to Hilbert than noneuclidean geometries were the logical paradoxes discovered by Bertrand Russell and his followers shortly after the turn of the century. These logical puzzlers are exemplified by the famous Barber Paradox: "The village barber shaves all those in the village who do not shave themselves. Who shaves the barber?" Tracing through the logical possibilities, we find that if the barber shaves himself, then he doesn't shave himself—and vice versa. Figure 6.7 gives a more contemporary view of the same kind of self-referential tangle.

Figure 6.7. *Paradoxical self-reference in modern form*

The standard methods of logical inference are too feeble to settle even such a seemingly simple question as the Barber Paradox. Nevertheless, these are precisely the tools upon which the methods used in constructing mathematical proofs ultimately rest, suggesting why Hilbert and others started getting concerned about the logical coherency of the mathematical enterprise. In Hilbert's own words, "Every definite mathematical problem must necessarily be susceptible of an exact settlement, either in the form of an actual answer to the question asked, or by a proof of the impossibility of its solution." But within the framework of classical logic, the Barber Paradox is just plain undecidable. So Hilbert's challenge was to find a way to formalize every mathematical truth in a way that would forever exclude the possibility of paradoxical statements appearing in mathematics in the way that Russell showed they could appear in ordinary language and logic.

But less than three years after Hilbert's Bologna address, the young Austrian logician Kurt Gödel astonished the mathematical world by publishing a revolutionary paper turning Hilbert's fondest dream into his greatest nightmare. We have already seen that our journey here in this book in pursuit of the limits to predictability and explanation in science and mathematics often touches on the myriad details, ramifications, and extensions of Gödel's work. The time has finally come to see exactly why. But before turning to these matters, let me first show how a statement of mathematics, arithmetic even, can be true—but unprovable, in a mathematical sense.

According to mathematical folklore, one day during the very brief grade-school career of "the Prince of Mathematicians," Karl Friedrich Gauss, the teacher grew annoyed with his students' unruly behavior and decided to silence them for a while by assigning a long calculation to perform. Specifically, the teacher told the class to add up all the numbers between 1 and 100. By the custom of the time, the first student to finish was supposed to write the answer on a slate and then put the slate face down on the teacher's desk. Entertaining the happy vision of long columns of numbers and frequent childish calculational errors, the teacher no doubt felt that this chore would occupy the class long enough for him to regain his sanity and peace of mind. Unfortunately, he hadn't counted on having a mathematical prodigy in the room, and within a few moments after the problem had been given, Gauss's slate slammed down on his desk. How did he do it?

Being considerably more than just a little bit cleverer than the teacher, Gauss saw immediately that the way to solve this problem was to separate the numbers from 1 to 100 into two groups, and then to write these two groups one below the other in the following way:

$$1 \quad 2 \quad 3 \quad 4 \quad 5 \ldots 50$$
$$100 \quad 99 \quad 98 \quad 97 \quad 96 \ldots 51$$

What Gauss noticed was that if he added the corresponding numbers from each group, the sum was always the same—101. And since the 100 numbers were divided into two groups of equal size, there must be 50 such pairs. Consequently, the sum of the numbers from 1 to 100 must be equal to 50×101, or 5,050. And it doesn't take much exercise of the imagination to see that Gauss's trick will work for any number the teacher might have chosen. If the teacher had given the number n, you just separate the integers from 1 to n into two groups of equal size (0 has to be thrown in to balance the groups if n happens to be odd), then write the two groups in ascending and descending order as above. The desired sum $1 + 2 + 3 + \ldots + n$ will then equal $(n/2) \times (n + 1)$.

Gauss's scheme constitutes a proof of this formula for an arbitrary, *but fixed*, whole number n. But it's not a proof that the formula holds for *every* positive integer n; just a proof for any fixed number the teacher may happen to call out. The usual proof of the general formula makes use of the principle of mathematical induction. We first verify that the formula holds for the case $n = 1$. Next we assume it holds for an arbitrary, but fixed, positive integer n. We then use this assumption to *deduce logically* that it holds for $n + 1$. Thus, we show that if it holds for $n = 1$, then it holds for $n = 2$. And if it holds for $n = 2$, it holds for $n = 3$, and so on. In fact, *all* proofs of this basic formula of arithmetic make use of an inductive argument of this sort in one way or another. This technique of mathematical induction, while not a tool of formal logical inference, is used extensively in mathematical arguments to allow us to infer a result for an infinite number of cases (all positive integers) from a finite set of conditions (the two cases $n = 1$ and $n = $ arbitrary, but fixed).

There are some philosophers of mathematics who argue that such nonconstructive and/or infinitary principles of inference like mathematical induction should not be admitted into mathematics as a tool of proof. So if we were to strip out the tool of induction from the logical proof mechanism of mathematics, the formula for the sum of the first n integers would no longer be provable for general n. Nevertheless, we would still be able to see "from the outside," so to speak, that the formula is true. What Gödel showed is that even playing with a full deck consisting of all the tools of logical inference and mathematical proof, including things like mathematical induction, there still exist true but unprovable mathematical statements. In short, there is an eternally unbridgeable gap between what can be proved and what's true.

As a consequence of Gödel's work, issues of prediction and explanation in mathematics center upon the following foundational questions:

I. Proof vs. Truth

What are the limits to mathematical proof?

II. Mathematical Reality

What does a mathematical "proof" prove?

Question I addresses the degree to which we can hope to narrow the gap between the universe of true mathematical statements and what's provable. But all mathematical truths, provable or otherwise, are statements about the existence of certain kinds of objects. So what kind of an existence does something like a hyperbolic triangle or a random number actually have? Thus, Question II asks us to give an account of what we are really talking about when we claim to have proved the "existence" of an object like an elliptic triangle or the formula for the sum of the first n integers. In cake-world terminology, we can think of these big questions as asking to what degree we can write down a recipe for every possible chocolate cake (Question I), and what kind of an existence a chocolate cake has if we give its recipe but have never actually baked it (Question II).

If our own existence were confined solely to the universe of cakes, these questions might seem to be at best amusing philosophical digressions. But unless you live in Vienna, your world is probably a bit broader in scope than the offerings of the corner coffeehouse and *Konditorei*. In particular, questions of prediction and explanation in the worlds of both science and mathematics ultimately come down to the kinds of answers we're able to provide for Questions I and II.

Since the idea of an axiomatic framework for all of mathematics was the starting point for Gödel's assault on proof, let's begin our story with a bit of background on Hilbert's Program for axiomatizing mathematical truth.

SPEAKING FORMALLY

In his famous epigram on the nature of mathematics, Bertrand Russell claimed that "pure mathematics is the subject in which we do not know what we are talking about, or whether what we are saying is true." This pithy remark summarizes the content of both Questions I and II, as well as striking to the heart of Hilbert's Program: the development of a purely syntactic framework for all of mathematics. There's more than a touch of irony in Russell's remark asserting the content-free nature of mathematics, since a prime force motivating Hilbert's Program was his feeling that the paradoxical element in things like Russell's own Barber Paradox was due to the *semantic* content in the statement of the paradox. Hilbert believed that the way to eliminate the possibility of such paradoxes arising in mathematics was to create an essentially "meaningless" framework within which to speak about the truth or falsity of mathematical statements. Such a framework is now termed a *formal system,* and it constitutes the historical jumping-off point for investigations of the gap between what can be proved and what is actually true in the universe of mathematics.

The "meaningless statements" of a formal system are composed of finite sequences of abstract *symbols.* The symbols are often termed the *alphabet* of the system, while the "words" of the system are usually called *symbol strings.* The symbols might be objects like ★ and ✛, or they might even be signs like 0 and 1. But in the latter case, it's absolutely essential to recognize that we're not talking yet about the *numbers* 0 and 1, but only the *numerals* 0 and 1. It's only when these symbols are given meaning as numbers that they acquire the properties we usually associate with the numbers 0 and 1. We'll come back to this point with a vengeance shortly. In a formal system, a finite number of these symbol strings are taken as the *axioms* of the system. To round things out, the system also has a finite number of *transformation rules.* These rules specify how a given string of symbols can be converted into another such string.

The general idea of proof within a formal system is to start from one of the axioms and apply a finite sequence of transformations, thereby converting the axiom into a succession of new strings, where each string is either an axiom or is derived from its predecessors by application of the transformation rules. The last string in such a sequence is called a *theorem* of the system. The totality of all theorems constitutes what can be proved within the system. But note carefully that these so-called statements don't actually say anything; they are just strings of abstract symbols. We'll get to how the theorems acquire meaning in a moment. But first let's see how this setup works with a simple example.

Suppose the symbols of our system are the three objects ★ (star), ✠ (maltese cross), and ♣ (shamrock). Let the two-element string ✠♣ be the sole axiom of the system. Letting x denote an arbitrary finite string of stars, crosses, and clouds, we take the transformation rules of our system to be:

Rule I: x♣ → x♣★
Rule II: ✠x → ✠xx
Rule III: ♣♣♣ → ★
Rule IV: ★★ → —

In these rules, → means "is replaced by." So, for instance, Rule I says that we can form a new string by appending a star to any string that ends in a shamrock. The interpretation of Rule IV is that anytime two stars appear together in a string, they can be dropped to form a new string. Let's see how these rules can be used to prove a theorem.

Starting with the single axiom ✠♣, we can deduce that the string ✠★♣ is a theorem by applying the transformation rules in the following order:

$$→ \;\; ✠♣ \;\; → \;\; ✠♣♣ \;\; → \;\; ✠♣♣♣♣ \;\; → \;\; ✠★♣$$
(Axiom)   (Rule II)   (Rule II)   (Rule III)

Such a sequence of steps, starting from an axiom and ending at a statement like ✠★♣, is termed a *proof sequence* for the theorem represented by the last string in the sequence. Observe that when applying Rule III at the final step, we could have replaced the last three ♣s from the preceding string rather than the first three, thereby ending up with the theorem ✠♣★ instead of ✠★♣. The perceptive reader will have also noted that all the intermediate strings obtained in moving from the axiom to the theorem begin with ✚. It's fairly evident from the axiom and the action of the transformation rules for this system that every string will have this property. This is a *metamathematical* property of the system, since it's a statement *about* the system rather than one made *in* the system itself. The distinction between what the system can say from the inside (its strings) and what we can say about the system from the outside (properties of the strings) is of the utmost importance for Gödel's results.

Comparing the workings of a Turing machine program and the operations we just went through using the transformation rules of a formal system, it doesn't look as if there's any important difference between the two. And so it is: Given any formal system $\mathcal{F}$, there is a Turing machine $\mathcal{M}$ such that the possible theorems of $\mathcal{F}$ coincide with the possible outputs of $\mathcal{M}$. Conversely, given any Turing machine, we can find a formal system such that the possible outputs of the machine are exactly the possible theorems of the formal system. The matchups showing this perfect correspondence between Turing machines and formal systems are given in Table 6.5.

Turing Machine	Formal System
tape symbols	alphabet
byte pattern	symbol string
input data	axioms
program	proof sequence
output	theorems

Table 6.5. Turing machine–formal system correspondence

We spoke earlier of Hilbert's famous *Entscheidungsproblem,* or Decision Problem, which asked if there is any algorithmic procedure for deciding if a given symbol string is or is not a theorem of a particular formal system. Using the "isomorphism" in Table 6.5 between Turing machines and formal systems, Turing was able to translate the Decision Problem involving theorems in a formal system into its equivalent expression in the language of machines. We have already seen that this computing equivalent is the Halting Problem, whose negative solution implies the same sad answer to the Decision Problem. Since about now the right question to be asking yourself is "What does all this meaningless symbol manipulation have to do with everyday reality?," let's quickly turn our attention from matters of form to those of content.

The answer to how we get from form to content can be given in one word: *interpretation*. In particular, for reasons that will become apparent in a moment, let's focus our interest right now on the slice of everyday reality consisting of mathematical facts. Then, depending on the kind of mathematical structure under consideration (e.g., euclidean geometry, elementary arithmetic, calculus, topology . . .), we have to make up a dictionary by which we can match up (i.e., interpret) the objects constituting that mathematical structure, things like points, lines, and numbers, with the abstract symbols, strings, and rules of the formal system that we want to employ to represent that structure. By this dictionary-construction step, we attach meaning, or semantic content, to the abstract, purely syntactic strings formed from the symbols of the formal system. Thereafter, all the theorems of the formal system can be interpreted as true statements about the associated mathematical objects. The diagram below illustrates this crucial distinction between the purely syntactic world of formal systems and the meaningful world of mathematics.

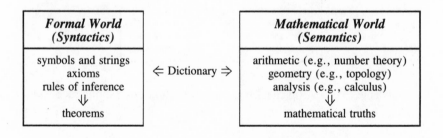

Before proceeding further, let me pause here for a moment to explain a possibly puzzling point about this interpretation step that could bother the attentive reader.

Originally, Hilbert suggested the idea of a formal system for getting at mathematical truth as a way of eliminating the possibility that logical paradoxes of the barbering sort could stick their ugly, unshaven faces into the realm of mathematics. The main selling point for formalization was the claim that these kinds of paradoxes stemmed from the semantic content of their expression in natural language. So if the symbols and strings of the formal system are completely meaningless, then the statements (symbol strings) should be paradox free. In particular, there should be no undecidable propositions. But if that argument is the main selling point for formal systems, then why are we all of a sudden trotting out this interpretation step, thereby injecting meaning back into the picture? Doesn't this dictionary-construction step undermine completely Hilbert's whole argument for formalization?

The key to the resolution of this apparent dilemma lies in putting the horse before the cart. Hilbert's Program involved *starting* with the formal system. The second step was then to bring out the mathematical structure of concern and show how to match its objects to the strings of the formal system, i.e., how to interpret the meaningful mathematical objects in terms of the meaningless formal ones. So we don't begin with the semantic-laden mathematical structure, but rather start with the purely syntactic world of the formal system. Hilbert's Program really amounted to trying to find a formal system that was above all free from internal contradictions, and whose theorems were in perfect correspondence with all the true facts of arithmetic. In essence, Hilbert didn't believe that any Russell-type paradoxes lurked in the world of mathematical truths, even though they might exist in the far fuzzier realm of natural language. And the way he thought we could prevent them from crossing the border separating ordinary language from mathematics was to formalize the entire universe of mathematical truth. Put simply, what Gödel showed was that Hilbert was dead wrong. There is no way to erect a barrier between mathematics and the demons of undecidability—even in the pristine world of pure numbers. Now let's get back to our story.

From what has gone before in our discussion of chocolate cakes—both virtual and real—the reader will recognize that the interpretation step linking mathematical and formal systems is actually nothing new. Earlier, we used the standardized binary strings of the ASCII code to symbolize, or code, the cake ingredients, as well as to code the final cakes themselves. These strings, of course, are composed of the content-free symbols 0 and 1, and acquire meanings like "two eggs," "a pinch of salt," or "*Sachertorte*" only by virtue of the dictionary titled *The ASCII Code*. The same thing happens in mathematics, except that by historical tradition, accident, convenience, and otherwise, different branches of mathematics have acquired their own characteristic coding schemes. These schemes make use of all the strange symbols like $\int$, Σ, $\leftrightarrow$, and ∇ that mystify, frustrate, and intimidate the uninitiated. But this symbolism is just for style. What's really important is that for every mathematical structure, there exists at least one dictionary linking it to a formal system.

Once this dictionary has been written and the associated interpretation established, then we can hope along with Hilbert that there will be a perfect, one-to-one correspondence between the true facts of the mathematical structure and the theorems of the formal system. Loosely speaking, Hilbert's dream was to find a formal system in which every mathematical truth translates into a theorem, and conversely. Such a system is termed *complete*. Moreover, if the mathematical structure is to avoid contradiction, a mathematical truth and its negation should never both translate to theorems, i.e., be provable in the formal system. Such a system in which no contradictory statements can be proved is termed *consistent*. With these preliminaries in hand, we can finally describe Gödel's wreckage of Hilbert's Program.

By the time of Hilbert's 1928 Bologna lecture, it was already known that the problem of the consistency of mathematics as a whole was reducible to the determination of the consistency of arithmetic. That is, to the properties and relations among the natural numbers (the positive integers 1, 2, 3, . . . , or what some people call the whole numbers). So the problem became to give a "theory of arithmetic," i.e., a formal system that was (1) finitely describable, (2) complete, (3) consistent, and (4) sufficiently powerful to represent all the statements that can be made about the natural numbers. By the term *finitely describable* what Hilbert meant was not only that the number and length of the axioms and rules of the system should be constructible in a finite number of steps, but also that every provable statement in the system, i.e., every theorem, should also be provable in a finite number of steps. This condition seems reasonable enough, since you don't really have a theory at all unless you can tell other people about it. And you certainly can't tell them about it if there are an infinite number of axioms, rules, and/or steps in a proof sequence.

A central question that arises in connection with any such formalization of arithmetic is to ask if there is a finite procedure by which we can decide the truth or falsity of every arithmetical statement. So, for example, if we make the statement "The sum of two odd numbers is always an even number," we want a finite procedure, essentially a computer program, that halts after a finite number of steps, telling us whether that statement is true or false, i.e., provable or not in some formal system powerful enough to encompass all possible statements of ordinary arithmetic. For example, in the ✛-★-⚜ formal system considered earlier, such a decision procedure is given by the far from obvious criterion: "A string is a theorem if and only if it begins with a ✛ and the number of ⚜s in the string is not divisible by 3." The question of the existence of a mechanical procedure or rule like this to decide every statement about arithmetic is Hilbert's famous Decision Problem, which we already know is unsolvable.

Hilbert was convinced that a formalization of arithmetic satisfying the foregoing desiderata was possible, and his Bologna manifesto challenged the international mathematical community to find or create it. It's somehow comforting to know how dramatically and definitively wrong even a man as great as Hilbert can be!

In 1931, less than three years after Hilbert's Bolognese call to arms, Kurt Gödel published the following metamathematical fact, perhaps the most famous mathematical (and philosophical) result of this century:

Gödel's Theorem—Informal Version

Arithmetic is not completely formalizable.

Remember that for a given mathematical structure like arithmetic, there are an infinite number of ways we can choose a finitary set of axioms and rules of a formal system in an attempt to mirror syntactically the mathematical truths of the structure. What Gödel's result says is that *none* of these choices will work; there does not and cannot exist a formal system satisfying all the requirements of Hilbert's Program. In short, there are no rules for generating *all* the truths about the natural numbers.

Gödel's result is shown graphically in Figure 6.8 for a given formal system **M** representing arithmetic. The entire square represents all possible statements that can be made about the natural numbers. Initially, the square is entirely gray. As we prove a statement true using the rules of the formal system **M**, we color that statement white; if we prove the statement false, we color it black. Gödel's Theorem says that there will always exist statements (or *Gödel sentences*) like **G** that are eternally doomed to a life in the shadow world of gray; it's impossible to eliminate the gray and color the entire square in black and white. And this result holds for *every* possible formal system **M**, provided

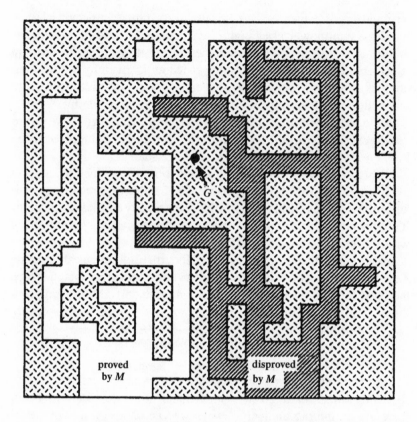

Figure 6.8. *Gödel's theorem in logic space*

only that the system is consistent; for every consistent formal system **M**, there is at least one statement **G** that cannot be proved or disproved in **M**. As in the rest of life, so it is in arithmetic too: There's no washing away the gray! We call a statement like **G** *undecidable* in **M**, since it can be neither proved nor disproved within the framework of that formal system. And if we add that undecidable statement **G** as an axiom, thereby creating a new formal system, the new system will have its own Gödel sentence. What's perhaps equally surprising is that for every such formal system **M**, the statement **G** can be constructed so that it is actually true—when looked at from outside the system. Consequently, while **G** is undecidable *within* **M**, it is actually true and can be seen to be true by jumping outside the system.

By his theorem, Gödel snuffed out once and for all Hilbert's flickering hope of providing a complete and total axiomatization of arithmetic, hence of mathematics. Since Gödel's Theorem represents one of the pinnacles of human intellectual achievement, not to mention forming the basis for a whole host of related developments in mathematics, philosophy, computer science, linguistics, and psychology, let's spend some time looking at how one could ever prove such a profound, mind-boggling result.

THE UNDECIDABLE

In March 1938 Hitler's troops invaded Austria in the so-called *Anschluss* with Germany. The subsequent rise of Nazi influence in all aspects of daily and academic life in Austria, coupled with the very down-to-earth fact that Gödel was declared eligible to be drafted into the German Army despite his always precarious health, made Vienna an increasingly difficult place for him to carry on his mathematical work. So despite the fact that he was not Jewish, Gödel left Austria and Europe forever in January 1940, emigrating via the Trans-Siberian Railway to the scholars' haven at the Institute for Advanced Study in Princeton, New Jersey, where he spent the remainder of his life.

In early 1948 Gödel decided to seek American citizenship. So in his characteristically thorough way, he began a detailed study of the U.S. Constitution in preparation for the citizenship examination. On the day before the exam Gödel called his friend the noted economist Oskar Morgenstern, saying with great excitement and consternation that he had discovered a logical flaw in the Constitution, a loophole by which the United States could be transformed into a dictatorship. Morgenstern, who along with Einstein was to serve as one of Gödel's witnesses at the examination the next day, told him that the possibility he had uncovered was extremely hypothetical and remote. He further cautioned Gödel not to bring the matter up the next day at the interview with the judge.

The following morning Einstein, Morgenstern, and Gödel drove down to the federal courthouse in the New Jersey state capital of Trenton, where the citizenship examination was to take place. As legend has it, Einstein and Morgenstern regaled Gödel with stories and jokes on the trip from Princeton to Trenton in order to take his mind off the upcoming test. At the interview itself the judge was suitably impressed by the sterling character and public personas of Gödel's witnesses, and broke with tradition by inviting them to sit in during the exam. The judge began by saying to Gödel, "Up to now you have held German citizenship." Gödel corrected this slight affront, noting that he was Austrian. Unfazed, the judge continued, "Anyhow, it was under an evil dictatorship . . . but fortunately, that's not possible in America." With the magic word *dictatorship* out of the bag, Gödel was not to be denied, crying out, "On the contrary, I know how that can happen. And I can prove it!" By all accounts it took the efforts of not only Einstein and Morgenstern but also the judge to calm Gödel down and prevent him from going into a detailed and lengthy discourse about his "discovery."

This story illustrates perfectly the legalistic workings of the kind of mind needed to look into the heart of Hilbert's Program and announce to the world that the emperor, or at least Hilbert, had temporarily lost his mind. Unfortunately, the full details of Gödel's Theorem are much too complicated for the space available here. But the basic ideas, while a bit tricky and devious, are still fairly easy to grasp even for those with no mathematical training. In fact, understanding the logic underlying Gödel's magnificent achievement has been described by some as being akin to a mystical or religious conversion experience. While I can't personally report having been transported to quite such sublime heights, with that kind of advertising it's hard for me to resist outlining the key steps in Gödel's path to "the theorem."

In arriving at his proof of the incompleteness of arithmetic, Gödel's first crucial observation was to recognize the importance of Hilbert's insight that every formalization of a branch of mathematics is itself a mathematical object in its own right. So if we create a formal system intended to capture the truths of arithmetic, that formal system can be studied not just as a set of mindless rules for manipulating symbols, but also as an object possessing mathematical, i.e., semantic, as well as syntactic properties. In particular, since Gödel was interested in the relationships between numbers, he showed how it would be possible to represent any formal system purporting to encompass arithmetic within arithmetic itself. In short, Gödel saw a way to mirror all statements about relationships between the natural numbers by using these very same numbers themselves.

This mirroring idea is probably more familiar in the context of ordinary language, where we use words *in* the English language to speak *about* language. For example, we use words to describe properties of words such as whether they are nouns or verbs, and we discuss the structure of, say, a treatise on English grammar, which consists of words, by employing other words of the English language. Thus, in both cases we are making use of language in two different ways: (1) as a collection of *uninterpreted* strings of alphabetic symbols that are manipulated according to the rules of English grammar and syntax, and (2) as a set of *interpreted* strings having a meaning within the context under discussion. So the key notion is that the very same objects can be considered in two quite distinct ways, opening up the possibility for that object actually to speak about itself. In passing, let me note that the very same dual-level idea pertains to the symbols and their interpretations in the genetic material (the DNA) of every living cell. What Gödel saw was how to do this same trick with mirrors using the natural numbers.

To understand Gödel's "mirroring" operation with numbers a little more clearly, consider the familiar situation at a bakery where the customers are given numbers on entering in order to indicate the sequence in which they will be served. Suppose Clint and Brigitte both want to have a slice of *Sachertorte* and haven't yet obtained a CCM. Thus, they go down to the local *Konditorei*, where upon entering Clint receives the service number 4, while Brigitte comes in a bit later and gets number 7. By this service-assignment scheme, the real-world fact that Clint will be served before Brigitte is "mirrored" in the purely arithmetical truth that 4 is less than 7. In this way a truth of the real world has been faithfully translated, or mirrored, by a truth of number theory. Gödel used a tricky variant of this kind of numbering scheme to code all possible statements about arithmetic using the language of arithmetic itself, thereby employing arithmetic both as an interpreted mathematical object and as an uninterpreted formal system with which to talk about itself. It's revealing to see how this *Gödel numbering* scheme actually works.

In their monumental three-volume treatise *Principia Mathematica,* Bertrand Russell and Alfred North Whitehead used the symbolism of logic to create a calculus capable of expressing the statements of arithmetic, geometry, and analysis—essentially all of classical mathematics. If you're ever tempted to dip into this work and see what "2 + 2 = 4" looks like in logical language, let me warn you that I once fell victim to the same temptation, and was ultimately buried in an impenetrable morass of abstract symbols and formulas that didn't come around to the proof of "1 + 1 = 2" until Volume Two! It's no wonder that philosopher and educator John Kemeny could describe the Russell-Whitehead work as "a masterpiece discussed by practically every philosopher and read by practically none." But for Gödel the *Principia* was a convenient starting point for his tail-swallowing idea of turning arithmetic back upon itself by coding all the symbols and statements of the Russell-Whitehead language in arithmetic. In this way Gödel was able to describe the results on each page of *Principia Mathematica* as a sequence of transformations of numbers.

To see how Gödel's method works, let's consider a somewhat streamlined version of the Russell-Whitehead language of symbolic logic due to Ernest Nagel and James R. Newman. In this language there are elementary signs and variables. To follow Gödel's scheme, suppose there are the ten logical signs shown in Table 6.6, each with its Gödel code number, an integer between 1 and 10.

Sign	Gödel Number	Meaning
~	1	not
∨	2	or
⊃	3	if . . . then
∃	4	there exists
=	5	equals
0	6	zero
s	7	the immediate successor of
(	8	punctuation
)	9	punctuation
'	10	punctuation

Table 6.6. Gödel numbering of the elementary logical signs

In addition to the elementary signs, the language of the *Principia* contains logical variables that are linked through the signs. These variables come in three different flavors, representing a kind of hierarchical ordering that depends upon the exact role the variable plays in the overall logical expression. Some variables are *numerical,* meaning that they can take on numerical values. For other variables we can substitute entire logical expressions or formulas (*sentential* variables). And, finally, we have what are called *predicate* variables, which express properties of numbers or numerical expressions like *prime, odd,* or *less than.* All the logical expressions and proof relations in *Principia Mathematica* can be written using combinations of these three types of variables, connecting them via the logical signs. For our streamlined version of *Principia*, there are only ten logical signs, although in the real case there are quite a few more. In this toy version of *Principia Mathematica*, Gödel's numbering system would code numerical variables by prime numbers greater than 10, sentential variables by the squares of prime numbers greater than 10, and predicate variables by the cubes of prime numbers greater than 10.

To see how this numbering process works in practice, consider the logical formula $(\exists x)(x = sy)$, which translated into plain English reads: "There exists a number x that is the immediate successor of the number y." Since x and y are numerical variables, the Gödel coding rules dictate that we make the assignment $x \to 11$, $y \to 13$, since 11 and 13 are the first two prime numbers larger than 10. The other symbols in the formula can be coded by substituting numbers using the correspondences in Table 6.6. Carrying out this coding yields the sequence of numbers (8, 4, 11, 9, 8, 11, 5, 7, 13, 9), formed by reading the logical expression symbol by symbol and substituting the appropriate number according to the coding rule. This sequence of ten numbers pins down the logical formula uniquely. But since number theory, i.e., arithmetic, is about numbers, we'd like to be able to represent the formula in an unambiguous way by a single number. Gödel's procedure for doing this is to take the first ten prime numbers (since there are ten symbols in the formula) and multiply them together, each prime number being raised to a power equal to the Gödel number of the corresponding element in the formula. Since the first ten prime numbers in order are 2, 3, 5, 7, 11, 13, 17, 19, 23, and 29, the final Gödel number for the above formula is

$$(\exists x)(x = sy)$$
$$\downarrow$$
$$2^8 \times 3^4 \times 5^{11} \times 7^9 \times 11^8 \times 13^{11} \times 17^5 \times 19^7 \times 23^{13} \times 29^9$$

I'll gladly leave it to the reader to compute the actual value of this quantity! Using this kind of numbering scheme, Gödel was able to attach a unique number to each and every statement and sequence of statements about arithmetic that could be expressed in the logical language of *Principia Mathematica*.

It's not hard to see that this Gödel numbering scheme doesn't differ much in spirit from the ASCII coding procedure we discussed earlier. The main difference is that the ASCII scheme is designed to code only at the single level of the individual alphanumeric symbols used in the English language. On the other hand, the Gödel scheme accounts for several levels of expression, allowing us to distinguish between the lowest level of a numerical variable, which is basically just the level of the ASCII code, and the higher levels of sentential and predicate variables representing entire strings or even properties of the lower-level variables, including the all-important proof relations between axioms and theorems. A key part of Gödel's route to incompleteness was to show how to code arithmetically these very distinct semantic levels of logical expression.

By Gödel's coding procedure every possible proposition about the natural numbers can itself be expressed as a number, thereby opening up the possibility of using arithmetic to examine its own truths. The overall process can be envisioned by appealing to the metaphor of a locomotive shunting boxcars back and forth in a freight yard. This idea, due to Douglas Hofstadter, is shown in Figure 6.9. In the upper part of the figure we see the boxcars with their uninterpreted numbers painted on the sides of the cars, while looking down from the bird's-eye view we see the interpreted symbols inside each car. The shuffling of the cars in the switching yard in accordance with the rules for manipulating logical symbols and formulas is mirrored by a corre-

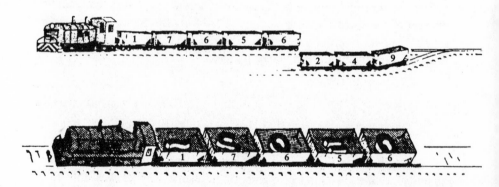

Figure 6.9. *Freight train view of Gödel numbering and transformation rules*

sponding transformation of natural numbers, i.e., statements of arithmetic—and vice versa.

Deep insight and profound results necessarily involve seeing the connection linking several ideas at once. In the proof of Gödel's Theorem there are two crucial notions that Gödel had to juggle simultaneously, Gödel numbering being the first. Now for the second Big Idea.

Logical paradoxes of the sort that worried Hilbert are all based on the notion of self-reference. A humorous illustration of a self-contradictory type of self-referential statement is shown in Figure 6.10. The granddaddy of all such conundrums is the so-called Epimenides Paradox, one version of which is

Figure 6.10. *A self-contradictory self-referential statement*

> This sentence is false.

What Gödel wanted to do was find a way to express such paradoxical self-referential statements within the framework of arithmetic. Gödel needed such a statement in order to display an exception to Hilbert's thesis that all true assertions should be provable in a formal system. However, a statement like the Epimenides Paradox involves the notion of truth, something that logician Alfred Tarski had already shown could not be captured within the confines of a formal system. Enter Gödel's Big Idea Number 2.

Instead of dealing with the eternally slippery notion of truth, Gödel had the insight to replace "truth" by something that is formalizable: the notion of *provability*. Thus, he translated the Epimenides Paradox above into the Gödel sentence:

> This statement is not provable.

This sentence, of course, is a self-referential claim about a particular "statement," the statement mentioned in the sentence. However, by his numbering scheme Gödel was able to code this assertion by a corresponding self-referential, metamathematical statement expressed in the language of arithmetic itself. Let's follow through the logical consequences of this mirroring.

If the statement is provable, then it's true; hence, what it says must be true and it's *not* provable. Thus, the statement and its negation are both provable, implying an inconsistency. On the other hand, if the statement is not provable then what it asserts is true. In this case the statement is true but unprovable, implying that the formal system is incomplete.

Gödel was able to show that for *any* consistent formal system powerful enough to allow us to express all statements of ordinary arithmetic, such a Gödel sentence must exist; consequently, the formalization must be incomplete. The bottom line then turns out to be that in *every* consistent formal system powerful enough to express all relationships among the whole numbers, there exists a statement that cannot be proved using the rules of the system. Nevertheless, that statement represents a true assertion about numbers, one that we can see is true by "jootsing," to use Douglas Hofstadter's colorful term for "jumping outside of the system." Almost as an aside, Gödel also showed how to construct an arithmetical statement **A**, which translates into the meta-mathematical claim "arithmetic is consistent." He then demonstrated that the statement **A** is not provable, implying that the consistency of arithmetic cannot be established by using any formal system representing arithmetic itself. Putting all these notions together, we come to

---

Gödel's Theorem—Formal Logic Version

For every consistent formalization of arithmetic, there exist arithmetic truths that are not provable within that formal system.

Since the steps leading up to Gödel's startling conclusions are both logically tricky and intricately intertwined, let me summarize the principal landmarks along the road in Table 6.7.

An indicator of the degree to which Gödel's results were unexpected can be found in the reaction to his original announcement of the theorem at a philosophy-of-science symposium in Königsberg, Germany, on September 7, 1930. Ironically, Königsberg happened to be Hilbert's hometown, which perhaps partially accounts for the lukewarm reception given to Gödel's presentation of his results. In fact, the transcript of the discussions at the meeting gives no indication whatsoever of Gödel's remarks, and there is no mention of Gödel at all in an article published later summarizing the papers given at the meeting! So like many belief-shattering ideas, Gödel's appears to have been so unexpected and revolutionary that even the professionals didn't at first understand what he had accomplished. But one participant who did see immediately the implications of the work was John von Neumann, who cornered Gödel after his talk and pressed him for more details—a case of genius recognizing genius, I suppose. Over the next few months Gödel spoke about his theorem on several occasions in Vienna, finally publishing his epoch-making paper "On Formally Undecidable Propositions of *Principia Mathematica* and Related Systems" in 1931. The rest is history.

Gödel's Theorem has many profound implications, both for science and for philosophy. Just as with Chaitin's Theorem, it's worth pausing for a moment to summarize what Gödel's conclusions have to say about the limits of human reasoning. When all the mathematical smoke

Gödel Numbering: Development of a coding scheme to translate every logical formula and proof sequence in *Principia Mathematica* into a "mirror-image" statement about the natural numbers.

Epimenides Paradox: Replace the notion of "truth" with that of "provability," thereby translating the Epimenides Paradox into the assertion "This statement is unprovable."

Gödel Sentence: Show that the sentence "This statement is unprovable" has an arithmetical counterpart, its Gödel sentence **G**, in every conceivable formalization of arithmetic.

Incompleteness: Prove that the Gödel sentence **G** must be true if the formal system is consistent.

No Escape Clause: Prove that even if additional axioms are added to form a new system in which **G** is provable, the new system with the additional axioms will have its own unprovable Gödel sentence.

Consistency: Construct an arithmetical statement asserting that "arithmetic is consistent." Prove that this arithmetical statement is not provable, thus showing that arithmetic *as a formal system* is too weak to prove its own consistency.

Table 6.7. The main steps in Gödel's proof

clears away, Gödel's message is that mankind will never know the final secret of the universe by "finitistic" or constructivistic thought alone; it's impossible for human beings ever to formulate a complete description of the natural numbers. There will always be arithmetic truths that escape our ability to fence them in by any kind of finite analysis. As Rudy Rucker has expressed it, Gödel's Theorem leaves scientists in a position similar to that of Joseph K. in Kafka's novel *The Trial*. We scurry about, running up and down endless corridors, buttonholing people, going in and out of offices, and, in general, conducting investigations. But we will never achieve ultimate success; there is no final verdict in the court of science leading to absolute truth. However, Rucker notes, "To understand the labyrinthine nature of the castle [i.e., court] is, somehow, to be free of it." And there's no understanding of the court of science that digs deeper into its foundations than the understanding given by Gödel's Theorem.

Having now seen Gödel's Theorem in its original formal-logic clothing we will find it of intellectual as well as pedagogical interest to return for a moment to the computer-oriented ideas of algorithms, programs, and complexity, and see how Gödel's result might be expressed today in those terms.

While I didn't emphasize the point in discussing Turing machines, one of the things that we could use such a computing device for, at least in principle, would be to search for all the true statements of arithmetic. From Turing's solution of the Halting Problem and its equivalence to Hilbert's Decision Problem, as well as from the faithful correspondence between Turing machines and formal systems, we know that there is no program that will ever print out all the true statements of arithmetic. Just for fun, let's rephrase Gödel's Theorem in these terms. Call a program P *correct* if it never lists a false statement of arithmetic. Then a truth omitted by P is a true statement of arithmetic not listed by P. With these definitions we have:

Gödel's Theorem—Computer Program Version

There is a computer program $P*$ such that if P is a correct program, then $P*$ applied to P yields a truth omitted by P.

Gödel's result can also be obtained from what amounts to a completely straightforward, almost trivial, corollary of Chaitin's Theorem on complexity, again appealing to the matchup between Turing machines and formal systems. Suppose we are given a consistent formal system F. Then Chaitin's Theorem says that there are numbers having complexity greater than F can prove. In other words, F is incomplete. This amounts to a one-line proof of Gödel's Theorem—Complexity Version, which was stated earlier in terms of Turing machine programs.

Remarkable as it is, Chaitin's Theorem on complexity is only the appetizer to a main course whipped up recently by Chef Chaitin showing that there are arithmetical facts that completely elude the bounds of finitary rules of reasoning. What Chaitin proved is that while we can clearly state these simple propositions, for all intents and purposes their truth or falsity might as well be settled by flipping a coin; they are completely and forever beyond the bounds of the human mind ever to resolve definitively. Let's complete our tour of the ins and outs of Gödel's Theorem with an account of this stunning result.

THE TENTH PROBLEM

If asked to name the top ten theorems of all time, just about every mathematician I know would reserve a place somewhere on the list for the Pythagorean Theorem, relating the lengths of the sides of a right triangle like the one shown in Figure 6.11. If a and b are the lengths of the short sides of such a triangle, c being the length of the hypot-

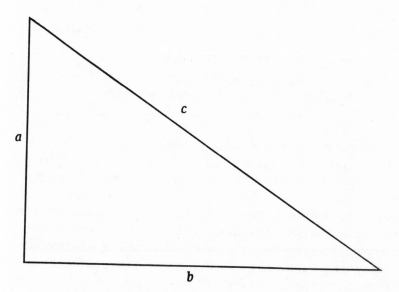

Figure 6.11. *The Pythagorean Theorem:* $a^2 + b^2 = c^2$

enuse, the Pythagorean Theorem says that the equation $a^2 + b^2 = c^2$ linking the quantities a, b, and c always holds.

The Pythagorean Theorem provides an example of a polynomial equation in three variables a, b, and c. The solution to this equation is a set of values for a, b, and c like $a = 1$, $b = 2$, $c = \sqrt{5}$ that satisfy the equation. Of special mathematical interest are the so-called *Diophantine equations*, polynomial equations for which we demand that the solutions be in whole numbers, unlike the example just given, which involves the noninteger quantity $\sqrt{5}$. To illustrate, the three quantities $a = 3$, $b = 4$, $c = 5$ form an integer solution to the equation. So when we consider the equation linking a, b, and c in the Pythagorean Theorem and admit only integer solutions like this, then we are thinking of it as a Diophantine equation. Consequently, the term *Diophantine* refers more to the character of the set of solutions we're interested in finding than it does to the equation itself.

The number of solutions of a given polynomial equation may vary from finite to infinite, depending upon whether or not we regard it as a Diophantine equation. For example, the Pythagorean Theorem's equation can be shown to have an infinite number of both noninteger and integer solutions. On the other hand, the equation $a^2 + b^2 = 4$ has only the four integer solutions $a = \pm 2$, $b = 0$ or $a = 0$, $b = \pm 2$, but an infinite number of noninteger solutions (e.g., a any real number between $+2$ and -2, $b = \sqrt{4 - a^2}$). So, regarded as a Diophantine equation, this equation has a finite solution set. But thought of as a general polynomial equation, the equation has an infinite number of solutions. As an aside, the matter of whether the Diophantine equation $x^n + y^n = z^n$ has *any* positive solution when n is an integer greater than 2 constitutes one of the most celebrated unsolved problems in mathematics, the famous Fermat Conjecture. Our concern with Diophantine equations here comes from the surprising connection between the nature of the set of solutions to Diophantine equations and the Halting Problem for a UTM.

Earlier we mentioned Hilbert's famous lecture to the 1900 International Congress of Mathematicians in Paris, where he outlined a set of problems for the coming century. The tenth problem on this list involved Diophantine equations. What Hilbert asked for was a general algorithm enabling us to decide whether or not an arbitrary Diophantine equation has any solution. For future reference, note carefully that Hilbert did not ask for a procedure to decide if the solution set was infinite, but only for an algorithm to determine if there is *any* solution.

It turns out that there exists an algorithm for listing the set of solutions to any Diophantine equation. So in principle all we have to do to decide whether the solution set is empty is to run this program, stopping the listing procedure if no solution turns up. The difficulty is that it might take a very long time (like forever!) to decide whether or not a solution will appear. For instance, the first integer solution of the simple-looking Diophantine equation $x^2 - 991y^2 - 1 = 0$ is $x = 379516400906811930638014896080$, $y = 12055735790331359447442538767$. How long would you be willing to punch keys on a calculator waiting for that pair to pop up? This example shows that to solve Hilbert's Tenth Problem we can't rely upon a brute-force search for the first solution—a solution might not exist or it might be so large that we'd get tired of looking. In either case, a direct search gives no guarantee of ever coming up with the correct answer about a particular equation's solvability. We need to do something a bit more clever.

While an undergraduate student in mathematics at the City College of New York shortly after World War II, Martin Davis read in one of his teacher Emil Post's articles that Hilbert's Tenth Problem "begs for an unsolvability proof." Following many years of effort by Davis, along with major contributions by Julia Robinson and Hilary Putnam, the whole issue boiled down to showing that if there existed even one Diophantine equation whose solutions behaved in a particularly explosive fashion, then Hilbert's Tenth Problem would be resolved in the negative. Unfortunately, no one was able to prove the existence of such an object until 1970, when Yuri Matyasevich, a twenty-two-year-old mathematician at the Steklov Mathematical Institute in Leningrad, found an example of the elusive type of equation. Amusingly, Matyasevich made crucial use of the famous Fibonacci sequence of numbers in constructing his solution to Hilbert's problem. This sequence, originally introduced by Leonardo of Pisa in 1202 to explain the explosive growth of a rabbit population in the wild, showed that apparently the well-known procreation habits of rabbits give rise to just the kind of rapid growth Matyasevich needed to create his equation and thus resolve negatively yet another of Hilbert's conjectures.

An interesting corollary of Matyasevich's proof is that there exists a polynomial such that as the variables a, b, c, and so on take on all possible nonnegative integer values, the positive values of the polynomial itself are exactly the set of prime numbers. To illustrate concretely this curious result, the To Dig Deeper section of this book gives such a polynomial involving twenty-six variables, whose positive values coincide with the set of prime numbers.

By now the reader should be highly sensitized to the connection between negative solutions to decision problems and Gödel's Theorem. So before continuing our pursuit of the connection between Diophantine equations and the Halting Problem, let's pause to give Gödel his due—again.

Gödel's Theorem—Diophantine Equation Version

There exists a Diophantine equation having no solution—
but no theory of mathematics can prove the equation's unsolvability.

Part of Matyasevich's celebrated solution to Hilbert's Tenth Problem focused attention on the little-known fact that any computation can be encoded as a polynomial. In other words, for every Turing machine there exists an equivalent Diophantine equation, and the properties of the solutions of this equation mirror precisely the computational capacities of the corresponding Turing machine. Thus, not only are formal systems and Turing machines abstractly identical, so are Turing machines and Diophantine equations. Chaitin's recent results on the randomness of arithmetic make heavy use of this fact within the context of a generalized type of Diophantine equation called an *exponential Diophantine equation*.

The standard kind of Diophantine equation we saw with the Pythagorean Theorem involves variables like a, b, and c that can be raised to some integer power (2 in the Pythagorean case). In an exponential Diophantine equation, the variables can be raised to the power of other variables. To illustrate the idea, $a^b + 5c^3 - d^{3e} = 0$ is such an equation, where we see the variables a and d raised to the power of other variables. Chaitin's work uses a family of such equations, each member of the family being singled out by the value of a single variable k (called a parameter) that ranges through the natural numbers. The equation $ka^2 + 3b^c = 0$ is an example of this kind of infinite family, since as we let the parameter k take on the values $k = 1, 2, 3, \ldots$, we obtain the individual exponential Diophantine equations $a^2 + 3b^c = 0$, $2a^2 + 3b^c = 0$, $3a^2 + 3b^c = 0$, and so on.

Chaitin's work is based upon a result of James Jones and Matyasevich's to the effect that it's possible to find such a family of exponential Diophantine equations with a single parameter k, such that the equation has a solution for a given value of k if and only if the kth computer program for a UTM (the program whose Gödel number is k) ever halts. Of course, this result shows clearly the complete equivalence between Hilbert's Tenth Problem on the solvability of Diophantine equations and the Halting Problem. Now let's see how Chaitin extended these ideas to show that there is just nothing certain in life— even in the world of numbers.

Buried deep within the Theoretical Physics Division of the IBM Research Laboratories in Yorktown Heights, New York, is a broomcloset-sized office, whose spartan furnishings consist of a bare desk, three empty bookshelves, a spotless blackboard, a Monet landscape reproduction on the wall, and a computer terminal. After having spent over twenty years as an IBM salesman, systems engineer, and programmer, Gregory Chaitin now calls this office home. And in 1987 it was from these stark surroundings that Chaitin hurled forth a lightning bolt so electrifying that the editors of the *Los Angeles Times* wrote in their June 18, 1988, editorial that "Chaitin's article makes the world shake just a little." And who'd be a better judge of what does and doesn't make the world shake than an Angeleno? But what kind of mathematical result could possibly send the general press into such a state of rapture? As it turns out, nothing less than a proof that the very structure of arithmetic itself is random. As what must surely stand as being about as close to the final word on mathematical truth, proof, and certainty as we'll ever get, let's see how Chaitin managed to extend Gödel's results to come up with such an astounding conclusion.

Suppose we have a UTM and consider the set of all possible programs that can be run on this machine. As we already know, every such program can be labeled by a string of 0s and 1s, so it's possible to "name" each program by its own personal ID number. Consequently, it makes sense to consider listing the programs, one after the other, and talk about the kth program on the list, where k ranges through the positive integers. Now consider the question: "If we pick a program from the list at random, what is the likelihood that it will halt when run on the UTM?" Or, equivalently, we could start with a fixed program for the UTM and ask the same question for an input string that's random. It turns out that this question is intimately tied up with the solvability of Diophantine equations, leading eventually to Chaitin's remarkable result.

The key step in Chaitin's route to ultimate randomness was to consider not whether a Diophantine equation has *some* solution, but the sharper question of whether the equation has an infinite or a finite number of solutions. The reason for asking this more detailed question is that the answers to the original query are not logically independent for different values of k. In other words, if we know whether some solution exists or not for a particular value of k, this information can be used to infer the answer for other values of k. But if we ask whether there are an infinite number of solutions or not, the answers are logically independent for each value of k; knowledge of the finiteness or not of the solution set for one value of k gives no information at all about the answer to the same question for another value.

Following this reformulation of the basic question, Chaitin's next step was a real *tour de force*. He proceeded to construct explicitly a particular exponential Diophantine equation family specified by a single parameter k, together with over seventeen thousand additional variables. Let's call this equation $\chi (k, y_1, y_2, \ldots, y_{17,000+}) = 0$, using the Greek symbol χ (chi) in Chaitin's honor. From this equation we can form a very special string of binary digits in the following manner: As k successively assumes the values $k = 1, 2, 3, \ldots$, we set the kth entry in our string to 1 if Chaitin's equation $\chi = 0$ has an infinite number of solutions for that value of k, while we set the kth entry to 0 if the equation has a finite number of solutions (including no solution). As we already know, the binary string we form by this procedure represents a single real number. Chaitin labeled this number by the last letter in the Greek alphabet, Ω (omega). And for good reason, too, as the properties of Ω show that it's about as good an approximation to "The End" as the human mind will ever make.

First of all, Chaitin showed that the quantity Ω is an uncomputable number. Furthermore, he proved that any program of finite complexity N can yield at most N of the binary digits of Ω. Consequently Ω is random, since there is no program shorter than Ω itself for producing all of its digits. Moreover, the digits of Ω are both statistically and logically independent. Finally, if we put a decimal point in front of Ω, it represents some decimal number between 0 and 1. When viewed this way, Ω can be interpreted as the probability that the UTM will halt if we present it with a randomly selected program. Or, as before, that a fixed program will halt if presented with a random input. Indeed, Chaitin constructed his equation precisely so that Ω would turn out to be this halting probability.

So while Turing considered the question of whether a given program would halt with a random input, Chaitin's extension produces the probability that a randomly chosen program will stop. As an aside, it's worth noting that the two extremes Ω equals zero or one cannot occur, since the first case would mean that no program ever halts, while the second would say that every program will halt. The trivial, but admissible, program STOP deals with the first case, while I'll leave it to the reader to construct an equally primitive program to deal with the second.

But the real bombshell, the one that shook up the *Los Angeles Times*'s editorial staff, is that the structure and properties of Ω show that arithmetic is fundamentally random. To see why, take some finite but "sufficiently large" integer. For example, some number greater than the Busy Beaver function value $BB(12)$ considered earlier. For values of k larger than this, there is no way to determine whether the kth digit of Ω is 0 or 1. And there are an infinite number of such undecidable digits, each corresponding to the following simple, definite arithmetical fact: For that value of k in Chaitin's equation $\chi = 0$, the equation has either a finite or an infinite number of solutions. But as far as human reasoning goes, which of the two possibilities is actually the case may as well be decided by flipping a coin; it is completely and forever undecidable, hence effectively random.

So Chaitin's work shows that there are an infinite number of arithmetic questions with definite answers that cannot be found using any axiomatic procedures; they do not and cannot correspond to theorems in any formal system. The answers to these questions are uncomputable and are not reducible to other mathematical facts. Extending Einstein's famous aphorism about God, dice, and the universe, Chaitin describes the situation by saying, "God not only plays dice in quantum mechanics, but even with the whole numbers." It's fitting to conclude this section with our final tribute to Gödel:

Gödel's Theorem—Dice-Throwing Version

There exists an uncomputable number Ω whose digits correspond to an infinite number of effectively random arithmetic facts.

This chapter is concerned with two Big Questions: "What are the limits to proof?" and "What is mathematical reality?" Gödel, Turing, and Chaitin have provided ample testimony showing that the mere following of rules will never generate the whole truth. Now it's time to ponder the second part of our dynamic duo.

THE TRUTH, THE WHOLE TRUTH, AND THE MATHEMATICIAN'S TRUTH

Awhile back, the scientific press carried a small filler piece alerting the world to the fact that researchers at the computer-manufacturing firm Amdahl had discovered that the number $391,581 \times 2^{216,193} - 1$ is prime. In addition to being the largest prime number yet found, this number is interesting from several standpoints, not the least of which is that it represents a *very* large, computable, nonrandom number. When I mentioned this achievement during the course of a lecture, one of the students in the back row looked up from his newspaper long enough to mutter, "So what? Why should anybody spend time looking for something as useless as the largest prime number? Who cares?" In response, after noting the fact that looking for such numbers is an excellent way for computer circuit designers to check the performance and accuracy of their experimental hardware, I went on to say that people look for such numbers for the same reason that other people climb mountains—because they're there. Or are they? Can we really say that the 65,087-decimal-digit "Amdahl number" is as real as, say, Mount Everest? Just what kind of a reality does a number like this actually have?

Unless you happen to be an unreconstructed solipsist, Mount Everest is definitely there; hence, certainly real. You can fall from it, die from cold and oxygen starvation on it, or climb it. There's little, if any, doubt about its reality. But numbers, or, more generally, mathematical constructions and proofs, seem to enjoy a different kind of existence. You can't touch them, weigh them, see them, or look at them. Of course, you can write numbers down in symbols and interact physically with the symbols in various ways. But in this case the medium is definitely *not* the message; the symbol is not the number being symbolized. So what is the nature of the kind of reality that mathematicians believe in? In short, how do mathematical results relate to anything that John and Jane Q. Public might think of as being "real"?

There is probably no number other than π that's more important and pops up in more places in mathematics than e, the base of natural logarithms. Its decimal expansion is $e = 2.718281828459045 \ldots ,$

a sequence that continues forever with no apparent pattern. Now consider the following statement about the number e:

(A) "The $10^{1,000}$th digit of e is a 4."

I'd be willing to bet all of my pension (which isn't saying much) that we'll never know if this statement is true. Nevertheless, the calculation could be carried out, at least in principle, and the answer obtained. I'm equally confident that most mathematicians would say that our inability to resolve the matter is due solely to our ignorance, and that *in reality* either the $10^{1,000}$th digit of e is or is not a 4.

Next consider the following claim:

(B) "The decimal expansion of the number e contains a run of $10^{1,000}$ 4s."

In this case we again have a computational procedure to verify the statement if it is true (just keep calculating the digits of e until the required string of 4s appears), but no procedure to verify its falsity.

Finally, consider the assertion:

(C) "The expansion of e contains an infinite number of 4s."

For this statement there is no finite computational procedure available for checking whether it's true or false.

So we have three statements A, B, and C making claims about properties of the number e. As we move from statement A to statement C, we move progressively from a situation in which just about everyone would agree that the statement is definitely true or false to one in which there are pretty strongly held, mutually contradictory views about the nature of the mathematical reality of the claimed sequence of 4s. To put it simply, if it could be established that statement C is undecidable, would you still *believe* that it's either true or false? In the words of Berkeley mathematician David Gale, "At what point does God leave off and man take over?"

Beginning with the set-theoretic paradoxes of Georg Cantor in the latter part of the nineteenth century, and further stimulated by the logical paradoxes of Bertrand Russell, mathematicians and philosophers began to ponder seriously the nature of what constitutes mathematical reality. To make contact with Gale's boundary between God and man, let's take a quick tour of the major positions.

*   *   *

One of the great events of the Gay Nineties, mathematically speaking at least, was the publication of Georg Cantor's pathbreaking work on the theory of infinite sets and transfinite numbers. What Cantor discovered was that there are different "styles" of infinity, an infinite number of them in fact. He labeled this collection of styles $\aleph_0$, $\aleph_1$, $\aleph_2$, . . . , using the first character of the Hebrew alphabet, $\aleph$ (read: aleph [ah-leff]-null, aleph-one, and so on). The first level, $\aleph_0$, denotes the kind of infinity we see in the whole numbers, called *countably infinite*. The next level, $\aleph_1$, or as it's more usually denoted c, is the infinity of the continuum, i.e., the number of points on the real number line. Since the natural numbers, 1, 2, 3, . . . , are properly contained in the set of real numbers and almost every real number involves an infinite sequence of natural numbers for its expression, we see that c is a level of infinity somehow "bigger" than that of the natural numbers. Level $\aleph_2$ *might* correspond to the infinity of all possible curves in the plane, and after that the sequence of $\aleph$s is of interest only to the kind of mathematician that even topologists and algebraists think lives in outer space.

Cantor's introduction of these levels of infinity was met with scorn and derision by the mathematical community of his day, typified by the famous after-dinner remark of the noted German mathematician Leopold Kronecker when he said, "God created the integers. The rest is the work of man." This reception of his life's work, together with an obsession with what has come to be termed Cantor's Continuum Hypothesis, drove Cantor mad—literally. Ironically, it was only a few years after publication of Cantor's major work in 1895 that Hilbert put his imprimatur on Cantor's ideas, reserving the coveted position as problem number one on his famous list for the Continuum Hypothesis. The problem is very easy to state: Are there any styles of infinity between the integers and the continuum, or, more symbolically, are there levels of infinity between $\aleph_0$ and c? The Continuum Hypothesis claims that the answer is no. But easy to pose is not necessarily easy to answer, and it was not until 1963 that the problem was finally laid to rest. We'll come to this solution in a moment. For now, the most important aspect of the Continuum Hypothesis is its role as a stimulus for a major reconsideration of what constitutes mathematical reality, as well as a reevaluation of what kinds of methods are admissible in trying to find it. More concretely, what kind of reality would a mathematical object like a set with an infinity of members between $\aleph_0$ and c have? Let's look at what the competing schools of mathematical philosophy have to say on this matter.

The philosopher and mathematician Nicholas Goodman has identified the central concern of the philosophy of mathematics as being to identify that which is "practically real" in the operational experience of mathematicians. To this end, Goodman invokes what he terms the Principle of Objectivity: If a concept X plays an important role in a theory, and if failure to acknowledge the role of X severely limits the theory, then X is practically real. At issue is the degree to which something that is practically real is objectively real. For example, in physics we talk about objects like quarks and strings that no one has ever observed directly. Yet their omission from the theories of elementary-particle physicists would deal these theories a severe blow. Hence, they are practically real. Moreover, a large number of physicists believe they are objectively real as well. Similarly, in geometry we deal with objects like triangles and circles. No one has ever seen a perfect triangle or the ideal circle (other than vicious circles and eternal triangles, of course). Nevertheless, geometry would be in bad shape if we couldn't make use of these objects. Consequently, they, too, are practically real. Are they also objectively real? It depends on whom you ask.

Historically, there are four main positions, or schools of thought, on what's objectively real in mathematics: *formalism, logicism, platonism,* and *intuitionism.* Each of these philosophical schools is based on certain foundational aspects of mathematical experience. To get a feel for the spectrum of possibilities for mathematical reality, let's take a brief look at the tenets of each group, along with its position regarding the Continuum Hypothesis.

• *Formalism:* We have already explored the formalist creed in some detail, consisting as it does of the view that mathematics is the formal manipulation of content-free symbols. Thus formalism is based on the idea of transformation rules for the shuffling-about of strings of symbols. In its current guise, formalism differs a bit from Hilbert's original conception in that Hilbert at least took the finite, combinatorial part of mathematics as being "true." But today a strict formalist would argue that the Pythagorean Theorem, for example, has no objective reality at all; it's just a string of meaningless symbols.

Continuum Hypothesis: There is no real number system outside what we create with our axioms. So, since there is no mathematical reality independent of these axioms, the Continuum Hypothesis is true or false only insofar as it can be settled within our current "best" axiomatic framework.

• *Logicism:* Logicists, like Bertrand Russell, hold to the position that mathematics consists of the kinds of truths derivable from logic by an interpreted formal system of rules. They deny that these truths are "about" anything; consequently, for a logicist mathematical truths must be true solely as a result of their internal structure and of their relations to one another. Of course, in such a view there is no room for anything like intuition, since a logicist would claim that there are no structures or concepts for the mathematician to have insight into.

Continuum Hypothesis: Basically, logicists hold to similar views as the formalists. The existence of a style of infinity between $\aleph_0$ and c is purely a question of whether such a level of infinity "fits in" with our existing logical structures and methods of inference.

• *Intuitionism:* This school, sometimes called *constructivism,* is a countermovement to logicism. The basic view is that mathematics consists of intuitive constructions and of the manipulations (mentally) of symbols representing these constructions. Intuitionists, who were originally led by the Dutch topologist L.E.J. Brouwer, accept the natural numbers as intuitively real. Every other mathematical concept or notion must be generated explicitly by a construction (read: algorithm) in order for it to be admissible. In particular, no argument based upon unrestricted use of the Law of the Excluded Middle is acceptable to an intuitionist; assertions may be true, false, or undecided. And, in general, statements are undecided unless they can be rendered true or false by an explicit construction making no appeal to *reductio ad absurdum* arguments. None of the statements A, B, or C given earlier about the properties of the decimal expansion of the number *e* would be true or false for an intuitionist until an actual calculation settled the matter. In particular, intuitionists would claim that statement C is forever undecidable, or even meaningless, since it cannot be settled by any conceivable constructive procedure. Thus, intuitionism asserts that mathematical objects exist only as a result of constructions starting with the natural numbers, and mathematical facts are true only if they follow from the results of such constructions.

Continuum Hypothesis: The question is meaningless. To speak of the existence of a level of infinity intermediate between that of the integers and the real numbers is without meaning until we produce a constructive procedure to "build" an infinite set having the asserted "style of infinity."

- *Platonism:* In Plato's philosophy the objects and notions of the phenomenological world are regarded as mere "shadows" on the wall of a cave, shadows cast by ideal, abstract objects inhabiting a universe outside ordinary space and time. But for Plato these ideal objects outside space and time are even more real than the more familiar objects of our physical and mental experience. Mathematical platonists like Gödel, René Thom, and Roger Penrose regard mathematical objects as also being inhabitants of this Platonic world. For such mathematicians, the content of mathematics consists of truths about these abstract structures, of the logical arguments establishing those truths, of the constructions underlying those arguments, and of the formal manipulation of symbols expressing such arguments and truths. There is nothing else. To a platonist, the Pythagorean Theorem would be a literal statement about the length of the sides of an idealized right triangle existing in the Platonic realm. The reality of this ideal triangle is just as real as, say, the reality of the physicist's quark or the sociobiologist's "selfish gene." And how do mathematicians make contact with this ethereal realm? According to Gödel, contact comes via the development of a sense of mathematical intuition.

Continuum Hypothesis: Such a level of infinity either definitely exists or definitely does not exist in the Platonic realm. If we can't resolve the matter within our current axiomatic framework, then those axioms are incomplete as a description of the set of real numbers. In short, they aren't powerful enough to tell us the whole truth, and we should direct attention to beefing up our axioms.

Before summarizing these various positions, it's worth noting that within the framework of the commonly accepted axioms of modern mathematics, the Continuum Hypothesis is truly undecidable. As early as 1937 Gödel himself showed that the hypothesis cannot be disproved using these axioms, and in 1963 Paul Cohen of Stanford demonstrated that it cannot be proved either. Thus the question can have a definite resolution only by extending and/or modifying the axiomatic system employed by most working mathematicians today. While many suggestions have been made as to how this might be done, no clear-cut consensus has emerged as yet showing that any of these candidates is superior to the standard system.

So that's the competition. Let me pause here to summarize the basic positions of each school in Table 6.8.

School	Methods and Objective Reality
Formalism	formal systems + symbol manipulation; only symbols are real
Logicism	logical structures + rules of inference; symbols are real
Intuitionism	feasibility of constructions; only natural numbers are real
Platonism	discovery of real objects by intuition and axiomatics

Table 6.8. Philosophies of mathematics

A large part of the difficulty with these philosophies is that, as a foundation for mathematics, each of them claims to be exhaustive. Moreover, each founders on a perceived need to see mathematics as being infallible, or, to put it more explicitly, to hold that mathematics generates knowledge that is certain, objective, and eternal. In view of the great difficulties each of these schools runs into when trying to shelter this collection of absolutes beneath its limited umbrella, mathematically inclined philosophers and philosophically oriented mathematicians have in recent times begun exploring the radical view that perhaps there is no fundamental difference between the practice of mathematics and that of the natural sciences. In short, mathematics is an *empirical* activity, and any viable philosophy for its foundations must respect this fact. Following up the implications of this claim leads us to a consideration of what's been termed the *quasi-empirical* approach to the foundations of mathematics.

During the Hungarian uprising of 1956, a ranking official in the Hungarian Ministry of Education fled across the border into Austria, later making his way to England. Eventually settling in Cambridge, this political refugee took up pursuit of a doctoral degree in philosophy, developing a dissertation around the theme that mathematics, like history, is fallible, and grows with criticism and correction of theories that are never totally free of the possibility of error. Unfortunately, the author of this novel thesis, Imre Lakatos, didn't live to see his work form the basis of a major upheaval in the philosophy-of-science community, particularly the mathematical branch, since he died in 1974 of a brain tumor at the relatively young age of fifty-two. Lakatos's ideas about the practice of mathematics were published posthumously in the 1976 volume *Proofs and Refutations,* which outlined a totally new view of what constitutes a mathematical proof.

The core of Lakatos's philosophy of mathematics is that the "proof" of a conjecture means giving explanations and various sorts of elaborations making the conjecture more and more plausible and convincing. At the same time, the mathematician sharpens and refines the conjecture by subjecting it to the pressure of looking for counterexamples that would falsify it. So, in Lakatos's view, the practice of mathematics constitutes a process of conjecture, refutation, growth, and discovery, a view having much in common with the ideas of Karl Popper about the ins and outs of the scientific enterprise in general.

This "quasi-empirical" vision of the mathematical process sees mathematicians using methods analogous to those of the physical scientist, except that conclusions are verified by a proof instead of being the product of observations. For example, consider the Fermat Conjecture, which claims that there are no positive solutions to the Diophantine equation $x^n + y^n = z^n$ for any values of the integer $n > 2$. If we agree to accept the conjecture because computers have failed to find a counterexample, then we would say that the Fermat Conjecture has been verified, or confirmed, by quasi-empirical methods.

It's crucial for Lakatos's arguments that he is able to find potential falsifiers for mathematical theories, beyond the usual logical falsifiers like inconsistency. In the natural sciences such potential falsifiers are the "hard facts" of measurement and observation. Lakatos makes the suggestion that the theorems of informal, i.e., quasi-empirical, mathematics can serve as falsifiers for more formal theories. Thus, computer investigations of the Fermat Conjecture would serve as a potential falsifier for an attempted disproof of the conjecture by more formal procedures.

In order to accept the quasi-empirical view of mathematical truth in which a particular proposition of pure mathematics is established by appeal to empirical evidence, we must abandon, or at least drastically modify, certain traditional beliefs about mathematics. Some of the beliefs called into question are:

A. All mathematical theorems are known a priori.
B. Mathematics, as opposed to the physical sciences, has no empirical content.
C. Mathematics relies only on proofs, while the natural sciences make use of experiments.
D. Mathematical theorems are certain to a degree that no fact of the natural sciences can match.

Dismissal of point A is a direct rejection of the platonist position, while denial of point B strikes a severe blow against both the formalist and the logicist views of mathematical reality. Interestingly, rejection of points C and D seems to my eye to support in a vague kind of way some of the arguments of the intuitionists, but not their notion of construction as the only admissible type of mathematical proof.

A striking illustration of the shifting views of what constitutes a proof in mathematics arose in 1976 with the computer-assisted "proof" by Kenneth Appel and Wolfgang Haken of the famous Four-Color Conjecture. This celebrated conjecture involved the claim that no more than four colors are needed to color any map drawn on a planar surface so that two adjacent countries having more than a single point in common (thus excluding contact like that between Arizona and Colorado) do not share the same color. The Four-Color Conjecture had resisted the efforts of mathematicians for over a hundred years, and was arguably the most famous unsolved problem in mathematics at the time of Appel and Haken's work.

The approach taken by Appel and Haken was based upon showing how the problem could be reduced to the matter of checking 1,936 special configurations. If each such configuration possessed certain properties, then the Four-Color Conjecture would be true. The work involved in looking through each of these configurations was far beyond what any human "computer" could accomplish in several lifetimes, so Appel and Haken wrote an ingenious and lengthy computer program to perform the computational drudgery. The program ran for more than twelve hundred hours on a state-of-the-art machine, which ultimately rendered the verdict that each configuration indeed possessed the requisite properties. And that's how the Four-Color Conjecture became the Four-Color Theorem.

The reaction of many mathematicians to the Appel and Haken proof is summed up in the sentiments of logician Reuben Hersh, who says that when he first heard about the proof he was very excited and eager to know more about the details. When told that the "method" boiled down to the brute-force checking by computer of a large number of different configurations, Hersh responded dejectedly, "So it just goes to show, it wasn't a good problem after all." Somehow mathematicians seem to long for more than just results from their proofs; they want insight. And the verification of a couple of thousand special cases by a computer smelled suspiciously like the kind of *ad hoc* exercise that ends up leading nowhere.

Hersh has been one of the most outspoken advocates of an intuition-based philosophy of mathematics. In a variety of books and articles he's argued that *all* the standard philosophical viewpoints considered above make use of intuition in an essential way. For instance, platonism regards mathematical objects as already existing things, living in some ideal, timeless realm. But Hersh echoes Gödel's view when he says that we need intuition to make contact with this nonmaterial reality. Similarly, formalists, who claim that only the rules of the game matter in mathematics and that mathematical objects have no "meaning," need some kind of intuition to infuse those very same objects with semantic content. As a result of such considerations, the fundamental question of mathematical epistemology becomes: What is mathematical intuition? An answer will be forthcoming only when philosophers and mathematicians free mathematics from the shackles of papal-like infallibility. On this perhaps surprising note, let's add up the score for mathematics in the prediction/explanation sweepstakes.

MAKING THE GRADE

Prediction

At the entrance to the Central Intelligence Agency headquarters building in Langley, Virginia, there is a large marble plaque into which is carved the biblical phrase: "Ye shall know the truth, and the truth shall make you free." Whenever I run across this bit of local color in some spy novel, it conjures up the image of a gigantic Universal Truth Machine filling up one of the deeper cellars of the building. After receiving agents' reports, analysts' opinions, and management prejudices, the machine clunks away on the data, eventually spitting out the current state of the world—CIA style, anyway.

Let's suppose for a moment that such a Universal Truth Machine did exist somewhere in the bowels of Langley (and, of course, deep beneath Dzerzhinsky Square in Moscow, too). Let the machine have a slot where a field agent's report is fed in. The machine then proceeds to scan the report and decide whether the report is true or not. If it is, the report is put on one pile for further consideration and action; if not, it's thrown on the scrap heap. Liberal congressmen, time-warped flower children, and CIA haters and baiters the world over can now have a little fun over at Spook Central by arranging for their favorite mole to slip a report into the slot stating: "The Universal Truth Machine will not say this report is true." Just feed this report into the slot, lean back, and wait for the smoke to start drifting up from the cellar! By now the reader will be sensitized to the chain of reasoning leading me to term this experiment "Gödel's Theorem—CIA Version."

It's exactly the fact that no such Universal Truth Machine can exist, even at CIA or KGB headquarters, that stands in the way of mathematics ever meriting an A$^+$ for prediction. The essence of scientific prediction is having a rule-based procedure for getting at the truth. And if there's any gap that's forever unbridgeable, it's the gap between proof in a formal mathematical system and mathematical truth. And, in fact, even if we do come up with a formal proof, Gödel's inconsistency result tells us that the proof itself cannot be totally trusted. So, in the final analysis the prediction of a mathematical truth ultimately comes down to intuition—the rock-bottom basis for every school of mathematical epistemology. In the words of the distinguished logician J. Barkley Rosser, "The average mathematician should not forget that intuition is the final authority." Fortunately, this intuition seems to be in pretty good shape, having been finely honed over several millennia of pondering geometric forms, numbers, and their many interconnections and relationships. With this comforting thought in mind, we come to the final grade for prediction in mathematics as:

Term Grade—Prediction: B

Explanation

Beyond any shadow of a doubt, one of the worst fates that can befall a taxpayer is to have his or her return selected "at random" by the Internal Revenue Service for one of the IRS's infamous no-holds-

barred audits. Such a procedure calls for the hapless taxpayer to produce documentary evidence supporting every single statement made on
the return, beginning with the name and address at the top and ending
with the signature at the bottom. This kind of line-by-line, take-
nothing-on-trust scrutiny looks suspiciously as if it may have been
suggested to the IRS by my undergraduate probability-theory instructor, who regularly inspected the proofs in my homework assignments
with the same sort of zeal under the same sort of microscope. In this
connection, I read recently that it's been estimated that to give a formal
demonstration of one of the great number theorist Ramanujan's conjectures, armed with only the rules of set theory and elementary logic,
would require about 2,000 pages. This gap of about 1,998 pages
between one of Ramanujan's results and my homework exercises says
something, I suppose, about the depths to which Ramanujan and I
plumbed in our respective prospectings for mathematical truth. But
2,000 pages or 2, the issue of explanation in mathematics comes down
to proof: You've explained a mathematical truth only when you've
given a good proof of it.

To further underscore the point, the December 20, 1988 issue of *The
New York Times*, in an article titled "Is a Math Proof a Proof If No One
Can Check It?," reported the results of a computer search for an object
called a finite projective plane of order 10. The search, which was
initiated to settle another long-standing mathematical conjecture, con-
sumed several thousand hours of time on a Cray supercomputer, eventually rendering the verdict that there are no such planes, thus
confirming the conjecture. What C.W.H. Lam, the author of this
search, did not tell the media was that the Cray is reported to have
undetected errors at the rate of approximately one per thousand hours
of operation. So it would certainly be reasonable to expect a few errors
during the course of the computer's work on this search. As Lam
remarked, "Imagine the expanded headline, 'Is a Math Proof a Proof
If No One Can Check It and It Contains Several Errors?' " So when
it comes to giving a "good" proof, how good is good enough?

By common consensus in the mathematical world, a good proof
displays three essential characteristics: A good proof is (1) *convincing,*
(2) *surveyable,* and (3) *formalizable.* The first requirement means
simply that most mathematicians believe it when they see it. The
philosopher Ludwig Wittgenstein held to the skeptical view that in
practice this was the *only* requirement for a mathematical proof, a good
indication of why he was a better philosopher than a mathematician.

Most mathematicians and philosophers of mathematics demand more than mere plausibility, or even belief. A proof must be able to be understood, studied, communicated, and verified by rational analysis. In short, it must be surveyable. Finally, formalizability means we can always find a suitable formal system in which an informal proof can be embedded and fleshed out into a formal proof.

These three features of a good proof reflect three very different aspects of the practice of mathematics, each of which is a crucial component of the way mathematics is actually done. That a proof must be convincing is part of the *anthropology* of mathematics, providing the key to understanding mathematics as a human activity. The *epistemology* of mathematics comes into play with the requirement that a proof be surveyable. We can't really say that we have created a genuine piece of knowledge unless it can be examined and verified by others; there are no private truths in mathematics. It is questions about surveyability, incidentally, that lie at the heart of the difficulty many mathematicians have in swallowing the computer-assisted proof of the Four-Color Conjecture. Finally, we invoke the *logic* of mathematics when we demand that every informal proof be capable of being formalized within the confines of a definite formal system.

When it comes to evaluating the degree to which mathematics delivers on the promise of providing scientific explanations for mathematical truths, matters hinge on whether or not our current proof methods offer systematic procedures or rules for generating good proofs. Weighing the competing claims on this score from the logicists to the quasi-empiricists, I come to the final judgment for explanation in mathematics as

Term Grade—Explanation: B⁺

Quite surprisingly, having fired what at first sight appear to be our biggest guns in the scientific search for certainty, the "canons" of mathematics, we end up concluding that mathematics offers no surer road to epistemological salvation than any of the other redwoods and Douglas firs in the broad forest of intellectual pursuit. Norbert Wiener summed up the situation concisely when he cautioned, "One of the chief duties of the mathematician in acting as an advisor to scientists is to discourage them from expecting too much from mathematics." It seems fitting somehow to conclude our pursuit of the mathematical muse with an extension of Wiener's remark, adding *and not just when advising scientists!*

THE LETTERS OF THE LAWS

What Can We Know for Sure?

My mind seems to have become a kind of machine for grinding general laws out of large collections of facts.

—CHARLES DARWIN

The most important problem does not lie in understanding the laws of the objective world and thus being able to explain it, but in applying the knowledge of these laws actively to change the world. —MAO TSE-TUNG

We can never finally know. I simply believe that some part of the human Self or Soul is not subject to the laws of space and time.

—CARL GUSTAV JUNG

ABSOLUTES? ZERO!

To those raised in the suffocating embrace of a can-do, the-impossible-just-takes-a-little-longer culture, with its emphasis on an almost mystical belief in the powers of the human spirit and mind to overcome virtually any obstacle, a tour of twentieth-century science must be quite a discouraging and depressing experience. If there's any message that modern science can be confident in trumpeting to the world, it's the sobering thought that there are limits—even to the human spirit. The age of absolutes, if it ever really existed, is now most definitely and permanently passé. Einstein's work buried once and for all the concepts of absolute space and time, while Heisenberg shot down the belief in absolutely precise measurement. Gödel, of course, stamped paid to the quaint and curious ideas of absolute proof and truth. Even more recently, we find sociobiologists trying valiantly (and with some measure of success) to terminate with extreme prejudice the incomprehensible notion of absolute free will. Moreover, chaos theorists have been making a tidy living of late telling us that even if we did know the mechanism, we still wouldn't know the phenomena. Taken as a whole, modern science has redrawn the map of human knowledge so that it now shows potholes and detours not only along every side street and back alley, but on all the major highways and byways as well.

But just as a game without rules isn't much of a game, so it is too with the prediction and explanation of natural and man-made events. It's the rules, or what we've called *laws,* that make the game exciting. And if there was ever a compact description of the distilled essence of what it means to "do science," that description is that doing science is searching for "lawful" descriptions of natural and human phenomena. From this perspective, we see that some types of limitations, like Gödel's Theorem constraining our ability to axiomatize the world, are limitations only on the degree to which we can construct a descriptive law for *every* phenomenon. Since this is just the sort of limitation that strikes directly at the heart of scientific prediction and explanation, let's examine the point in more detail using Figure S.1, a slight variant of the diagram for a modeling relation given in Chapter One (page 32).

Our leitmotif throughout this book has been that the kinds of "laws" entering into the *natural system* side of the diagram are the stuff of which scientifically based methods of prediction and explanation are made. Generally, in science these natural laws are translated, or en-

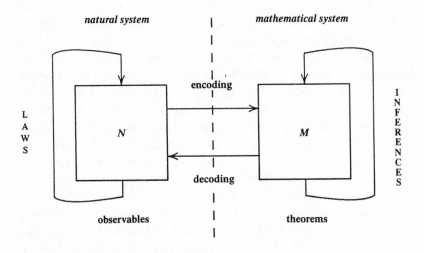

Figure S.1. *The modeling relation*

coded, into mathematical language for the simple reason that only on the *mathematical system* side of the diagram do we have a set of tools for systematically generating new true statements (theorems) from old: the rules of logical inference. We extensively explored this interplay between the two sides of the diagram in the first and last chapters, so it needs no further elaboration here other than to say that the presence of the tools of logical inference on the right-hand side of the diagram is probably the biggest selling point for the preeminent position mathematics has always occupied as *the* universal language of choice for scientific expression.

But we also saw in the last chapter that every mathematical system we can put into the box on the right-side of the diagram (i.e., every formal system) is completely equivalent to a program for a universal Turing machine. Thus, by the encoding from the laws of nature to the rules of inference of formal systems, we come to the inescapable conclusion that predicting and/or explaining—scientific style—is tantamount to the writing (and running) of an appropriate program for a UTM. In short, every scientific scheme for predicting and/or explaining ultimately comes down to following the set of rules encoded in a Turing machine program. So the issue of the degree to which we can predict and explain comes down to a question of computability, i.e., the carrying-out of a computation. This line of argument ultimately leads to the equation "prediction/explanation scheme = program," at least when we're speaking scientifically. But, by definition, this means that every prediction/explanation scheme must be mathematically embodied in a computable function.

The key question raised by the computability imperative is: "Are there natural or human phenomena that are intrinsically uncomputable?" Or, put another way, "Do there exist 'incompressible' natural or human phenomena?" On general mathematical grounds, we know that the computable functions constitute a very small subset of the set of all possible functions. Therefore it's perfectly plausible, likely even, that the "true" mathematical descriptions of many observed phenomena are indeed uncomputable. And, in fact, arguments have been presented in the scientific literature claiming that phenomena ranging from turbulent fluid flow to human consciousness can be properly described only by using such uncomputable functions. Clearly, if such claims are true, then the Turing-Church Thesis is definitely false for physical and human systems. More importantly, for such processes the very idea of scientific prediction makes no sense, since if uncomputable phenomena do indeed exist, then they are inherently random—at least to within the currently understood capabilities of the human mind to comprehend and deal with them rationally.

But to explore adequately the distinction between computable and uncomputable phenomena—or, equivalently, phenomena that are simple or complex—would require another volume at least the size of this one. So instead of wandering off into that wilderness of mirrors, let me try to summarize graphically what's been learned in *this* book about the degree to which science can confidently predict and/or explain events of everyday concern. Figure S.2 depicts the grades we've assigned throughout this "semester," along with a few areas we didn't look into that are given here as benchmarks of comparison. The reader should be well sensitized by now to the interpretation of these grades as being an ordinal representation of the degree to which science is able to serve up

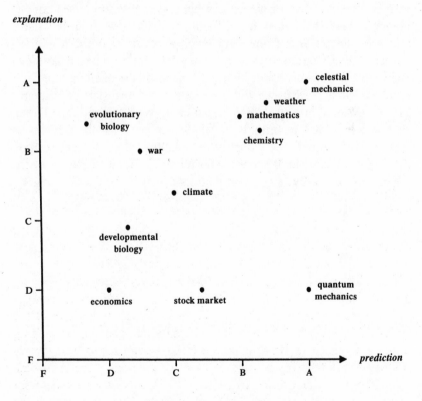

Figure S.2. *Scientific predictability and explainability*

computable functions capturing the empirical evidence available for the phenomenon at hand.

The diagram makes it evident, I think, that it's in those areas of the natural sciences least susceptible to human influence that we have the best "programs" for prediction and explanation. As we move away from hard physics and astronomy and into the Jell-O–like realm of biology, our capabilities for prediction and explanation begin to deteriorate. And by the time we reach the almost totally gaseous state of economics and the other social sciences, there's far more "social" than "science" in our capacity to say what's next and why.

At this late moment in our narrative, it should hardly be necessary to note that the above assessments are tentative, hence subject to revision of a possibly dramatic kind. One of the hallmarks distinguishing science from pseudoscience and religion is that in science all knowledge is provisional. So as time goes on, and we gain deeper insight into the ways of nature and humans, we'll surely see considerable jockeying for position in Figure S.2, along with an inevitable and pronounced drift from entry-level positions near the lower left corner of the diagram toward the state of scientific bliss at the upper right. But if not only Gödel but also much of the contemporary scientific world is correct, we will never attain that final state of academic grace enshrined in a straight-A report card. With this ultimate limitation in mind, we can fittingly conclude our quest for the predictable and explainable with the words of the quantum physicist and cosmologist John Archibald Wheeler, who remarked about the laws of the universe: "The only law is that there is no law."

TO DIG DEEPER

CHAPTER ONE

General References

So much has been written by so many on the topics of uncertainty, explanation, prediction, causality, and all the other toys of the philosopher of science that it's hard to know where to enter this minefield of the intellect. So let me just list a couple of introductory volumes that I have found useful:

Bunge, M. *Causality and Modern Science,* 3rd Revised Edition. New York: Dover, 1979.
Kemeny, J. *A Philosopher Looks at Science.* Princeton, NJ: Van Nostrand, 1959.

The Kemeny volume is directed toward undergraduates, giving the philosophical perspective of one of America's best-known and most-respected educators. The Bunge volume, on the other hand, is a bit tougher sledding, aimed at a more advanced reader. Nevertheless, it is still quite accessible, the rewards being well worth the extra effort.

The Laws of the Game

Thorp's David-and-Goliath battle with the casinos is recounted with great relish and style in the "blackjack bible":

Thorp, E. *Beat the Dealer.* New York: Random House, 1962.

The intervening decades have seen numerous additional volumes appear devoted to polishing Thorp's apple to a little brighter shine. Two of the best are

Griffin, P. *The Theory of Blackjack.* Las Vegas: Gambler's Book Club Press, 1979.
Uston, K. *The Big Player.* New York: Holt, Rinehart and Winston, 1977.

Griffin is a professor of mathematics in California, and his book looks at the game of twenty-one purely from the academic point of view. If your interests are in a very readable, yet technically complete, account of how the winning strategies of Thorp were developed, then this is the book for you. Incidentally, Griffin's work shows that the high-low ratio discussed in the text is only one stage in a hierarchy of increasingly complex twenty-one strategies opened up by Thorp's pioneering work. Thus, just like the Japanese game of go, twenty-one has its own virtually limitless levels of play, of which the Thorp "ten-count" strategy is only a relatively low rung on the ladder. The Uston book is a horse of an entirely different color. It tells the tale of a team of card counters, showing the advantages of team play over going it alone. It also illustrates in the most graphic terms imaginable the lengths to which the casino owners will go in order to ban proficient players from the tables for no other reason than their being too good! All in all, a vivid portrayal of how the casinos trapped themselves by offering a game of skill to the public and then tried to prevent players from participating—if they were too skillful. When the first Atlantic City casinos opened in the late 1970s, Uston led the charge against the dubious legality of this kind of ham-handed, oafish "solution" to the counting problem, initiating a legal challenge that finally resulted in a compromise of sorts between the card counters and the casinos.

The question of what it means to be "random" is discussed in an informal, yet very insightful, manner by the famed probability theorist Mark Kac in

Kac, M. "What is Random?" *American Scientist,* 71 (July–August 1983), 405–406.
Kac, M. "More on Randomness." *American Scientist,* 72 (May–June 1984), 282–283.

For introductory discussions on the process of science and the development of scientific theories, including the problem of discerning laws of nature from empirical relationships, see

Barrow, J. *The World Within the World.* Oxford: Oxford University Press, 1988.
Chalmers, A. F. *What Is This Thing Called Science?,* 2nd Edition. Milton Keynes, U.K.: Open University Press, 1982.
Swartz, N. *The Concept of Physical Law.* Cambridge: Cambridge University Press, 1985.
Ziman, J. *An Introduction to Science Studies.* Cambridge: Cambridge University Press, 1984.

The most important tool of theoretical science is the mathematical model. Two recent accounts of the relationship between the real world and the world of mathematics, exploiting the diagram in Figure 1.2, are found in the works

Casti, J. *Alternate Realities: Mathematical Models of Nature and Man.* New York: Wiley, 1989.
Rosen, R. *Anticipatory Systems.* Oxford: Pergamon Press, 1985.

Some social scientists have argued that human cultures differ in the ways they see the world, even to the extent of having their own modes of logic. This relativistic claim helps to account for a lot of the antagonism people often express toward science, since it supports the view that science is just another form of culture-bound intellectual imperialism. Interestingly enough, recent experimental evidence suggests otherwise, indicating that not only all humans, but most likely all mammals share the same fundamental cognitive machinery and use the same processes of inference. For an introductory account of this work, see

Dunbar, R. "Common Ground for Thought." *New Scientist,* January 7, 1989, pp. 48–50.

The Why of Things

For a much more complete account of the Oaxaca quake and the role played by Karen McNally's group in gathering the data to confirm the Latham group's prediction, the reader should consult

Judson, H. F. *The Search For Solutions,* pp. 145–151. New York: Holt, Rinehart and Winston, 1980.

Another highly politically charged earthquake prediction was made in 1979 by research physicist Brian Brady, who claimed that Peru would effectively cease to exist on or about June 28, 1981. As we know, the Earth did not move for Brian Brady on that date, and the following day the newspapers in Lima ran the headline PERU, SI! BRADY, NO! A gripping account of the origin of this prediction, as well as the reactions of the scientific community and the governments of the United States and Peru, is given in the book

Olson, R., with B. Podesta and J. Nigg. *The Politics of Earthquake Prediction.* Princeton, NJ: Princeton University Press, 1988.

Geophysicists, just like the rest of the scientific community, have not been idle when it comes to looking for chaotic behavior in earthly processes. For a discussion of recent work showing that the appearance of earthquakes may follow a chaotic path, and hence be inherently unpredictable, see

Scholtz, C. "Global Perspectives of Chaos." *Nature,* April 6, 1989, p. 459.

The ideas of causality, correlation, and determination discussed here are covered in much more detail in the Bunge book cited above under general references. Ideas along the same lines, but more for professional reading, are presented in

Hempel, C. *Explanation and Theory Construction.* Glencoe, IL: Free Press, 1974.
Humphreys, P. *The Chances of Explanation.* Princeton, NJ: Princeton University Press, 1989.
Salmon, W. *Scientific Explanation and the Causal Structure of the World.* Princeton, NJ: Princeton University Press, 1984.
Suppes, P. *Probabilistic Metaphysics.* Oxford: Basil Blackwell, 1984.

Scientific explanation from the viewpoint of distinguishing spatial patterns from random configurations is treated in a very readable fashion in the short volume

Katz, M. *Templets and the Explanation of Complex Patterns.* Cambridge: Cambridge University Press, 1986.

While the story told in the text about the appearance of storks and babies is intended to emphasize the lack of any kind of causal relation between the two, digging a little deeper into the matter reverses this conclusion. It turns out that the community involved was one of mostly new houses with young couples living in them. Moreover, storks don't like to nest beside chimneys that other storks have used in the past. Thus, there was a common cause: new houses occupied on the inside by young couples who had children and occupied on the outside by storks. This example just goes to show that what looks like causality or noncausality at one level can easily shift polarity when examined under the power of a higher-resolution microscope.

Polishing the Crystal Ball

Soothsayers and their ingenious methods have probably been with us since prehistoric times. For an entertaining account of various "predictors," their methods, and their results, see

Fisher, J. *Predictions.* New York: Van Nostrand Reinhold, 1980.
Wallechinsky, D., A. Wallace, and I. Wallace. *The Book of Predictions.* New York: Morrow, 1981.

The science fiction writers have had a field day speculating about the possibilities of seeing into the future, usually under the guise of various sorts of time travel schemes. While Silverberg's *The Stochastic Man* mentioned in the text is my personal favorite, probably the most famous sci-fi work along these lines is Isaac Asimov's *Foundation* series. In these volumes the psychohistorian Hari Seldon predicts that the Galactic Empire of a million worlds is about to decay, and that its decline will leave the galaxy in a state of anarchy for thirty thousand years. Consequently, he sets up two Foundations at opposite ends of the galaxy and . . . Well, maybe it's better if I let Asimov tell it! For those who haven't read these volumes, they are gathered together in

Asimov, I. *The Foundation Trilogy.* New York: Ballantine, 1983.

Strictly speaking, scientific prediction as we have defined it here involves *deductive* inferences from scientific laws, whereas inductive reasoning is used to arrive at candidates for the lawful relationships themselves, as is depicted in Figure 1.1. Thus, Goodman's Grue-Bleen Paradox, addressing as it does inductive inferences, is not strictly relevant to the problem of prediction. However, it certainly is relevant to the problem of how much faith to put in the laws by which predictions are made; hence its discussion here. For Goodman's own account of the paradox, see

Goodman, N. *Fact, Fiction, and Forecast,* 4th Edition. Cambridge, MA: Harvard University Press, 1983.

The Good, the Bad and the Probable

Excellent introductory accounts of the mysteries of probability and statistics are available in many places. Some volumes that I've found useful through the years are

Feller, W. *An Introduction to Probability Theory and Its Applications,* 3rd Edition. New York: Wiley, 1968.
Freud, J., and F. Williams. *Elementary Business Statistics: The Modern Approach,* 3rd Edition. Englewood Cliffs, NJ: Prentice-Hall, 1977.
Gnedenko, B. *The Theory of Probability.* Moscow: Mir Publishing Co., 1973.

Feller's book is the absolute all-time classic in the area, a work upon which several generations of advanced students have cut their teeth. But it's a bit tougher going than the others, although the numerous illustrative examples are highly recommended as motivational material while the reader consults lower-level treatments. The Freud and Williams book is aimed at lower-division undergrads, while the Gnedenko volume is for upper-division students.

Imprecision as a source of uncertainty has not been entirely neglected from the scientific standpoint. Several attempts to create formal structures adequate for addressing imprecision are on the record, perhaps the best publicized being the theory of fuzzy sets introduced by Lotfi Zadeh in the mid-1960s. Some recent reference works in this direction are

Dubois, D., and H. Prade. *Possibility Theory*. New York: Plenum, 1988.
Klir, G., and T. Folger. *Fuzzy Sets, Uncertainty, and Information*. Englewood Cliffs, NJ: Prentice-Hall, 1988.
Yager, R., ed. *Fuzzy Sets and Applications; Selected Papers by L. A. Zadeh*. New York: Wiley, 1987.

As a counterpoint to these alternatives to the use of probability theory for characterizing uncertainty, the reactionary members of the "International Society of Probabilists" have argued that the *only* satisfactory description of uncertainty is—probability theory! They throw down the challenge that anything that can be done by alternative methods for handling uncertainty can be done better by probability theory. These arguments are presented in the paper

Lindley, D. "The Probability Approach to the Treatment of Uncertainty in Artificial Intelligence and Expert Systems." *Statistical Science*, 2, No. 1 (1987), 17–24.

A fairly convincing refutation of this extreme claim is given in

Klir, G. "Is There More to Uncertainty Than Some Probability Theorists Might Have Us Believe?" *International Journal of General Systems*, 15 (1989), 347–378.

The Tracks of Time

Differential equations are truly the lingua franca of theoretical scientists everywhere. Given these equations' ubiquitous role in the formal description of natural and human affairs, it's unfortunate that expository treatments are not required reading for non–science majors in universities. For those sufficiently motivated nonscientists, a very accessible and brief account not only of differential equations, but also of their connection with chaos, catastrophes, randomness, and the fate of the solar system can be found in the outstanding book

Ekeland, I. *Mathematics and the Unexpected.* Chicago: University of Chicago Press, 1988.

For a more textbookish account, two of the best sources at the introductory level are

Arnold, V. *Ordinary Differential Equations.* Cambridge, MA: MIT Press, 1973.
Hirsch, M., and S. Smale. *Differential Equations, Dynamical Systems, and Linear Algebra.* New York: Academic Press, 1974.

More detailed technical discussions of dynamical systems are presented in

Guckenheimer, J., and P. Holmes. *Nonlinear Oscillations, Dynamical Systems, and Bifurcations of Vector Fields.* New York: Springer, 1983.
Irwin, M. *Smooth Dynamical Systems.* New York: Academic Press, 1980.
Lichtenberg, A., and M. Lieberman. *Regular and Stochastic Motion.* New York: Springer, 1983.

The classical dynamical systems have fixed points and limit cycles as their attractors; "modern" dynamical processes have strange attractors. The transition between the two is a type of attractor termed *quasiperiodic motion,* which was only briefly mentioned in the text. Quasiperiodic motion is sort of a combination of several different limit cycles, and cannot occur for simple planar systems. To envision what this kind of attractor looks like, think of a doughnutlike manifold (technically, a torus). Quasiperiodic motion is a trajectory on this doughnut that winds around the surface and through the hole in the center, coming arbitrarily close to every point on the torus without ever coming back to the same point twice. For the interested reader, detailed accounts are available in the above volumes.

Volterra's classical paper on predator-prey dynamics was originally published in French as

Volterra, V. "Principes de Biologie Mathématique." *Acta Biotheoretica,* 3 (1937). (English translation available in *Mathematical Essays on Growth and the Emergence of Form,* P. Antonelli, ed., pp. 269–309. Edmonton, Alberta: University of Alberta Press, 1985.)

A good discussion of the periodic nature of the trajectories of Volterra's system is presented in the Hirsch-Smale book cited above.

The Mathematics of the Unexpected

The question of the stability of the solar system is still far from having a clear-cut answer, although recent work indicates that the planetary motions are indeed chaotic. In particular, the predictability of the orbits of the inner planets, including the Earth, is lost within a few tens of millions of years. For a discussion of these results, see the papers

Laskar, J. "A Numerical Experiment on the Chaotic Behavior of the Solar System." *Nature*, March 16, 1989, pp. 237–238.
Murray, C. "Is the Solar System Stable?" *New Scientist*, November 25, 1989, pp. 60–63.

In an interesting related development, mathematician Andrew Prentice of Monash University in Australia has shown recently how to use Laplace's theory for the origin of planets to predict the number and properties of the moons orbiting the planets Jupiter, Saturn, and Uranus. For an account of his ideas, see

"Mathematician Predicts a Multitude of Moons," *New Scientist*, August 5, 1989, p. 29.

General treatments of both the Lyapunov and general structural stability problems presented in the text are given in the Guckenheimer and Holmes book cited in the preceding section. See also the biologically motivated treatment in

Rosen, R. *Dynamical Systems Theory in Biology: Stability Theory and Its Applications.* New York: Wiley, 1970.

The question of stability in all its many guises is definitely one of the pillars upon which mathematical modeling of the real world rests. Some, like mathematician René Thom, have argued that since every observation and measurement is subject to some error, models whose character changes under small perturbations are useless as a proper description of nature. Others question Thom's position, claiming that the kind of instability seen in chaotic systems is the true way of nature and that virtually all systems are unstable in the mathematical sense. Thom argues his position in his well-known book on catastrophe theory:

Thom, R. *Structural Stability and Morphogenesis.* Reading, MA: Addison-Wesley, 1975.

Without a doubt, the heated discussion surrounding the pros and cons of catastrophe theory as a vehicle for mathematically capturing the unexpected and the discontinuous was the most contentious issue in applied mathematics during the past couple of decades. A representative sampling of quotes from the opponents of catastrophe theory gives the flavor of the attack against Thom:

> Catastrophe theory is one of many attempts that have been made to deduce the world by thought alone . . . an appealing dream for mathematicians, but a dream that cannot come true.
> —RAPHAEL ZAHLER and HECTOR SUSSMAN, in *Nature*

> Exaggerated, not wholly honest . . . the height of scientific irresponsibility . . .
> —MARK KAC, in *Science*

> Catastrophe theory actually provides no new information about anything. And . . . it can lead to dangerously wrong conclusions.
> —JAMES CROLL, in *New Scientist*

To these broadsides, Thom poignantly responds:

> Many of my assertions depend on pure speculation and may be treated as daydreams. . . . At a time when so many scholars in the world are calculating, is it not desirable that some, who can, dream?

For those wishing to see for themselves just what Thom really *did* say, the source is Thom's book referenced above.

Thom has also been a tireless contributor to journals and conference proceedings, extolling the virtues of catastrophe theory as a language for theoretical biology and linguistics. Some of his speculations in these directions are collected in

Thom, R. *Mathematical Models of Morphogenesis*. Chichester, U.K.: Ellis Horwood, 1983.
Thom, R. *Semio Physics: A Sketch*. Redwood City, CA: Addison-Wesley, 1990.

For a layman's introduction to the whole theory, as well as to the controversy, the best source is

Woodcock, A., and M. Davis. *Catastrophe Theory*. New York: Dutton, 1978.

As noted in the text, no one questions the mathematics underlying catastrophe theory, only the way it has been applied to practical problems—especially in the areas of biology and social science. The primary focus of many of these complaints has been Christopher Zeeman, who has acted as Thom's Boswell in promoting the general ideas of catastrophe theory in applied areas. Many of Zeeman's models, as well as some fascinating interchanges with Thom, are given in

Zeeman, E. C. *Catastrophe Theory: Selected Papers 1972–1977*. Reading, MA: Addison-Wesley, 1977.

In somewhat more techncal terms, catastrophe theory deals with the degenerate critical points of a smooth function $V(x_1, x_2, \ldots, x_n)$. A small perturbation of the function V can destroy the topological character of such types of critical points. Thom's theory shows how to embed V within a *family* of functions, so that within the space of families of smooth functions the topological nature of the family containing V cannot be destroyed by small changes. Such families are characterized by parameters, and one of Thom's major achievements was to work out the minimal number of parameters necessary to stably embed an unstable function. The characteristic names of the elementary catastrophes, like the "cusp" shown in the text, arise from looking at the regions within the space of these parameters corresponding to the boundaries between the stable and the embedded unstable functions, i.e., the regions in parameter space where there is a discontinuous change of behavior within the overall family. Technical accounts of these matters are found in

Casti, J. *Alternate Realities: Mathematical Models of Nature and Man*. New York: Wiley, 1989.
Gilmore, R. *Catastrophe Theory for Scientists and Engineers*. New York: Wiley, 1981.
Poston, T., and I. Stewart. *Catastrophe Theory and Its Applications*. London: Pitman, 1978.

A Strangeness in the Attraction

Population ecology has been a fruitful source of real-world application of chaos, probably because it's one of the few areas where extensive amounts of the right kind of data are available to check the predictions of the theory empirically. Here's a sampling of this literature, starting with Robert May's classic 1976 paper:

May, R. "Simple Mathematical Models with Very Complicated Dynamics." *Nature*, 261 (1976), 459–467.
Oster, G. "Predicting Populations." *American Naturalist*, 21 (1981), 831–844.

Schaffer, W. "Can Nonlinear Dynamics Elucidate Mechanisms in Ecology and Epidemiology?" *IMA Journal of Mathematics Applied in Medicine and Biology*, 2 (1985), 221–252.

The literature on chaos is by now so large that it's impossible to do anything other than give some general pointers. In this regard, a good starting point is the introduction given in Chapter 5 of the Casti book noted above. Other easy-to-digest introductions are the articles

Crutchfield, J., et al. "Chaos." *Scientific American*, 225 (December 1986), 46–57.
Ford, J. "How Random Is a Coin Toss?" *Physics Today*, April 1983, pp. 40–47.
Jensen, R. "Classical Chaos." *American Scientist*, 75 (March–April 1987), 168–181.

The following two compendiums are highly recommended as sources for many of the pioneering articles establishing chaos as an identifiable academic discipline:

Cvitanović, P. *Universality in Chaos*. Bristol, U.K.: Adam Hilger, 1984.
Hao, Bai-Lin. *Chaos*. Singapore: World Scientific, 1984.

For the general reader there is the immensely successful journalistic account given in

Gleick, J. *Chaos*. New York: Viking, 1987.

However, my own tastes lean more toward the very informative and entertaining introductory discussion provided in

Stewart, I. *Does God Play Dice?* Oxford: Basil Blackwell, 1989.

Borges's famous story about the Library of Babel, as well as many other stories of a similar phantasmagorical bent, can be found in the collection

Borges, J. *Labyrinths*. New York: New Directions, 1964.

CHAPTER TWO

General References

Patterns, superstitions, legends, traditions, and folklore about the weather have fascinated people down through the ages. Two very informative, entirely nontechnical, and highly entertaining volumes on such matters are

Dolan, E. *The Old Farmer's Almanac of Weather Lore.* Dublin, NH: Yankee Books, 1988.
Lockhart, G. *The Weather Companion.* New York: Wiley, 1988.

The affairs of humans and the climate have always been strongly intertwined, and never more so than today. For a sampling of work touching on all aspects of this symbiosis, see

Currie, R. "Lunar Tides and the Wealth of Nations." *New Scientist,* November 5, 1988, pp. 52–55.
Ladurie, E. *Times of Feast, Times of Famine: A History of Climate Since the Year 1000.* New York: Doubleday, 1971.
Maunder, W. *The Uncertainty Business: Risks and Opportunities in Weather and Climate.* London: Methuen, 1986.
Rind, D., A. Rosenzweig, and C. Rosenzweig. "Modelling the Future? A Joint Venture." *Nature,* 334 (August 11, 1988), 483–486.
Winkless, N., and I. Browning. *Climate and the Affairs of Men.* New York: Harper's Magazine Press, 1975.

A Tower, a Boy, and a Girl

Further information about the Tower of the Winds is given in the Lockhart book above. For a very readable account of the work of Gilbert Walker, the Southern Oscillation, and the work of Cane and Zebiak on predicting El Niños, see the article

Zebiak, S. "Ill Winds." *The Sciences,* March–April 1989, pp. 27–31.

Other accounts of the El Niño–La Niña phenomena and the associated side effects leading to things like the summer 1988 drought in the United States include

Namias, J. "Cold Waters and Hot Summers." *Nature,* 338 (March 2, 1989), 15–16.
Philander, G. "El Niño and La Niña." *American Scientist,* September–October 1989, pp. 451–459.
Philander, G. *El Niño, La Niña, and the Southern Oscillation.* Orlando, FL: Academic Press, 1990.
Rasmussen, E. "El Niño and Variations in Climate." *American Scientist,* 73 (March–April 1985), 168–177.

Recently, the Indian Meteorological Department has developed a "monsoon predictor" that it claims can predict two months in advance not only whether the monsoon will be good or bad, but whether total rainfall will be more or less than the normal 88 centimeters. More information about this model is given in

Jayaraman, K. "Monsoon Prediction Model." *Nature*, 342 (November 2, 1989), 4.

As noted in the text, the Zebiak and Cane El Niño prediction was the culmination of years of work by many investigators, each putting one piece of the El Niño puzzle into the overall picture. Here's a brief chronology of the highpoints:

1. Gilbert Walker notes the Southern Oscillation signal in surface pressure.
2. Jacob Bjerknes and others discover associated atmospheric "tele-connections."
3. In the 1970s Adrian Gill develops some simple analytic models of the "Walker circulation," which is a tropical circulation driven by a localized convection.
4. At about the same time, Jim O'Brien and others begin to realize the importance of fast large-scale waves in the equatorial ocean and their connection with El Niño.
5. George Philander discovers an instability of the coupled atmosphere-ocean system that many now believe is the key to understanding how El Niño maintains itself.
6. Rapid progress ensues in the development of computer models of the atmosphere-ocean system, of which the one by Zebiak and Cane is the first to be used to make an actual prediction of El Niño.

It's recently been suggested that El Niño events may have been responsible for the decline of at least two early Peruvian civilizations. For an account, see

"El Niño Events Devastated Two Ancient Civilizations." *New Scientist*, March 3, 1990, p. 31.

The Weather Machine

Introductory discussions of the general process of weather formation can be found in almost every book on the weather. Two good places to look are the Dolan and Lockhart books already cited. Slightly more technical, but still very accessible, accounts that I found helpful are

Atkinson, B., and A. Gadd. *A Modern Guide to Forecasting Weather*. London: Beazley, 1986.

Hughes, J. "The Copernican Legacy for Meteorology," in *The Heritage of Copernicus*, J. Neymann, ed., pp. 332–353. Cambridge, MA: MIT Press, 1974.

A Tempest in a Transistor

A good summary of the historical origin of numerical weather forecasting, including a more complete discussion of Richardson and his work on numerical weather prediction, can be found in the article

Thompson, P.D. "The Mathematics of Meteorology," in *Mathematics Today*, L. A. Steen, ed., pp. 127–152. New York: Springer, 1978.

The precise citation for Richardson's own pioneering book is

Richardson, L. F. *Weather Prediction by Numerical Processes*. Cambridge: Cambridge University Press, 1922.

In addition to accounting properly for the Courant condition, another crucial factor contributing to the success of the Institute for Advanced Study weather-forecasting model was a condition discovered by Jule Charney. He found that the fundamental dynamical law governing the large-scale motions of the atmosphere is the principle of absolute vorticity conservation. What this means is that the product of the spin of a fluid element around its vertical axis and the area of its horizontal cross section must remain constant. This is a condition familiar to all ice skaters and fans of ballet, where rotation can be speeded up or slowed down simply by drawing in or throwing out the arms. Using this principle, Charney was able to derive a single equation for the "reduced" hydrodynamical flow, thereby dramatically decreasing the computing burden associated with making a forecast. An account of this work, as well as a discussion of the entire IAS Meteorology Project, can be found in the book

Goldstine, H. *The Computer from Pascal to von Neumann*. Princeton, NJ: Princeton University Press, 1972.

The precise form of the differential equations used in GCMs varies from research center to research center, and from textbook to textbook. But they all include the general features discussed in the text. Two excellent sources for a detailed technical discussion of all the terms, equations, numerical schemes, and difficulties are

Cullen, M. "Current Progress and Prospects in Numerical Techniques for Weather Prediction Models." *Journal of Computational Physics*, 50 (1983), 1–37.
Haltiner, G., and R. Williams. *Numerical Prediction and Dynamic Meteorology*, 2nd Edition. New York: Wiley, 1980.

For the mathematically inclined, here is what a reasonably generic mathematical model of the atmosphere looks like:

$$\partial V/\partial t + V \cdot \nabla V + \omega \partial V/\partial p + f \cdot k \times V + \nabla \phi = F \quad \text{(motion)}$$
$$\nabla \cdot V + \partial \omega/\partial p = 0 \quad \text{(continuity)}$$
$$\partial T/\partial t + V \cdot \nabla T + \omega \partial T/\partial p - \kappa T\omega/p = Q \quad \text{(thermodynamic)}$$
$$\partial q/\partial t + \nabla q + \omega \partial q/\partial p = P \quad \text{(moisture)}$$
$$\partial \phi/\partial p + RT/p = 0 \quad \text{(hydrostatic)}$$

The quantities V, T, q, p, and ϕ are the horizontal wind vector, temperature, humidity mixing ratio, pressure, and geopotential height, respectively. The terms $V \cdot \nabla$ and $\nabla \cdot V$ are the horizontal advection and two-dimensional divergence operators, $\omega = dp/dt$ is the vertical velocity equivalent in pressure coordinates, and κ is the unit vertical vector. Further, we have the Coriolis parameter $f = 2\Omega \sin \theta$, where Ω is the Earth's rotation speed at the latitude θ. The symbols F, Q, and P stand for processes such as the frictional dissipation, diabatic heating, evaporation, and precipitation, which have to be parameterized.

The results from the British Meteorological Office model, as well as a good general account of the achievements and problems in numerical weather prediction, are given in

Mason, J. "Numerical Weather Prediction." *Proceedings of the Royal Society of London A*, 407 (1986), 51–60.

Both the objective and the subjective utility of the ECMWF predictions are discussed in the Cullen paper noted earlier, while the Australian rainfall computations are considered in

Brown, J. "Operational Numerical Weather Prediction." *Reviews in Geophysics*, 25 (1987), 312–322.

Finally, the results for the sea-level pressure predictions can be found in the following first-rate introductory textbook on climate modeling, which is notable not only for its exposition of all aspects of the problem, but also for its BASIC computer models, which can be run on a home computer. For all this, as well as much, much more, see

Henderson-Sellers, A., and K. McGuffie. *A Climate Modelling Primer*. Chichester, U.K.: Wiley, 1987.

In abstract terms, the problem of filtering is the following: We are given a finite time series of observations (say, real numbers) $X = \{x_0, x_1, \ldots, x_T\}$ (the "signal"), where each observation x_t is assumed to be corrupted by noise. Thus $x_t = m_t + n_t$, where $m_t = $ the "message" at time t and $n_t = $ the "noise." The problem is to determine the best estimate of the message process $M = \{m_0, m_1, \ldots, m_T\}$. In short, the question is how to "filter out" the noise when we know only the signal process X and the statistical properties of the noise process $N = \{n_0, n_1, \ldots, n_T\}$—but not the actual noisy components n_t themselves. Mathematically, there are many different ways to interpret what's "best," although in the linear case solved by Wiener they all turn out to be more or less equivalent.

If we let $\hat{x}_t$ denote the best estimate of the message at time t, the linear filtering rule of Wiener says that we must have $\hat{x}_t = \Sigma_{i=0}^{t} a_i x_i$, where the quantities $\{a_j\}$ are determined from the statistics of the noise process. In other words, the optimal linear estimator of the message at time t is obtained by just adding up all the observations up to time t, suitably weighted by the quantities $\{a_j\}$. As it turns out, Wiener also solved an additional problem using the same techniques. This is the question of how to optimally *extrapolate*, i.e., predict, the message for some time $s > T$ on the basis of the observations available up to time T.

Lorenz had just such a set of observations: noisy measurements of various quantities pertaining to the weather. What he wanted to do was find the optimal estimate of the weather at some future time on the basis of all the data available at the moment. Mathematically, he wanted to find a future weather quantity y as some function of the past observed data. Symbolically,

$$y_s = \mathcal{F}(x_0, x_1, \ldots, x_T), \ s > T$$

The claim (hope) of the statistical weather-forecasting community was that the best possible way to choose the function $\mathcal{F}$ was to let it be a summation as above. That is, the weather people hoped that Wiener's results for the linear case were the best possible way to filter and extrapolate the observations. Lorenz rightly thought otherwise. And when the problem is stated in these terms, the only puzzling aspect of the whole business is why everyone didn't agree with him. For those interested in looking a little deeper into the mathematical and computational aspects of filtering, good sources are

Casti, J. *Nonlinear System Theory*. New York: Academic Press, 1985.
Hazewinkel, M., and J. Willems, eds. *Stochastic Systems: The Mathematics of Filtering and Identification and Applications*. Dordrecht, Netherlands: Reidel, 1981.

For those curious about the exact form of the differential equations that constitute what in the world of chaos are called the Lorenz equations, they are given by

$$dX/dt = \sigma(Y - X)$$
$$dY/dt = rX - Y - XZ$$
$$dZ/dt = XY - bZ$$

where σ, r, and b are parameters. Roughly speaking, the variable X measures the rate of convective overturning in the atmosphere, while Y and Z represent the horizontal and vertical temperature variation, respectively. The three parameters σ, r, and b are respectively proportional to the Prandtl number, the Rayleigh number, and some physical properties of the region under consideration. For a wide range of values of the parameters, including the values $\sigma = 10$, $b = \frac{8}{3}$, $r = 28$, this system of equations exhibits a strange attractor. For a personal account of the historical development of these equations, the best source is Lorenz's own discussion in his Craaford Prize Lecture presented to the Royal Swedish Academy of Sciences in 1983. The published version of this lecture is

Lorenz, E. "Irregularity: A Fundamental Property of the Atmosphere." *Tellus*, 36A (1984), 98–110.

For a detailed mathematical account of the almost limitless varieties of behavior the Lorenz equations can display, see

Sparrow, C. *The Lorenz Equations: Bifurcations, Chaos, and Strange Attractors*. New York: Springer, 1982.

Good introductory presentations of chaotic behavior in weather systems are given in

Palmer, T. "A Weather Eye on Unpredictability." *New Scientist*, November 11, 1989, pp. 56–59.
Pool, R. "Is Something Strange About the Weather?" *Science*, 243 (March 10, 1989), 1290–1293.

The work by Tsonis and Elsner on uncovering a strange attractor in the wind dynamics is reported in

Tsonis, A., and J. Elsner. "The Weather Attractor over Very Short Timescales." *Nature,* 333 (June 9, 1988), 545–546.

This work was critically reviewed by dynamical system theorist Itamar Procaccia, who concluded that Tsonis and Elsner's results show that either there is something fundamental in atmospheric behavior that we don't understand, or their method of analysis doesn't apply to this kind of situation. Procaccia claims that in order to get a reliable computation of the correlation dimension, the quantity used by Tsonis and Elsner to conclude the system has a strange attractor, it would be necessary to have about 10 million data points; Tsonis and Elsner had 3,960. For the full discussion, see

Procaccia, I. "Complex or Just Complicated?" *Nature,* 333 (June 9, 1988), 498–499.

Forecast errors are always the sum of the error due to the imprecision in the initial conditions and the error due to approximations and/or omissions in the underlying mathematical model. More details of the text discussion of these two sources of error and the rate at which they destroy the credibility of the prediction are found in the Mason article cited above.

The Cold and the Dark, the Warm and the Wet

A rather extensive account of the Maxwell-Wheeler Energy Cycle can be found in

Steiger, B. *A Roadmap of Time.* Englewood Cliffs, NJ: Prentice-Hall, 1975.

In addition to the Henderson-Sellers and McGuffie textbook noted earlier, a surprisingly good layman's introduction to some of the problems and schools of thought in climate modeling is given by the U.S. Central Intelligence Agency in the unclassified report

"Study of Climatological Research as It Pertains to Intelligence Problems." CIA Office of Research and Development, August 1974.

As part of the benefits of the Freedom of Information Act, useful reports like this are now readily accessible. This particular one can be found reprinted as an appendix in the following volume, which is itself a worthwhile source of information about matters pertaining to a new ice age:

The Weather Conspiracy: The Coming of the New Ice Age. A Report of the Impact Team. New York: Ballantine, 1977.

While there is strong empirical evidence in support of some kind of eleven-year cycle in climatic conditions, this periodic fluctuation may not be attributable to the solar sunspot cycle at all, but to factors internal to the nonlinearity of atmospheric dynamics. For an account of this point of view, see

Geller, M. "Variations Without Forcing." *Nature,* 342 (November 2, 1989), 15–16.

For an excellent presentation in both words and diagrams of the Milankovitch cycle, see the Henderson-Sellers and McGuffie book mentioned above. A good discussion of the work of the Imbrie group on carbon dioxide and ice ages and their implications for global warming can be found in

Gribbin, J. "The End of the Ice Ages?" *New Scientist,* June 17, 1989, pp. 48–52.

The work by Overpeck and his co-workers on implicating the Laurentide Ice Sheet in the nonlinear behavior of the onset and disappearance of ice ages is reported in

Overpeck, J., et al. "Climate Change in the Circum–North Atlantic Region During the Last Deglaciation." *Nature,* 338 (April 13, 1989), 553–557.

The citation of the original paper by Crutzen and Birks on the possible darkening of the Sun due to smoke and dust from a nuclear exchange is

Crutzen, P., and J. Birks. "The Atmosphere After a Nuclear War: Twilight at Noon." *Ambio,* 11 (1982), 114–125.

The much-ballyhooed TTAPS paper, which brought the smoke and dust problem to the media's attention, as well as creating the colorful phrase *nuclear winter* (attributable to the paper's first author, Richard Turco), is

Turco, R., O. B. Toon, T. P. Ackerman, J. B. Pollack, and C. Sagan. "Nuclear Winter: Global Consequences of Multiple Nuclear Explosions." *Science,* 222 (December 23, 1983), 1283–1292.

This paper is reprinted as an appendix to the following general-audience book relating the proceedings of a U.S.-U.S.S.R. conference on the long-term global environmental and biological implications of nuclear war:

Ehrlich, P., C. Sagan, D. Kennedy, and W. O. Roberts. *The Cold and the Dark.* New York: Norton, 1984.

To my mind, the best treatment of the overall problem is

Greene, O., I. Percival, and I. Ridge. *Nuclear Winter.* Cambridge: Polity Press, 1985.

The state of thinking in the climatological community about the effects of such a war, leading to the phrase *nuclear fall* (or *autumn*), is summarized in the review paper

Schneider, S., and S. Thompson. "Simulating the Climatic Effects of Nuclear War." *Nature,* 333 (May 19, 1988), 221–227.

The nuclear autumn studies were based on the assumption that the particles of airborne soot would be spherical in shape. Recently, Jenny Nelson of Bristol University in the United Kingdom pointed out that the particles would more likely be "fractal," resulting in making them more efficient at blocking solar heat. Thus, it may well be nuclear winter after all. For a firsthand account of this theory, see

Nelson, J. "Fractility of Soot Smoke: Implications for the Severity of Nuclear Winter." *Nature,* 339 (June 22, 1989), 611–613.

A good survey of the state of knowledge in the climatological world about the greenhouse effect is presented in the volumes

Schneider, S. *Global Warming.* San Francisco: Sierra Club Books, 1989.
Seitz, F., R. Jastrow, and W. Nierenberg, *Scientific Perspectives on the Greenhouse Problem.* Washington, DC: George C. Marshall Institute, 1989.

The latter study concludes by saying that solar variability might provide a better explanation for the hundred-year rise in average temperature than increased concentrations of carbon dioxide. Other good references on the overall problem include

Barron, E. "Earth's Shrouded Future." *The Sciences,* September–October 1989, pp. 14–20.
Bolin, B., J. Jäger, and B. Doos, eds. *The Greenhouse Effect, Climate Change and Ecosystems: A Synthesis of Present Knowledge.* Chichester, U.K.: Wiley, 1986.
Boyle, S., and J. Ardill. *The Greenhouse Effect: A Practical Guide to the World's Changing Climate.* London: New English Library, 1989.

Gilchrist, A. "Numerical Weather Prediction and Climate Simulation." *Reports on Progress in Physics*, 51 (1988), 1205–1226.

Hansen, J., and A. Lacis. "Sun and Dust Versus Greenhouse Gases: An Assessment of Their Relative Roles in Global Climate Change." *Nature*, 346 (August 23, 1990), 713–719.

MacCracken, M., and F. Luther, eds. *Projecting the Climatic Effects of Increased Carbon Dioxide*. Washington, DC: U.S. Department of Energy, 1985.

McKibben, B. "Is the World Getting Hotter?" *The New York Review of Books*, December 8, 1988, pp. 7–11.

Pain, S. "No Escape from the Global Greenhouse." *New Scientist*, November 12, 1988, pp. 38–43.

Pearce, F. *Turning Up the Heat*. London: The Bodley Head, 1989.

Raval, A., and V. Ramanathan. "Observational Determination of the Greenhouse Effect." *Nature*, 342 (December 14, 1989), 758–761.

A lot of recent work on the greenhouse effect has emphasized the negative feedback influence of clouds. The basic theme of this work is that atmospheric pollution over the oceans may reduce rainfall, thereby making the cloud cover last longer. This, in turn, leads to a reduction of incident solar radiation, thus tending to counterbalance the heat-trapping effects of sulfur dioxide and carbon dioxide. For a discussion of these theories, see

Mitchell, J., C. Senior, and W. Ingram. "CO_2 and Climate: A Missing Feedback." *Nature*, 341 (September 14, 1989), 132–134.

Wigley, T. "Possible Climatic Change Due to SO_2-Derived Cloud Condensation Nuclei." *Nature*, 339 (June 1, 1989), 365–367.

A radical view suggesting that we might well enjoy a "greenhouse paradise," with cattle grazing in the Sahara and crops growing in the deserts of Central Asia, is championed by Mikhail Budyko. For details, see

"Soviet Climatologist Predicts Greenhouse 'Paradise.' " *New Scientist*, August 26, 1989, p. 24.

Further discussion of the Amazonian region climate-prediction experiment can be found in the paper

Henderson-Sellers, A. "Effects of Change in Land Use on Climate in the Humid Tropics," in *The Geophysiology of Amazonia*, R. Dickinson, ed., pp. 463–493. New York: Wiley, 1987.

Several years ago James Lovelock and Lynn Margulis advanced the Gaia Hypothesis, claiming that life shapes the environment as much as the other way around. Treatments of the details of this controversial theory and its implications for greenhouse phenomena are found in

Allaby, M. *A Guide to Gaia.* London: Macdonald, 1989.
Myers, N., ed. *The Gaia Atlas of Planet Management.* London: Pan Books, 1985.
Pearce, F. "Gaia: A Revolution Comes of Age." *New Scientist,* March 17, 1989, pp. 32–33.

Making the Grade

For an account of the text discussion of the differing predictions of the competing CO_2 models, see

Barnett, T. P. "Beware Greenhouse Confusion." *Nature,* 343 (February 22, 1990), 696–697.
Stevens, W. "A Race to Assess Global Warming." *International Herald Tribune,* February 9, 1989.

It's of considerable interest to note the many climatologists who dispute the predictions of global warming. For instance, at a 1989 meeting at Harvard, Thomas Karl of the U.S. National Climatic Data Center stated that he has a "small degree of confidence in the link [between atmospheric gases like carbon dioxide and global warming]." This remark was made in response to James Hansen's assertion that he has a "high degree of confidence" in the same link. For another skeptical view, see

Gavaghan, H. "Effect of Global Warming on Sea Levels Overestimated." *New Scientist,* December 16, 1989, p. 11.

For a summary of the Schneider-Lindzen debate, see

Aldhous, P. "Hot Air—or What?" *Nature,* 345 (June 14, 1990), 562.

CHAPTER THREE

General References

The strongest possible testimony to the stranglehold the mechanist position has on the mainline developmental biology community is given by looking at the available textbooks in the field. Almost without exception, such volumes entirely omit discussions of the various organicist positions. Nevertheless, there is much to recommend some of these volumes, especially as a statement of exactly what the mechanist views really are. A text of this sort that I found particularly useful in preparing this chapter is

Gilbert, S. *Developmental Biology,* 2nd Edition. Sunderland, MA: Sinauer Associates, 1988.

Two other excellent introductions to all the problems of modern biology, including very accessible accounts for laymen of the problems of developmental biology, are

Arthur, W. *Theories of Life.* London: Penguin, 1987.
Smith, John Maynard. *The Problems of Biology.* Oxford: Oxford University Press, 1986.

From an artistic point of view, biological forms hold an irresistible attraction. An intriguing attempt to marry art and biology is given in

"Art and the New Biology: Biological Forms and Patterns." Special issue of *Leonardo,* 22 (1989).

Finally, for the more technically inclined, the following book summarizes the current state of play for many of the most interesting theoretical questions in developmental biology today:

Goodwin, B., and P. Saunders, eds. *Theoretical Biology: Epigenetic and Evolutionary Order from Complex Systems.* Edinburgh: Edinburgh University Press, 1989.

From Blobs to Babies

An illuminating introductory discussion of the positions held by the classical philosophers on the problem of form is given in the volume

Sheldrake, R. *The Presence of the Past.* New York: Times Books, 1988.

This volume includes a general account of the theory of preformationism, as well as the vitalist position of Driesch, the germ plasm theory of Weismann and its closely related mechanist theory, in addition to an introduction to the overall position of organicism. However, given the book's main goal, which is the explication of Sheldrake's hypothesis of formative causation, the volume does not go into detail on competing organicist views like those of Goodwin and Thom.

For a good account of the rational morphologists, see the chapter on biology in the classic volume

Cassirer, E. *The Problem of Knowledge*. New Haven, CT: Yale University Press, 1950.

The best-chronicled attempt to relate an organism's ontogenetic path to its phylogenetic history is what's called Haeckel's Law, which was briefly mentioned in the text. The short version of this "law" is that "ontogeny recapitulates phylogeny." What this means is that each stage in an individual organism's developmental pathway mirrors one of the stages in the evolutionary history of the species to which the organism belongs. As an example, at one stage in its development the human embryo possesses something like the gills of a fish. Haeckel's Law claims that this observation is explainable by the fact that the species *Homo sapiens* originally evolved from fish, with the gill stage being an ancestral reminder of this fact. Nowadays, Haeckel's Law is pretty much dismissed in view of the many counterexamples that have been discovered. For an account, see

Gould, S. J. *Ontogeny and Phylogeny*. Cambridge, MA: Harvard University Press, 1977.
Rosen, R. *Optimality Principles in Biology*. London: Butterworth, 1967.

The Genocentric View of the World

More information about Sydney Brenner and his role in the discovery of the genetic code can be found in the interviews

"The Entry of Molecular Biology," in *Imagined Worlds*, P. Andersen and D. Cadbury, eds. London: Ariel Books, 1985.
"No Zombie Biologist," in *A Passion for Science*, L. Wolpert, ed. Oxford: Oxford University Press, 1988.

The way the cell goes about its chemical business during the process of protein synthesis is discussed in just about every book on modern biology. A particularly entertaining and informative account of the whole story in cartoon format, including the Jacob-Monod theory, the Central Dogma, and all the rest can be found in

Rosenfeld, I., E. Ziff, and B. Van Loon. *DNA for Beginners*. London: Writers and Readers Press, 1983.

The work of the Brenner group on mapping the developmental history of *C. elegans* is summarized in

Lewin, R. "Why Is Development So Illogical?" *Science*, 224 (June 22, 1989), 1327–1329.

A good view of the molecular biological perspective on development is available in

de Pomerai, D. *From Gene to Animal*. Cambridge: Cambridge University Press, 1985.

The Gene Machine

An excellent general survey of the ideas underlying modeling developmental systems by both mathematical and computational means is presented in the book

Ransom, R. *Computers and Embryos: Models in Developmental Biology*. Chichester, U.K.: Wiley, 1981.

Dawkins's account of his travels through Biomorph Land can be found in his popular volume on evolutionary theory

Dawkins, R. *The Blind Watchmaker*. London: Longman, 1986.

For a more technical discussion of experiments, along with much more material on the Los Alamos meeting on artificial life, see

Langton, C., ed. *Artificial Life*. Reading, MA: Addison-Wesley, 1988.

Since it plays a pivotal role in the argument supporting the mainline mechanist position, Wolpert's French Flag Problem is discussed in just about every book on developmental biology. A good account is given in the Gilbert volume cited under general references, as well as in the Ransom book noted earlier in this section. For Wolpert's original article on the topic, see

Wolpert, L. "Positional Information and Pattern." *Journal of Theoretical Biology*, 25 (1969), 1–49.

A sympathetic portrayal of Alan Turing's tortured life, including a rather detailed discussion of his work on pattern formation in morphogenesis, can be found in the prize-winning biography

Hodges, A. *Alan Turing: The Enigma*. London: Burnett Books, 1983.

For a detailed discussion of reaction-diffusion models of morphogenesis, the mathematically inclined should consult

Meinhardt, H. *Models of Biological Pattern Formation*. London: Academic Press, 1982.

Meinhardt, H. "Tailoring and Coupling of Reaction-Diffusion Systems to Obtain Reproducible Complex Pattern Formation During Development of the Higher Organisms." *Applied Mathematics and Computation*, 23 (1989), 103–135.

It's worth pointing out that the much more publicized recent work of Ilya Prigogine and his followers on far-from-equilibrium thermodynamics represents a major extension of the basic reaction-diffusion idea, one that has also been employed to study biological pattern formation. The interested reader can consult the following volume for the flavor of these efforts:

Nicolis, G., and I. Prigogine. *Self-Organization in Nonequilibrium Systems*. New York: Wiley, 1977.

A semitechnical account of Edelman's ideas on development is given in his books

Edelman, G. *Neural Darwinism: The Theory of Neuronal Group Selection*. New York: Basic Books, 1987.

Edelman, G. *Topobiology: An Introduction to Molecular Embryology*. New York: Basic Books, 1988.

In reviewing this latter volume in the April 27, 1989 issue of *The New York Review of Books*, Richard Lewontin noted that Edelman appears to see the difficulty in development as being the problem of how the one-dimensional information in cellular DNA can give rise to a three-dimensional organism. Lewontin argues that this is not the problem at all, since one-dimensional information is regularly used to generate three-dimensional objects, e.g., when one writes down instructions for some spatiotemporal activity using a one-dimensional string of words. Lewontin's claim is that the real problem is one of size: The DNA sequence of protein codes is just way too small to tell every cell where it should be and when; in short, there's just not enough DNA to go around.

An interesting account, circa the early 1970s, of the way mechanists thought about using a computer as a metaphor for a developing organism can be found in

Arbib, M. "Automata Theory in the Context of Theoretical Embryology," in *Foundations of Mathematical Biology*, Volume 2, R. Rosen, ed., pp. 141–215. New York: Academic Press, 1972.

Going Round in Cylinders

Wainwright's arguments for why living organisms should be expected to develop cylindrically shaped bodies are given in his immensely enlightening book

Wainwright, S. *Axis and Circumference*. Cambridge, MA: Harvard University Press, 1988.

Other books employing principles of classical hydrodynamics, mechanics, and optics to argue in a top-down fashion why organisms look the way they do include

Alexander, R. *Optima for Animals*. London: Edward Arnold, 1982.
Huntley, H. *The Divine Proportion*. New York: Dover, 1970.
Tributsch, H. *How Life Learned to Live*. Cambridge, MA: MIT Press, 1982.

The Huntley volume is notable for its focus upon the so-called *spira mirabilis,* the logarithmic spiral, a shape that appears in many living objects ranging from the chambered nautilus to pinecones. The relation between this ubiquitous curve and the Fibonacci number sequence is especially intriguing, and is discussed in great detail in the following work:

Cook, T. *The Curves of Life*. New York: Dover, 1979.

Allometric relations are considered in the Gilbert text noted under general references, as well as in the Rosen book on optimality principles in biology, also cited above.

The Fields of the Forms

Recent accounts of the rational morphological notion of the "typical form" representing the tetrapod limb are found in the articles

Oster, G., et al. "Evolution and Morphogenetic Rules: The Shape of the Vertebrate Limb in Ontogeny and Phylogeny." *Evolution,* 42 (1988), 862–884.
Shubin, N., and P. Alberch. "A Morphogenetic Approach to the Origin and Basic Organization of the Tetrapod Limb." *Evolutionary Biology,* 20 (1986), 319–387.

The classic work by D'Arcy Thompson in which he almost single-handedly kept the rational morphological view of development alive during the "dark ages" of unrestrained mechanism is

Thompson, D. *On Growth and Form*. Cambridge: Cambridge University Press, 1917 (abridged edition, J. Tyler Bonner, ed., 1971).

Structuralist biology takes as its general aim to make the order of a unified system intelligible, and to provide a set of rules or laws with generative power that can account for the range of possible forms belonging to a particular set of organisms. The manifesto of the modern structuralist school of biology was laid down in the paper

Webster, G., and B. Goodwin. "The Origin of Species: A Structuralist Approach." *Journal of Social and Biological Structures*, 5 (1982), 15–47.

Brian Goodwin has been a tireless worker in pushing forward the organicist position on development. The reader can get the flavor of his views in the following articles:

Goodwin, B. "Developing Organisms as Self-organizing Fields," in *Mathematical Essays on Growth and the Emergence of Form*, P. Antonelli, ed., pp. 185–200. Edmonton, Alberta: University of Alberta Press, 1985.
Goodwin, B. "Morphogenesis and Heredity," in *Evolutionary Processes and Metaphors*, M.-W. Ho and S. Fox, eds., pp. 145–162. Chichester, U.K.: Wiley, 1988.
Goodwin, B. "Organisms and Minds as Dynamic Forms." *Leonardo*, 22 (1989), 27–31.

In mathematical clothing, Laplace's equation for an electric field $u(x, y)$ in some two-dimensional spatial region R is

$$\frac{\partial^2 u}{\partial x^2} + \frac{\partial^2 u}{\partial y^2} = 0, \ (x, y) \in R,$$

$$u(x, y) = f(x, y) \text{ on } \partial R$$

Here $f(x, y)$ is the prescribed value of the field on the boundary of the region R. As noted in the text, without the boundary condition the equation generally has an infinite number of solutions in R. But once the boundary condition has been specified, all nonuniqueness in the solution disappears. Organicists claim that the role of the genes in development is exactly this: to specify the boundary conditions for the relevant morphogenetic fields.

The hypothesis of formative causation, which so incensed the editors of *Nature*, is laid out in detail in

Sheldrake, R. *A New Science of Life: The Hypothesis of Formative Causation*. London: Blond and Briggs, 1981.

A new edition, with an appendix containing comments, reviews, and discussion prompted by the first edition, was published in 1985. A slightly less technical version of the theory for the general reader is presented in the Sheldrake volume cited earlier. A television interview with Sheldrake, in which he illuminates the idea of morphic resonance as well as suggests its connection with things like Jung's collective unconscious, is reprinted in

Rawlence, C., ed., *About Time,* pp. 193–199. London: Jonathan Cape, 1985.

Richard Dawkins is one of the many biologists who think that Sheldrake's ideas are nonsense. For a brief indication of why, see

Dawkins, R. "Books for Scraping?" *New Scientist,* October 8, 1988, p. 65.

Formal Catastrophes

For primary references on catastrophe theory, along with a discussion of the backlash from the mathematical community, the reader is referred to the bibliographic material cited for Chapter One. The famous Zeeman lecture at the 1974 International Congress of Mathematicians in Vancouver, British Columbia is available in written form in

Zeeman, E. C. "Levels of Structure in Catastrophe Theory Illustrated by Applications in the Social and Biological Sciences." *Proceedings of the International Congress of Mathematicians,* pp. 533–546. Vancouver: Canadian Mathematical Congress, 1975.

Extensive details of Zeeman's model of cellular differentiation, along with a host of additional material, are given in

Zeeman, E. C. "Primary and Secondary Waves in Developmental Biology." *Lectures on Mathematics in the Life Sciences,* Volume 7, pp. 69–161. Providence, RI: American Mathematical Society, 1974.

Both of these papers, as well as many more relating to other areas of application of catastrophe theory, are reprinted in the book

Zeeman, E. C. *Catastrophe Theory: Selected Papers, 1972–1977.* Reading, MA: Addison-Wesley, 1977.

"Wad" Waddington was a man who seemed to be interested in just about everything. The flavor of the man and his ideas can be found in the biographical sketch

Schubert, G. "Epigenetic Evolutionary Theory: Waddington in Retrospect." *Journal of Social and Biological Structures*, 8 (1985), 233–253.

For a spectrum of material showing why Waddington was one of the leaders of the charge toward putting modern mathematics to work in the cause of biology, see the four-volume classic

Waddington, C. H., ed. *Towards a Theoretical Biology*. Chicago: Aldine Press, 1968–1972 (in four volumes).

For a discussion of the spatial and temporal interpretations of the seven elementary catastrophes in Table 3.4, the reader should consult Thom's catastrophe theory "bibles" already cited for Chapter One, as well as

Thom, R. "Topological Models in Biology." *Topology*, 8 (1969), 313–335.

CHAPTER FOUR

General References

It's hard to think of an area in which so much has been written by so many who appear actually to know so little as the stock market. Nevertheless, there is some wheat in all this chaff. Two of the best treatments I've found for the general reader are

Johnson, M. *The Random Walk and Beyond*. New York: Wiley, 1988.
Malkiel, B. *A Random Walk Down Wall Street*, 4th Edition. New York: Norton, 1985.

Each of these books gives an excellent overview of all aspects of the ways and whys of the market, the Johnson book being a bit more technical, while the Malkiel volume is very breezy and anecdotal. But both are easily accessible to the uninitiated, providing the kind of overview that every investor should carefully digest before putting even one cent into the market.

Another volume for the general reader that's well worth consulting for its detailed consideration of the "group think" psychology underpinning market behavior is

Dreman, D. *Psychology and the Stock Market*. New York: AMACOM, 1977.

A more academic account of the role that popular opinion and psychology plays in the volatility of market prices is found in

Shiller, R. *Market Volatility*. Cambridge, MA: MIT Press, 1989.

For mainline academic finance—textbook style—a good, relatively recent reference is

Haugen, R. *Introductory Investment Theory*. Englewood Cliffs, NJ: Prentice-Hall, 1987.

Finally, for a lot of useful terminological as well as informational wisdom about the market, the reader should consult

Scott, D. *Wall Street Words*. Boston: Houghton-Mifflin, 1988.

A Bull in a Bowl

The Super Bowl Indicator is discussed in many places, including the Johnson volume cited above. Interestingly, there is also a converse indicator for using the market's behavior to predict the outcome of the game. It works as follows: If the DJIA is down from the end of November until the Friday before the Super Bowl, then the team that ranks first alphabetically (by the name of its hometown) will win; if the DJIA is up, then the team that is alphabetically second will win. For the 1989 game, the DJIA stood at 2238 on the Wednesday before the game, well above its 2114 at the end of November 1988. Prediction: San Francisco should prevail over Cincinnati, which indeed it did by a count of 20–16. Including the 1989 Super Bowl, this converse indicator has worked an astonishing thirteen times out of fifteen—a success rate comparable to the direct indicator itself. For football fanatics wanting further details on this converse indicator, see

Norris, F. "The Super Bowl Indicator Works in Both Directions." *International Herald Tribune*, January 20, 1989.

Virtually every general-investor type of stock market book talks about the different kinds of indexes employed to measure market movements. What these books often leave unsaid is the fact that even an index like the S&P 500 or the Wilshire 5000 that includes a very large number of stocks is still a very limited sample of the overall "market." This fact is used by many academics in various kinds of critiques of ideas like beta and CAPM that rely on some measure of the market *as a whole*. Some useful discussion along these lines is given in the Johnson book noted under general references.

Walking the Street—Randomly

An English translation of Bachelier's remarkable dissertation is given in

Cootner, P., ed. *The Random Character of Stock Market Prices*. Cambridge, MA: MIT Press, 1964.

For those interested in seeing why the finance and statistics communities so uniformly adopted both the weak and semistrong random-walk theories in the 1960s, this volume is the place to turn. It contains reprints of a number of pioneering papers, starting with Bachelier's thesis, almost all of which strongly argue the RWT.

For an intriguing account of Bachelier's life as an academic in France espousing an unfashionable idea, the reader should look at Mandelbrot's fractals "bible":

Mandelbrot, B. *The Fractal Geometry of Nature*. New York: Freeman, 1983.

The deliberations of Senator McIntyre's Banking Committee are reported in the August 16, 1967, issue of *The New York Times*. The story is also recounted in the following volume treating stock market forecasting alongside schemes for beating the horses:

Fabricand, B. *The Science of Winning*. New York: Van Nostrand Reinhold, 1979.

Looking For a Beta Way

An excellent account of the principles of diversification, together with lots of examples, is given in the Johnson book noted earlier. It's of considerable practical interest to note the theoretical results showing that a portfolio of ten to fifteen well-chosen stocks can reduce specific risk to essentially zero. Thus, it's not necessary to invest vast sums of capital and buy the market to get rid of this kind of risk; it's a task well within the purse of the average investor—and that's why the market won't pay you a premium for doing it!

The CAPM, together with its associated notion of beta, represents the most fashionable idea in finance during the 1970s. The Malkiel and Johnson books give excellent introductory accounts. Those hungering for the gory details, should turn to the comprehensive assessment of the entire idea given by Jensen in 1979:

Jensen, M. "Tests of Capital Market Theory and Implications of the Evidence," in *Handbook of Financial Economics*, J. L. Bickster, ed. Amsterdam: North-Holland, 1979.

The CAPM itself appears to have originated with Stanford economist William F. Sharpe. The source article is

Sharpe, W. "Capital Assets Prices: A Theory of Market Equilibrium Under Conditions of Risk." *Journal of Finance*, 19 (1964), 425–442.

The Infomaniacs

A good profile of Arnold Bernhard, as well as the history and philosophy of *The Value Line Investment Survey*, is given in

Brimelow, P. "Order in the Ranks." *Barron's*, June 3, 1985, pp. 6–7.

A thorough facts-and-figures account of the success of the amazing Mr. Bernhard is provided in the book by Johnson cited under general references. For a history of the development of the Value Line rating scheme itself, see

"The Value Line Ranking System: A 25th Anniversary Perspective." *The Value Line Investment Survey*, April 20, 1990.

The low P/E study by Basu is reported in

Basu, S. "Investment Performance of Common Stocks in Relation to Their Price/Earnings Ratios: A Test of the Efficient Market Hypothesis." *Journal of Finance*, 32 (1977), 663–682.

Reinganum's pioneering work on the small-firms effect is reported in

Reinganum, M. "Portfolio Strategies Based on Market Capitalization." *Journal of Portfolio Management*, Winter 1983.

For a rather thorough up-to-date account of the entire small-firms anomaly, see Section III of

Dimson, E., ed. *Stock Market Anomalies*. Cambridge: Cambridge University Press, 1988.

Where Have All the Gurus Gone?

A journalistic account of Robert Prechter and the Elliott Wave Theory can be found in

Crossen, C. "Wave Theory Wins Robert Prechter Title of Wall Street Guru." *Wall Street Journal*, March 18, 1987.

"The source" for the ins and outs of the Elliott theory is the volume

Frost, A., and R. Prechter. *Elliott Wave Principle*. Gainesville, GA: New Classics Library, 1985.

For an update on Prechter and Frost's views, see

Norris, F. "These Two Differ On How to Ride the Elliott Wave." *International Herald Tribune*, February 16, 1989.

Incidentally, the "differences" between Prechter and Frost implied by this article's title have subsequently been resolved, as both men now see the same dismal future: short-term prosperity followed by a massive downturn in the market lasting till the mid-1990s.

For those wondering about the methods and techniques of technical analysis in general, by far the most complete and up-to-date account is the following volume by Eng. This book covers not only the old standby methods of the chartist, but also all the other technical methods ranging from astrological cycles to the Elliott Wave Theory. Moreover, the book not only gives the theory behind the methods, but also shows how the methods work in practice. And, if this were not enough, references to original sources as well as to computer programs for your PC complete the picture. Truly a must-have volume for every stock market aficionado—even those who don't believe in technical analysis!

Eng, W. *The Technical Analysis of Stocks, Options, and Futures*. Chicago: Probus, 1988.

The January Barometer, as well as a host of other timing anomalies, is covered in great statistical detail in the popular work

Hirsch, Y. *Don't Sell Stocks on Monday*. New York: Penguin, 1987.

For a quick account of the monthly effect, see the Hirsch book above. More technical details are presented in the paper

Ariel, R. "Evidence on Intra-Month Seasonality in Stock Returns," in *Stock Market Anomalies*, E. Dimson, ed. Cambridge: Cambridge University Press, 1988, pp. 109–119.

Not So Great Expectations

Muth's original paper outlining the concept of rational expectations is

Muth, J. "Rational Expectations and the Theory of Price Movements." *Econometrica*, 29, (1961), 315–335.

A semitechnical treatment of the topic, so well written that even the nontechnically inclined will get a lot out of it, is

Sheffrin, S. *Rational Expectations*. Cambridge: Cambridge University Press, 1983.

Clarity in Chaos

The story about Josiah Willard Gibbs is recounted within the context of the irrationality of speculative booms and busts in

Montroll, E., and W. Badger. *Introduction to Quantitative Aspects of Social Phenomena*. New York: Gordon and Breach, 1974.

In addition to its excellent summary of many speculative manias ranging from the Tulipmania in Holland to the Wall Street Mania of 1929, this book is notable for its own treatment of stock price fluctuations. Unfortunately, the authors (both physicists, incidentally) wrote at a time when both the weak RWT and the EMH were in full favor, with the consequent foreordained conclusions about beating the market. Nevertheless, their treatment is interesting, if for no other reason than that it illustrates the fascination that the mathematically trained have always had with the market.

Mandelbrot's ideas about infinite-variance distributions to describe price fluctuations are summarized in his fractal book cited earlier. A somewhat more complete (and easier-to-understand) treatment is found in

Mandelbrot, B. "The Many Faces of Scaling: Fractals, Geometry of Nature, and Economics," in *Self-Organization and Dissipative Structures*, W. Schieve and P. Allen, eds., pp. 91–109. Austin, TX: University of Texas Press, 1982.

As noted in the text, Mandelbrot's ideas date back much further than these citations. Perhaps the first account of the Lévy stable distributions as a solution to the statistical discrepancy of speculative price data is

Mandelbrot, B. "The Variation of Some Other Speculative Prices." *Journal of Business*, 40 (1967), 393–413.

Some of Mandelbrot's ideas have been called into question by results of Blatterberg and Gonedes showing that the normal distribution is a better fit for stock prices over the longer term than for daily returns. This result directly contradicts what would be expected from Mandelbrot's assumptions of a nonnormal Lévy stable law. For an account see

Fama, E. *Foundations of Finance*, pp. 26–35. New York: Basic Books, 1976.

The "toy market" example and the gold price study, as well as an excellent summary of the relevance of the tools of dynamical system theory for economic phenomena, can be found in

Frank, M., and T. Stengos. "Chaotic Dynamics in Economic Time Series." *Journal of Economic Surveys*, 2 (1988), 103–133.

Some of the other recent literature emphasizing the system-theoretic point of view for economic processes includes

Brock, W. "Introduction to Chaos and Other Aspects of Nonlinearity," in *Differential Equations, Stability, and Chaos in Dynamic Economics*, W. Brock and A. Malliaris, eds. New York: North-Holland, 1988.
Brock, W. "Nonlinearity and Complex Dynamics in Economics and Finance," in *The Economy as an Evolving Complex System*, P. Anderson, K. Arrow, and D. Pines, eds., pp. 77–97. Reading, MA: Addison-Wesley, 1988.
Brock, W., and C. Sayers. "Is the Business Cycle Characterized by Deterministic Chaos?" *Journal of Monetary Economics*, 22 (1988), 71–90.
Savit, R. "Chaos on the Trading Floor." *New Scientist*, August 11, 1990, 48–51.
Scheinkman, J., and B. LeBaron. "Nonlinear Dynamics and Stock Returns." *Journal of Business*, 62 (1989), 311–337.

For an excellent up-to-date summary of the implications of chaos for modeling in economics and finance, see

Brock, W. "Chaos and Complexity in Economic and Financial Science," in *Acting Under Uncertainty: Multidisciplinary Conceptions*, G. von Furstenberg, ed., pp. 421–447. Boston: Kluwer Academic, 1990.
Brock, W. "Causality, Chaos, Explanation and Prediction in Economics and Finance," in *Beyond Belief: Randomness, Prediction and Explanation in Science*, J. Casti and A. Karlquist, eds., pp. 230–279. Boca Raton, FL: CRC Press, 1991.

As a precautionary note to overly enthusiastic system theorists, Blake LeBaron has conducted extensive tests on both real and simulated stock price data, concluding that "the nature of the nonlinearities may not remain stationary long enough for researchers to reliably detect them." A complete account is given in

LeBaron, B. "The Changing Structure of Stock Returns." Preprint, Department of Economics, University of Wisconsin, Madison, WI, July 1988.

Making the Grade

For more details on Milton Friedman's views of "good modeling," the reader should have a look at

Friedman, M. "The Methodology of Positive Economics," in *Essays on Positive Economics*, p. 15. Chicago: University of Chicago Press, 1953.

CHAPTER FIVE

General References

Of all the topics I've ever looked into, war is without a doubt the one with the largest, most diffuse literature. Probably because the subject touches the life of everyone involved, every academic discipline from anthropology to zoology has its own theory of why wars break out. So believe me when I say that trying to distill the essence of this voluminous literature into a chapter-length account of why, how, and when wars begin is not an exercise for the fainthearted. Nevertheless, there are some reliable guideposts to point the way for the uninitiated and adventurous. Here is one that I found useful in preparing this chapter:

Wright, Q. *A Study of War,* 2nd Edition. Chicago: University of Chicago Press, 1964.

This two-volume treatise, along with Karl von Clausewitz's classic, *On War,* doubtlessly represents the pinnacle of the war analyst's art. Quincy Wright's encyclopedic treatment covers everything from the phenomena of war itself to the prediction and control of war, employing the kind of legalistic slant we would expect from an expert on international law, which he was. Of course, Clausewitz's work is well known to generations of war scholars and the general public alike, needing no citation here.

An illuminating consideration of many aspects of the phenomenon of war is offered from a historian's perspective in the collection of essays

Howard, M. *The Causes of War*, 2nd Edition. Cambridge, MA: Harvard University Press, 1983.

Another historian's perspective on war, especially interesting for the detailed discussion of power distribution and redistribution since the Renaissance, is the panoramic best seller

Kennedy, P. *The Rise and Fall of the Great Powers*. New York: Random House, 1988.

A good overview of many of the issues in the war prediction business as seen by today's international relations experts is given in the collection

Rotberg, R., and T. Rabb, eds. *The Origin and Prevention of Major Wars*. Cambridge: Cambridge University Press, 1988.

For those readers curious about the hot spots in today's world, as well as for those wishing a source for the empirical data underpinning any of the power distribution models, I advise taking a look at the following works:

Dunnigan, J., and A. Bay. *A Quick and Dirty Guide to War*. New York: Quill, 1986.
Keegan, J., and A. Wheatcroft. *Zones of Conflict: An Atlas of Future Wars*. London: Jonathan Cape, 1986.

When it comes to actually waging war, the world's military machines don't seem to be managed any better than other human organizations. A couple of accounts of military incompetence of a high order that have given me several hours worth of laughs are

Dixon, N. *On the Psychology of Military Incompetence*. London: Jonathan Cape, 1976.
Fair, C. *From the Jaws of Victory*. New York: Simon and Schuster, 1971.

Cleopatra's Nose and the Wickedness of Hegel

I've borrowed the colorful terminology forming the title of this section from the lecture "Causation in History" by the Oxbridge scholar E. H. Carr. This lecture gives one of the easiest-to-digest, most enlightening accounts I know of about the problem of transferring the notion of causation as used in the physical sciences into events taking place in the social realm. I highly commend this lecture to the reader's attention. Its written form is available in

Carr, E. H. *What Is History?* London: Penguin, 1987.

For those looking for less academically oriented introductions to the enormous difficulties involved in mathematically predicting historical trends and events, it's hard to beat Isaac Asimov's science fiction classic, the *Foundation* series. Of special interest in this connection is the overture volume:

Asimov, I. *Prelude to Foundation.* New York: Doubleday, 1988.

Casus Belli

When it comes to crises of any sort, no accounts can really compete with those given by the participants themselves, at least when it comes to conveying the flavor and tension of the situation. In this regard, the memoir by Robert F. Kennedy remains the definitive portrayal of the Cuban missile crisis. See

Kennedy, R. *Thirteen Days: A Memoir of the Cuban Missile Crisis.* New York: Norton, 1969.

Ned Lebow's classification of crises and their relationship to international politics is discussed at great length in his work

Lebow, R. N. *Between War and Peace.* Baltimore, MD: Johns Hopkins University Press, 1981.

The crisis cube was first presented in

Hermann, C. "International Crisis as a Situational Variable," in *International Politics and Foreign Policy,* Revised Edition. New York: The Free Press, 1969.

The empirical observations summarizing the general features of modern wars are presented along with a great deal of amplification in

Luard, E. *Conflict and Peace in the Modern International System,* 2nd Edition. Albany, NY: State University of New York Press, 1988.

A Tide in the Affairs of Nations

The paper Richardson submitted to the American journal was later published as

Richardson, L. F. "Generalized Foreign Politics," *British Journal of Psychology Monograph Supplements,* No. 23, 1939.

Much of Richardson's work on arms races and determinants of war, including a consideration of the stability of multipolar worlds, is found in his two posthumously published works:

Richardson, L. F. *Arms and Insecurity.* Pittsburgh, PA: The Boxwood Press, 1960.
Richardson, L. F. *Statistics of Deadly Quarrels.* Pittsburgh, PA: The Boxwood Press, 1960.

A good elementary account of Richardson's model and its role in today's world of conflict research is given in

Rapoport, A. *The Origins of Violence.* New York: Paragon House, 1989.

In this volume, Rapoport makes the important observation that Richardson's model is probably not of great value in predicting the outbreak of war, at least in its original form. Its real value lies more in its pioneering role in promoting a new way of looking at international relations as a systematic interaction between states, analyzable by formal mathematical means.

The treatment by Choucri and North on master variables and their role underlying war is given in the article

Choucri, N., and R. North. "Roots of War: The Master Variables," in *The Quest for Peace,* R. Väyrynen, ed., pp. 204–216. London: Sage Publishing Company, 1987.

For details on the O&K study comparing various power distribution theories, see

Organski, A., and J. Kugler. *The War Ledger.* Chicago: University of Chicago Press, 1980.

In addition to providing a very clear account of the competing theories, O&K look into the question of who will win a war that's already under way, as well as problems of nuclear arsenals. Perhaps surprisingly, they conclude that in less than two decades losers make up for their losses, and *all* combatants find themselves where they would have been if no war had occurred.

The treatment in the text of Colinvaux's ecological theory of the way history happens only skims the surface of his fascinating idea. For the details of why he thinks that expansion of "niche space" is the key to human history—including wars—Colinvaux's Tansley Lecture at the University of Southampton in 1981 is particularly rewarding reading. Both the theory and the lecture can be found in

Colinvaux, P. *The Fate of Nations.* New York: Simon and Schuster, 1980.

For the mathematically inclined, Richardson's model for an n-nation world can be formulated abstractly as the set of constant-coefficient linear differential equations

$$\frac{dx}{dt} = Ax + f, \quad x(0) = x_0,$$

where the state vector $x \in R^n$, $A \in R^{n \times n}$ is an $n \times n$ coefficient matrix whose entries represent the threat and security parameters for the n nations, and $f \in R^n$ is a vector of grievance parameters. As is well known from the stability theory of differential equations, this system has an equilibrium at the point x^* satisfying the equation $Ax^* + f = 0$. This representation makes it clear that the balance-of-power equilibrium point depends on the level of the grievance coefficients f. As is also well known, the equilibrium point x^* is stable if and only if all the characteristic roots of A have a negative real part—i.e., they lie in the left half of the complex plane. The condition given in the text involving the threat and security parameters is just a special case for the two-nation situation of this much more general criterion, which is valid for any number of nations n.

Mathematical explorations of generalized versions of Richardson's equations involving the addition of nonlinear terms, random perturbations, different notions of stability, and other academic finery are legion. Two good sources for some of these exercises are

Gillespie, J., and D. Zinnes, eds. *Mathematical Systems in International Relations Research.* New York: Praeger, 1977.
Hollist, W. Ladd, ed. *Exploring Competitive Arms Processes.* New York: Marcel Dekker, 1978.

An excellent recent study of the driving forces behind arms races, especially the issue of technological determinism—the idea that what is technically possible will be done versus the notion that "politics is in command"—is presented in the collection

Gleditsch, N., and O. Njølstad, eds. *Arms Races: Technological and Political Dynamics.* London: Sage Publications, 1990.

The empirical results using Richardson's model for the U.S.-U.S.S.R. and Arab-Israeli arms buildups are taken from

Taagepera, R., et al. "Soviet-American and Israeli-Arab Arms Races and the Richardson Model." *General Systems,* XX (1975), 151–158.

It's clear that in their decisions to go to war, governments are always constrained by factors in both their internal and external environments. Given the dramatic changes in the global system over the past century or so, new constraints have entered that affect the traditional elements of power politics. The degree to which these factors influence governments in their decisions about war was the question that William Domke set out to address, and that we answered only superficially in the text. For a complete account of what Domke discovered, his book on this matter is essential reading:

Domke, W. *War and the Changing Global System.* New Haven, CT: Yale University Press, 1988.

Eyeball to Eyeball

In its December 29, 1985 issue, *The New York Times Magazine* called *Balance of Power* "the most sophisticated strategic simulation in America, other than Pentagon war games." To see why, the computer-game-crazy reader is urged to consult the designer's account of how he created the game, what relations he used to determine "prestige points," and how the savvy international operator must operate in order to do in the opposition. Few game designers have taken the time to write a separate book about how their game works and why; Chris Crawford, designer of *Balance of Power,* is in that select group. His story is found in

Crawford, C. *Balance of Power: International Politics as the Ultimate Global Game.* Redmond, WA; Microsoft Press, 1986.

As for those "Pentagon war games," the reader can do no better than to consult the general-audience account of the origin and development of military simulations, computer and otherwise, given in

Allen, T. *War Games.* New York: McGraw-Hill, 1987.

The detailed postmortem of the Cuban missile crisis by Graham Allison has by now come to be heralded as a classic by those in the decision-analysis community. Making use of the detailed information available on the crisis, along with firsthand accounts by the participants themselves, Allison showed convincingly, and for the first time, that real decisionmakers in real crises definitely do not always behave like Rational Actors. For anyone even slightly interested in decisionmaking in the real world, Allison's study makes for fascinating reading. It can be found in

Allison, G. *Essence of Decision*. Boston: Little, Brown, 1971.

One of the pillars upon which the RAND Corporation built its reputation in the world of theoretical systems analysis and applied mathematics is its work in developing John von Neumann and Oskar Morgenstern's theory of games. The RAND work, of course, was directed toward the kind of "games" arising in the military and political arenas, not those of the economic world, which originally stimulated von Neumann and Morgenstern. Following in the footsteps of the RAND mathematicians, modern game theorists have developed the application of game-theoretic ideas in political decisionmaking to a high art. An excellent recent account showing how superpower concerns like arms races, arms control treaties, and deterrence all fit into the game-theoretic mold is

Brams, S. *Superpower Games*. New Haven, CT: Yale University Press, 1985.

Specific results for the case of the arms race are found in

Brams, S., M. Davis, and P. Straffin. "The Geometry of the Arms Race." *Journal of Conflict Resolution*, 23 (1979), 567–588.

For a general-reader introduction to games of strategy as mathematicians use the term, I highly recommend the following works:

Colman, A. *Game Theory and Experimental Games*. Oxford: Pergamon Press, 1982.
Williams, J. *The Compleat Strategyst*. New York: McGraw-Hill, 1954.

The Prisoner's Dilemma game is so ubiquitous in modern life that it has acquired a literature all its own, quite separate from the consideration of general games of strategy. An especially interesting recent contribution to this literature is the work of Robert Axelrod at the University of Michigan, who conducted a series of computer experiments using different strategies in a sequence of interactions with the Prisoner's Dilemma payoff structure. Axelrod was interested in discovering whether there were strategies that would lead to the emergence of cooperative behavior. In other words, could cooperation come about rationally in a Prisoner's Dilemma situation if the participants were forced to interact many times, rather than just once? For the answer, including its intimate relationship to the TIT-FOR-TAT strategy mentioned in the text, the reader is urged to examine Axelrod's account:

Axelrod, R. *Evolution of Cooperation*. New York: Basic Books, 1984.

Axelrod's "plain vanilla" model of the evolution of cooperation has been extended in several directions: more than two players, more than two choices of action, variation in the payoff structure, uncertainty. A survey of results obtained from these variations is given in

Axelrod, R., and D. Dion. "The Further Evolution of Cooperation." *Science*, 242 (December 9, 1988), 1385–1390.

The classic account of expected utility theory is found in von Neumann and Morgenstern's treatise on game theory:

von Neumann, J., and O. Morgenstern. *Theory of Games and Economic Behavior*. Princeton, NJ: Princeton University Press, 1947.

An excellent critique of EUT, emphasizing the nontransitivity of decisionmakers' preferences, using both example and precept, is

Tversky, A., and W. Kahneman. "The Framing of Decisions and the Psychology of Choice." *Science*, 211 (1981), 453–458.

Bueno de Mesquita's work in applying EUT to international affairs can be found in

Bueno de Mesquita, B. *The War Trap*. New Haven, CT: Yale University Press, 1981.
Bueno de Mesquita, B. "The Contribution of Expected Utility Theory to the Study of International Conflict," in *The Origin of Prevention of Major Wars*, R. Rotberg and T. Rabb, eds., pp. 53–76. Cambridge: Cambridge University Press, 1988.

A recent paper examining the effects of arms races on the occurrence of war using the EUT perspective is

Morrow, J. "A Twist of Truth: A Reexamination of the Effects of Arms Races on the Occurrence of War." *Journal of Conflict Resolution*, 33 (September 1989), 500–529.

In this study, Morrow concludes that swings in military superiority between the competing powers create a motivation for war in order to exploit temporary advantages. Risk-taking leaders are more prone to initiate such an arms race war, while risk-averse leaders are more likely to fail to respond to such threats.

Wargasms as Chaostrophes

Herman Kahn's penchant for hyperbole was legend in the community of strategic analysts. Comparing Kahn's attitude toward hostile criticism of contradictions in his book to Walt Whitman, one RAND colleague remarked that "[Herman] was vast. He contained multitudes," a reference not only to Kahn's intellectual ambitions, but also to the fact that Kahn probably tilted the scales somewhere in the 300-pound range. Despite the contradictions, his book still makes interesting reading today. I recommend the revised, paperback edition:

Kahn, H. *On Thermonuclear War*. New York: The Free Press, 1969.

See also Kahn's updated version of scenario building for nuclear war given in

Kahn, H. *Thinking About the Unthinkable in the 1980s*. New York: Simon and Schuster, 1984.

A particularly graphic scenario constructed around the outbreak of the next world war is the best seller

Hackett, J. *The Third World War*. London: Sidgwick and Jackson, 1978.

However, I think a much less visible, but more realistic, scenario for World War III is that given in

Bidwell, S. *World War III*. London: Hamlyn, 1978.

For those curious about what kind of people advise the government on when, where, and how to use its nuclear arsenal, two fascinating books that tell the story are

Herken, G. *Counsels of War*. New York: Alfred Knopf, 1985.
Kaplan, F. *The Wizards of Armageddon*. New York: Simon and Schuster, 1983.

The reader is cautioned, however, that both of these books share a common problem: Since they concentrate on the analysts, they make it appear that the analysts had a great deal more authority and responsibility than was actually the case. This community of analysts may indeed have had influence, but it did not include the actual people charged with the responsibility of making the decisions. As an indicator of the types of thoughts these "wizards" are thinking when they are engaged in peering into the abyss, see

Schelling, T. *The Strategy of Conflict*. Cambridge, MA: Harvard University Press, 1980.

The Holt group's work on using catastrophe theory as a mathematical metaphor for the outbreak of war was originally published as

Holt, R., B. Job, and L. Markus. "Catastrophe Theory and the Study of War." *Journal of Conflict Resolution*, 22 (1978), 171–208.

The simplified model of how chaotic behavior can arise in the armaments race by introduction of an SDI may be found in

Saperstein, A., and G. Mayer-Kress. "A Nonlinear Dynamical Model of the Impact of SDI on the Arms Race." *Journal of Conflict Resolution*, 32 (1988), 636–670.

CHAPTER SIX

General References

Perhaps not surprisingly, compared to physicists and biologists, research mathematicians have made relatively few attempts to explain the meaning, concerns, and methods of their profession to the general reader. Two outstanding efforts in this direction that I can recommend unreservedly are the volumes

Davis, P., and R. Hersh. *The Mathematical Experience*. Boston: Birkhäuser, 1980.
Stewart, I. *The Problems of Mathematics*. New York: Oxford University Press, 1987.

To the best of my knowledge, the first account of Gödel's Theorem written expressly for the general reader, and still one of the best, is the short volume

Nagel, E., and J. R. Newman. *Gödel's Proof*. New York: New York University Press, 1958.

This work notwithstanding, Gödel's results remained more or less buried in academic obscurity until the appearance of the Pulitzer Prize–winning account of the theorem and its implications given in

Hofstadter, D. *Gödel, Escher, Bach: An Eternal Golden Braid.* New York: Basic Books, 1979.

A good place to begin digging into the motivations, ideas, and weaknesses of formalism, logicism, intuitionism, and platonism is

Kline, M. *Mathematics: The Loss of Certainty.* New York: Oxford University Press, 1980.

For a dip into the original literature on these competing positions, as well as for amplifying discussions and subsequent developments, I found the following collection of great value:

Benacerraf, P., and H. Putnam, eds. *The Philosophy of Mathematics: Selected Readings,* 2nd Edition. Cambridge: Cambridge University Press, 1983.

For a thorough examination of the currently popular quasi-empirical view of the foundations of mathematics, see the collection of reprints

Tymoczko, T., ed. *New Directions in the Philosophy of Mathematics.* Boston: Birkhäuser, 1986.

Let Them Eat *Sachertorte*

Since *Sachertorte* plays such a pivotal role in the deliberations of this chapter, here's a simple recipe for those who would like to try their hand at simulating a *Sachertorte* Machine. I should point out, however, that this recipe is not the same one used at Demel's or at the cake's birthplace, the Hotel Sacher in Vienna.

Sachertorte

$\frac{1}{3}$ cup butter (*at room temperature*)	$\frac{1}{2}$ cup plus 1 tablespoon sifted flour
6 tablespoons granulated sugar	5 egg whites
3 ounces semisweet chocolate, melted	$2\frac{1}{2}$ tablespoons apricot jam
4 egg yolks	

1. Preheat oven to moderate (325° F). Grease and lightly flour a deep 8-inch spring-form pan.
2. Cream the butter, add the sugar gradually, and cream until fluffy. Add the chocolate and mix thoroughly, scraping the bottom of the bowl several times.
3. Add the egg yolks one at a time and mix well after each addition. Stir in the flour until no particles show.

4. Beat the egg whites until stiff but not dry and gently fold them into the batter until no whites show.

5. Turn the batter into the prepared pan and bake on the lower shelf of the oven until the cake shrinks from the sides of the pan and rebounds to the touch when pressed gently in the center, or about $1\frac{1}{4}$ hours.

6. Let the cake stand ten minutes on a cooling rack before turning out of the pan. Turn the cake out on the rack, turn right side up, and let it finish cooling.

7. Stand the rack and cake on waxed paper and spread the top of the cake with jam. Pour any desired chocolate icing over the cake and spread it quickly to coat the top and sides.

Turing Around

An excellent introductory account of the circle of problems surrounding computation, formal systems, Turing machines, the Halting Problem, Gödel's Theorem, complexity, and Hilbert's Tenth Problem is available in the article

Davis, M. "What Is a Computation?" in *Mathematics Today: Twelve Informal Essays*, L. A. Steen, ed., pp. 241–267. New York: Springer, 1978.

For a general-readership development of the idea and workings of a Turing machine, see

Hoffman, P. *Archimedes' Revenge*. New York: Norton, 1988.
Rucker, R. *Mind Tools*. Boston: Houghton-Mifflin, 1987.

For a more technical account of Turing machines and their connections not only with decision problems but also languages, the reader is directed to the textbook

Davis, M., and E. Weyuker. *Computability, Complexity, and Languages*. Orlando, FL.: Academic Press, 1983.

A very stimulating collection of essays reviewing current knowledge about Turing machines and their many ramifications in other areas is

Herken, R., ed. *The Universal Turing Machine*. Oxford: Oxford University Press, 1988.

The Turing machine program given in Table 6.2 enables the machine to decide if the string of 1s and 2s given on the input tape read the same forward and backward, i.e., if the string constitutes a *palindrome*.

For more details on the construction and operation of a UTM, the reader should see either Rucker's *Mind Tools* (referenced above) or his *Infinity and the Mind* (referenced below).

The Turing-Church Thesis lies at the heart of the currently fashionable artificial-intelligence debate, which revolves about the question of whether or not a computer can think like a human being. *If* human thought processes can be shown to all be "effective," and *if* the Turing-Church Thesis is correct, then it necessarily follows that there is no barrier, at least in principle, between the "thought processes" of machines and those of humans. But both of these ifs are very big ifs indeed, and no one has yet been able to give a knockdown argument resolving either half of this conundrum. For an account of the current state of play, as well as for an extensive bibliography on the whole issue, see Chapter Five of

Casti, J. *Paradigms Lost: Images of Man in the Mirror of Science.* New York: Morrow, 1989. Paperback edition, New York: Avon, 1990.

A much more technical, philosophically oriented approach to the implications of the Turing-Church Thesis for both psychology and the philosophy of mathematics is presented in

Webb, J. *Mechanism, Mentalism, and Metamathematics.* Dordrecht, Holland: Reidel, 1980.

In this same connection, see also

Arbib, M. *Brains, Machines, and Mathematics,* 2nd Edition. New York: Springer, 1987.
Penrose, R. *The Emperor's New Mind.* Oxford: Oxford University Press, 1989.

The Busy Beaver Game was dreamed up by Tibor Rado of Ohio State University in the early 1960s. A compact, introductory discussion of what's currently known about this problem and about the Busy Beaver function can be found in the articles

Brady, A. "The Busy Beaver Game and the Meaning of Life," in *The Universal Turing Machine,* R. Herken,ed., pp. 259–277. Oxford: Oxford University Press, 1988.
Dewdney, A. "Busy Beavers," in *The Armchair Universe,* pp. 160–171. New York: Freeman, 1988.

In 1973 Bruno Weimann discovered that the four-state Busy Beaver can write thirteen 1s on the tape before halting. Thus, $BB(4) = 13$. So far no one knows the value $BB(5)$, although in 1984 George Uhing showed that $BB(5) \geq 1,915$. The program establishing this remarkable result follows.

	Symbol Read	
State	0	1
A	1, R, B	1, L, C
B	0, L, A	0, L, D
C	1, L, A	1, L, STOP
D	1, L, B	1, R, E
E	0. R, D	0, R, B

Uhing's 5-state Turing machine program
for the Busy Beaver Game

Here is a slick proof due to Ian Stewart showing the unsolvability of the Halting Problem. Suppose such a Halting Algorithm exists and let d be the input data. Consider the following UTM program:

1. Check to see if d is the code for a UTM program P. If not, go back to the start and repeat.
2. If d is the code for such a program P, double the input string to get $d \cdot d$.
3. Use the assumed Halting Algorithm for the UTM with input data $d \cdot d$. If it stops, go back to the beginning of this step and repeat.
4. Otherwise, halt.

Call the above program H. Now since H is a program, it has its own code h. Thus, we can ask, "Does H halt for input h?" It surely gets past step 1, since by definition h is the code for the program H. And H gets past step 3 as well, if and only if the UTM doesn't halt with input $h \cdot h$. Thus we conclude that H halts with input data h if and only if the UTM does not halt with input data $h \cdot h$. But the UTM simulates a program P by starting with the input data $P \cdot d$, and then behaving just like P operating on input data d. Therefore, we see that P halts with input data d if and only if the UTM halts with input data $P \cdot d$. So if we put $P = H$ and $d = h$, then we find that H halts with input data h if and only if the UTM halts with input data $h \cdot h$—a direct contradiction of the result obtained a moment ago. Thus we conclude that there is no such Halting Algorithm. This proof, along with much, much more about the state of modern mathematics, can be found in Stewart's book on the problems of modern mathematics noted under General References.

The Importance of Being Arbitrary

The citation for Solomonoff's original paper on the complexity of scientific theories is

Solomonoff, R. "A Formal Theory of Inductive Inference." *Information and Control*, 7 (1964), 224–254.

The complete story of Chaitin's independent discovery of algorithmic complexity and its connection with randomness is contained in his collection of papers

Chaitin, G. *Information, Randomness, and Incompleteness*, 2nd Edition. Singapore: World Scientific, 1990.

Quite independently of both Chaitin and Solomonoff, the famous Russian mathematician Andrei Kolmogorov also hit upon the idea of defining the randomness of a number by the length of the shortest computer program required to calculate it. His ideas were presented in

Kolmogorov, A. "Three Approaches to the Quantitative Definition of Information." *Problems in Information Transmission*, 1 (1965), 3–11.

The original formulation of Berry's Paradox involved a statement like "the smallest number that cannot be expressed in fewer than thirteen words." Since the preceding phrase contains twelve words, the paradox follows for exactly the same reasons as given for the more general phrase used in the text. A fairly complete account of the Berry Paradox and its relationship to complexity and Gödelian logic is available in the Rucker book *Infinity and the Mind* noted below.

The Limits to Proof

Hilbert's famous list of twenty-three problems presented at the 1900 International Congress of Mathematicians in Paris has served to direct and motivate a good deal of twentieth-century mathematics—just as

Hilbert hoped. An English translation of Hilbert's original presentation, together with an assessment by contemporary mathematicians as to where we stand today on each of the problems, is given in

Mathematical Developments Arising from Hilbert Problems. Proceedings of the Symposia in Pure Mathematics, Vol. 28. Providence, RI: American Mathematical Society, 1976.

An additional feature of the foregoing volume that mathematically inclined readers will find of interest is the inclusion of a collection of problems for the twenty-first century submitted by many of today's most prominent and productive mathematicians.

An introductory, general-reader account of noneuclidean geometry, as well as many other areas of mathematics, including Gödel's proof and Russell's paradoxes, can be found in

Guillen, M. Bridges to Infinity. London: Rider, 1984.

Speaking Formally

A simple, easy-to-understand introduction to formal systems is given in Hofstadter's treatise cited earlier, as well as in

Levine, H., and H. Rheingold. The Cognitive Connection. Englewood Cliffs, NJ: Prentice-Hall, 1987.

For a more technical account emphasizing the connections between formal systems and languages, see the book

Moll, R., M. Arbib, and A. Kfoury. An Introduction to Formal Language Theory. New York: Springer, 1988.

The star–maltese cross–shamrock system introduced in the text is a recasting of the MIU-system originally presented in Hofstadter's volume on Gödel. For a proof of the decision procedure given for this system, as well as for a discussion of some other results related to it, see the article

Swanson, L., and R. McEliece, "A Simple Decision Procedure for Hofstadter's MIU-System." Mathematical Intelligencer, 10, No. 2 (1988), 48–49.

The Undecidable

An English translation of Gödel's pioneering paper, as well as an enlightening biographical account of his life, can be found in the first volume of Gödel's collected works:

Feferman, S., et al., eds. *Kurt Gödel: Collected Works*, Vol. 1. New York: Oxford University Press, 1986.

An assessment of Gödel's Theorem from both a philosophical and a mathematical point of view is contained in the collection of reprints

Shanker, S., ed. *Gödel's Theorem in Focus*. London: Croom Helm, 1988.

People often wonder whether or not long-standing, seemingly intractable mathematical questions like Goldbach's Conjecture (every even number is the sum of two primes) are undecidable in the same way that Cantor's Continuum Hypothesis turned out to be undecidable. Musings of this sort give rise to the consideration of whether or not Gödel's results really matter to mathematics, in the sense that there are important mathematical questions that are truly undecidable. With the recent work of Chaitin and others, the comforting belief that there are no such problems seems a lot less comforting than it used to. For a discussion of some other "real" mathematical queries that are genuinely undecidable, see

Kolata, G. "Does Gödel's Theorem Matter to Mathematics?" *Science,* 218 (November 19, 1982), 779–780.

Many details of Gödel's personality, views on life, and philosophy, as well as an assessment of both his mathematical and philosophical work, are found in the following book written by the well-known mathematical logician Hao Wang, who was a long-time acquaintance of Gödel's:

Wang, H. *Reflections on Kurt Gödel*. Cambridge, MA: MIT Press, 1987.

Additional information about Gödel's life is given in

Dawson, J. "Kurt Gödel in Sharper Focus." *Mathematical Intelligencer,* 6, No. 4 (1984), 9–17.
Kreisel, G. "Kurt Gödel: 1906–1978." *Biographical Memoirs of Fellows of the Royal Society,* 26 (1980), 148–224.

The text discussion of "mirroring" and Gödel numbering follows that given in the Nagel and Newman book noted above. Hofstadter's switching-yard metaphor for Gödel numbering and transformations in a formal system can be found in the expository paper

Hofstadter, D. "Analogies and Metaphors to Explain Gödel's Theorem." *College Mathematics Journal,* 13 (March 1982), 98–114.

The discussion by Rudy Rucker likening Gödel's Theorem to the plight of Joseph K. in his frustrated wanderings through Kafka's *The Trial* may be found in the very enlightening, but slightly technical, book

Rucker, R. *Infinity and the Mind*. Boston: Birkhäuser, 1982.

In connection with Gödel as a person, this book is especially recommended for its account of several meetings that Rucker had with Gödel in the years shortly before Gödel's death in January 1978.

The Tenth Problem

A very easy-to-understand, illuminating discussion of Hilbert's Tenth Problem is given in Chapter Six of

Devlin, K. *Mathematics: The New Golden Age*. London: Penguin, 1988.

A somewhat more technical account is presented in the Davis article "What Is a Computation?" noted above, as well as in the volume

Salomaa, A. *Computation and Automata*. Cambridge: Cambridge University Press, 1985.

Each of the foregoing sources also gives a good account of Matyasevich's resolution of the problem.

In our discussion of Turing machines we introduced the idea of a computable number—one whose digits can be successively calculated by some UTM program. This idea can be extended to sets of whole numbers by saying that a set is computable if, given any integer in the set as input, the program prints a 1 and halts. But if the given number is not in the set, the program prints a 0 and stops. It turns out that this notion is a bit too strong for many purposes, and it's convenient to introduce a weaker version. We say that a set of integers is *listable* if there is a program that, given any integer as input, prints a 1 and stops if the integer is in the set. But if the integer is not in the set, the program may print a 0 and halt or it may not stop at all. So the difference between a set's being computable and being listable is that if the set is listable, the program may or may not halt. But the program always stops when the set is computable. Obviously, computable sets are listable—but not conversely. This distinction forms the basis for an attack mounted on Hilbert's Tenth Problem by Martin Davis. Here is an outline of his strategy.

Davis's idea was to prove that for every listable set of integers S, there is a corresponding polynomial $P_S (k, y_1, \ldots, y_n)$ with integer coefficients, such that a positive integer k^* belongs to the set S if and only if the solution set of the Diophantine equation $P_S (k^*, y_1, \ldots, y_n) = 0$ is not empty, i.e., the equation has at least one solution in integers. In short, the solvability or unsolvability of the equation $P_S (k, y_1, \ldots, y_n) = 0$ serves as a decision procedure for membership in the listable set S. Here we subscript the polynomial with a small S to indicate that there may be a different polynomial for each listable set S. Davis showed that Hilbert's Tenth Problem can be resolved negatively if such a polynomial can be found for every listable set of integers.

The logical chain of reasoning underwriting Davis's approach to the Tenth Problem is composed of the following links:

A. Suppose there were a Diophantine decision algorithm of the type that Hilbert wanted, and let S be some listable but not computable set of integers.
B. Then by the assumed existence of the algorithm, there is a Turing machine program (call it $\mathcal{D}$ for Diophantine) which, given the integer k^* as input, halts with output 1 if the Diophantine equation $P_S (k^*, y_1, \ldots, y_n) = 0$ has a solution, and halts with output 0 if there is no solution.
C. But the relationship between S and P_S implies that the existence of such a program $\mathcal{D}$ would mean that S is computable, since $\mathcal{D}$ definitely stops with a 0 or a 1 as output.
D. But this contradicts the assumption that the set S is not computable. Hence, no such program $\mathcal{D}$ can exist. That is, there is no algorithm of the sort sought by Hilbert and the Tenth Problem is settled negatively.

Unfortunately, Davis was unable to prove the existence of such a polynomial P_S for every listable set S. However, later work by Davis, Julia Robinson, and Hilary Putnam showed that if there were even one Diophantine equation whose solutions grew at an exponentially increasing rate in just the right way, then Davis's polynomial P_S would have to exist. An example of just this sort of equation was what Yuri Matyasevich constructed in 1970.

An interesting corollary of Matyasevich's proof is that for any listable set of natural numbers S, there exists a polynomial $P_S (y_1, \ldots, y_n)$ with integer coefficients such that as the variables $y_1, \ldots, y_n$ range over the nonnegative integers, the positive values of the polynomial are exactly the set S. To illustrate this result, here is the promised polynomial equation in the twenty-six letters of the alphabet, whose positive values are the set of prime numbers:

$$P(a, b, \ldots, z) =$$
$$(k + 2)\{1 - [wz + h + j - q]^2$$
$$- [(gk + 2g + k + 1)(h + j) + h - z]^2$$
$$- [2n + p + q + z - e]^2$$
$$- [16(k + 1)^3(k + 2)(n + 1)^2 + 1 - f^2]^2$$
$$- [e^3(e + 2)(a + 1)^2 + 1 - o^2]^2$$
$$- [(a^2 - 1)y^2 + 1 - x^2]^2 - [16r^2y^4(a^2 - 1) + 1 - u^2]^2$$
$$- [((a + u^2(u^2 - a))^2 - 1)(n + 4dy)^2 + 1 - (x + cu)^2]^2$$
$$- [n + l + v - y]^2 - [(a^2 - 1)l^2 + 1 - m^2]^2$$
$$- [ai + k + 1 - l - i]^2$$
$$- [p + l(a - n - 1) + b(2an + 2a - n^2 - 2n - 2) - m]^2$$
$$- [q + y(a - p - 1) + s(2ap + 2a - p^2 - 2p - 2) - x]^2$$
$$- [z + pl(a - p) + t(2ap - p^2 - 1) - pm]^2\}$$

As the letters a through z run through all the nonnegative integers, the polynomial P takes on positive and negative integer values. The positive values are exactly the set of prime numbers; the negative values may or may not be the negatives of primes. Incidentally, the reader will note that the expression for P is given in terms of two factors, seeming to contradict the definition of a prime number as one that has no factors other than itself and 1. The apparent contradiction is resolved by noting that the formula produces only positive values when the factor $(k + 2)$ is a prime and the second factor equals 1. This polynomial for primes was first published by James Jones, Daihachiro Sato, Hideo Wada, and Douglas Wiens in 1977.

An introductory account of Chaitin's fabulous Diophantine equation straight from the horse's mouth, so to speak, is found in

Chaitin, G. "Randomness in Arithmetic." *Scientific American,* 259 (July 1988), 80–85.

Chaitin, G. "A Random Walk in Arithmetic." *New Scientist,* March 24, 1990, pp. 44–46.

Creation of Chaitin's "monster" equation followed the flow chart below, involving the creation of a sequence of machine-language and LISP programs:

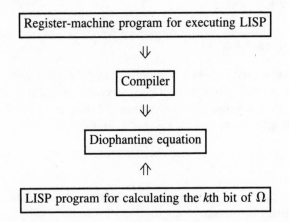

The technical details surrounding this monumental intellectual and programming effort are given in the book

Chaitin, G. *Algorithmic Information Theory*. Cambridge: Cambridge University Press, 1987.

The Truth, the Whole Truth, and the Mathematician's Truth

A very readable discussion of what the different schools of mathematical philosophy have to say about our statements A, B, and C concerning the properties of numbers like π and e is given in the very stimulating article (from which I've paraphrased the title of this section):

Gale, D. "The Truth and Nothing But the Truth." *Mathematical Intelligencer*, 11, No. 3 (1989), 62–67.

See also the discussion of the degree to which mathematics is an arbitrary logical construct given in

Ruelle, D. "Is Our Mathematics Natural? The Case of Equilibrium Statistical Mechanics." *Bulletin of the American Mathematical Society*, 19 (1988), 259–268.

The various schools of mathematical philosophy are treated in some detail in the Davis and Hersh, Kline, Benacerraf and Putnam, and Tymoczko books already cited. Goodman's account of the Principle of Objectivity is found in

Goodman, N. "Mathematics as an Objective Science." *American Mathematical Monthly*, 86 (1979), 540–551.

The mathematician-turned-philosopher Ernst Snapper has argued that the process of doing mathematics involves the creation of classes and the proof of theorems. He has examined how each of the competing philosophical schools sees these two activities in

Snapper, E. "What Do We Do When We Do Mathematics?" *Mathematical Intelligencer*, 10, No. 4 (1988), 53–58.

The quasi-empirical approach to mathematical philosophy was originally outlined in the novel doctoral dissertation

Lakatos, I. *Proofs and Refutations: The Logic of Mathematical Discovery*. Cambridge: Cambridge University Press, 1976.

Further developments of Lakatos's thesis are recounted in the essays in the Tymoczko volume cited above. Of special note in this connection is the very close relation between the idea of a mathematical proof and that of verifying a computer program, i.e., proving that the program is really implementing the algorithm the programmer thinks it is. These intertwining themes are explored in the article

Barwise, J. "Mathematical Proofs of Computer System Correctness." *Notices of the American Mathematical Society*, 36 (September 1989), 844–851.

The computer-assisted resolution of the Four-Color Conjecture, along with a detailed account of the problem's history, can be found in

Appel, K., and W. Haken. *Every Planar Map Is Four Colorable*. Providence, RI: American Mathematical Society, Contemporary Mathematics, Vol. 98, 1989.

Saaty, T., and P. Kainen. *The Four-Color Problem: Assaults and Conquest*. New York: McGraw-Hill, 1977 (New York: Dover reprint, 1986).

The philosophical implications of computer proofs, with special reference to the Four-Color Theorem, are explored in

Tymoczko, T. "The Four-Color Problem and Its Philosophical Significance." *Journal of Philosophy*, 76, No. 2 (1979), 57–83.

Making the Grade

Some very interesting observations regarding mathematical proof by computer is given by C.W.H. Lam, seeker of the projective plane of order 10, in

Lam, C.W.H. "How Reliable Is a Computer-Based Proof?" *Mathematical Intelligencer,* 12 (1990), 8–12.

CREDITS

Grateful acknowledgment is made to the following individuals and publishers for permission to reproduce material used in creating the figures in this book. Every effort has been made to locate the copyright holders of material used here. Omissions brought to our attention will be corrected in future editions.

Academic Press for Figure 1.6, which is reproduced from M. Hirsch and S. Smale, *Differential Equations, Dynamical Systems, and Linear Algebra*, 1974, and for Figure 3.10, which is reproduced from H. Meinhardt, *Models of Biological Pattern Formation*, 1982.

Cambridge University Press for Figure 1.7, which is reproduced from J. Maynard Smith, *Models in Ecology*, 1974; for Figure 1.9, which is reproduced from P. Saunders, *An Introduction to Catastrophe Theory*, 1980; for Figure 3.13, which is reproduced from D'Arcy Thompson, *On Growth and Form*, 1942; and for Figure 4.10, which is reproduced from *Stock Market Anomalies*, E. Dimson, ed., 1988.

Grafton Books for Figure 2.1, which is reproduced from F. Pearce, *Turning Up the Heat*, 1989.

Basil Blackwell, Ltd., for Figures 2.2 and 2.17, which are reproduced from O. Greene, I. Percival, and I. Ridge, *Nuclear Winter*, 1985.

John Wiley & Sons for Figures 2.3, 2.8, 2.12, and 2.18, which are reproduced from A. Henderson-Sellers, *A Climate Modelling Primer*, 1987; for Figures 3.8 and 3.9, which are reproduced from R. Ransom, *Computers and Embryos*, 1981; and for Figures 4.1 and 4.2, which are reproduced from M. Johnson, *The Random Walk and Beyond*, 1988.

New Scientist magazine for Figures 2.4 and 2.14.

Carl Kirkpatrick for Figure 2.5.

The Royal Society for Figures 2.9 and 2.15, which are reproduced from J. Mason, "Numerical Weather Prediction," *Proceedings of the Royal Society of London A*, 407 (1986), 51–60.

Prentice-Hall, Inc., for Figure 2.16, which is reproduced from B. Steiger, *A Roadmap of Time*, 1975.

Sinauer Associates Inc., for Figure 3.1, which is reproduced from S. F. Gilbert, *Developmental Biology*, 2nd Edition, 1988.

Blackie & Sons, Ltd., for Figure 3.3, which is reproduced from P. Calow, *Evolutionary Principles*, 1983.

Longman Group, Ltd., for Figures 3.4, 3.5, 3.6, and 3.7, which are reproduced from R. Dawkins, *The Blind Watchmaker*, 1986.

Oxford University Press for Figure 3.11, which is reproduced from J. Maynard Smith, *The Problems of Biology*, 1986.

University of Alberta Press for Figures 3.14 and 3.15, which are reproduced from *Mathematical Essays on Growth and the Emergence of Form*, P. Antonelli, ed., 1985.

Century Hutchinson, Ltd., for Figures 3.16, 3.17, and 3.19, which are reproduced from R. Sheldrake, *A New Science of Life*, 1985.

E. C. Zeeman for Figure 3.18.

E. P. Dutton, Inc., for Figure 3.20, which is reproduced from T. Woodcock and M. Davis, *Catastrophe Theory*, 1978.

Random House, Inc., for Figures 3.2 and 3.21, which are reproduced from R. Sheldrake, *The Presence of the Past*, 1988.

Value Line, Inc., for Figure 4.3.

New Classics Library, Inc., for Figures 4.4–4.7, which are reproduced from R. Prechter and C. Frost, *Elliott Wave Principle*, 5th Edition, 1985.

McGraw-Hill Book Co. for Figure 4.8, which is reproduced from R. Teweles, et al., *The Commodity Futures Game*, Abridged Edition, 1977.

W. W. Norton, Inc., for Figure 4.9, which is reproduced from B. Malkiel, *A Random Walk Down Wall Street*, 4th Edition, 1985.

Benoit Mandelbrot for Figure 4.11, which is taken from his book *The Fractal Geometry of Nature*. New York: Freeman, 1983.

Sage Publications for Figures 5.6 and 5.7, which are taken from R. Holt, B. Job, and L. Markus, "Catastrophe Theory and the Study of War," *Journal of Conflict Resolution*, 22 (1978), 171–208, and for Figures 5.8 and 5.9, which are from A. Saperstein and G. Mayer-Kress, "A Nonlinear Dynamical Model of the Impact of SDI on the Arms Race," *Journal of Conflict Resolution*, 32 (1988), 636–670.

Society for General Systems Research for Figure 5.4, which is reproduced from *General Systems*, XX (1975), 154.

Penguin Books for Figure 6.2, which is reproduced from K. Devlin, *Mathematics: The New Golden Age*, 1988.

Houghton Mifflin Company for Figures 6.3, 6.4, and 6.8, which are reproduced from R. Rucker, *Mind Tools*, 1987.

University of Chicago Press for Figures 6.7 and 6.10, which are reproduced from J. Allen Paulos, *Mathematics and Humor*, 1980.

Douglas Hofstadter for Figure 6.9.

INDEX

Page numbers in *italics* refer to figures and tables.